The Great Arch

Brian Doyle

To the memory of
Philip Abrams

The Great Arch

English State Formation as Cultural Revolution

PHILIP CORRIGAN and DEREK SAYER

With a Foreword
by
G. E. Aylmer

Basil Blackwell

First published 1985

Basil Blackwell Ltd
108 Cowley Road, Oxford OX4 1JF, UK

Basil Blackwell Inc.
432 Park Avenue South, Suite 1505,
New York, NY 10016, USA

British Library Cataloguing in Publication Data
Corrigan, Philip
The great arch: state formation, cultural revolution and rise of
capitalism.
1. England—Social life and customs
I. Title   II. Sayer, Derek
942   DA110

ISBN 0-631-14054-9
ISBN 0-631-14055-7 Pbk

Library of Congress Cataloging in Publication Data
Corrigan, Philip Richard D.
The great arch.

Bibliography: p.
Includes index.
1. Great Britain—Politics and government—19th
century—Addresses, essays, lectures. 2. Great Britain—
Social conditions—19th century—Addresses, essays,
lectures. 3. Social classes—Great Britain—History
19th century—Addresses, essays, lectures.
I. Sayer, Derek.   II. Title.
JN216.C67   1985   941.081   85-7409

ISBN 0-631-14054-9
ISBN 0-631-14055-7 (pbk.)

Typeset by Katerprint Co. Ltd., Oxford
Printed in Great Britain by The Bath Press Ltd, Bath

Contents

Foreword

The Great Arch is emphatically not a conventional history book. Nonetheless, as a historian I am pleased to have been asked to write a Foreword to it, because I believe it would be a misfortune if it were not read by historians among others.

The authors, sociologists at Toronto and Glasgow respectively, have written an extended analytical survey. Their theme is the formation of the English state from Anglo-Saxon times to the later nineteenth century. Essentially they see 'state formation as cultural revolution', and in their view 'moral regulation is co-extensive with state formation and state forms are always animated and legitimated by a particular moral ethos.' The modern English state, as it has emerged over many centuries, is seen as co-terminous with the nation, likewise with a bourgeois-capitalist economic system and a patriarchal, male-dominated social order. The intellectual debts which they acknowledge are, among the founders of social science, primarily to Marx, next to Durkheim and then to Weber; among modern writers on English history and culture, to Christopher Hill, E. P. Thompson, Raymond Williams and above all the late Philip Abrams (whose pupils they both were). The influence of Norbert Elias and Michel Foucault is also evident, but not obtrusively so.

The book burns with political passion. This is most evident in the Introduction, the Epilogue and the Afterthoughts. Much of the intervening chapters is taken up with a closely reasoned discussion of developments over the centuries, where the authors' contemporary political commitment intrudes very little. One may indeed not share their viewpoint, but still greatly admire the achievement. This is a work of courage, scope and immense thoroughness. Moreover the argument is presented lucidly and cogently, while the difficulties and limitations of the evidence are seldom if ever concealed or glossed over. The sheer quantity of material assimilated compels respect. Yet at the same time the pattern imposed upon it is always of the authors' making and never merely derivative. Their authorship is also remarkable as an intellectual partnership. The reader will be hard put to decide where Corrigan begins and Sayer leaves off, or vice versa. No doubt there are minor differences in tone and style detectable between them, but their intellectual consonance is unusually complete and the joint authorship much nearer than is usual in such partnerships to true identity as writers.

How far it is possible to be persuaded of the historical case put forward without accepting the conclusions drawn from it, must be left to each individual reader. But, like the present writer, each will surely learn much, both from the text and the bibliography. To the many apposite quotations, cited from a remarkable range of authors, I would only suggest adding James Madison in *Federalist*, 51:

But what is government itself, but the greatest of all reflections on human nature? If men were angels, no government would be necessary. If angels were to govern men, neither external nor internal controls on government would be necessary. In framing a government which is to be administered by men over men, the great difficulty lies in this; you must first enable the government to control the governed; and in the next place oblige it to control itself.

No doubt the present authors would wish to controvert the use of the male gender, but that may not be thought altogether to dispose of the argument. *The Great Arch* deserves to be taken very seriously. It presents a challenging case which cannot be brushed aside, and at the very least demands a serious, reasoned response.

G. E. Aylmer

Acknowledgements

This book has been long in the making, and owes much to many people. Our very considerable debts to many historians – whose primary researches we extensively rely upon – and sociologists will be evident from our references and bibliography. We both owe much to the late Philip Abrams, who encouraged our work over many years, and to whose memory this book is dedicated.

Since 1982 we have been involved in a discussion group on the formation of the English state, meeting annually at St Peter's College, Oxford, and have benefited greatly from both the papers and discussions at its sessions. Earlier versions of parts of this book have been presented as papers at the Universities of Chicago, Dar Es Salaam, Sussex and Toronto, and to the 1981 Manchester Round Table; we would like to thank participants for their interest and comments. Kim Pickin and Sean Magee, of Basil Blackwell, deserve our thanks for their unfailingly supportive editorial work throughout. We would also like to acknowledge the support of the University of Glasgow in its provision of departmentally located word-processing facilities for academic use; a frequently revised manuscript, by authors living and working on different sides of the Atlantic, would have been very much more cumbersome to produce without this technology.

Special thanks are due to Michael Clanchy, Jason Ditton and David Loades, who were kind enough to read and give detailed comments on parts of the manuscript, and to Gerald Aylmer, who read it all and gave much useful advice. Apart from saving us from several errors, their encouragement of our general project is deeply appreciated. It goes without saying that the responsibility for any remaining errors, as well as for the overall argument of the book – historical, sociological and political – is our own.

Philip Corrigan, Toronto, Ontario, Canada
Derek Sayer, Glasgow, Scotland

A national economy is a political space, transformed by the state as a result of the necessities and innovations of economic life, into a coherent, unified economic space whose combined activities may tend in the same direction. Only England managed this exploit at an early date. In reference to England the term *revolution* recurs: agricultural, political, financial and industrial revolutions. To this list must be added – giving it whatever name you choose – the revolution that created England's national market.

Fernand Braudel (1977: 99)

Let us now put the pieces back and start the game with a different move. In this case we will suppose that 1832 happened as it did, but (less plausibly) 1640 did not – that the Laudian reaction was less provocative, that Charles capitulated before the Grand Remonstrance, and that a circumscribed constitutional monarchy was established, bloodlessly, in 1640, without Marston Moor, the Leveller ferment, the execution of the King, and the Glorious Revolution. In this event the model-builders would be wholly at a loss for *the* Revolution; and, paradoxically, might perforce be better historians, for they would have to construct, from the Wars of the Roses, the Tudor Monarchy (is there a premature Robespierre in Henry VIII, a dictatorship of the bourgeoisie?), the attainder of royal ministers, the religious conflicts of the sixteenth and seventeenth centuries, and from 1832, pieces of that great arch which in fact, in the epochal sense, make up the bourgeois revolution.

I am objecting to a model which concentrates attention upon one dramatic episode – *the* Revolution – to which all that goes before and after must be related; and which insists upon an ideal type of this Revolution against which all others may be judged. Minds which thirst for a tidy platonism very soon become impatient with actual history.

E. P. Thompson (1965: 47)

Introduction

There is a war on. It is an undeclared civil war instigated by Mr Scargill, his squads of pickets, and his political associates against the rest of society. The enemy within dares insurrection against legitimate authority. The challenge can be met in only one way if the values of liberal democracy and liberty under the law are to prevail – by enforcing the surrender of Mr Scargill and the national executive of the mineworkers' union.

Only by that outcome, declared and plainly recognized, will the militant left be checked, the path of extra-parliamentary politics blocked, the criminal conspiracy to intimidate citizens at their places of work and in their homes defeated, the will of trade unions to challenge the policies of the elected government broken, and their ability to frustrate necessary changes in the economic order significantly reduced.

Thus *The Times* (2 August 1984), editorializing in the depths of the 1984–5 British miners' strike. The crunch, of course, is in the last clause: 'necessary changes in the economic order'. One way of describing what this book is about is to say that it is concerned with how forms of social order were historically constructed, within which such descriptions could plausibly be sustained: the butchering of mining communities seen as mere economic necessity, their defence as something akin to treason.

Social theory has long acknowledged some sort of connection between state formation and the rise of modern capitalism, both in general terms and in the specific case of England: that is our empirical focus in this book. For Max Weber, 'it is the closed nation state which afforded to capitalism its chance of development'; for Karl Marx, bourgeois society 'must assert itself in its external relations as nationality and internally must organise itself as state'.[1] That the triumph of modern capitalist civilization involved a wholesale cultural revolution too – a revolution as much in the way the world was made sense of as in how goods were produced and exchanged – is also widely recognized, whether in sociological,[2] Marxist[3] or feminist[4] literature.

But the relation between state formation and cultural revolution in the long making of bourgeois civilization, whether for England or more generally, is less often marked. Neither the profoundly cultural content of state institutions and activities nor the nature and extent of state regulation of cultural forms are adequately addressed in much of the literature. Still less is state formation grasped as the cultural revolution we shall argue it centrally is. Social theory, both Marxist and sociological, often rests content with demonstration in general theoretical terms of the functionality of the nation state to capitalist production, seeing this as an end to analysis rather than a mere prelude to historical inquiry. Within historical writing itself, state formation is often hived off into the specialized sub-disciplines of constitutional or administrative history. Marxists have in addition all too frequently been inclined to comprehend 'the State' simply as an organ of coercion, Lenin's 'bodies of armed men, prisons, etc.,'[5] a mere reflex of supposedly 'economic' power, or to 'lose' it in a critical or bland empiricism of institutional biography, bureaucratic lineage, or local imposition. Much of the recent Marxist 'turn', influenced by a particular reading of Gramsci, which stresses the activity of establishing and reproducing 'consensus', remains marred by the same dichotomy between theoretical or empirical paradigms. Worse still there is now a rabid idealism in some such work which forgets the degree of mutuality between consensus and coercion in state formation. In none of these approaches is the meaning of state activities, forms, routines and rituals – for the constitution and regulation of social identities, ultimately of our subjectivities – adequately apprehended. Yet, we shall argue, state formation plays a major role in orchestrating this constitutive regulation, both by what it is and by what it does.

Questions of meaning are more conventionally seen as belonging to a separate realm, the historiography or sociology of 'culture'. But parallel criticisms can be made here. Where it is not overtly idealist, the history of self-developing ideas, or simply ahistorical and unempirical, cultural analysis has usually had little room for consideration of state regulation. There is a persistent empiricism in histories of culture – providing rich resources but dangerously reproducing a conventional separation of cultural reality from material life. This separation is hardly remedied by inflating the meaning of culture metaphorically (as a kind of add-on effect, remarkably similar to much treatment of gender, ethnicity, language competence, age and so on) as in discussions of 'the culture of' the factory, of work, of schooling, etc. There are, of course, exceptions on both sides.

What this book attempts is simultaneously to grasp state forms culturally and cultural forms as state-regulated. Our original plan was to give equal attention to both state formation and capitalism's wider cultural revolution. Considerations of space, however, have obliged us to concentrate on the former. We offer, in essence, an argument about English state formation, presented through a framework of historical narrative spanning the eleventh to the late nineteenth centuries. The context of that narrative is a double making: of rulers and ruled, of the rights of the former and the wrongs of the latter. Property and discipline are two sides of this one coin. The content of our narrative is a third making (and we stress it needs to be seen as a making, a construction): of the routines and rituals of rule, through which the first two makings are organized – not caused, but organized. Fundamental to this is their legitimation, in Weber's sense as that which confers authority on power. Though we deal here to some extent with state regulation of cultural forms, we cannot be said to have anatomized capitalism's cultural revolution in its wider contexts.[6] We insist, however – and this is the central, and most distinctive, argument of this study – that state formation itself is cultural revolution.

Let us elaborate a little (though what we have to say is best conveyed by the empirical and historical material which follows). The repertoire of activities and institutions conventionally identified as 'the State' are cultural forms, and cultural forms, moreover, of particular centrality to bourgeois civilization. Marx, who did not reduce the state to 'bodies of armed men', grasped this when he wrote in an early essay that 'the abstration of the *state as such* belongs only to modern times, because the abstraction of private life belongs only to modern times. The abstraction of the *political state* is a modern product.'[7] States, if the pun be forgiven, *state*; the arcane rituals of a court of law, the formulae of royal assent to an Act of Parliament, visits of school inspectors, are all statements. They define, in great detail, acceptable forms and images of social activity and individual and collective identity; they regulate, in empirically specifiable ways, much – very much, by the twentieth century – of social life. Indeed, in this sense 'the State' never stops talking.

We mean this very broadly indeed. What counts as 'politics' evidently receives much of its definition from the institutions of state (Parliament, parties, elections) through which it is organized, so that, for instance, the distinction between 'political' and 'industrial' strikes (or, much more generally, between 'public' and 'private' life) becomes second nature within our culture. But much else is nuanced, inflected, shaped too. Out of the vast range of human social capacities – possible ways in which social life could be lived – state activities more or less forcibly 'encourage' some whilst suppressing, marginalizing, eroding, undermining others. Schooling for instance comes to stand for education, policing for order, voting for political participation. Fundamental social classifications, like age and gender, are enshrined in law, embedded in institutions, routinized in administrative procedures and symbolized in rituals of state. Certain forms of activity are given the official seal of approval, others are situated beyond the pale. This has cumulative, and enormous, cultural consequences; consequences for how people identify (in many cases, *have to* identify) themselves and their 'place' in the world.

In contrast to much theorizing, we wish to stress at the outset that the specifics of state formation, and the forms of cultural relations which states regulate (normally naturalized or presented in terms of increasing 'provision' and 'access') hurt as much as they help. They are differential in their constitution (whose interests they further) and their effect (on whom, and how, they are imposed). In contrast to much empirical history, we seek to generalize this experience of painfulness beyond its normal depiction in terms of personal or group 'exceptionality': this is how politics and culture work within capitalism – a capitalism, we should also make clear at the start, which has always been integrally patriarchal.

We call this *moral regulation*: a project of normalizing, rendering natural, taken for granted, in a word 'obvious', what are in fact ontological and epistemological premises of a particular and historical form of social order. Moral regulation is coextensive with state formation, and state forms are always animated and legitimated by a particular moral ethos. Centrally, state agencies attempt to give unitary and unifying expression to what are in reality multifaceted and differential historical experiences of groups within society, denying their particularity. The reality is that bourgeois society is systematically unequal, it is structured along lines of class, gender, ethnicity, age, religion, occupation, locality. States act to erase the recognition and expression of these differences through what should properly be conceived of as a double disruption.

On the one hand, state formation is a totalizing project, representing people as members of a particular community – an 'illusory community', as Marx described it. This community is epitomized as the nation, which claims people's primary social identification and loyalty (and to which, as is most graphically illustrated in wartime, all other ties are subordinated). Nationality, conversely, allows categorization of 'others' – within as well as without (consider the House

Un-American Activities Committee during the McCarthyite era in the United States, or Margaret Thatcher's identification in 1984 of striking miners as 'the enemy within') – as 'alien'. This is a hugely powerful repertoire and rhetoric of rule. On the other hand, as Foucault has observed, state formation equally (and no less powerfully) individualizes people in quite definite and specific ways. We are registered within the state community as citizens, voters, taxpayers, ratepayers, jurors, parents, consumers, homeowners – individuals. In both aspects of this representation alternative modes of collective *and* individual identification (and comprehension), and the social, political and personal practices they could sustain, are denied legitimacy. One thing we hope to show in this book is the immense material weight given to such cultural forms by the very routines and rituals of state. They are embodied in the former and broadcast in the latter, made to appear as – to quote Herbert Butterfield on the Whig interpretation of history – 'part of the landscape of English life, like our country lanes or our November mists or our historic inns' (quoted in Kenyon 1981: 1407). State agencies are not of course the only means through which such moral regulation occurs, but they are central to it. 'The State' is as much 'the concentrated and organized force of society' (Marx 1867: 751) in the cultural sense as in the economic, concerting wider forms of regulation and modes of social discipline through which capitalist relations of production and patriarchal relations of reproduction are organized.

Emile Durkheim – a much neglected theorist, not least by the left, of the moral conditions of the bourgeois order and the role of state formation in creating and sustaining them – grasped this cultural dimension of state activity only too well:

Let us see how the state can be defined. It is a group of officials *sui generis*, within which representations and acts of volition involving the collectivity are worked out, although they are not the product of the collectivity. It is not accurate to say that the state embodies the collective consciousness [*conscience collective*], for that goes beyond the state at every point. . . . The representations that derive from the state are always more conscious of themselves, of their causes and their aims. They have been concerted in a way that is less obscured. The collective agency which plans them realizes better what is it about. . . . Strictly speaking, the state is the very organ of social thought. (1904: 49–50)

Durkheim concludes that the state 'is above all, supremely, the organ of moral discipline' (ibid.: 72)

Durkheim is clear, in these quotes and elsewhere, that 'the State' is not free-floating; it does not spin its 'representations' (of itself, of 'society', of individuals) out of thin air. It is, to begin with, parasitic upon the wider *conscience collective*, which it conversely regulates. The latter notion is an important one in Durkheim. The French *conscience* translates either as consciousness or as conscience, and Durkeheim intended the notion to have both cognitive and evaluative connotations. So do we: collective representations – ways in which we are collectively represented to ourselves, and in which 'permissible' parameters and forms of individual identity are defined and symbolized for us – are simultaneously descriptive and moral. Typically they present particular moral orders as description.

To this we would add an emphatic materialist – and historical – rider. The *conscience collective* itself is not free-floating either. Forms of social consciousness are anchored in historical experiences, and the material relations upon which they rest. In bourgeois society these are relations of inequality, domination and subordination, and social experiences in consequence differ from different standpoints in the social structure. This means, among other things, that the 'same' unifying representations from the perspective of 'the State' may well be differentially understood from 'below'. Examples we will encounter include notions of 'English' 'liberties', or 'democracy', or Protestantism, all of which are sites of protracted social struggle as to what they mean and for whom. We should not, in other words, take the state's statements at face value.

'The State' claims to speak from what Marx derided as 'so-called contemplation from the standpoint of society'. This:

means nothing more than the overlooking of the *differences* which express the *social relation* (relation of bourgeois society). Society does not consist of individuals, but expresses the sum of interrelations, the relations within which these individuals stand. As if someone were to say: Seen from the perspective of society, there are no slaves and no citizens: both are human beings. Rather, they are that outside society. To be a slave, to be a citizen, are social characteristics, relations between human beings. (1858: 264–5)

We are dealing with social individuals, in particular, historically constructed relations. This has two implications missing from Durkheim's account. First, the *conscience* in question – as Marx also stressed[8] – is always that of a dominant class, gender, race, delineating and idealizing its conditions of rule, in the final analysis as rules of individual conduct. Second, making this *conscience* genuinely collective is always an accomplishment, a struggle, against other ways of seeing, other moralities, which express the historical experiences of the dominated. And because society is not factually a unity these can never be finally erased. The moral discipline effected by state formation is therefore not, neutrally, about 'integrating society'. It is about enforcing rule.

Neither the shape of the state, nor oppositional cultures, can be properly understood outwith the context of the mutually formative (and continuing) struggle between them: in other words, historically. Too often these have been sundered. State forms have been understood within state formation's own universalizing vocabularies, without reference to what they are formed *against*; an evident vice of Whiggish history, but no less so of varieties of Marxism (and other sociologies) which comprehend 'the State' in abstracted and functional terms. Oppositional cultures are conversely comprehended through the grid of the various selective traditions imposed as if they were all there is to say and know about 'culture'. Where they are not outlawed as positive dangers to 'social health', they emerge as parochial, quaint, outmoded, cranky, in a word vernacular [9] – objects, at best, for a patronizing sentimentalism and nostalgia – without the salience of such depictions once being seen as having anything to do with state regulation. The third terms missing here are contradiction and struggle. It is the triadic interweaving of nation/state/culture, first understood historically, materially, relationally – as forms of claim, not neutral descriptions – and second understood as facets of the same kaleidoscope of knowledge/power relations, that we hope to make visible; turning, in this way, what are taken as answers into questions, above all questions as to the obviousness of certain identifications of, and relations between, human beings.

This brings us to a final preliminary point we wish to make about 'the' state, which is both a substantive and a methodological one. In a paper delivered to the 1977 BSA annual conference, disarmingly entitled 'Notes on the difficulty of studying the state',[10] Philip Abrams argued for abandoning the study of anything called 'the State' in favour of studying what he called 'politically organized subjection'. His reasoning was that both orthodox political science and Marxism had been hypnotized – by the dominant forms of capitalist civilization themselves, Marx's 'natural, self-understood forms of social life' (1867: 75) – into attributing to the *idea* of the state too much concreteness. As Marx realized, 'the State' is in an important sense an illusion. Of course, institutions of government are real enough. But 'the' state is in large part an ideological construct, a fiction: 'the state is at most a message of domination – an ideological artefact attributing unity, structure and independence to the disunited, structureless and dependent workings of the practice of government.' A feature we shall often find is illustrated here: descriptive names (seemingly neutral, natural, universal, obvious) are in fact impositional claims. The idea of the state, as Weber stressed,[11] is a *claim* to legitimacy, a means by which politically organized subjection is simultaneously accomplished and concealed, and it is constituted in large part by the activities of institutions of government themselves. Turning Durkheim on his head, Abrams argues that 'in this context we might say that the state is the distinctive collective misrepresentation of capitalist societies.' He elaborates, in terms which go far towards defining the project of this book:

The state, then, is not an object akin to the human ear. Nor is it even an object akin to human marriage. It is a third-order object, an ideological project. It is first and foremost an exercise in legitimation – and what is being legitimated is, we may assume, something which if seen directly and as itself would be illegitimate, an unacceptable domination. Why else all the legitimation-work? The state, in sum, is a bid to elicit support for or tolerance of the insupportable and intolerable by presenting them as something other than themselves, namely, legitimate, disinterested domination. The study of the state, seen thus, would begin with the cardinal activity involved in the serious presentation of the state: the legitimating of the illegitimate. The immediately present institutions of the 'state system' – and in particular their coercive functions – are the principal object of that task. The crux of the task is to over-accredit them as an integrated expression of common interest cleanly dissociated from all sectional interests and the structures – class, church, race and so forth – associated with them. The agencies in question, especially administrative and judicial and educational agencies, are made into state agencies as part of some quite historically specific process of subjection; and made precisely as an alternative reading and cover for that process. . . . Not to see the state as in the first instance an exercise in legitimation is . . . surely to participate in the mystification which is the vital point in the construction of the state. (1977: 15)

We aim to go behind the 'idea of the state', to show it as a construction, to decode its 'message of domination'. We are hardly the first to attempt this. State formation is something that has ever been contested by those whom it seeks to regulate and rule. It is, first and foremost, their resistance that makes visible the conditions and limits of bourgeois civilization, the particularity and fragility of its seemingly neutral and timeless social forms. This applies as much to 'the State' – the form of forms, *the* distinctive collective (mis)representation of capitalist societies – as elsewhere. Such practical criticism is a form of knowledge, and like all knowledge, inseparable from its forms of production (whence derived?) and presentation (how said and shown?). It is also, profoundly, a moral critique: what such struggles show again and again is the exact ways in which the regulated social forms of bourgeois civilization effect real, painful, harmful restrictions on human capacities. Such 'general knowledge' – disarmed by legitimate disciplines, denied by curricular forms, diluted in its being refused the accolade of scholarship, dissipated as 'empirical examples' in a thousand doctoral dissertations – is the 'classic ground' for an understanding of bourgeois civilization that does not simply parrot its 'encouraged' self-images, as well as for any feasible or desirable social transformation. We say this with some force here, because our own account, focusing as it does 'from above' on the intricate machinery of state formation and moral regulation, otherwise risks replicating the apparent coherence, the systematic, 'solid' features of that image in which the bourgeoisie try to make their world.

But state formation (the implications and consequences of policy, the very shape of 'the State') and state forms (the meaning of those routines and rituals, the total repertoire, the very weight of 'the State') are also made visible and coherently named from above. We do not have to subscribe to an evolutionary or cybernetic teleology or to over-inflate the systematic intentions or controlling competence of the agents involved to say this. But the same species of bad faith is involved in systematically ignoring – as is commonly done – the organized project of those with the social power to define, as is entailed in explaining enduring patterns of subordination by the 'false consciousness' of the subordinated. This is not a justification for conspiracy theory (though there is more than a grain of truth in Thomas More's description in his *Utopia* (1515: 132–3) of such a 'conspiracy' in the sixteenth century, and again in Adam Smith's discussion of government as a 'combination of the rich' in the 1760s!). It is a recognition of how the sharing of a certain moral and categorical framework orients action, in both its objectives and its forms, an argument for taking *agency* seriously. Particularly in our later chapters, we will give more space to such orientations to action, the animating philosophies of state, than is often done.

Our approach also draws on 'classical' sociological perspectives, in ways that should briefly be indicated here since we do not discuss them again before our concluding Afterthoughts to this book. Our major and most evident debt – congruent with that we acknowledged first, the practical criticism of a multitude of social struggles – is to Marx; though a Marx many of his followers would doubtless disavow (not least because of our refusal to see state formation or cultural revolution as 'superstructures')![12]

From Durkheim we have taken our central emphasis on moral authority:

The problem of sociology – if we can speak of a sociological problem – consists in seeking, among the different forms of external constraint, the different forms of moral authority corresponding to them *and discovering the causes which have determined these latter*. (Durkheim 1912: 208, n.4; a response to critics. Emphasis added)

But we have 'turned' that insight in at least three ways. We have sought to understand the conceptions of moral authority held by the socially powerful, and not see these simply as *ad hoc* justifications; to see there a recognition that the modes of control, or as we would prefer of regulation, have themselves to be morally justified even as they act to obscure the forms of power that make them thinkable in the first place. We have tried – a materialist emphasis – to make sense of how what became nameable as 'the machinery of government' is moralized not simply by overt and separate justification, but centrally in the combination of the mundane routines (which tend to drop below visibility in many accounts) and the magnificent rituals (too easily dismissed as decorative, or, following – but not comprehending – Bagehot, as 'dignified') of state. And we take the last part of Durkheim's statement – which we have emphasized – very seriously in inquiring through what shifts and changes did it become possible for the socially powerful to begin to think, see and act differently, recognizing in those changes (at various points in our historical narrative) resources for major shifts in the categories of political thought.

From Weber we have also taken much, not least his fruitful insistence on understanding authority as legitimated power. But particularly, we have tried to see ways in which we can extend his significant suggestions about 'the State' being the self-defined site, or set of sights and personnel, of claims – successful claims – to the monopoly of the legitimate use of force. State formation always returns to such a project of monopolization. 'The State' seeks to stand alone in its authority claims to be the only legitimate agency equally for this or that form of knowledge, provision, regulation or – that wonderfully neutral word – 'administration'. This is as much a part of the sinews of legitimated power as monopoly of the means of physical force (with which, of course, it is inextricably intertwined). In a sense it is the growing success of such claims that enables 'the State' to be named, as impersonal power, Hobbes's 'Mortall God', in the first place. Following through the shifts in the means of legitimation – above all, though not exclusively, the system of justice and the forms of political representation (together with, for a large part of our period, religion) – is a major theme of our narrative. We have tried not to forget that the essence of any claim is that it is contestable.

Enough by way of necessary general preliminaries. There will be little more overt 'theorization' before the concluding section of this book, where we will take up some wider issues of state formation in the social theory and historiography of capitalist civilization in the light of English historical experience. In the meantime our narrative will, we hope, speak for itself, fleshing out these brief and assertive suggestions. We take our title, *The Great Arch*, from a metaphor E. P. Thompson uses (quoted on p. ix) to characterize the reality of bourgeois revolution in England – a story of centuries-long embourgeoisement of England's dominant classes (and proletarianization of the ruled, the two being inseparable), complexly facilitated by the protracted making of a nation state through a series of what we will characterize as 'long waves' of revolution in government. Our specific focus in this book is on the latter; we cannot begin to tell the whole story in a work of this length.

This last point is important. We do not, in this book, pretend to provide a general history (or explanation) of either capitalism in England or the making of the English ruling class; we have a more limited topic, albeit one we would argue is central to the understanding of both. Valuable historical accounts of this wider context exist, which we see our own work as complementing and extending – if sometimes challenging, in their emphases.[13] Nor, equally importantly, do we claim to offer the kind of comprehensive narrative history of state formation one would expect from constitutional or administrative histories. If only for reasons of space, we have been selective in what we cover; each chapter here could have been a substantial book. We present, rather, a perspective on state formation as cultural revolution, a historiographic argument – no more, no less – about the 'classic ground' of capitalist civilization, in order, we hope, to shed further light on both the nature and origins of that civilization – not only in England – and the real peculiarities of the English. What we offer here is not, then, claimed as definitive: this is an essay – an attempt – in historical sociology, rather than a history in the conventional sense.

Finally, two particular clarifications – notices of areas insufficiently discussed, but nonetheless highly pertinent to our themes – need to be made at the outset. First, this book deals with English state formation in England. Not Britain, Great Britain, the British Isles, or the United Kingdom; not Wales, Scotland, Ireland, India, North and Central America, Australasia, Africa.[14] English state forms were expanded into all these areas, and imposed on their peoples, during the period covered in this book, and the 'imperial' qualities of English state formation were a fundamental aspect of both its materiality and its imagery. We say something about the latter, though not nearly as much as we would have liked. What we do not have space to discuss is the differential way English state forms were imposed, and experienced, outside England itself.

Second, as we have mentioned already, the state formation sketched here was and is more generally differentiated in its 'design', considered from above, and its 'meaning' – experience – considered from below. Just as the consequences and the contestation were and are different in Wales and Scotland (or Ireland and India), so too were and are different groups within England itself 'organized', in part by, but as much against, the 'same' forms of state, governance, regulation and rule. Above all, official politics as a separate sphere (and thus also the quality of the 'political nation') was a construction, as perspective and personnel, of male, white, Protestant, English propertied classes; a form of their organization and a central form through which they ruled others. We try wherever possible to signify this differential character of nation/state construction in our text, but the very focus of our narrative – on that 'political nation', on history 'from above' – constantly risks 'overlooking' exactly those outside and below. We should recall throughout that these are the majority.

One particular differentiated and differentiating facet of English state formation calls for strong and very general emphasis in this context; for so deeply embedded is it that it routinely goes unremarked. This particular notion of the proper public realm organizes, like a prismatic lens, other 'spheres' – notably those contrasting realms of 'the private': familial, dependent and domestic for most women and children; 'independent' and workplace- or task-related for most men. Of course across both lie further defining divisions – the kind of family form (and domestic duties) for aristocratic and later for high bourgeois 'ladies' is to be as clearly distinguished as the workplace 'occupations' of landed aristocracy, gentry and, later, capitalist entrepreneurs. But the gendered meta-organization of space and time, and the consequent attempt to regulate social identities along clearly demarcated gender divisions is worthy of very general mention – as a constitutive feature of all known capitalist civilizations – at the start. It has been a major effort and multiple effect of state formation in England. Across the period, the centrepiece of the social fabric was the family, its patriarchal order and society reflecting that of society as a whole; it has been (as it continues to be)[15] a major organizing metaphor of state. The pervasive masculinity of 'the State' is a feature which has been neglected in almost all studies until the last ten or fifteen years.[16] Yet consider, for a minute, what it means – for social identities, for subjectivities – to have had persisting lineages, routinized practices and normalized institutions which were exclusively (in all senses of the word) male for eight or nine hundred years.

This is not, then, history from below; the better side of the story goes untold, and that it does should be remembered throughout. As to why, we can do worse than quote Perry Anderson's concluding remarks to the Introduction to the second of his two very valuable volumes on state formation (though we would cavil at his overly neat separation of 'levels' of society):

A last word is perhaps needed on the choice of the *State* itself as a central theme for reflection. Today, when 'history from below' has become the watchword in both Marxist and non-Marxist circles, and has produced major gains in our understanding of the past, it is nevertheless necessary to recall one of the basic axioms of historical materialism: that secular struggle between classes is ultimately resolved at the *political* – not at the economic or cultural – level of society. In other words, it is the construction and destruction of States which seal the basic shifts in the relations of production, so long as classes subsist. A 'history from above' – of the intricate machinery of class domination – is thus no less essential than a 'history from below': indeed, without it the latter in the end becomes one-sided (if the better side). (1974b: 11)

Hobbes has said that laws without the sword are but bits of parchment . . . but without the laws the sword is but a piece of iron.

Samuel Taylor Coleridge, *The Friend*, 1809

I'd like to underline the fact that the state's power (and that's one of the reasons for its strength) is both an individualizing and a totalizing form of power.

Michel Foucault, 'The Subject and Power' (1982: 777)

There is not that thing in the world of more grave and urgent importance throughout the whole life of man, than is discipline. The flourishing and decaying of all civil societies, all the movements and turnings of human occasions are moved to and fro upon the axle of discipline. . . . Nor is there any sociable perfection in this life, civil or sacred, that can be above discipline: but she is that which with her musical chords preserves and holds all the parts thereof together. . . . Discipline is not only the removal of disorder, but if any visible shape can be given to divine things, the very visible shape and image of virtue.

John Milton, 1641 (quoted in Hill 1964: 218)

1

'A Remarkably Centralized Country': State Formation in Medieval England

> So narrowly did he cause the survey to be made that there was not one single hide nor rood of land, nor – it is shameful to tell, but he thought it no shame to do – was there an ox, cow, or swine that was not set down in the writ.
>
> *The Anglo-Saxon Chronicle*, on the Domesday survey

On 8 April 1960 General de Gaulle addressed both Houses of Parliament in Westminster Hall. Speaking of England – somewhat ruefully, one imagines – he asked this: 'At the worst moments, who ever contested the legitimacy or the authority of the state?' Radicals might demur. Ideologists of the wonders of Englishness might be more inclined to pose the matter in terms of the long pedigree of English democracy. But the general had a point. James Campbell et al. (from whom we borrow the anecdote) expand on it:

The origins of the security of the English state lie in the length of its history. This is the determinative contrast between England and the other great states of Europe. In no other has there been such continuity in the exercise of effective authority over so wide an area for so long. Cnut's writ ran from Yorkshire to Sussex and from Norfolk to Cheshire. So has that of all his successors, brief intervals of civil war apart. Continuity in the exercise of power brought with it, and was sustained by, continuity in the institutions of government. (1982: 240)

England, in Marc Bloch's words, 'was a truly unified state much earlier than any continental kingdom' (1967: 430); this is the first peculiarity of English state formation we wish to stress here. This 'unification' is the 'real relations' of and for not just the legitimacy (i.e. the formation of the key ideology) of 'the State' in England, but also the English state form imposed by conquest and brutal savagery in and on Wales, Scotland, Ireland, India, and it eventuates in that 'British Empire' which in 1933 covered over 23 per cent of the land surface of the globe and ruled a quarter of the world's population. George V's last words (as he lay dying, and according to *The Times*) in 1936 were 'How is the Empire?' 'The peculiarities of the English' are not some local instance of merely antiquarian interest.

But of equal importance is a second 'peculiarity'. That central state capacity in England was from the start – and for most of the period covered in this book – based upon a high degree of involvement of local ruling elites in the exercise of governance. Elaborate central bureaucratic structures did not emerge until very late in the day. Instead, major institutions of rule – Parliament, the whole panoply of shire government, the apparatus of justice – rested upon what Bloch calls 'that collaboration of the well-to-do classes in power, so characteristic of the English polity as long ago as the middle ages' (1967: 371). The institution of justices of the peace, dating from the early fourteenth century and surviving to the present day – Maitland's 'country gentlemen commissioned by the King' (1897: 209) – is symptomatic of this, and in some ways a metaphor for much of what was most peculiar, and characteristic, in English state formation. For Gleason JPs 'symbolize the polity of England' (1969: 1).

This relation between central state and local ruling class relates to a peculiarity of the English upper classes themselves, again noted by Bloch. 'In the French or German sense of the word, medieval England had no nobility; that is to say that among the free men there was no intrinsically superior class enjoying a privileged legal status of its own, transmitted by descent . . . [the ruling class] remained, as a whole, more of a "social" than a "legal" class . . . too ill-defined not to remain largely open' (1967: 330–1). This in part relates to the strength of the monarchy, which successfully sought to keep knighthood open and which in the later middle ages frequently buttressed gentry as a counterweight to the peerage. Perry Anderson comments on 'the exceptionally early demilitarization of the noble class . . . [which] allowed a gradual conversion of the aristocracy to commercial activities long before any comparable ruling class in Europe', so that by the seventeenth century the English landowning class was 'unusually civilian in background, commercial in occupation, and commoner in rank' (1974b: 127). From the middle ages onwards, England possessed what was for the time an extremely broad and unusually open political nation, sharing in the exercise of power. Bloch, Cam, Loades and others have sketched its contours at various times in its history.[1]

It goes without saying, of course, that this 'political nation' was an extremely small proportion of the English people as a whole (and even more so when state formation was extended to engulf the Welsh, Scots, Irish, Indian and other peoples). It was also resolutely male until 1918. Bloch is clear that the other side of the 'openness' in the middle ages was greater control over the peasantry – not least because of the strength of central authority in England – than most continental lords could exercise (1967: 270–4). It is as well to recall throughout our account this other story, which is not usually recounted along with the fables about 'the Oldest Democracy', 'the Mother of Parliaments', and the rest. Recall that the 'Great Reform Act' of 1832 increased the electorate by 280,814 men in England and Wales. In 1833 one in five men in England and Wales, one in eight men in Scotland, and one in twenty men in Ireland could vote. In 1886 the total electorate for England, Wales and Scotland was 1,902,270 men out of a total population (in 1891) of around 33 million, some 17 million of whom were female. Full franchise democracy (one adult person one vote) arrives only *in 1950* with the cessation of plural, privilege and property voting (all of Ireland is excluded from this statement),[2] with the far from inconsequential 'residues' of the House of Lords and the City of London![3]

The third feature of English state formation that deserves emphasis at the beginning of this survey is the peculiar flexibility of English state forms.[4] A superficial view of English constitutional history will reveal a very Whiggish continuity. Most of the great institutions of state – Parliament, the law, the Privy Council, the Crown itself – have their origins well back in the middle ages. Such continuities of form are indeed remarkable, and probably unparalleled elsewhere. The rhetorics surrounding this formal continuity have been, and remain, important cultural resources in the business of ruling. But beneath the apparent continuities lie important breaks, indeed revolutions in state formation. In this book we will trace what we might call the 'long waves' of English state formation: moments or periods of substantial revolution in government, above all the Norman/Angevin period, the 1530s, the seventeenth-century civil wars, and the 1830s – followed by longer periods of consolidation and eventual stalling. But what is worth remarking at the outset is the singular capacity of English state forms to accommodate substantial changes whilst appearing to preserve an unbroken evolutionary link with the past. It is of the utmost significance for an understanding of English political culture that the major Henrician statutes of the 1530s could invariably commence with some variant of 'It has always been the case that . . .', or that the revolutionaries of the seventeenth century could take their stand on the historic rights of Parliament and the liberties of freeborn Englishmen under Magna Carta and the common law.

The peculiarities we have touched upon so far are evidently connected with one another. England's precocious centralization around a comparatively strong crown limited the 'parcellization of sovereignty' typical of feudal polities. Monarchical strength forced the medieval ruling class to exercise its power more through evolving state forms than was normally the case elsewhere, and at the same time kept that ruling class relatively open and broadly based. Conversely, this made for the development of a broad political nation, and established forms of ruling, which were to limit any royal pretensions to absolutism. Through time, the social composition of the political nation was to change. But English state forms proved sufficiently flexible and deeply rooted to accommodate such shifts, and indeed often to serve as vehicles for them.

It is usual to date the first true 'revolution in government' in England from after the Norman conquest. But some resources for English state formation are older. The land conquered by William was already divided, in an orderly way, into shires and hundreds. Northumberland, Cumberland, Westmoreland, Durham and Rutland were created after 1066, but 'otherwise, a map showing the English shires as they were until 1974 represents to an astonishing degree the administrative geography of the early eleventh century' (J. Campbell 1980: 117n.). The division of the country into shires, each under a royal official, the sheriff, permitted an unusual degree of general control and uniformity of administrative action. The distribution of parishes – key units of local administration for most of our period – shows similar continuity from the twelfth to the nineteenth centuries.

Virtually all land was divided into hides for assessment purposes. The great Domesday survey of 1086 – for Maitland 'a magnificent exploit, an exploit which has no parallel in the history of Europe' (1897: 9), for James Campbell an 'incomparable' survey, 'proving England to have been a formidably organized state' (1980: 117) – probably stood in an Anglo-Saxon tradition familiar with large-scale surveys. Administrative use of written records goes back at least to the eighth century, while Anglo-Saxon Kings used letters (sealed and unsealed) for administrative purposes from the ninth century at the latest.

One important index of the central capability of the Anglo-Saxon state was its ability to tax. Levies of Danegeld are recorded 12 or 13 times between 845 and 926, and evidently 'rulers who could raise such taxes were powerful in a way that their successors, south of the channel, are not known to have been' (J. Campbell 1980: 130). Likewise with coinage, 'the English kings were running the earliest known, and the best, example of the system of *renovatio monetae* which by 1200 had come into use in many states from Poland to Portugal' (Campbell 1975: 40). Within this system the Crown could insist on all payments to itself being in coin of the current issue, which was replaced septennially. Campbell suggestes this was highly lucrative. He also offers evidence of central fiscal planning being executed 'in an elaborate and orderly way at local level' (1975: 40; cf. his 1980). Another indication of Anglo-Saxon state power, amply confirmed by archaeological evidence, is the extent of the fortress system.

Maitland long ago pointed to the importance of the Anglo-Saxon institution of the shire court for the subsequent evolution of both local government and, indirectly, Parliament (the early MPs were representatives of county courts). 'We must learn to think', he says, 'of the county as an organised unity which has long had a common life, common rights, and common duties' (1897: 44; cf. Elton 1974b: 41). Campbell et al argue that the post-conquest survival of these courts and the free classes who participated in them 'may well have done much to determine the later history of England' (1982: 245; cf. Bloch 1967: 371). Norman rulers also adapted Anglo-Saxon institutions of policing (frankpledge) and military service (the fyrd).

Overall, Campbell draws a strong contrast between tenth-century England and twelfth-century Capetian France.

In the one there is a reduction to uniformity; in the other the superimposition of royal government on whatever already existed, with as a consequence the France of the *ancien régime*, in some ways formidably united, in others with anomalies numberless and, for example, far more provincial distinctions in law than anyone has found in eleventh century England. (1975: 53)

The late Anglo-Saxon state, he considers, was not 'specious in its uniformity or rudimentary in its precocity. It was uniform and sophisticated and reflected not only power, but intelligence.' (1975: 54). Indeed he goes so far as to argue that it reveals 'a capacity for change and for order hardly matched until the nineteenth century' (ibid: 43), exhibiting fewer provincial variations in law and administration than did most European states in the eighteenth century. This legacy, on which the Normans and their successors were to build, was to have long-term consequences: 'if, ultimately, England avoided the fate of the rest of *ancien regime* Europe, it was largely thanks to a framework established by a régime yet more ancient' (ibid.: 54).

But most authorities would agree[5] that it was above all the Conquest which created a monarchy that was, in Perry Anderson's words, 'unrivalled in its authority and efficacy throughout Europe' (1974b: 113). Military conquest allowed a wholesale change in the ownership of manors, and this was to be an important basis for the monarchy's strength. Domesday records only two major English landowners, whilst by 1087 only one bishop and two major abbots were English.

Tenants in chief generally held land in many parts of the country, rather than the huge territorial principalities of the great Anglo-Saxon earls; though even here the Anglo-Saxons were already distinct in having no equivalent of *comités*, nobles whose authority over a county became hereditary. Within any shire royal power normally remained stronger than that of any single subject. The main exceptions to this were the Earldoms of Chester and of Shrewsbury, and the Prince Bishopric of Durham, border regions all. In addition, tenants in chief were very numerous in England. Bloch has pointed to the pardox entailed here. 'Although, in certain respects, no state was more completely feudal, the feudalism was of such a kind as ultimately to enhance the prestige of the Crown. In this country where every piece of land was a tenement, the King was literally the lord of all the lords' (1967: 430).

Monarchical strength allowed government of the counties by directly appointed royal officials, the sheriffs. Again in origin this institution is Anglo-Saxon. It was to sheriffs, rather than tenants in chief as such, that execution of major judicial powers, levying of troops and raising of taxes actually belonged. The great Norman barons were generally limited to enjoying a part of the profits of justice in the counties whose titles they bore. For a time, especially during Stephen's reign, the office of sheriff threatened to become hereditary in some of the great baronial families. But the Angevins succeeded in checking this potentially disintegrative tendency. In 1170 Henry II was able to sack all his sheriffs, subject their performance to an inquest, and reappoint only a few. Again Bloch catches the wider significance: 'because the public office was not completely identified with the fief, England was a truly unified state much earlier than any continental kingdom' (1967: 430).

Later the importance of the sheriff was to decline, with the monarchy relying more in the shires on justices of the peace, and, by the Elizabethan period, lords lieutenant and their deputies. By 1494 JPs were empowered to entertain complaints against sheriffs and extortions practised by them and their county courts, and to convict sheriffs and their officers summarily. But throughout the period it is the overall pattern we wish to stress. The disintegrative parcellization of sovereignty normal to feudalism is checked. The Crown is able to govern in the counties by agents acting for, and removable by, itself – albeit, importantly, agents drawn from the local political nation.

Under this unusually strong monarchy there developed important innovations in the actual conduct of government. 'The greatest result of the Norman Conquest', according to Plucknett, 'was the introduction of precise and orderly methods in the government and law of England' (1956: 11). Aylmer dates the most significant changes from c.1080 to c.1230 (1961: 422ff.). Central branches of administration began to go, in Tout's phrase, 'out of court' – to evolve into specialized institutions, independent of the King's immediate household and Curia Regis, and permanently based in London, rather than being peripatetic with the King. This happened first with the Exchequer, early in the twelfth century. In connection with finance, we should also note the early commutation, for the monetary payment known as scutage, of feudal obligations to military service – scutage was first collected in 1159 – and the first central taxation of personal property, the Saladin tithe of 1188. Separate records of Exchequer business, the tallies and the Pipe Roll, were kept from the reign of Henry I. By 1400, according to Kirby (1957), there were 'careers' established in the Exchequer. From the reigns of Henry II and Richard I onwards Curia's judicial business likewise became centred on Westminster in what became the central courts of common law.

Parallel to this institutional development was an immense increase in the keeping of written records, making literacy more and more a prerequisite for all administrators and leading to the early development of a 'clerisy' located in routines of administration. This 'official documentary system' is unparalleled in its coverage, continuity and comprehensiveness.[6] It reveals the very weight and shape of ruling – above all the central capability of governance possessed by the English ruling classes from the eleventh century onwards. The power involved in recording, preserving and retrieving 'facts' – defining realities – is one that grows rapidly by being used; behind the individual records is a formal authority which establishes routines and rituals, each buttressing the other.

What matters here are the *forms* of government that are being created. These are – for the time – remarkably orderly, thorough, precise, detailed, and national. One sign of this is the tradition, in medieval England, of surveys and 'inquiries'. We have already touched on Domesday. We might mention, at this point, the latter's immense significance as punishment – it was, as Maitland says (1897: 9; cf. Clanchy 1979: 18ff.), an exploit possible only in a conquered country. We should also record that other, *anti*-state tradition which also looks back to the Anglo-Saxons, and smouldered on for nine centuries: the oppositional historical vision (with its own conception of English 'liberties') of the Norman Yoke (see Hill's superb 1954). There were to be subsequent, if less spectacular, surveys throughout the medieval and early modern periods – the 1274 survey that began the Hundred Rolls records, the Quo Warranto survey of 1279, the 1291 valuation of church lands, Edward III's ministerial inquiries of 1340–1, Henry VIII's Valor Ecclesiasticus. The fact that such surveys were possible says much about the capability of the evolving English state. But more than this: through this form of action, rights (especially property rights) and powers (especially royal/state powers) are being defined.

Take, for instance, Quo Warranto. According to Michael Clanchy,

> no inquiry by any medieval government ever exceeded in scope and detail the survey inaugurated by Edward I in 1279, which immediately preceded the Quo Warranto prosecutions. Commissioners in each county were instructed to list by name and have written down in books all villages and hamlets and every type of tenement whatsoever, whether of the rich or the poor, whether royal or otherwise. The stated purpose of this survey was to settle questions of ownership once and for all. (1979: 6)

There are two points about this inquiry (and others like it) which need particular emphasis. First, it establishes that royal property differs in quality from any other. The monarch has the right to take any land (or its fruits) for which there is no proof that it truly belongs to those who use it. This form of alienating land to the monarch is remarkably similar to that used in the engrossing and enclosure movements of Tudor and later times, in its insistence on provision of legitimate title. Holdsworth (1972: vol. 1, 87ff.) is quite clear that such inquiries materialized kingship as particular powers. Second, the making of such inquiries also challenged alternative notions of legitimacy: not just customary right since 'time immemorial', but equally warrant by the sword. There is much to be drawn, as Clanchy does with great lucidity, from Earl Warenne waving his rusty sword and exclaiming, 'This, my Lords, is my warrant!' (1979: 21f.) – warriors against writers, custom against law, locality against centre, in short, the encroachment of control and regulation upon open, fluid relations.

Exactly the same applies to forms of familial relation; from a very early date these too are regulated in routinized ways. Bastardy, of course, long carried legal impedimenta (and in Tudor times female, though more rarely male, offenders were publicly whipped (Williams 1979: 209–10; Marchant 1969: 223–5)); the connection with stabilization of property is evident. Conversely marriage had to be a public and formal act, at least for legal purposes. Banns had to be read from 1200, and the ceremony held in public (usually at the church door); only marriages contracted *in facie ecclesiae* – certified as such where necessary by the bishop – were recognized in common law. Regulation continues in later centuries. After 1538 marriages had to be recorded in parish registers. By Lord Hardwicke's Act of 1753 publication of banns or purchase of a licence, the presence of two witnesses, and registration were made compulsory; falsification of the register of marriages was made a capital offence. Civil marriage – in a register office or other registered building, such as a nonconformist chapel – was introduced by statute in 1836. The secular equivalent of reading of the banns (until 1856) was notification to three successive weekly meetings of the Poor Law Board of Guardians. Baker calls 'common law marriage' as a description for 'unlicensed' cohabitation 'one of the most absurd solecisms of the twentieth century' (1979: 395). Here state regulation has actively and continuously enforced definition of 'acceptable' forms of social relationship. Diana Barker notes that marriage is unique among supposed contracts between adults in the degree to which its precise form (monogamous, heterosexual, for most of our period lifelong, dependent) is thus specified: 'there can be no bargaining between spouses, since the state declares what marriage shall be. It is not, in fact, a contract between the spouses, but rather they agree together to accept a certain (externally defined) status' (1978: 254). On the legal position of women within this marriage form, we shall have more to say below.

Clanchy's *From memory to written record* (1979) also brings out some crucial wider connections between 'literacy' and 'lawfulness' (we shall discuss 'the law' in more detail shortly) of relevance both to medieval and to later state formation. From an early date state activities focus coherently and cumulatively to regulate all forms of 'making public' – printing and publishing, dramatic performance, singing, speaking and/or reading aloud, preaching, graphic and other visual depictions, and so on. The double forms used here are significant: *licensing* approved individuals or places (and often examining and registering their products before they are made public), thereby criminalizing the unlicensed, and *regulation* by the criteria required if the status of proper, approved, acceptable and/or legalized was to be granted. Much of this activity can be understood in terms of making public (e.g. proper publications versus 'ephemeral material'; legitimate theatre versus travelling players) and thereby restricting access. Costs and prices regulate within and in part because of these prior and accompanying regulations – it is significant that the words 'cheap' and 'vulgar' (along with, as we have mentioned above, vernacular) can be used pejoratively.

Equally important are the deep roots of 'the clerisy' in the linkage of literacy and legality. The state formation we have sketched so far entailed the early development of lay, as well as ecclesiastical, clerks in the business of ruling routines. This term 'clerk' extends through to the later nineteenth century and beyond as a status term (as residually it still does in clerk to the justices of the peace, town clerk, clerk of the Privy Council, etc.). It was for centuries written into legal classifications in the privilege of 'benefit of clergy', which we will discuss in more detail below. But 'clerisy' develops across and above these later divisions and distinctions as relating more generally to the power of the word, and of all words what could be more powerful than 'the State'?

Who does not know what a poor and worthless creature man would be if it were not for the unity of human nature being preserved from age to age through the godlike form of the State. (S. T. Coleridge, quoted in Knights 1978: 42)

What is significant is the degree to which the sense of 'clerisy' in Knights' illuminating study (of the nineteenth century) obscures the embodiment of clerisy within – indeed, *as* – state servants, in that and many preceding centuries. Perhaps more significant is how literary lawfulness by such located members of the clerisy is embedded in the official documentary system and regulates the wider culture. Much of this is suggested but not developed by M. Cohen (1977) and M. Bisseret (1979) in their studies of linguistic practice from the mid-seventeenth century onwards. Finally, legal power is related directly to language use, first because some forms of words have to be used (and not only in court proceedings) though the restricted code of the latter – Latin, law French, precise and arcane forms of writ and plea – was a persistent means of rule and area of cultural struggle over the centuries (see Baker 1979: 183–91), and second because many words came to be legally defined, by both statute and case law. These centrally include gender terms, which we will explore in more detail below.

The other side of this revolution in government, deserving of equal weight, is the constraints this development of regular institutions, routines, rules and rituals of government placed upon the Crown itself, as well as upon other parties contending for a share in power. Already in 1215 Magna Carta acknowledged that the king operated within certain forms, his power was categorized through notions of its proper exercise. Gerald Aylmer, echoing Bloch's more general point made above, shows how from the reigns of John and Henry III onwards a 'classical' pattern of conflict, classical in the sense that it persisted without fundamental change for centuries, was emerging within state structures, over rival views of what the administrative system should be (1961: 425ff.). The Crown tended to rely on the king's personal servants and household agencies, while the magnates preferred the Council as an agency of administrative supervision, and control of established 'out of court' departments through their own nominees. This conflict was not resolved until the Tudor period. But the important point here is that both parties were constrained by developing state formation, to which their conflicts in turn contributed. Where this kind of dialectic is most apparent is in two central institutions of the English constitution: Parliament and the law.

The origins of Parliament are both ancient and contentious.[7] There is controversy over whether it was initially a representative assembly, called to discuss affairs of the realm and vote taxes, or rather an enlarged session of Council, whose main job was to decide pleas brought by petition – an embryonic political assembly, or a mere court. For Elton 'it was both – both a political and judicial body, or rather an occasion . . . on which all the affairs of government came together to be exercised in a meeting of the realm' (1974b: 20). Parliament originally had the same 'double root' as the Curia Regis. Under Henry III, the older idea of the feudal honour of England – the king and his tenants in chief – was gradually being superseded by that of the realm – the *universitas* or *communitas Angliae* – in which all men with an 'interest' in the kingdom, not just tenants in chief, could claim a voice. We mean men: there were to be no female MPs elected before 1919 or sitting before 1922, and their total has never exceeded 28; Glanvill expressed contemporary opinion when he wrote that women 'are not able, have no need to, and are not accustomed to serving their lord the King, either in the army or in any other royal service' (quoted in Shahar 1983: 11). Concurrently the establishment of regular courts of law divided pleas into those which were routine and those demanding special attention by the king. 'The English Parliament resulted from the necessity to find a new opportunity to amalgamate the political and judicial tasks once discharged by the Curia Regis' (Elton 1974b: 21). Hence the development of writs of summons to 'treat' with the king. Most business at this early stage was still the hearing of private pleas.

By the time of Edward I calling of Parliaments had become irregularly habitual. Still, at this stage, Parliament was 'a good way from being a real or a defined institution' (ibid.: 21). Membership was variable and at the pleasure of the Crown – representatives of shires and boroughs, for instance, were called to only 13 of Edward's 52 Parliaments. Procedure and forms of record remained haphazard. It was during the fourteenth century that Parliament gradually lost its judicial character of a court for private suits, and developed into a more clearly 'political' assembly.

Under Edward I, Parliament had remained essentially a royal instrument of government, and the permanent Council formed the animating instrument within it. This reflected the king's strength. Edward II's reign, by contrast, was the most troubled since Stephen's. 'In effect, the baronial opposition to Edward II took over the Parliament' (ibid.: 22). The core of Parliament was effectively transferred from the permanent Council to the lords of the Parliament, who in turn – like the king himself – sought support from lower down the social scale. This resulted in representatives of the communities being summoned with greater regularity. By the Statute of York of 1322 (whose interpretation, however, is controversial) matters touching the state of the king and the kingdom 'shall be treated, granted and established in Parliament by our lord the King, and with the consent of the prelates, earls, barons and of the commonalty of the kingdom'. Parliament 'was now, in the main, a political assembly of the great men of the realm, and representatives of the shires, boroughs, and the lower clergy were commonly called to attend and assent at meetings' (ibid.: 22–3). By the 1330s, as Cam (1945) shows, petitioning was becoming bifurcated: private or highly particular petitions going from Chancery clerks to auditors and thence to appropriate officials; common petitions to the clerk of the Parliament for reference to the King in Council or the lords of the Council with or without the discussion of the Commons, though the latter in 1327 protested about any bills coming forth which they had not properly examined.

Cam also shows the way that, from an early date, the Commons was being manipulated. Magnates and others used the Commons to 'apparently initiate' as common issues what were sectional points: 'The law against poachers of 1315 and the Ordinance on maximum prices of 1315 were instigated by the magnates and can fairly be ranked as class legislation' (ibid.: 187). Autocratic and despotic, as well as plainly sectional, legislation was originated in the Commons to give it a claim to being 'of the commonwealth of the realm'. Neale (1924: 151–3) shows the later Commons being used in the same way and argues against simplistic readings of the lower House's 'initiatives'. Nonetheless there is one change Cam notes which is significant: although 69 of 70 statutes of Henry V arise from petitions, this is true of only 17 of 114 Acts of Henry VII.

Elton sees the year 1340 as marking 'the end of a truly formative period' (1974b: 23). In that year representatives of the lower clergy withdrew to Convocations, and representatives of the shires and boroughs came together in a common body, prefiguring the later House of Commons. In 1340, too, the Parliamentary rolls acquired regularity of form and became a continuous record, distinct from both the plea rolls of the royal courts and the archives of the king's Council. Edward III's French wars and the crisis of 1340–1 accelerated the development of Parliament, his pressing need for money forcing him into alliance with the Lords of the Parliament and dependence on the Commons. The Crown's need for assent to taxation was to be a major factor in the growth of Parliamentary power throughout its history. Edward III's reign:

witnessed the achievement of the characteristic bases of Parliamentary power. Not only was the body recognised as the only proper source of consent for taxation, but by about 1340 it was also becoming doctrine that ordinances made in response to petitions in Parliament were superior to all other forms of legislation; in 1376, in the Good Parliament, the role of the institution as the effective weapon against misgovernment was consolidated in the processes against Edward's ministers. (Elton 1974b: 24)

The events around 1340 are illustrative of a more general way in which at times of crisis forms of expressing power can become solidified. This momentum was sustained in the reigns of Richard II and Henry IV.

During the fifteenth century the Commons evolved from petitioners whose demands the king submitted to the Lords of the Parliament, for their advice, to being essential assentors to legislation. In 1399 the Commons denied any right to assent; in 1414 they claimed it, but Henry V was unsympathetic; by 1460 their assent was regularly recorded. By the 1450s references to a lower and higher House were commonplace. Edward IV wooed the Commons and from the start treated them as constitutionally equivalent to the lords. Signs of the changes underway are again shown in forms of record. From 1484, the public business of Parliament is no longer recorded as a list of petitions, but simply as a list of statutes. There is a parallel shift in the form of impeachment proceedings. After the mid-fifteenth century, instead of the Commons acting as prosecutors in trials held before the Lords, there develops joint legislative action through Acts of Attainder. By 1489 the judges could declare an attainder invalid because it lacked Commons' assent.

Consent is important not just at the level of who assented – or was deemed to assent – but equally in terms of how that consent was expressed. The formalization of Parliament as the proper body to give the consent of the realm was an important aspect of its evolution, with far-reaching implications. Cam is clear on the early availability of Parliament as a forum through which public demand and grievance could be expressed, this simultaneously restricting the legitimate forms through which political statements came to be made (1945). By the early seventeenth-century Parliament had secured a virtual monopoly of consent. This was undoubtedly convenient for the Crown. But it also had other consequences: notably, it could leave a considerable vacuum when, as in the 1630s, Parliament did not meet for long periods. Again we see how forms of government which strengthened the Crown could also become, under certain circumstances, a basis from which 'the State' could come to be viewed as something distinct from the monarch.

The English Parliament was distinctive in several ways. It was, in Perry Anderson's phrase, 'singleton and conglomerate' (1974b: 114–15; cf. Elton 1974b: 37ff.). From the beginning it was a national assembly – it had no regional competitors. What were represented in it were localities – communities. As Cam shows (1962: 273f.), England was the first polity organized through an explicit theory and practice of representation. The communities brought into the organization we have come to know as 'the State' were as follows: 1110, the vill; 1166, the shires and hundreds; 1226, cathedral chapters; 1254, diocesan clergy; 1258 barons, and in 1265 boroughs. This 154-year history bears comparison with the 120 years (1832–1950) devoted to extending the franchise. We should also note – and this again is a contrast with most continental assemblies – that from 1294 to 1872 the writs ordering elections specifically denied the possibility of representatives in Parliament being delegates of the communities they 'represented' (see Edwards 1934).

It is important, also, that what was represented was not, as in comparable European bodies, the three conventional social estates. The tripartite organic social classification – those who pray, those who fight, those who work – was widespread throughout feudal Europe,[8] and its partial displacement in England, as an organizing code for institutional forms, is of a piece with other peculiarities. The clergy were not represented in Parliament as a body at all, after 1340, when the lower clergy withdrew to Convocations. Such prelates as continued to be present sat as tenants in chief of the Crown or royal officials and not in any special ecclesiastical capacity. The Parliamentary peerage were not elected by their kind and did not represent the nobility as an estate. They did not even coincide with tenants in chief, but can in fact only be defined circularly as those directly summoned by Parliamentary writ. They were, in essence, king's councillors, 'the enlarged General Council of the realm' (Elton 1974b: 36). The Commons, finally, did not correspond to the European 'third estate'. In an estate-based structure, knights of the shire would have sat with the Lords – they did not. But nor did the line between Lords of the Parliament and knights of the shire correspond to that of higher and lesser nobility. Men – as, of course, they always were – sat in one Parliament by individual summons, and the next as knights of the shire. 'From the start the Commons did not represent a class or classes; they represented communes, the units of local government under the king' (Fryde and Miller 1970a: 9; cf. Cam 1962).

All this made for the early development of a conception of Parliament as a representative national assembly. In 1309 the Commons described themselves as 'knights and folk of the boroughs who came to the King's Parliament at the King's command and for the people'. Chief Justice Thorpe wrote in 1366 that Parliament represents 'the body of the realm' (Elton 1974b: 36). By 1480, it was being asserted that Acts of Parliament were universally binding 'forasmuch as every man is party and privy to the Parliament' (ibid.: 37); 'a man was there . . . "a public, a councillor, to the whole State" (Cam 1962: 278). By the 1520s, this notion was commonplace. It reflected a reality. By the standards of the time, the English Parliament was unusually representative – of, at least, those we have referred to as the political nation (a crucial caveat). The Lords retained much of the character of an extended General Council. The Commons were unusual in the degree to which the communities they represented coincided with the administrative divisions of the realm – the ancient structure of the shires – in the case of the knights, and in the number of towns represented by borough members. Finally, by contemporary standards the English House of Commons was properly elected to an extent unknown elsewhere. Knights were elected by freeholders of the shire, a body large enough to merit franchise restriction by the introduction of a 40-shilling qualification in 1429. In the boroughs the qualification was usually all burgage tenants or all who paid certain local taxes. The House was unusually large by European standards, the largest in Europe both absolutely and relative to population by the end of Elizabeth's reign.

We should again stress, however, that it was the political nation, not the people, who participated in all this. The English theory is of virtual representation: MPs represent all because they speak for all, not because they are chosen by all. MPs were not delegates; the franchise was limited (and was further restricted after the 1660s); and as we have shown, universal adult suffrage was long resisted. What we have, in this 'political nation', is a very slowly expanding social–political–moral category, always doubly 'seated', locally (and/or in terms of an interest, e.g. 'We of the Manufacturing Interest') and centrally. Whilst it is conventional to think of lines of representation vertically, as local to central, we also have to understand the horizontality of this system. Whatever blurring there may have been at the boundaries of the political nation – mere money-making versus social standing – there was always a clear baseline; those under it were to be spoken for/against. They emphatically were not us. This is quite graphic even in the late nineteenth-century (around the 1867–84 extensions) when 'suddenly' Gladstone, Mill, Spencer all 'recognize' the working class as 'like ourselves', and therefore, generally, worthy of the vote.[9]

Elton has a final emphasis very pertinent to our argument. Against the tradition of historiography which constantly looks – teleologically – to Parliament as a counterweight to the Crown, and focuses on moments of political conflict between the two, he has consistently stressed 'the early and continuous efficacy of the English Parliament as an active business organization, especially as distinguishing it from representative institutions elsewhere' (1974b: 14). 'From first to last, Parliament has been an instrument of action, a body which *does* things and achieves ends' (ibid.: 8; cf. his 1971). Elton sees the vitality of the institution, and its survival and expansion in the sixteenth and seventeenth centuries when so many of its European counterparts were in abeyance or decline, as stemming largely from this. Parliament was important for the propertied classes, in facilitating their private affairs. Kings and queens found Parliament most valuable as a routinized expression of the assent of the realm (or that portion of it which mattered, 'speaking for' the rest) – particularly to taxation. The non-delegate character of Parliamentary representatives, their *plena potestas*, full powers to commit the communities they represented, was crucial to this, and contrasts with most comparable continental bodies. The business-like nature of Parliament is above all evident in the regularity of its organization – records, routines, rules, standardized forms and formulae – from an early date (see Elton 1974b: 49–50).

Parliament, and with it a theory and practice of representation, thus became a significant means of organizing consensus within a restricted political nation. The whole subsequent history of state formation takes this 'organized consensus' as central. Consider, in the light of what we have sketched, this quotation from 1974:

Probably the worst aspect of the threatening political battle is that, whether or not there is an election, the essential struggle will take place outside Parliament. For three hundred years [i.e. since 1688?] the British people have managed to keep almost all their main struggles within the parliamentary arena. As new social groups have sought political influence commensurate with their changing position in the social structure, they have been able to find it inside the House of Commons, fighting their fights within the rules of parliamentary order and avoiding class conflict. The decision of the Labour Party to go into Parliament as representatives of the broad mass of organised working people was the greatest single victory for the orderliness and humanity of the parliamentary process . . . the fabric of the nation is in some danger. (Butt 1974: 14)

Within England, and this is shown very well in the long complex history of trades unions, to be active outside this 'official politics' (in terms of the central or local state forms) was to be semi-criminal, precisely in a neat double sense an 'outside agitator'. But this system of official politics – normalized to become politics as such – and all its rituals of ruling itself requires contextualization. If this form of rule represents consensus, then justice represents coercion. And it is precisely that mythic entity 'the law' – as discourse, practice and institution – which unifies both. Who could ever be above/outwith 'the law'? Only outlaws (who could also, as in the Robin Hood stories, be popular and anti-state heroes). Those 'outside the law' form potential or actual 'enemies of the state', whether most women,[10] lay preachers, gypsies, Catholics, aliens, trades unionists, and through to today 'the Irish' (in the context of the Prevention of Terrorism Act). Those outside the political nation suffer 'justice'. The organized classifications of 'the law' concern us as much as systems of representation.

Consideration of the law and legal institutions is also fundamental to our discussion for other reasons. Jurisdiction – literally, speaking the law – was pivotal to all feudal polities: in Perry Anderson's words (1974a: 153) 'justice was the ordinary name of power'.[11] Growth of a nationally unified system of law is indicative of the limitation of 'parcellization of sovereignty', bespeaking the declining power of feudal lords individually vis-à-vis the Crown, if not as a class vis-à-vis the peasants. Max Weber insisted on the indispensability of a stable, rational legal system for the development of modern capitalist economy.[12] Ideas of the rule of law and the equality of citizens before it were to become central to the values, aspirations and ideological legitimations (the etymology of the very word speaks volumes, lawfulness becoming a generic term for that which 'authorizes' power!) of the bourgeoisie.[13] It is, then, of considerable significance that:

Compared with the rest of Europe, England and its Common Law were precocious. The system of writs ... and the attendant procedure and terminology, the developed notion of pleas of the Crown with all the machinery for the discovery and trial of criminals, the existence of central and itinerant royal courts capable of subjecting the whole nation to the King's law and government – all these things were unique to England. (Baker 1979: 27)

The Norman Conquest initially occasioned few changes in English law. The most significant, from our viewpoint, are the Conqueror's severance of ecclesiastical from temporal jurisdiction, and his requirement that loyalty to the king overrode all other feudal obligations. But the strong Norman–Angevin monarchy was a fertile soil in which a national system of law could grow. The origins of the common law as such lie in the twelfth century. A surviving text of around 1118, *The laws of Henry I*, cites three distinct systems of law as still operating in England – the law of Wessex, the law of Mercia, and the Danelaw – with considerable variations between counties within each. Sixty years later, the treatise traditionally ascribed to Henry II's justiciar, Ranulf Glanvill, though still acknowledging local variation, gives unquestioned primacy to the customs of the king's court – the *jus et consuetudo regis*, the law and custom of the realm. As often, theory follows practice: one of the things which most matters about Glanvill, reflecting the changing circumstances of the century, is that the theory is written down at all. The same is true of another document of the period, *The dialogue of the Exchequer*, which describes in detail the Exchequer's work. It is similarly significant – to jump ahead of our narrative for a minute – that studies of the law through cases were (along with religious works) amongst the first books to be printed in England, in the 1490s.

During Henry II's reign the judicial business of the Curia Regis first followed the Exchequer out of court, settling down at Westminster in what was later to be known as the Court of Common Pleas. This court developed under Richard I (an absentee king – through most of his reign England was governed by justiciars), was temporarily abolished under John, but was revived and given protection in Magna Carta. Common Pleas was 'the court which more than any other made the medieval common law' (Baker 1979: 35). It had jurisdiction over all suits in which the king had no interest, that is, all real actions (actions involving immovable property) and all personal actions not alleging breach of the peace. Henry took under his protection the seisin (possession) of all freeholders, providing in his court new remedies (novel disseisin, mort d'ancestor, darein) for all who were disturbed in their possession. Common Pleas increasingly became the major court of first instance. 'The consequence of this was a rapid development of law common to the whole land; local variations are gradually suppressed; we come to have a common law' (Maitland 1897: 13). Maitland may paint in broad brush strokes here, but his general point is valid. This should not, incidentally, be seen in terms simply of an aggressive Crown subduing local variation. The royal courts were attractive to litigants from the start because of their more effective process and execution and (after 1200) their written records, as against the vagaries and uncertainties of local courts. Milsom brings out a crucial wider implication of this development: 'the relationship between lord and tenants was subjected to the superior jurisdiction of royal courts and so became one of reciprocal private rights rather than of dependent allocation. . . . The transfer of jurisdiction made abstract rights out of claims to be allotted what was at the management's disposal' (1981: 5). The establishment and transformation, through the centuries, of 'private rights', and the wider connection of state formation and the individualization of social relationships, will be central themes of this book.

Suits in which the king did have an interest continued, initially, to be heard before the king and his advisers (coram rege). Business coram rege was first separately recorded in 1200, and regularly recorded after 1234. Within a generation what was to be known as the Court of King's Bench had evolved into a fully fledged court beside Common Pleas, with defined and separate jurisdiction. Though in later centuries King's Bench extended its jurisdiction into the civil arena, its major jurisdiction in the middle ages was over all criminal cases. By the fourteenth century King's Bench too was domiciled in Westminster Hall. The Exchequer developed a common law jurisdiction later, to become one of the major central courts; Chancery developed a distinctive 'equity' jurisdiction and procedures of its own.

Henry II also developed the germs of what was to become the assize system. Though there were occasional earlier precedents for itinerant justices, these had not been systematic. In 1166 Henry appointed two justices to tour England, and in 1176 he organized itinerant justices into six circuits of assize. These were known as Justices in Eyre. 'General Eyres' periodically visited every county, investigating crimes, unexplained deaths, misconduct by officials, feudal and fiscal rights of the Crown, and private disputes: 'they were not merely law courts: they were itinerant government' (Baker 1979: 15). Parallel to General Eyres, and probably of ultimately greater significance for the development of the assize system (see Cockburn 1972: 16ff.), there grew up more limited commissions. The commission as such is very important as a political form: commissions of widely varied sorts were to be much used over the centuries.

Visits of General Eyres to the counties were relatively infrequent (one in every six or seven years on average), while litigation in the central courts at Westminster was expensive and often impractical, since presentment of crimes and trial by jury required the presence of at least twelve local men. Commissions – 'ad hoc grants of judicial authority by letters patent under the great seal of England' (Baker 1979: 19) – attempted to compromise evolving central justice with the need for local investigation and trial. The major commissions, developed in the twelfth and thirteenth centuries, were oyer and terminer (to inquire into, hear and try offences specified), gaol delivery (to try or release prisoners in a given gaol), and petty assizes (for civil cases). These were supplemented by the so-called nisi prius system, developed during the twelfth century and put on a regular footing after 1285. Under this arrangement local juries were summoned to appear at the central courts at Westminster on a certain day unless first (*nisi prius*) justices shall have come to the county to receive their verdicts and transmit them back to Westminster.

During the thirteenth century these various activities coalesced into the regular assizes system. General Eyres as such fell into desuetude. It became usual for commission members to be men of law. After 1340 they had to be justices of Common Pleas or King's Bench, or sergeants-at-law. In 1293 the commissioners were organized into four regular circuits, extended to six in 1328. Statutes of 1299 and 1328 obliged assize commissioners to deliver gaols, and it became usual for them to be given general commissions of oyer and terminer.

All this settled into a routine. Twice a year two judges or sergeants would be assigned to each of the six circuits, through which they would ride with their clerks and records during the vacation. At each county town, or other appointed place, the commissions would be read out in public and the Justices would proceed to take the Assizes, deliver the gaol, try any other prisoners accused before them, and try the other civil cases at nisi prius. (Baker 1979: 20)

This 'routine' was to prove remarkably durable. It lasted, in essentials, until 1971. Bacon called justices of assize 'glasses or mirrors of state'. It was a two-way mirroring: they were the king's mouth and ears; and the eyes of the kingdom. All justices of assize were addressed before going on circuit by the monarch or the Lord Keeper; after 1715 these instructions were printed. We will exemplify the substance of some of their 'charges' below. From 1346 they were to oversee sheriffs, escheators, bailiffs and jurors; after 1489 they handled appeals for redress about which magistrates had been unable to remain impartial. Lord Keeper Bacon, addressing them in Star Chamber in 1617, called them 'the planets of the kingdom':

and no doubt you have a great stroke in the frame of this government, as the other have in the great frame of the world. Do therefore as they do; move always and be carried with the motion of your first mover, which is your Sovereign. (quoted in Cockburn 1972: 151)

'From Henry II's reign onwards', Michael Clanchy writes, 'the legal system had a fixed identity because of its set procedures. Bureaucracy set in fast and the forms of the possessory assizes and the main elements of the criminal law remained in being until the 19th century' (1983: 154). The crux lies in the development of standardized and regular procedures, like the forms of writ. Pollock and Maitland see this 'new, written and authoritative formalism' as 'an English peculiarity . . . for the like of which we shall look in vain elsewhere', made posible by 'the exceptional vigour of the English kingship' (1968: II, 558). Such procedures routinized justice, and made litigation in the royal courts easier (contributing to the decline of most other courts; manorial courts, in the middle ages, being a partial, and significant, exception, as we will see shortly). They also had another far-reaching effect:

Without being aware of it, Henry had achieved what Max Weber refers to as the 'routinisation of charisma'. The majestic power of the King, symbolised by his seal showing him seated crowned on his throne, was disseminated throughout the kingdom [as later throughout the empire] in thousands of royal writs containing his orders. (Clanchy 1983: 156)

Equally, however, this centralized system continued to depend upon local opinion and involvement. The essential decisions were made by local juries. More generally, the whole system fitted into the existing and ancient fabric of sheriffs, counties and hundreds – grand juries originally represented hundreds, writs were generally addressed to sheriffs, the assizes sat in the day and place of the county court. The evolution of the common law is a prime instance of both the relation between centre and locality and the novel uses of old forms we have pointed to as more general features of English state formation.

Magna Carta is generally reckoned the beginning of statute law, and is important here for its resonance down the centuries. It enunciated the famous principle that 'no freeman shall be arrested, or imprisoned, or dispossessed, or outlawed, or exiled, or in any way ruined, except by lawful judgement of his peers or by the law of the land' (quoted in Clanchy 1983: 196) – save, in other words, by 'due process'. After all caveats, according to Clanchy (ibid.: 198), it remains a highly original document. 'For better or worse', he concludes, 'England was . . . the first country in Europe to have a written constitution, whereby people's rights were enshrined in an official document disseminated and recited throughout the land'.[14] Magna Carta was issued in four versions (1215, 1216, 1217, 1225) and repeatedly confirmed by later kings.

Of course we should qualify 'people' here as we have done for the 'political nation' above; and a more general observation is called for. The law was organized by (as it organized) social classifications of both class and gender. Villeins, the bulk of the peasants, were excluded from the public courts in matters affecting relations with their lord, where they were subject to his jurisdiction, exercised in the manorial court. As Bloch puts it, with the rise of 'public' justice:

a new dividing line whose practical importance was evident to all was drawn through English society. On the one hand, there were the true subjects of the

King to whom was extended, at all times, the protection of his courts; on the other, there was the mass of the peasantry, largely abandoned to the jurisdiction of the lord of the manor. (1967: 272)

In the case of gender, such structuring went very deep and was to last for a very long time indeed; we are not fully rid of it yet.

Blackstone, writing in the eighteenth century, accurately summarized the position of married women in English law when he stated: 'The very being or legal existence of a woman is suspended during the marriage, or at least is incorporated into that of the husband' (quoted in Baker 1979: 395). This was of course an unsustainable fiction, like many such social classifications. Women (like villeins) had criminal responsibility – they could feel the weight of the law, and a husband could not be executed for his wife's crimes. But a married woman could neither own property nor make contracts in her own right. Under common law all her property passed to the husband on marriage: her chattels (personal property) for his absolute use and disposal; her real property for his use (including alienating its fruits) for the duration of the marriage, or, if children were born, his lifetime. By the sixteenth century this uncompromising doctrine could be slightly modified by the equitable concept of separate use, whereby property could be settled for the wife's use alone: even here, from the eighteenth century the device of 'restraint upon anticipation' could prevent the wife alienating such property while married. But this protected the women of the landed classes only. Not until 1870 was the doctrine of separate use extended to wages. Only by statutes of 1935 and 1949 was a wife given the same absolute rights to own property as a man. Nor did she gain equivalent legal rights to make contracts until 1935. The logic here was impeccably summarized by Beaumanoir: 'the dumb, the deaf, the insane, and the female cannot draw up a contract, neither alone nor through a representative, since they are subservient to the authority of others' (quoted in Shahar 1983: 92).

A wife could not sue or be sued at common law in her own name alone; in particular, she could not sue her husband (in most areas she still cannot). The latter was in English law her baron. Murder of a husband was petty treason (as was murder of a master by his servant), not simple homicide, until 1828. Petty treason carried the penalty of death by burning and, like all treasons (and unlike, in the middle ages, murder), was not subject to benefit of clergy. The latter – the right of 'clerics' (in practice this category was fictionally extended to embrace all male literates) to be tried in ecclesiastical courts, which could not impose the death penalty – was in any case, before the late sixteenth century, an exclusively male privilege. In petty treason we see very clearly how *particular* hierarchic and patriarchal conceptions – ruling images – of family and political community are made to mirror one another. Before 1857, divorce by Act of Parliament – the only kind of divorce available – was not only a prerogative of the rich, it was also almost entirely a prerogative of rich men. In only four cases (out of some three hundred petitions in total in the eighteenth and nineteenth centuries) were divorces granted to female petitioners. The first occurred in 1801 and involved the husband's adultery with his wife's sister; the other three concerned bigamy or incest; a woman's plea on grounds of her husband's repeated infidelity and violence (he regularly whipped her) was rejected in 1848. After 1857, where a man could obtain divorce through the courts on grounds of adultery, a woman had also to prove cruelty or desertion (until 1923). In cases of separation women had no rights of custody or access to their children before 1839, when limited rights were granted. In common law, sons inherit before sisters born before them. We could continue.

In both these cases a much more general feature of state formation is evident, exactly as it is in the 'representative' claims and practices of Parliament. Construction of national forms and projection of unifying imagery – the *common* law – on one level, goes hand in hand with the establishment and manipulation of detailed and differentiated social classifications on another. The law – or any other state form – rules through both; or better, through their interplay, the universalistic claims of the former legitimating and at the same time obscuring the selecting and differentiating practices of the latter. In general it behoves us to remember that the 'rights of freeborn Englishmen' were emphatically rights of (some) freeborn, English, men.

In the same connection, we should note that in criminal trials common law procedures were heavily weighted against the accused. Prisoners who refused to plead were subjected to the grisly torture of *peine forte et dure* – being pressed to death with heavy weights – abolished only in 1772, and then replaced by automatic conviction (until 1827); the last instance of pressing occurred in Cambridge in 1741 (Baker 1979: 416). Until 1702 an accused's right to call witnesses was doubted, and they were not sworn; not until 1867 could defence witnesses deposit evidence before trial or be bound to attend it (a right the prosecution had enjoyed since at least the 1550s). Accused were not, normally, allowed legal counsel in either preparing a case or cross-examining prosecution witnesses, until 1692 for treason and 1836 for felony. Most trials remained very speedy affairs, several capital cases being 'disposed of' at a single sitting, well into the nineteenth century.

Other early statutes worth noting here deal with enclosure and engrossing (1235, 1267, 1285 and so on) and – often 'of uncertain date'

– the regulation of weights and measures. Statute law is the most visibly Erastian of all legal forms; what is most interesting, however, in the English context, is its articulation with common law, the two being cemented in a generalizing conception of the 'rule of law'. English law plays on two rhetorics of authority: the custom, common sense, pragmatics, of 'case law', and the origins of statute in Parliament, representing 'the body of the realm'. This is a wonderfully flexible repertoire: case law can be superseded by statute, statute 'interpreted' in the courts, without legitimacy ever being lost. Legitimacy is conferred less by particular statutes or rulings than by the very forms of lawfulness as such. Holdsworth considered this 'a far more efficient protector of constitutional government than an unalterable fundamental law' (1924: 17), providing a 'legal mould, and the legal forms and concepts . . . the media of public discussion' (ibid.: 39). This is a very important insight.

To return to our narrative. The next reign, that of Henry III, was 'the golden age of judge-made law' (Maitland 1897: 18). Business in the royal courts increased and the greater part of the common law – especially the land law – took shape. It is this that is recorded in the treatise ascribed to Bracton (c.1250–60), which cites over 500 decisions of the king's judges. In substance, as well as form, the law is achieving fixity. By the end of the reign, in Maitland's view, 'it is more and more felt that for new laws the consent of the estates of the realm, at all events of the baronage, is necessary' (ibid.: 17). The first 13 years of the next reign, Edward I's, saw unparalleled legislative activity, comparable only with the 1530s and the 1830s. Thereafter:

we may turn page after page of the statute book of any century from the 14th to the 18th, both inclusive, without finding any change of note made in the law of property, or the law of contract, or the law about thefts and murders, or the law as to how property may be recovered or contracts enforced, or the law as to how persons accused of theft or murder may be punished. (ibid.)

This needs considerable qualification: although the forms of the law remained the same, it was in fact frequently updated, the use of fictions being one indication of this. However, Edward I's statutes do mark the beginnings of the principle that changes in the law require the assent of Parliament; though Chief Justice Hengham, in this reign, illustrated the point we drew from Holdsworth above when he told learned counsel not to gloss a statute, with the words 'we know it better than you, because we made it' (Plucknett 1949: 73). In our own time, the judgements and writings of Lord Denning indicate a not dissimilar perspective on the law.

The final secular judicial institution we wish to consider here is the justices of the peace (JPs). During the thirteenth century, knights had been assigned to keep the peace in the shires, sometimes elected by the county court. Initially this was a policing rather than a judicial function, but it became common for them to be employed on special commissions of oyer and terminer and gaol delivery between Eyres. Their functions were systematized and regularized by statute under Edward III. They had powers to 'keep the peace' – to arrest, commit to gaol, demand sureties for good behaviour – and to try most crimes (other than treason); in effect, a general commission of oyer and terminer, though they were directed to leave the more difficult cases for the assizes. A statute of 1388 required them to hold 'sessions of the peace' quarterly – quarter sessions, as they became known. These too survived until 1971. Between quarter sessions, JPs exercised powers of summary conviction (i.e. without a jury) for minor crimes at petty sessions.

Additionally, JPs came to exercise substantial quasi-governmental power. They became perhaps the key form of rule at local level. Especially after 1349 (the labour crisis following the Black Death) they were given wide powers to compel labourers to work at legal wages. Putnam sees the Statute(s) of Labourers (1349–51) as representing 'assertion by the government of its right to legislate in economic matters for the whole country on a scale previously unheard of' (1908: 7; cf. her 1906); their administration was largely in JPs' hands. JPs could intervene extensively in master/servant relations, for instance under statutes of 1464 and 1467 relating to the cloth industry. The 1601 Poor Law administration was under their control, likewise the new highway system. 'More and more the Quarter Sessions of the Peace began to supplant the old county courts as the real governing assembly of the shire,' becoming 'not merely a criminal court for the whole county, but also a governmental assembly, a board with governmental and administrative powers' (Maitland 1897: 208, 233). Features of the 1349–51 labour statutes and the 1563 Statute of Artificers remained in force until the nineteenth century, and features of the 1601 Poor Law until the present day.

JPs again show the typical central/local relationship. They were commissioned by the Crown, the form of commission being settled under Richard II. Many petitions to Parliament demanding election of JPs by freeholders were denied. And JPs were carefully watched over by the king's Council – the 1388 statute, for instance, threatening punishment if sessions are not held. At the same time, JPs are drawn from the ranks of the local political nation. A statute of 1439 required them to have lands or tenements to the value of £20 p.a. – that is, ten times the qualification for the Parliamentary franchise. In 1732 this was raised to £100. Here – as with other institutions of local government throughout our period – there is a perennial concern with appointment of what the nineteenth century was to call 'fit and proper persons'.[15] Maitland summarizes:

> Country gentlemen commissioned by the King are to keep the peace of the shire, are to constitute a court of quarter sessions with a high criminal jurisdiction, are to punish the pettier offenders in a summary way, are to exercise miscellaneous governmental powers and police powers – to fix the legal rate of wages for instance. They were to be substantial men. (1897: 209)

In short, 'the local government of England was to be government by country gentlemen' (ibid.: 495) – acting in the king's name, though as often as not in their own interests.

A word should also be said here on ecclesiastical courts, and religious regulation more generally. Before the Conquest ecclesiastical and temporal jurisdictions were not distinct; William I separated them in 1072. Thereafter, there were two parallel systems of courts in England, with the ecclesiastical courts administering canon law. 'Benefit of clergy', referred to above, was one legacy of this separation. From archdeacons' and bishops' courts at diocese level, appeal in the ecclesiastical courts lay to the Chancery Court of York or the Court of Arches at Canterbury, and thence (until the 1530s) to Rome. Conflicts over jurisdictional boundaries in the middle ages are too involved to go into in detail here; suffice it to say that by the early fourteenth century the Church had unquestioned jurisdiction over marriage and bastardy, succession to personal property, and punishment of 'mortal sin' – centrally fornication and adultery. Before the sixteenth century, ecclesiastical courts also handled slander. Church courts – their powers, as we shall see, in some respects strengthened at the Reformation, at the same time as the Church was itself Erastianized – exercised 'a pervasive jurisdiction over the lives of most ordinary people: over family matters and wills, sexual offences, defamation and breach of faith' (Baker 1979: 112; cf. Marchant 1969, Hill 1964: chs 8, 9).

We can do no more here than signal wider state involvement in regulation of and through religion in the medieval period, notably around Lollardy. We find, in the Lollard rising of 1431, alternative social visions intertwined with religious differences; this is first clear in Sir John Oldcastle's rising of 1414 (McFarlane 1952; Aston 1960; Hilton 1973). Hilton sees connections between the 1381 Peasant Revolt and Lollardy 'provided we regard Lollardy as something wider than the following of Wycliff. After all, Ball was first imprisoned for illicitly preaching in the 1360s' (1973: 313; cf. p. 230ff.). As Aston shows (1960: 313f.), in 1400, the year before the institution of death by burning for heresy, Henry IV urged sheriffs to ban any but licensed preachers, illicit conventicles and confederations. In short, all unauthorized meetings and assemblies were banned. This is especially relevant for two reasons: Aston's argument about how 'Lollardy' became a kind of catch-all category of demon (like, later, Ranter, Leveller, Jacobin, Revolutionist, Socialist, Communist, Marxist – agitators all) shows how, from heretics, 'Lollards' became criminals, then 'traitors and enemies of the King' by 1431 (1960: 280); Christopher Hill, conversely, has traced lineages from Lollardy to the Levellers, from one alternative vision of society to another (1978b; cf. his 1954, 1964, 1975: chs 2, 6, 8). If any one Lollard statement would have been 'impossible' for dominant groups in the fifteenth century, it was that 'any layman can teach and preach the gospel anywhere' (Aston 1960: 287) – especially when this was to be done in English (McFarlane 1952: 122f.).

We should note the extent – before the ritualized public executions of heretics by burning (carried out *by the civil power*) – of public support for Lollardy: mayors, clerks, justices, and the attempt to generalize this support by appeals to Parliament (McFarlane 1952: 132ff.). Already by 1377 papal letters warned the secular authorities of England that such theological malpractices as Lollardy had implications for earthly rulers. Aston shows (p. 313ff.) how heresy became extended to any doctrine that challenged authority, and how, after 1414, secular officials were responsible for combating it with the aid of bishops, who had the right of immediate arrest. Lollardy shows the secular implications of theological disputes, especially where the form of knowledge is to be generalized, to make mysteries known, to free doctrine from a small group of specialists. From Lollardy, if not before, the state is involved in regulating into silence, eccentricity, marginality or crime all doctrines and practices within the realm of cultural life that provide glimpses of an alternative set of social relations. The weary task of 'eternal vigilance' has begun. It is not without irony that after the 1530s the name and heritage of Wycliff was to be invoked in legitimation of state-centred English Protestant nationalism, as in Council's propagandist use of Foxe's *Book of martyrs*. We shall examine this in later chapters.

Before leaving this brief survey of aspects of state formation in medieval England, a final cautionary note needs to be sounded. The actual effectiveness of governance during the middle ages varied enormously from reign to reign, and was rarely as great as a bald sketch of institutional forms such as we have given might suggest. The disintegrative potentialities of feudalism and 'bastard feudalism' were never far beneath the surface. Lawlessness was often rife, particularly in the further flung regions of the realm. Law enforcement was invariably less than perfect and at times extremely corrupt. Under weak monarchs the state machinery itself could become means of pursuing disintegrative private quarrels, as happened under Henry VI. Throughout the period, the effectiveness of central government depended crucially upon both the strength and abilities of the individual monarch and his maintenance of good relations with the political nation, in particular with the great magnates. In the turmoils of the mid and late fifteenth century, much of what we have described was to break down. We would still argue, however, that by the end of the middle ages institutional forms and political traditions had been constructed in England which made it singular in important respects, and which were to serve as resources in the sixteenth- and seventeenth-century revolutions we will go on to examine in subsequent chapters. The 'Complaint' of Cade's rebels in 1450 is revealing:

Item, they say that our sovereign lord is above his laws to his pleasure and he may make it and break it as him list without any distinction. The contrary is true and else he should not have sworn to keep it. . . .

Item, they say that the King should live upon his commons, and that their bodies and goods are the King's; the contrary is true, for then needed he never Parliament to sit to ask for goods of his commons. (quoted in Loades 1977: 37–8)

This has almost a seventeenth-century feel about it. By 1450, expectations were there, a distinct national political culture was in the making. This culture cannot be divorced from the process of state formation we have sketched so far.

2

'This Realm of England is an Empire': The Revolution of the 1530s

> This realm of England is an Empire, and so hath been accepted in the world, governed by one Supreme Head and King having the dignity and royal estate of the imperial Crown of the same, unto whom a body politic, compact of all sorts and degrees of people divided in terms and by names of Spirituality and Temporality, be bounden and owe next to God a natural and humble obedience.
> Preamble to Act of Appeals 1533, quoted in Elton 1974c: 160–1

The 'Tudor revolution' in government remains highly contentious.[1] Elton has been charged with exaggerating both what happened in the 1530s and its long-term significance. The Marxist tradition has in general (Christopher Hill being a partial exception) downplayed 1530s, preferring to seek the 'real' bourgeois revolution in the next century. For Perry Anderson, the Tudor state was an infant absolutism. On most points we would side with Elton against his critics. This is not to say that we think the events of the 1530s were a 'bourgeois revolution' or the Tudor state a 'bourgeois state'. They were not. Our argument is rather that the Henrician revolution was of immense importance in developing the national state forms and political culture within (and in part, through) which capitalism was eventually able to triumph. It was crucial to creating that 'national economic space' – which is first of all political and cultural – insisted upon by Braudel.

Before we look at the 1530s themselves, a word or two needs to be said on the preceding reign. Trevelyan might have exaggerated when he described the Wars of the Roses as 'a bleeding operation performed by the nobility on its own body' (1962: 199) – neither that class, nor its power, were destroyed. But Loades's more careful judgement is apposite: by the time of Henry VII's accession, 'there was no clientage system of national scope which could be mobilised by anyone who had the will to oppose him' (1977: 102). There was no basis for concerted baronial opposition to the king. In this climate, Henry was able to restore the authority of the Crown.

He did this, largely, by refurbishing the traditional machinery of government, especially the Council and the courts, and by even-handed and extensive – if unprofligate – use of patronage. A major innovation was the Council of the North. But it was thoroughness – 'constant, meticulous, and well-informed administrative pressure' (ibid.: 119) – that was the hallmark of the reign. Royal finance was put on a sounder footing. JPs' powers were extended, at the expense of the sheriffs, and the first handbook for their work was issued, probably with official approval, in 1506. Henry developed an impressive intelligence network.[2] The 'great evils' of bastard feudalism – livery, maintenance and embracery – were gradually curbed. The Acts of 1487 and 1504 against liveries – in both their appearance of blanket prohibition and their provision for royally sanctioned, licensed, exemptions – served further to assert the uniqueness of royal power. On his death, Henry bequeathed his son 'a working Council and an administration capable of governing the realm in his name' (ibid.: 123). This restoration of royal authority is an important background to the Tudor revolution: in terms of Sir John Fortescue's famous contrast between *dominium regale* and *dominium politicum et regale*, it requires the former to obtain the latter. Or, better, the latter is made possible through a particular route to the former (cf. Koeningsberger 1977).

Council was to be a core institution of Tudor rule. It has been studied in detail by Gladish (1915), while Strayer (1970: 92ff.) places it in a comparative context, stressing the social origins of members and the possibility of 'career' officials. Loades gives the composition of Council: about 'a quarter were peers, a similar number lawyers and household officials, whilst almost half were ecclesiastics of various ranks' (1977: 115). Although some 227 men are listed as Council members for the whole of Henry VII's reign, their involvement varied greatly, and average attendance – where the records survive – was seven; Mackie (1952) suggests that under twenty were regularly consulted. Loades also indicates the existence of 'committees', both semi-permanent and *ad hoc*, within the Council. The king normally presided at meetings in person. In all, the Council was 'the great nerve centre and clearing house for all kinds of business' (Loades 1977: 115).

A more general shift during this period also needs remarking. Partly because of the way Henry VII handled patronage, and partly because of the increase in what Loades calls the 'density' of government during his reign, by its close the nobility had become 'more dependent upon, and more involved in, the work of central government than ever before' (ibid.: 119). This is of great importance to state formation. Manred – the ability to command personal retinues – gradually lost its importance, and wealth and political influence came to mean far more.

Relations of 'service' were being reconstructed as those of patron and client. Factional struggles came increasingly to be fought out – for office, for influence – within the arena of the developing state.

Now to the revolution of the 1530s. Karl Marx once wrote that bourgeois society 'must assert itself in its external relations as nationality and internally must organise itself as state' (Marx and Engels 1846: 89). This decade is of momentous significance in this two-sided construction of nation/state. For Elton, 'the essential ingredient of the Tudor revolution was the concept of national sovereignty' (1974c: 160). This sovereignty was established in the break with Rome, in the denial of the authority of any 'foreign potentates' within England. But it was far from being just an external matter. The corollary was an immense strengthening of the authority and visibility of the state internally. It became the claimed first focus of political loyalty, against both transnational and more localized alternatives; both the Pope and the Earl of Derby. If, in Christopher Hill's phrase, 'the Reformation in England was an act of state' (1956a: 32) – which is not to gainsay either the genuineness of conviction of Protestant reformers, or Cromwell's sympathy for their cause (see Elton 1972: 34ff.; 1973) – one of its lasting consequences was a huge boost to the instruments of state through which it was effected. It is not without significance that 'the State' first comes to be spoken of impersonally, as the repository of political loyalty, precisely in the 1530s.[3] The shift, in both its external and internal facets, is admirably exemplified by the preamble to the 1533 Act of Appeals, drafted by Thomas Cromwell himself, which we quoted at the head of this chapter.

Nationalization, and Erastianization, of the Church – the decisive shift from its being the Church in England, archiepiscopal provinces of the Universal Church of Rome, to the Church of England, under the supremacy of the Crown – was in Loades's words 'undoubtedly the greatest single augmentation which royal authority has ever received' (1977: 175). In purely financial terms, the ensuing dissolution of the monasteries yielded the Crown something like 10 per cent of the landed wealth of the realm, with an annual income (£136,000) over three times the previous royal income from land, together with first fruits and tenths (c.£40,000) and plate and bullion valued in excess of £1 million (ibid.: 174; Hill 1956a: 32–3). Most of the appropriated land was of course fairly rapidly sold off (Coleman (1977: 43) reckons three-quarters by 1558 and the remainder by 1640), largely ending up in the hands of the gentry, with consequences for the rise of capitalist agriculture recognized by commentators from Marx (1867: ch. 27) onwards. The sales also in the end fatally weakened the financial independence of the Crown, increasing its dependence on Parliament.

But quite as important, from our point of view, is the fact that the royal supremacy gave the Crown both greatly extended opportunities for patronage, and control over what was at the time the most extensive apparatus of propaganda (the pulpit) and moral regulation (the Church courts) in the land. Canon law was not abolished in the 1530s, despite claims to that effect; it is more accurate to say it was Erastianized. The Canons of 1604 defined the 'bawdy courts' as competent for 'adultery, whoredom, incest, drunkenness, swearing, ribaldry, usury' and 'any other uncleanness and wickedness of life' including sabbath-breaking and not taking communion at Easter (Hill 1964: 291; cf. Marchant 1969). High Commission (the supreme ecclesiastical court) had responsibilities for censorship after 1611, which embraced all 'books pamphlets and portraitures offensive to the state' (Hill 1964: 334). The Elizabethan Act of Supremacy empowered it to fine and imprison, and pursue miscreants throughout the land. In other words, it made use of secular instruments and penalties for religious crimes (extending the medieval precedents set in dealing with Lollardy). Marchant describes High Commission as 'the longest of the long arms of Church law' (1969: 34); Hill considers it 'one of the many instruments of the Tudor state for centralization, for imposing national uniformity' (1964: 333–4).

'Tudor and Stuart preachers', as L. B. Wright argues, 'were the sociologists of the day' (1943). Their sermons were tracts for the citizen and the state. Cromwell's administration took meticulous care to secure the loyalty of clergy (for instance, the oath-taking of 1534–5) and to 'tune the pulpits', requiring regular preaching of the royal supremacy (and going so far as to supply specimen sermons 'for priests unlearned'). It was the establishment of a *state* Church in the 1530s that laid the ground for that potent fusion of Protestantism and nationalism which was to prove so important to subsequent English history:

in the long run the consequences which followed from the break with Rome were momentous. 'Religion', as Sir Lewis Namier used to say, 'is a sixteenth century word for nationalism'. . . .

For 250 years protestantism and patriotism were closely interwoven. . . . John Foxe's *Acts and Monuments* popularised a national historical myth which saw God's Englishmen from Wyclif's day (at least) fighting against Anti-Christ, who in the sixteenth century was represented by the pope and Spain. The Spanish Armada in 1588, Guy Fawkes' plot in 1605, the Irish revolt of 1641, the Popish Plot of 1679, all fitted into this pattern. . . . For 250 years protestantism strengthened patriotism, and the existence of an internal (papist) enemy, as well as the neighbouring popish Irish, helped to bind Englishmen together in national unity. The struggle of pious protestants to extend English religion and English civilisation, first to the 'dark corners' of England and Wales, then to Ireland and the Highlands of Scotland, was a struggle to extend the values of London, and so to reinforce England's national security. It was no accident that Leland, so interested in the development of internal communications, was also a keen protestant, a friend of Thomas Cromwell, and intended his *Itinerary* as a contribution to English patriotism. (Hill 1969a: 36, 42; cf. his 1963)

The seeds of the notion of England as an elect nation, enjoying God's special favour, are present in the officially inspired or sanctioned propaganda of the 1530s themselves (see Elton 1972: ch. 4 for examples).

Christina Larner has argued that Christianity, whether Protestant or Counter-Reformation, served between the Reformation and the industrial revolution as 'the world's first political ideology', replacing older kinship and feudal ties:

From the late fifteenth century the evangelisation of the populace coincided with the development of what can loosely be called nation states. Nation states could not depend on the old ties to bind their people to them. Like all new regimes they demanded both ideological conformity and moral cleansing. Ideological conformity in the sixteenth century meant overt adherence to the form of Christianity preferred within the regime concerned. (1982: 35–6; cf. her 1981)

In this context, the purely Erastian character of the Reformation in England – it is generally agreed that the expansion of Protestantism was the consequence, not the cause, of the English Reformation – becomes particularly significant.

Equally important is the impact of the supremacy for conceptions of kingship. Myers captures this well:

the breach with Rome brought out the unmedieval idea that the King was supreme in every sphere of life, and that England was a self-sufficient empire, with Henry as its emperor, subject to no other authority on earth. Henceforth, the King would be addressed not as 'Your Grace', a form of address which he shared with archbishops and dukes, but as 'Your Majesty', a unique being exalted above all others in both Church and state. (1952: 193–4)

Augmentation of the authority of the Crown, in other words, was as much conceptual and symbolic as material. For Elton, the difference lies 'less in the real power exercised by the king ... than in the potential power released by the establishment of national sovereignty' (1974c: 160). But this potential was enormous.

Papal pretensions were not the only threat to the sovereign's 'plenary, whole and entire power, pre-eminence, authority, prerogative and jurisdiction', nor the only bastion to fall to the Crown in the 1530s. The decade saw a more wholesale centralization of jurisdiction. By statutes of 1534 and 1536 the Welsh marcher lordships were abolished, and Wales itself juridically and administratively 'incorporated' into the English system, with the whole panoply of shire government, assize circuits, JPs and (in 1543) MPs. In 1536 a statute – the wording is significant in its use of conservative rhetoric for revolutionary purposes – 'for recontinuing certain liberties and franchises heretofore taken from the Crown' reserved pardons for all treasons and felonies and appointment of all judges and justices throughout the realm to the king, and provided for all judicial process to run in his name throughout the land. 'All franchisal rights of any consequence were destroyed: for the first time, the whole realm, without qualification, became subject to government from Westminster' (Elton 1974c: 176). In the next year, following the defeat of the Pilgrimage of Grace, a new Council of the North was set up with common law and equity jurisdiction throughout the northern counties: it was 'a permanent body dominated by royal officials and controlled from the centre' (ibid.). Loades summarizes the overall impact of these moves:

By the end of 1536 the realm of England was jurisdictionally united as never before under the authority of the King, and the complex hierarchy of powers which had checked and limited the medieval monarchy had disappeared. Men at all levels of society were to become increasingly aware of the intrusive presence of the central government. (1977: 175)

That intrusive presence was manifested in various ways. Whether or not, as Elton argues, the 1530s represent a generalized shift from 'household' to 'bureaucratic' methods of government, there can be no doubt the reforms heralded an increase in its density. Cromwell's new revenue courts may or may not have embodied a new, 'departmental' form of financial organization; what is beyond contention is that they 'covered the country with a new network of royal officials, Surveyors, Receivers, Auditors and others . . . [which] added a new dimension to the Crown's patronage and created as many additional sources of information and agents of control' (ibid.: 173). It is a commonplace that Thomas Cromwell's intelligence-gathering was unprecedented in its scope and efficiency and unrivalled before the days of Cecil and Walsingham. We need however to be careful here. There is little evidence to suggest Cromwell had (or Tudor state resources could have financed) the vast spy network of hostile legend. Rather, he relied for information on the reconstructed patron/client structure of Tudor society and enlarged loyalty to the Crown. What distinguished his regime was the pressure put upon local officials and others to bring disaffection to the notice of the centre, and the assiduousness with which such incoming information was followed up through the processes of the law. The Crown remained dependent, in the final analysis, on the consent and co-operation of the local political nation, in particular the gentry.

The scope of treason was extended by Acts of 1534 and 1536, principally to compass treason by word as well as overt deed. Refusal to take the oath of supremacy became treasonable. At the same time, and the point is important, treason was brought more fully under the common law.[4] Between 1532 and 1540, 883 people were tried and 308 of them executed for treason (if we exclude those taken in open rebellion, the figure falls to 110, with a further 17 probable); 63 of these died for speaking words against the supremacy (Elton 1972: ch. 9; Loades 1977: 163n.). The government also extended its control over the spoken and written word by preventative measures. Cromwell made strenuous efforts to control the licensing of preachers, at one time contemplating the use of royal (as opposed to bishops') licences with nationwide effect. Sustained attempts were made to suppress opposition writings; a proclamation of 1536 required surrender of any publication hostile to the authority of the Crown. Another, of 1538, went further, banning the import of books in English without royal licence, and requiring prior licence of all domestic publications, by the Council or their appointees. This marked 'the beginning of an effective censorship, a policy continuously maintained, with varying success, till after the revolution of 1688' (Elton 1972: 221). No Index of prohibited writings as such was attempted until 1546.

The other side of this policy was the positive propaganda campaign waged by the government to defend the revolution and prepare the ground for its successive stages. A variety of methods were used: the pulpit; printed tracts, in both English and Latin, for learned and unlearned audiences; dissemination and public display of the great reforming statutes themselves, with their propagandist preambles, throughout the realm. Justices of assize were charged in 1538 publicly to declare at their sessions 'the treasons traitorously committed against us and our laws by the late Bishop of Rochester and Sir Thomas More' (Elton 1972: 241). In all, this was 'the first such campaign mounted by any government in any state of Europe' (ibid.: 206). The wider context of this was a more general stiffening of moral regulation. Cromwell did not confine his attention to overtly political disaffection – in Elton's words, 'what was at stake for him was a whole social policy' (ibid.: 79). In 1538 he had the Lord Chancellor assemble JPs in Star Chamber, 'specially giving them charge for bruiting of news, vagabonds and unlawful games' (ibid.). State concern with 'idle time' was to resound down the centuries, as we will see.

A final indicator of the increasing presence of government calls for particular mention. Thomas Cromwell's second set of Injunctions for the Clergy, of September 1538, required – apart from the placing of an English Bible in every church – the keeping of registers, in every parish, of all baptisms, marriages and burials. Historians are inclined to see in parish registers an invaluable data-base, as indeed they are. Contemporaries saw them differently. They provoked widespread resentment, and people feared their use for taxation purposes. Cromwell's own justification, responding to such fears, is interesting. The registers were being instituted, he said, 'for the avoiding of sundry strifes, processes and contentions rising upon age, lineal descents, title of inheritance, legitimation of bastardy, and for knowledge of whether any person is our subject or no'; 'and also', he added, 'for sundry other causes' (Elton 1972: 259–60). Concern with property and concern with rule are equally witnessed here. Registers are not merely a technical device, they materialize new sorts of claims of a state over its subjects. The Elizabethan Poor Law, for example, was to rely for its administration on the kind of detailed knowledge of individuals the registers supplied. Less well known, but equally indicative, Cromwell also attempted compulsory registration of land conveyances (Palliser 1983: 319).

In the 1530s, then, the sheer weight of government increased mightily. In turn this both concretized and contributed to changing, more 'modern', conceptions of the nature of the state and of subjects' relations to it, of political community and loyalty, so that for instance it became possible to speak of 'the State' impersonally. The reforms were systematic in quality, they move in particular directions – an observation that can be made without entering the murky waters of who drafted which clauses or the murkier waters of intentions and 'planning'. In the long run we would regard this as more important for the history of state formation in England than the fine details of Elton's arguments concerning the alleged transition under Cromwell from household to bureaucratic methods of government. Certainly we can see, from the 1530s on, a regularization in the functioning of the Privy Council (formalized, with a clerk and minute book, around 1540) and a growth in the importance of the office of Secretary of State. Arguably certain of the institutions developed by Cromwell (like the new revenue courts) did embody relatively novel forms of bureaucratic organization – though the system of government as a whole remained haphazard in many ways, and the personality of the monarch continued to be crucial to its functioning. But little of this was totally unprecedented, and not all Cromwell's reforms survived his fall. Here Elton's critics do have a point – but this is not the aspect of his argument most germane to our case.

The final feature of Elton's thesis we do wish to focus on is his view of the kind of sovereignty being constructed in England in the 1530s, and its implications for the two institutions we highlighted in our discussion of the medieval period – Parliament and the law. In Christopher Hill's words, 'the English Reformation was enacted by statute' (1969a: 35). The jurisdictional revolution detailed above was accomplished by statute. Enforcement of the revolution depended largely upon the authority of statute, most evidently so in the case of the Treason Acts. Cromwell even sought to ground royal proclamations in statutory authority (see Elton 1974c: 169–70). Parliament was, in fine, *the* central instrument of Thomas Cromwell's revolution. The Parliament of 1533–9 had the heaviest legislative programme that had yet been seen, and one which was to remain unsurpassed until the 1830s (Loades 1977: 173; cf. Lehmberg 1970); some 677 statutes were passed in Henry VIII's reign as a whole, 'occupying almost as much space as all the preceding legislation from Magna Carta onwards' (Baker 1979: 179).

This is important, for several reasons. First, it to our mind at least convincingly demolishes any thought that Henry VIII was attempting to construct a personal despotism. He knew what he was talking about when in 1543 he said 'we at no time stand so highly in our estate royal as in the time of Parliament' (quoted in Myers 1952: 199). Certainly the 1530s massively enhanced the authority of the Crown. But because, throughout, the instrument of revolution was Parliament and statute, this was done at the cost of limiting the personal power of the monarch (as the Stuarts were to discover in the next century). The monarchy that emerged was constitutional rather than in any sense absolutist, it had increasingly to operate within defined forms. Holdsworth quotes Bacon to good effect when he speaks of how law made 'the ordinary power of the King more definite and regular – his acts and grants are limited by law, and we argue them every day' (1972: vol. 4, 201).

Second, the prestige, authority and centrality of Parliament itself were greatly strengthened by its role in the revolution. This is especially true of the Commons. Parliaments become more regular. There are notable developments in Parliamentary procedure – committees first begin to be used, Commons journals appear in the 1540s. The Commons struggle for privileges – freedom of speech, freedom from arrest at a private suit – and for the power of an autonomous court in ordering its own affairs date from around the same time. Both Lords and Commons move towards becoming clear Houses of

Parliament, in their modern sense. Importantly, in terms of the point made earlier regarding the English Parliament's character as a business organization sharing in government, the Parliament of 1532 marks the first instance of an extensive *government* legislative programme (as opposed to Acts produced in response to Bills introduced by private members) (Elton 1974c: 172).

Against all this – and the qualification is important – we should also note that between 1509 and 1603 there were 43 years without a Parliament, 26 of them in Elizabeth's reign (contrasting with 42 such years between 1327 and 1485). Roskell argues that when Charles I said of the Commons in 1642 that it was 'never intended for any share in Government, or the choosing of them that should govern' (1964: 313n.), he was echoing Elizabeth, who had the Lord Keeper tell the Commons that as to 'liberty of speech, her Majesty commands me to tell you, that to say Yea or No to Bills . . . is the very True Liberty of the House', rather than 'to speak . . . of all causes . . . and to frame a form of religion or a State of government as to their idle brains shall seem fitting' (ibid.: 309–10; cf. Neale 1924: 168). Roskell also argues that many powers and rights remained with the monarch, remained royal rather than Parliamentary. Not until 1694 (with the Triennial Act) did Parliament become a truly regular institution (though from 1689 it had to meet annually to renew the Mutiny Act). Not until 1679 did it challenge – and by the Act of Settlement of 1701 overcome – the right of royal pardon to nullify its impeachment. Not until 1678 did the Commons gain the right to initiate all money bills – and these could still be rejected by the Lords, until 1861, a right not secured by statute until 1911. Audit was not firmly established as a working principle until 1667 and as a power *of the Commons* until 1861–6, strengthened in 1912.

Similar points can be made about the common law. Parliament, in Elton's words, 'legalized' the Refomation not in the nebulous sense of providing assent, but 'in the severely practical sense of making possible the prosecution of those who opposed the royal policy' (1974c: 166). It is of the utmost importance that for the most part the revolution *was* defended through the processes of the common law – as is most evident in the treatment of treason. Cromwell, himself a common lawyer by training, was punctiliously legalistic. We have argued above that both Parliament and the common law were in important ways peculiar, and precociously unifying features of the medieval English polity (which also inseparably operated on and through social classifications of class and gender difference). The 1530s, far from attempting a personal despotism, enormously consolidated the power of both:

if we go by what was actually done, the triumph of the common law is manifest. Indeed it was Cromwell's administration which saved the medieval common law, as it saved the medieval Parliament, and used both in the service of the modern state. The use of Parliament meant enforcement through the courts of the common law to whom the statutes of the 1530s opened up a great and important new field. (ibid.: 169)

Once again some qualification – whilst endorsing the general point – is called for. The enhancing of the power of the Crown by the 1530s revolution also facilitated the rise of 'prerogative courts' – Star Chamber and the rest – outwith, and in increasingly uneasy relationship with, the courts of common law.

The third point we would draw here from Elton is more philosophical, but crucial in considering the construction of the 'modern' state. He detects, in the 1530s, a profound shift in the competence of statute (and therefore the status of Parliament, as its author). The medieval conception of law had in general been a highly conservative one; laws, natural and divine, were 'disclosed'. What was so revolutionary about the 1530s was the notion that Parliaments *make* laws, and on earth there is nothing an Act of Parliament cannot do, even in spheres previously considered the province of spiritual authority. Statute is omnicompetent. Coke, in the next century, wrote that Parliamentary power in making statutes 'is so transcendent and so absolute that it cannot be confined either for causes or persons within any bounds' (quoted in Baker 1979: 181). Extending our earlier points on 'lawfulness' and 'literacy' – and another indication of the solidification of central state power during this period – Baker observes that

with this new concept of legislation came a new reverence [not an unprecedented one, we would argue] for the written text. Legislative texts were now drawn with such skill by Crown lawyers, in advance of Parliament, and explained in such extensive and explicit preambles, that the judges were manifestly being discouraged from the creative exegesis they had bestowed on medieval statutes. (1979: 180)

For Elton this enhanced conception/practice of statute law marks the decisive break between medieval and modern conceptions and practice of government:

The establishment of the royal supremacy over the Church, the expulsion of the pope, the assertion of the unlimited sovereignty of statute destroyed the foundations of medieval polity and society and put something new in their place. Thomas More knew well why he opposed the voice of Christendom to an Act of Parliament, and Thomas Cromwell knew equally well what his assertion of the omnicompetence of Parliament meant. They both knew they were witnessing a revolution. (1953: 426–7)

Just how profound a revolution they were witnessing is well expressed by Myers:

These great changes shook men out of their acceptance of the traditional limitations of Parliament's functions. Henry had united spiritual to temporal authority; before a century had passed the claim would be made – inconceivable in medieval England – that both could be exercised through Parliament alone. (1952: 199)

3

An Elect Nation:
The Elizabethan Consolidation

This England never did, nor never shall
Lie at the proud foot of a conqueror,
But when it first did help to wound itself.
Now these her princes are come home again,
Come the three corners of the world in arms,
And we shall shock them; naught shall make us rue,
If England to itself do rest but true.

William Shakespeare, King John, V, vii

For government, though high, and low, and lower,
Put into parts, doth keep in one consent,
Congreeing in a full and natural close,
Like music.

William Shakespeare, Henry V, I, ii

We have spoken of the 'long waves' of English state formation –
periods of revolution being interspersed with longer periods of
consolidation and conservation. The years after the early 1550s were
one such period of conservation. This does not imply either stasis –
consolidation can be an active process – or tranquillity. The reign of
Elizabeth was bedevilled by plots and intrigue, not to mention the
conflict with Spain. But little in the area of state formation could be
described as revolutionary during these years. Indeed, they culminate
in a positive stalling, of which failures of attempts as reform in the
1620s are one indication.[1] Roy Strong has noted the importance of
1615 as a dividing line: 'for the Elizabethans, all history led up to
them. For the Stuarts all roads finally led back to Elizabeth' (1977).
Hill similarly divides the 50 or so years after 1588 into a lively and a
relatively barren sequence of 25 years, the latter drawing on the forms
and traditions of the former (1965: 11ff. 213ff.). Both are pointing, of
course, to the cult of Gloriana – the personalization of an era. And
that queen 'was – in the most primitive sense of the term – a profound

conservative. Not to act, not to move, never to change – these were the instinctive royal impulses, even in moments of urgent crisis' (MacCaffrey 1963: 26).

We will begin by developing a theme we touched on in connection with the 1530s: religion and its part in the making of a distinctive English national identity. How England was made Protestant is also instructive for what it reveals about the capacity and workings of the machinery of the Tudor state. The minority of Edward VI gave Protestant reformers their head, pushing the English Church doctrinally far beyond the state in which Henry had left it. By contrast, Mary did much for the Protestant cause, by default. Her Spanish marriage and Habsburg predilections (leading her to lose Calais in 1558) were widely unpopular. Her restoration of Catholicism ran up against both the fears of the beneficiaries of Henry's sale of Church lands, and a wider anti-clericalism amongst the gentry – upon whose co-operation the effectiveness of her persecutions ultimately depended. The persecutions themselves – the burnings of Cranmer and Ridley, and so on – helped create a potent Protestant martyrology, celebrated in such books as Foxe's *Acts and monuments of the English martyrs*. Protestantism, from being 'associated with continental influences ... became the spearhead of patriotic resistance to Spanish domination, and a faith for which men and women were prepared to die' (Loades 1977: 238–9). The ideology of England as an elect nation – prefigured, as we have seen, in some of the propaganda of the 1530s – was explicitly formulated by exiles from the Marian persecution. Others began to develop doctrines of justified resistance to rulers, of conscience above authority, which were to echo down into the seventeenth century.

The immediate background to the Elizabethan Church settlement of 1559 need not detain us further here. Suffice it to say that a straightforward restoration of the conservative Henrician Church was not on the cards. Doctrinally, the Protestant Prayer Book of 1552 was restored with only minor amendments. Jurisdictionally, the settlement created a nakedly Erastian Church, governed by royal commission. There is a fine symbolism, for students of the state/Church relation, in the Anglican *Book of Common Prayer* beginning with an Act of Parliament, the Act of Uniformity. The powers of High Commission, as mentioned above, were strengthened.

Following Elizabeth's accession, all Mary's bishops were replaced by Protestants (though not necessarily radical ones); in most cases the Marian incumbents refused to accept the 1559 settlement. Consistent attempts were made thereafter to build up a trained cohort of Protestant clergy at lower levels. The government steadily extended control over the universities of Oxford and Cambridge, most colleges being transformed into Protestant institutions by 1570 or so, with a view to producing a committed clerical elite. No one could enter the universities without first taking the oath of supremacy. Lower down the educational scale, schoolmasters had to be licensed by bishops, and it was forbidden to educate one's children abroad or employ unlicensed tutors. Ecclesiastical visitations and commissions were used to purge survivals of old rituals, images and ornaments at parish level. The Crown used its own network of patronage to buttress the Protestant cause, for instance remodelling the Commission of the Peace. Propaganda – a re-edition of the Edwardian Homilies, commanded to be read from in churches every Sunday, Cecil's commissioning and printing of Jewel's *Apologia Ecclesiae Anglicanae* – also played its part. Foxe's *Book of martyrs* was published in an English edition in 1563, and ordered by Council to be set up beside the English Bible in churches and public places. The second English edition, in 1570, explicitly embraced the myth of England as an elect nation. After the Bible, Foxe's works were the most widely read books in sixteenth-century England.[2] Council even turned its attention to the political content of school grammar books. Drama, also, was censored, the queen at the beginning of her reign forbidding all plays dealing with religion or contemporary government. By 1580 the Corpus Christi plays at York had disappeared.

In the first decade of the reign, however, there was little by way of direct repression of Catholics. Elizabeth herself was no religious radical. But events were to push her further than she might otherwise have wished to go. The (pro-Catholic) Rebellion of the Northern Earls in 1569 was put down with relative ease and with a good deal of exemplary brutality – indicating, amongst other things, the growth of Tudor state capacity: the Pilgrimage of Grace, thirty years before, had posed a much more serious threat to royal authority. But the aftermath of the rising was, from our point of view, more important than the rebellion itself. Pope Pius V threw his weight behind the rebel cause with the Bull *Regnans in Excelsis*. This excommunicated Elizabeth, declaring her a heretic and no true queen. Effectively the Bull made sedition a religious duty for all English Catholics, and gave crusader status to any Catholic prince who made war on Elizabeth, deserving Catholics' loyalty and support. Parliament responded by making it treason to import or publish any papal Bull, to deny Elizabeth's title or to call her schismatic; the evangelical 39 Articles of 1563 now became the official doctrine of the English Church; and anyone leaving the country for more than six months stood to forfeit their lands.

Pius's Bull had another, further-reaching consequence which he almost certainly did not intend. By posing the issue of loyalty so starkly – faith versus queen and country – *Regnans in Excelsis* helped drive English Catholics into the position of being a well-defined, and increasingly an outcast, recusant minority, and cut the ground from under the moderate religious conservatism that had been so influential in the first decade of the reign. Occasional conformity became less and less of an option, and Catholicism increasingly a ghetto – and largely upper-class – religion, cut off from its popular roots. Papal involvement in seditious intrigues over the next decade served further to isolate the English Catholics and to strengthen the hand of Protestants around the queen.

It was against this background that Catholic seminary priests (and later, Jesuits) began arriving in England from 1574 onwards. Repression intensified. In 1575 Council, which had previously left the problem of recusancy largely to local agencies, initiated a campaign against prominent Catholic laymen. A general census of recusants was ordered – and 'remarkably careful, individual attention was given to each of these individual recusants. The attack was aimed at selected and influential targets' (Williams 1979: 276). Gradually important positions in the counties became closed to Catholics. Commissions of the Peace were more methodically purged, assize judges were ordered to administer the oath of supremacy to all JPs.

In 1581 reconciliation to the Catholic Church became high treason for both priest and penitent, and penalties for absence from church were steeply increased. The number of executions rose sharply: 4 in 1581, 11 in 1582, a further 89 by 1590. Yet more penal legislation was passed after the assassination of William of Orange in 1584. Council's propaganda machinery was extremely active throughout the 1580s. The so-called 'bloody questions', requiring suspects in their answers effectively to betray their faith or admit themselves traitors, were widely administered, and the results of interrogations regularly published in the cause of whipping up anti-Catholic feeling. The cumulative effect of all we have sketched was, in Loades's words, that:

> By the time that she eventually went to war with the champion of the counter-reformation, England was a protestant country in a sense which she had certainly not been in 1550, or 1559, or even in 1569. The catholic church had paid a very heavy price for salvaging a small proportion of its flock. (1977: 289)

England was at war with Spain from 1585. Unsurprisingly, anti-Catholic repression increased still further. An Act of 1585 (anticipated in a proclamation of 1582) made the very fact of Roman ordination treasonable – the first time in English history that a conviction for treason could be grounded on status alone, without overt deed or word. Enforcement of recusancy fines was tightened up. Following the execution of Mary Queen of Scots in 1587, Philip of Spain advanced his own claim to the English throne, supported by Allen, the exiled cardinal of England. In the Armada year of 1588 over 30 Catholics were executed. In 1591 special commissions were set up to track down Catholic priests and their abettors. Cecil and Walsingham also used paid, professional secret agents to provide information on recusants – a new development in policing methods. In 1593 further laws were passed, exiling landless recusants and confining those with lands to a five-mile radius of their homes. It is, perhaps, not surprising that by the time Elizabeth died England was vociferously Protestant, nor that identities of Church and state, political and religious communities, were so closely tied together, each echoing back the other.

Before we leave religion, a word needs to be said about Puritanism – a concept more difficult, incidentally, to apply here than to the next century. The Anglican Church, as we have seen, moved doctrinally away from Catholicism, and to the extent that it did so this gave some succour to the Puritan cause and attracted Puritan support for royal policy. But Elizabeth remained unremittingly – and successfully – hostile to extreme Puritanism, especially in matters touching Church government, the episcopal hierarchy. By 1593 a Bill could pass Parliament imposing on Protestant nonconformists penalties similar to those for recusants. In part this was because the radical Puritans lost support in high places: there is clear evidence that erstwhile sympathizers feared the political implications of full-blooded Protestant radicalism. But it was equally a consequence of the successful self-definition, in the course of the reign, of the Anglican Church itself, and its association with the nation state. It seemed the living embodiment of England as the elect nation, the defeat of the Armada being the ultimate sign of God's favour. By the end of the reign a theologian of the stature of Hooker was able to give respectability to the distinctive, non-Puritan Protestantism of the Anglican Church, making it seem something much more than a sordidly Erastian compromise. He did so, moreover, in terms highly germane to our inquiry:

We hold that . . . there is not any man of the Church of England but the same man is also a member of the commonwealth; nor any man a member of the commonwealth that is not also of the Church of England. (Loades 1977: 324)

Mainstream Protestantism was thus harnessed to the purposes of state, to the mutual benefit of both. Puritanism, like recusancy, was for the time being driven into the wilderness.

The extension of the identification of Church and state, from Elizabeth through to Coleridge's famous and subtle treatment in *On the Constitution of the Church and State according to the Idea of each* (1830), is significant for at least three reasons. First, it serves to remind us of the sanctified and religious forms of much English official (and unofficial) politics, from coronations and Prayers in Parliament through to the texts and iconography of banners in the Durham miners' gala. There is much efficiency in these dignified parts of the constitution! Second, the features of the Christian religion accentuated and formalized in the established Church draw attention to the same authority claims and selecting practices in official politics. Third, to make a contrary emphasis, no set of beliefs and rituals is all of a piece, at any one time it may be selectively drawn upon in terms of different historical experiences (priests and bishops are not among the most loved figures of Christian religion), and over time its meaning has changed. E. P. Thompson shows this with great sensitivity in his discussion of Methodism (1968: ch. 11), as does Christopher Hill in his wonderful *The world turned upside down* (1975). Thus Coleridge argues coherently against treating people as things (reification), as he also argues against unregulated commerce – mere money-making. This radical Toryism continues to provide critical resources against capitalism: against monetarism's miseries as against earlier factory building. Raymond Williams has surveyed this sort of linkage, in English culture, of conservative and radical critiques of capitalism from Burke to D. H. Lawrence and beyond (1958). For others, from Lollardy through the Levellers to the Ranters, Quakers, and on to those who sought Heaven on Earth as socialism, Christianity could provide a means to criticize power, authority, corruption, exploitation and oppression through a social gospel, as it continues to do in present-day Latin American liberation theology. Christianity as political ideology has ever been a two-edged sword.

Returning to the Tudors, closely bound up with religious regulation was glorification of monarchy and exhortation of obedience to the Crown. Beginning with Henry VIII, this reached its peak under Elizabeth. Medieval theorists like Aquinas had taught that resistance to tyranny or misgovernment was permissible; Parliament had itself held the deposition of Richard II to be justified. Only under the Tudors did the doctrine of the duty of absolute obedience fully evolve. Cromwell, Cecil and others made it a central platform of state propaganda. Printed homilies on obedience were issued for reading from pulpits; the earliest, of 1547, stated that 'the high power and authority of Kings, with their making of laws, judgements, and officers, are the ordinances, not of man, but of God' (quoted in Williams 1979: 352). In the main sixteenth-century religious radicals and conservatives alike agreed on the sinfulness of rebellion; Latimer,

Ridley and Cranmer died unresisting in accord with this code. Hooker ably theorized the doctrine in his *Laws of ecclesiastical polity*.

This elevation – one might almost say, deification – of the monarchy was also encouraged by means other than the word.[3] 'The support that [monarchy] derived from portraiture, ceremonial, pageantry, and panegyric' was an essential ingredient of Tudor and Stuart state power (ibid.: 361). Royal portraits were commissioned, and their style shifted from those of the middle ages. Holbein depicted Henry VIII as the physical embodiment of authority, towering above mere mortals; Rubens painted James VII in the guise of the four Virtues triumphing over the four Vices. Elizabeth had herself portrayed against the background of the Armada, or standing on a map of England. She also forbade, by a proclamation of 1563, any representation of her person other than authorized ones. Copies of such portraits were made to hang in country houses, much as, in many states today, photographs of presidents adorn all 'official' buildings. When images of saints were removed from the chancel arches of parish churches, they were often replaced by the royal coat of arms. It is not simply Erastianism that is signified here; it is equally a sanctification of secular power.

The royal court projected a conscious brilliance, and the Crown sought to impress the wider populace by elaborately stage-managed entries, progresses and pageants. The imagery surrounding Elizabeth's entry into London for her coronation is particularly revealing:

Along the route 'scaffolds' had been erected with symbolic scenes, from which children, 'in costly apparel', spoke appropriate verses. At Gracechurch Street, for instance, was an ark in which sat persons representing the Queen's ancestors, with the roses of York and Lancaster united into a single branch. By the Conduit was a pageant entitled 'the Seat of Worthy Governance', with a royal throne resting upon the four virtues each of which was treading down its complementary vice. In the final pageant, in Fleet Street, Elizabeth herself was represented as Deborah, consulting with her Estates for the restoration of good government in Israel: the protestant message was here made very clear. (Williams 1979: 365)

After 1570 the anniversary of Elizabeth's accession became a public holiday, rung in by bells and celebrated with bonfires, wine and ballads.

Elizabeth herself was hailed as Pandora, Gloriana, Cynthia, Belphoebe, Astraea – classical and biblical imagery were equally exploited. She was even compared to the Virgin Mary, and called (by Spenser among others) a saint in her own lifetime. Spenser's *Faerie Queen* was the apotheosis of all this. The poem celebrates monarchy, order, justice and the struggle against popery, all of these incarnated in

Elizabeth's person; Spenser – in an interesting anticipation of Milton[4] – conceived it 'to fashion a gentleman or noble person in vertuous and gentle discipline' (quoted in Williams 1979: 367). Similar emphases on order and authority are plain in Shakespeare's plays.[5] As Penry Williams notes, the point about such works is that they are great literature and not just hack propaganda; as such they 'witness more effectively than anything else to the emotional power of the symbols and the allegories upon which they were drawing and to the firm foundations laid for monarchy in the public imagination of the time' (ibid.: 368).

Awareness of the power of symbolism and ritual surrounded other institutions of state too. Take, for instance, the assizes:

At the border of the first county on each circuit the judges were met by trumpeters and the sheriff's bailiff and, several miles from the assize town, by the sheriff himself, other local officers, and representatives of the county gentry. The ensuing cavalcade, throughout this period and, indeed, well into the nineteenth century, was one of some magnificence, attended by pike- and liverymen specially clothed for the occasion. Welcomed into town with bells, music, and occasionally, a Latin oration, the judges went first to their lodgings. There they received leading members of the local gentry who probably reported on the state of the county. Thus forewarned, the judges, now robed again and again attended by the sheriff and his men, passed to the church where the local minister read prayers and the sheriff's chaplain delivered a sermon. (Cockburn 1972: 65)

Assize sermons were often printed, and during the sixteenth and seventeenth centuries Council exercised itself with their content and the appointment of assize chaplains – often a London incumbent was drafted in. After the service all solemnly processed to the Crown Court. Here judges sat on a raised bench, with county notables ranked in descending order of importance on either side and to the front. After the swearing in of the grand jury one of the judges would read their charge 'telling the cause of their coming, giving a good lesson unto the people' (ibid.: 67) – such orations, high in tone and replete with learned allusions, served as vehicles for the transmission of official attitudes. The 'Public Peace', royal supremacy, and the evils of Rome were prevalent themes. A seventeenth-century source speaks of 'lordly judges' riding circuit 'to frighten people with their bloody robes, state, and pomp' (ibid.: 3). The whole occasion was conceived as an exercise in public education. One cannot underestimate the importance of what Bagehot was later to call these 'dignified' parts of the constitution. Certainly the Tudor state did not.

There can be little doubt that by the end of Elizabeth's reign England had become more peaceable, more governable, than a century before.

One measure of Tudor success here is that in the 'crisis decade' of the 1590s – one of warfare, poverty, and famine, ending a century in which population grew, prices inflated (by around 300 per cent in the case of corn), real wages fell (by some 50 per cent), rents rose, and many people found themselves without land or work – actual disorder was 'remarkably slight in comparison with other areas of Europe or with England's own experience fifty years before'.[6] There are various dimensions to this pacification.

Over the Tudor period as a whole aristocratic and gentry violence declined. There were a variety of reasons for this, discussed at length by Lawrence Stone (1965a). Amongst them were the decline of continental military involvement and shift to naval power, with a consequent demilitarization of the nobility: by 1576 only a quarter of the peerage had seen active service. There is a general cultural shift to be observed here away from 'warrior' paradigms of aristocracy, a civilizing process (cf. Elias 1939) of considerable importance: 'Most of the landowning class was, during the Tudor epoch, turning away from its traditional training in arms to an education at the universities or the Inns of Court' (Williams 1979: 241). Regarding the latter, of 1,300 JPs (out of a total of some 15,000) examined by Gleason, only 9 out of 128 in 1562 had been to a university or Inn or both; for 1636 the comparable figure was 129 out of 183. The Inns of Court and universities need to be seen as forms and agencies of socialization. Holdsworth argued that 'the education, the discipline, the whole life of the Inns of Court was collegiate in the best sense of the word' (quoted in Gleason 1969: 91). But perhaps most importantly, as noted earlier, state formation was itself shifting the basis of aristocratic power from manred to political influence and office. The signs of this pacification – slow and uneven as it undoubtedly was – are evident from mid-century on. The last great English magnate castle, Kenilworth, was built in the mid-1570s, and even then was an anachronism. Noblemen and gentlemen turned increasingly to litigation rather than brawling to resolve their disputes: in the first year of Elizabeth's reign, Star Chamber heard 67 cases; in the last, 732. Wales and the Marches, traditionally lawless areas, were thought by contemporaries to have been pacified under Elizabeth.

One state measure does deserve particular emphasis in this context, the 1573 reorganization of the militia. This required trained bands to be recruited from the traditional shire muster, equipped with modern weaponry, paid, and drilled for ten days per year at the expense of their shires. These bands were under the control of lords lieutenant of the counties. Council concurrently established county armouries, under deputy lieutenants. The latter – showing once again the typical pattern – were appointed by the lieutenants, but the Crown exercised a veto. The consequence was to cut the Crown's dependence for defence on aristocratic retinues and arms, rapidly accelerating the decline of both. The aristocracy, in brief, ceased to have any military function. This was a decisive step towards one of the defining features of a modern state:[7] 'the deployment of armed force . . . became almost exclusively the prerogative of the state, and those who controlled it did so by virtue of authority delegated by the Crown' (Loades 1977: 296). Penry Williams qualifies this (1979: 436ff.) by pointing out that nobles who had once led bands of liveried servants now commanded the militia as lords lieutenant – a command they often considered theirs by right – while in 1642 and 1688 local militias were to be raised against the Crown. Certainly 'the decline of retaining and the development of the militia did not replace unfettered magnate power by omnipotent state control' – things were more complex than that (before 1573 as much as after). Nonetheless there is an important shift to be registered from private magnate, commanding his own servants, to lord lieutenant, acting under royal commission – not least in the 'tradition' of county regiments (related to geographical areas and particular aristocrats and officered by gentlemen) that survived various military reorganizations until the 1970s. The 1573 measures are symptomatic both of the extent of national state formation and, equally importantly, of the kind of state, still heavily dependent upon the local political nation, still without a standing army or large central bureaucracy, that was being constructed in Tudor England.

Certain legal developments are also worth recording. Over the Tudor period, the number of felonies – capital crimes – increased. One significant addition was withchcraft (Acts of 1542 and 1563). This is important, for two main reasons. First, it exemplifies the case made earlier for the ideological role of Christianity during this period. Whilst, as Christina Larner puts it, witch-beliefs are endemic to pre-industrial societies, witch-hunting is not (1982: 44); the key shift is the increased concern of the emergent and religiously sanctified nation state with people's beliefs. Witchcraft is henceforth a secular crime, to be tried in civil courts. The 'demonic pact' (a witch's supposed carnal copulation with the Devil) was 'an act of apostasy with political significance for the state. For witches were deemed to be in conspiracy not only with the Devil, but with each other to attack the godly state' (ibid.: 51–2). Conversely,

Witchcraft was particularly economical in a law and order crisis – or panic – in that it represented not merely particular misdemeanours or individual crimes, but total evil – total hostility to the community, the church, the state, and God. (ibid.: 41)

The witch was as much a focus of collective representations as the figure of the Virgin Queen; both symbols are instructive. Second, witchcraft was overwhelmingly a female crime (though not exclusively so, fairy tales notwithstanding; it is revealing that the stereotypes should 'overlook' this). It thus further exemplifies that structuring by gender of society and its self-images through state routines which we have remarked before. Dominant cultural images of women and their 'proper place' in the order of things are well illustrated here. Daughters of Eve were dangerous; women not under patriarchal authority were particularly dangerous. Across Europe, the largest single category of convicted witches, who were ritually burned to death, were old, single women.[8] The sixteenth century also sees the beginnings of the long masculinization of healing.

Penal legislation against seditious rumour and libel grew apace during this period. Most liberties and franchises had disappeared in the 1530s; gradually assault was also made upon the right of sanctuary. Benefit of clergy was progressively withdrawn from certain categories of crime (1489 onwards) and offender (from 1532). After 1576 those successfully claiming benefit of clergy were imprisoned by the civil power, not the Church. In this period, also, the power and jurisdiction grew of the so-called prerogative courts, most notably Star Chamber. The latter acted upon information by the Attorney-General and tried summarily, i.e. without a jury; in Baker's words 'this gave the Crown a distinct advantage in prosecutions of an unpopular character, and the court was used to suppress sedition and other political offences' (1979: 103). Star Chamber left an enduring legacy: the laws of criminal libel, conspiracy, forgery and perjury were largely its creation. Its suppression in 1641 did not do away with 'political misdemeanours'; they could still be prosecuted, and by information, but in King's Bench.

A particularly unsavoury side of Tudor justice was the growth of torture as an instrument of judicial process – it was regularly used on Catholics after 1570, and before that on suspected thieves and murderers, and on gypsies (see Langbein 1977) – and of physical mutilation as a form of punishment. To instance two areas of abiding concern to the state, vagrants lost ears and were branded, whilst authors of seditious tracts had their right hands cut off. A proclamation of 1538 made assault on royal officials punishable by the loss of both hands. These were not medieval survivals, but emphatically instruments of the nascent modern state: torture had been largely unknown in England between 1310 and the reign of Edward IV, and the use of mutilation was rare in the later middle ages. The Tudors also adopted a somewhat cavalier attitude to *habeas corpus*. Under Elizabeth recusants were imprisoned without trial in the Fleet, and the judges in 1591 held this to be lawful where 'reasons of state' were at issue. The Tudors may, as Elton argues, have ruled largely (but see

Williams 1979: 394ff.) through the law, but it is as well to remember that that law was frequently brutal and, as we have indicated above, routinely weighted against the accused. Brutality is too gentle a word for the onslaught against gypsies, the most threatening outgroup of the time.[9]

Let us turn, finally, to the area of economic and social regulation.[10] On paper the Tudors created a formidable machinery of controls, far outreaching anything known in the medieval period. Over 300 'economic' statutes were passed by the Tudors, some 250 of these penal in their provisions. Statutes were supplemented by an unending stream of proclamations and letters of instruction from Council and royal officials. In some cases – customs, grain commissioners – new bureaucratic machinery was established. The Crown also made extensive use of patents, licences and monopolies, particularly under Elizabeth. The extent to which the state was ever pursuing a consistent policy, the degree to which regulation was actually enforced, and its overall effects, however, are all matters of debate amongst Tudor historians.

The field of economic regulation in which Tudor governments were most successful was probably that of foreign trade. Government intervened extensively at all levels of the textile trade, then England's major export (and, through customs, an important source of royal revenue). Crown policy was crucial to the outcome of rivalries between English and foreign merchants – the Hanseatic merchants being effectively ousted in the 1560s – and to the direction of English cloth exports. Government also played a key role in the establishment of the great chartered trading companies, including the East India Company, founded by royal charter in 1600. By the end of the century foreign trade was overwhelmingly concentrated in the hands of a few London monopolies, a direct consequence of state regulation.

Domestically, Tudor governments attempted to stimulate industry by issuing patents to foreigners with wanted skills – an import-substitution policy – and later, especially under Elizabeth, to Englishmen. Historians differ as to the ultimate economic benefit. Certainly under Elizabeth the system ramified beyond any purely economic objectives, to become primarily a means of boosting Crown revenues and rewarding favourites. By the end of the century strong opposition to monopolies had surfaced in Parliament. One important area where state policy was both fairly consistent and reasonably successful was the regulation of corn supply.[11]

It is important, here, not to dissociate a narrowly construed 'economic history' from both state formation and reformation *and* a precisely focused, if diffused, moral–political philosophy.[12] The fusion of these normally separated areas can be seen in studies of social structure by T. K. Rabb and F. F. Foster. Rabb extends our earlier points drawn from Bloch: the involvement of English peers with trade 'set them apart from their peers on the continent . . . their participation in commerce revealed a cohesiveness and flexibility in the upper levels of England's social structure' (1967: 13). Rabb nationally, and Foster, who focuses on London, are able to relate this to a specifically moral revolution, in which people like Hakluyt and his followers 'defined and invoked a national spirit' (ibid.: 101), and a new literature – of travels, sermons and epic vision – propelled forward a new cosmography and new conceptions of history. Such visions energized new forms like the joint-stock companies. Rabb's tables (e.g. ibid.: 104) show that in 1584 13.2 per cent of MPs were investors, in 1604 31.2 per cent (the 1604 Commons is significant in that 35.2 per cent of *new* MPs were investors), and in 1628 20.7 per cent. Foster examines the 'deliberative regularity' of the elite of Elizabethan London: meetings which began at 8.00 a.m. or earlier at which 'not only material goods and conditions, but the whole moral condition of human beings was subject to thorough examination'. He argues that in this set of rituals of ruling the 'force of law . . . emanated not so much from certain courts, or even very conducively from particular laws, as from the authority of those entrusted with its creation and protection' (1977: 89).

Statutory regulation of the labour market[13] had been a feature of English polity from before the Statute of Labourers of 1349–51. A statute of 1389 had imposed national maximum wages, empowering JPs to assess actual rates: this was re-enacted twice in the fifteenth century and again under Henry VIII. The Elizabethan Statute of Artificers of 1563 attempted more detailed regulation. It provided for JPs to determine maximum wages for each shire; amongst its other provisions were prohibition of servants quitting their masters without due cause, and compulsory employment (gendered: men in husbandry, women in domestic service) of the unemployed. JPs were undoubtedly active in making assessments, and whilst wages frequently exceeded the legal maxima, they stayed well below the rising cost of living.

The Poor Law – actually a series of measures from the early sixteenth century onwards, codified in statutes of 1597 and 1601 – has been viewed by Marxists (beginning with Marx himself) in terms of structuring of the labour market, habituating the poor and dispossessed to wage labour. Again the history is a long one. Penal legislation against 'sturdy vagabonds' had existed since the time of Richard II. Under the Tudors repressive legislation grew; we cannot rehearse all its details here. Of note, for its moral message, is the statute of 1531 which denounced 'idleness' as 'the mother and root of all vices'. This provided for vagabonds to the whipped and for the 'impotent' poor to be licensed by JPs. Licensing is a new departure, indicative of growing state involvement (and of a piece with other 1530s reforms). Over the next 40 years vagrancy remained of central concern – as it was indeed to be for the next 400 – and the unholy trinity of rogues, vagabonds and sturdy beggars variously subject to whipping, branding, boring through the ears, enslavement, service in the king's galleys, and execution. Gypsies, living symbols of a particular kind of 'indiscipline' and 'immorality', were treated particularly harshly. In the postwar period Lambarde – author of *Eirenarcha, or the office of the justice of the peace* (1581) and *Duties of constables* (1602), as well as works on Commons procedure and the high courts of justice, and a central figure of the time – bemoaned 'swarms of vagrant and flying beggars' (Cockburn 1977: 62). Flying beggars? Flying pickets?

The Elizabethan period saw 'a methodical extension of the role of the state' (Williams 1979: 200) in this area of regulation. Major new developments, and pillars of the Poor Law until the nineteenth century, were first, the introduction of a compulsory parish poor rate, levied by Overseers of the Poor under the supervision of JPs; second, the provision of work (so that, in the words of the 1576 Act, rogues 'may not have any just excuse in saying that they cannot get any service or work'); and third, the building of 'Houses of Correction' – mandatory in each shire between 1576 and 1597, and again after 1610 – to which vagrants could be summarily committed (after being duly whipped) by constables and other parish officials. But for the 'idle' poor – a strongly moral category, central to debate and legislation in the area from then till now – 'the form of repression swung back and forth from savagery to mere.severity' (ibid.: 203). During the 1590s the government empowered provost-marshals, originally purely military officials, to suppress vagrants under martial law. Privy Council demanded, and got, systematic searches for vagrants in 1570–1 and again after 1588. Another index of this fear of the 'many-headed monster' was the perennial campaign against unlicensed alehouses, seen – as they were again to be in the nineteenth century – as dens of potential sedition, rumour-mongering and revolt (see ibid.: 210–11; cf. Hill 1966, E. and S. Yeo 1981, Corrigan and Gillespie 1974).

Although the years after 1550 saw relatively little by way of revolutionary innovation in state formation, they were very important in consolidating and extending the revolution of the 1530s; even if the momentum was ultimately to stall. Key institutions of government matured – the Privy Council, the system of county government, Parliament. Council, in particular, developed.[14] Under Elizabeth an 'inner Council', with the growing power of Secretaries of State, began with about 19 members meeting on Tuesdays, Thursdays and Saturdays, and by the 1590s was meeting most days, with four to six councillors. By 1600 the Council had a definite structure of secretary, clerks, registrar and a keeper of office; it often met on Sundays starting at 7 or 8 a.m., and had begun to delegate work to committees and officials. In her excellent narrative of the Secretaries of State, Evans (1923: ch. 4) notes new developments in James VI/I's reign: the Secretary no longer moving with the king in 1615, and the conventionalization during that decade of one Secretary travelling with the king, one remaining in the metropolis. Many commentators point to the growing systematization of office practice and the longevity of office holding, the beginnings of fully fledged state service.

At local level, however, the gentry and voluntary service remained crucial. As Aylmer has argued,

In the localities the will of the central government depended for its execution on the voluntary co-operation of a hierarchy of part-time unpaid officials: Lord and Deputy Lieutenants, Sheriffs, Justices of the Peace, High and Petty Constables, Overseers of the Poor, and Churchwardens. Without their co-operation the central government was helpless. (1961: 7)

Parliament was one crystallization of this structure of rule. 'The entire membership of the Council sat in one of the two houses' (MacCaffrey 1963: 34ff.); so too did representatives of local elites. Parliament also, and increasingly as we move into the seventeenth century, provides a prism through which we can glimpse emergent contradictions in that structure. We have already indicated ambivalences in the post-1530s status of Parliament. They are evident in Thomas Smith, who could both (in his *Discourse on the commonwealth of England* of 1565) see Parliament as 'the most high and absolute power of the realm of England ... the power of the whole realm, both the head and the body' (quoted in Elton 1963: 128–9), *and* (in 1560) write 'What can a commonwealth desire more than peace, liberty, quietness, little taking of base money, and few Parliaments?' (quoted in Roskell 1964: 304). Parliament was one focus of what David Matthews considers 'the bureaucratic class, constantly shifting in its form and emphasis and varying in its methods of recruitment, that was to provide an element of continuity in social structure' (1948: 1) between the seventeenth and the nineteenth centuries; a 'ruling class' (ibid.: 9) centred upon the 'county officials' who 'provided a fulcrum for administrative action' (ibid.: 3). At the same time the state had other foci, around Crown,

Council and the royal household: we have here some of the basis for subsequent 'Court/Country' divisions, which were – like earlier and later struggles – in part conflicts over what forms the state should take.

Over this period, the general density of government increased. A notable feature of Tudor and early Stuart[15] government was the use of commission. Commissions, whether permanent parts of the machinery of government (Commissions of the Peace, lords lieutenant) or *ad hoc* (grain commissions, religious visitations), were major instruments of both information-gathering and policy-enforcement; 'taken together the commissions show the steady growth of state intervention in national life' (Williams 1979: 418). They are also a typically 'English' device in both their flexibility and their central/local relation. Such institutional development was matched by ideological consolidation, on a scale unknown previously. In some ways the most important feature of this period is the visibly increasing *definition* of a nation/state community; here the link between nationalism and religion, focused on the monarchy, is central. So are the battery of often coercive means through which this was organized. Too much stress on the intermittent effectiveness of Tudor policy-enforcement can obscure this point. It is not so much the fine detail of enforcement of this or that statute or proclamation that matters, as the steady, exemplary and cumulative weight of growing state regulation. It is in this context, as much as that of any direct fostering of capitalist enterprise, that Tudor economic regulation should be evaluated. The overall effect of all this was to give 'the State' a palpability and presence it had not enjoyed before.

Two signs of the times – contrasting, but in their different ways equally revealing – will serve to close this brief survey of the Elizabethan consolidation. The later sixteenth century saw an unprecedented explosion in the making of maps. Nowell produced manuscript maps of England in the 1560s, and Saxton published a complete set of county maps between 1574 and 1579. Camden's *Britannia*, an account of the whole realm, appeared in 1586. Burghley patronized both Nowell and Saxton, and kept a complete set of framed county maps in his house. If anyone applied to the Privy Council for leave to travel abroad, it is said, Burghley 'would first examine him of England. And, if he found him ignorant, would bid him stay at home, and know his own country first' (Palliser 1983: 8–9). Beale's *Treatise of the office of Councillor and Principal Secretary to her Majesty* (1592), written for a particular individual in the expectation that he would become Principal Secretary, recommends Thomas Smith's *Discourse*, and maps of the world and of England ('with a particular note of the division of the shires ... and what noblemen, gentlemen, and others be residing in every one of them').[16] The detail is clearly that of administration: to make rule possible. Elizabeth, meantime, could rely sufficiently on her burgeoning machinery of government, in this increasingly known and integrated state, not to have to travel, in the whole 44 years of her reign, further north or west than Stafford, Shrewsbury and Bristol.

4

Mortall God Enthroned:
One Bourgeois Revolution (of Many)

That the said Charles Stuart, being admitted King of England,
and therein trusted with a limited power to govern by and
according to the laws of the land, and not otherwise; and by his
trust, oath, and office, being obliged to use the power committed
to him for the good and benefit of the people, and for the
preservation of their rights and liberties; yet, nevertheless, out of
a wicked design to erect and uphold in himself an unlimited and
tyrannical power to rule according to his will, and to overthrow
the rights and liberties of the people, yea, to take away and make
void the foundations thereof, and of all redress and remedy of
misgovernment, which by the fundamental constitutions of this
kingdom were reserved on the people's behalf in the right and
power of frequent and successive Parliaments, or national meetings of Council; he, the said Charles Stuart, for accomplishment
of such his designs, and for the protecting of himself and his
adherents in his and their wicked practices, to the same ends hath
traitoriously and maliciously levied war against the present
Parliament, and the people therein represented.

from 'The Charge against the King', 20 January
1649, printed in Gardiner 1979: 371–2

The origins of the Civil War, and the question of its connection (or
otherwise) with wider social and economic changes – in particular, the
rise of capitalism – have been the topic of perennial debate.[1] Marxists
have tended to seek the 'bourgeois revolution' here. For Christopher
Hill, 'the 1640s and 50s marked the end of medieval and Tudor
England . . . in agrarian relations the middle ages were brought to an
end in 1646 . . . in trade, colonial and foreign policy, the end of the
middle ages in England came in 1650–51 . . . the middle ages in
industry and internal trade also ended in 1641 . . . in finance the
middle ages in England ended in 1643 . . . 1641 was no less a turning
point for the church than for the state' (1969a: 135, 146, 155, 169,
190). Hill sees the destruction of the royal bureaucracy in 1640–1 as

'the most decisive single event in British history' (ibid.: 98). On the other hand Gerald Aylmer can find no major state-structural change of the revolutionary years that persisted, apart, of course, from the abolition of High Commission, Star Chamber, the Court of Wards and the Council of the North (1961). In many ways the Restoration was, apparently, just that.

We cannot do justice to these debates here. Nor do we have any pretensions to 'explaining' the Civil War. But some points do require making, particularly around the paradox introduced in the last paragraph. Where the origins of the Civil War have been sought in more than mere 'accident', these debates have most often been organized around gentry/peerage or Court/Country distinctions.[2] One way of reconstructing how these issues might more usefully be examined has been provided by Zagorin, who argues:

English social structure was being reshaped during the sixteenth and seventeenth centuries . . . [the consequence] was to give . . . men in a position to deploy capital in agriculture, trade, and industry – the command of social life. By the end of the seventeenth century these changes had stamped upon the aristocracy of titled and armigerous landlords who continued to form the apex of the social and political hierarchy a new character that set them apart from their contemporaries in every other European monarchy. . . . There does not seem to be anything in these changes, however, that necessarily requires . . . the economic decline of the Elizabethan peerage. . . . Nor is it profitable in this connection to distinguish peers from gentry, gentry from wealthy merchants, or gentry engaged exclusively in agriculture from those occupied also in commercial or industrial enterprise. Neither is it very material that the rise or progress of landed families should often have been made possible by the gains derived from trade and office. . . . The class whose formation is the present focus of interest was being continuously recruited, and it naturally comprised diverse elements as to status, wealth, and source of income. But despite these and other differences its members were species of the same genus. They constituted a single economic class, for what they had in common was the possession of capital that they employed for the end of profit and further accumulation. (in Stone 1965b: 49–52)

Simply to counterpose a supposedly feudal peerage[3] and a homogeneously capitalist gentry will not do. The embourgeoisement Zagorin points to was affecting both classes. By 1640 land – whether owned by peers, gentry, merchants or even the more prosperous yeomen – was much more clearly becoming *capital*, a profit-yielding investment, rather than primarily a source of service, or followers, or loyalty. There were 'improving peers' to be found (as well as 'backwoods gentry'). The 'aristocratic' crisis discussed by Lawrence Stone[4] indeed needs to be seen as part of a general crisis which is the making of capitalism in England, but it was less a financial crisis than a complex crisis of legitimacy – a cultural crisis. Both the growing commercialization of landlord/tenant relationships and Tudor state centralization itself had progressively eroded specifically feudal bases of aristocratic power and authority: manred, and the ideologies of obligation and allegiance bound up with it. The 1573 militia measures, discussed above, were one symptom of this. These factors are important deep-seated elements in the background to the mid-century upheavals. This is not to say they are in any mechanical sense their causes, nor that there was any 'inevitability' about their course or outcome.

At the heart of the notion of 'Country' Hexter locates a group he calls 'country magnates'. These were neither Trevor-Roper's 'fat court gentry', nor his 'declining mere gentry', nor yet Tawney's 'hard-bitten' proto-capitalist gentry. They typically had large landholdings, and drew their income mainly from land rather than office. Country magnates' salient feature, for Hexter – and it is one which is highly germane to our concerns – is this. They:

> provided the realm with the most important part of that 'self-government at the King's command' which is the most significant trait of the English polity. They were the Deputy Lieutenants. They were the Sheriffs. They were JPs. They were the commissioners in the counties . . . it was these same men who came to Parliament from the counties and the boroughs to make up the larger part of the membership of the House of Commons. This majority of local magnates seems to have increased right up to 1640, so that in the House of Commons of the Long Parliament all other groups appear as auxiliaries. (in Stone 1965b: 38)

Morrill offers a related emphasis in his study of the northern gentry. By the early seventeenth century, he argues,

> a new conception of gentility had totally supplanted the old one. Much less emphasis was now placed on the ranking within rural society, and the new concept was intended to give a common strength and purpose to all those titles. The new conception was an adaptation of Aristotle's definition of the citizen as a man whose wealth and leisure freed him from material preoccupations for the task of equipping himself to govern the *polis*, the state . . . The gentry were the governors. (1979: 71)

This 'Country' cause drew support from outwith the traditional political nation too: provincial merchants, incensed by London privileges, craftsmen angered by merchant control over manufacture and trade, and many of the 'middling sort' in town and country. Many gentry sympathized with criticism of the London companies: '[trade]

difficulties presented them as JPs with immense problems of poor relief and the maintenance of order, and [its] prosperity was bound up with their own as woolgrowers and landlords of spinners and weavers' (Manning 1978: 160). The work of Manning, Sharp (1980), and Hirst (1975) shows the extensive pressure, before 1640, on gentlemen MPs from below.

We need to see such formations as 'Court' and 'Country' as 'historic blocs' – formed, defined (and self-defined) through real historical experiences – rather than as cardboard cutouts mechanically representing 'economic interests' (or as clear political 'parties'). Such reductionism is found on both sides of these debates. In the case of 'Country', we are dealing with a bloc, rooted in, but reaching out beyond, the political nation, formed around, in sum, exclusion from 'Court' – office, favour, privilege – and perceived threats to their social power, particularly to their property rights, represented by the use of the royal prerogative. 'Country's' composition needs to be explained not abstractly but in terms of the history of the first half of the seventeenth century, not least the history of state forms them-selves. In Zagorin's sense their mode of life was indeed increasingly a bourgeois one, but their particular formation is not adequately or sufficiently explained by this alone. Nor, therefore, are the events of 1640 on. It did, however, colour their aspirations: they sought a particular sort of freedom from the incubus of court and a polity within which they would have 'presence' and 'visibility' commen-surate with both the facts of their economic power and its modali-ties.

Typically of such political formations, 'Country' had a strong, and totalizing, sense of their 'virtues', their self-defined worth and the actualization of that worthiness in the world. Significantly, this was expressed in terms of *English* values and traditions. Similar contours can also be found in later struggles, notably the claim from those considering themselves 'worthy men' against royal powers and appointees, against 'Old Corruption', in the Economical Reforms movement of the 1780s, and the later movements for radical reform of the state apparatuses and their operating ideologies from the 1830s onwards. As the 'new men' of the early and middle seventeenth century could consider 'Improvement' their right, so too could the bourgeois radicals of the 1830s speak of and work for 'a national system of Improvement'.

We thus think Zagorin correct in seeing the conflict of 1640–2 as one originally internal to the ruling classes,[5] and the measures of those years as initiatives coming from within the ranks of the political nation:

It is striking with what unanimity representatives of England's dominant class in Parliament went to work in 1640–42 to repudiate all that the King had done. Amidst wide agreement, men who not two years later were to take opposing sides in the civil war abolished some of the highest prerogative powers of the Crown and struck down forever the system of paternal rule, with its infringement on vested property interests: ship money, consiliar courts, patents of monopoly, forest laws, and enclosure commissions. (Zagorin, in Stone 1965b: 54)

We need also to be aware of the dynamics of conflict, and the pressures from below. The battle-lines after 1642 did not correspond to the former Court/Country split; and Hill (1959, 1969a, 1980b) has persuasively argued that in the Civil War economically 'progressive' elements – the economically advanced areas of the south and east, the big towns (though not always their ruling oligarchies), the ports, the Navy, the mass of Londoners, and the manufacturing areas of the counties – supported Parliament. But it remains worthy of pause that it is usually just these 1640–2 measures – passed with unanimity by representatives of key sectors of the traditional political nation, if Zagorin is right – that are most often hailed as amongst the most enduringly bourgeois political legacies of the revolution.

One other argument in the gentry controversy is particularly pertinent to our themes. Trevor-Roper – notoriously – saw both Puritanism and recusancy as an economic reflex of the 'Outs', those excluded from the court orbit: a staggering piece of economic reductionism (1953). In fact whatever the deeper roots of 'aristocratic' crisis, much of the hostility attached to the court focused on its supposed papist leanings. Aylmer, whilst denying that the events of 1640–9 can plausibly be explained as happening 'because a defined body of people set out to introduce and impose one particular kind of Church settlement', is clear that 'without the great anti-Catholic phobia and all its ramifications, it is . . . hard to see that these events would have happened as they did' (1980a: 157). By 1640 some 20 per cent of the peerage was Catholic. What was seen as lack of diplomatic and economic patriotism – detente with Spain, run-down of the Navy, failure to support the Protestant cause in the Thirty Years War – was extremely unpopular with the Country group. Lawrence Stone sees Laud's policies on ritual and doctrine as the 'final instrument which brought the edifice to the ground' (1965b: 64).

What Trevor-Roper wholly overlooks is how Protestantism linked with other key elements in Country's charges – notably of Charles I's autocracy and arbitrariness: ship money, prerogative courts, the attempt to rule without Parliament, and so on – as a major component in conceptions of national identity, conceptions deeply anchored in the way of life of the 'natural rulers', whose formation we have sufficiently explored above. These conceptions were forms through which the opposition to the king both defined their own identity and articulated their social vision. Hexter touches a very important point when he argues that:

From the Apology of the Commons in 1604 to the Declaration of Rights in 1688 their ['the rich country gentlemen who fill the House of Commons'] line of action is consistent, clear, and effective. And the latter document is not an assertion of the social supremacy of the middle-class gentry or the political supremacy of the House of Commons; it is precisely what on the face of it it appears to be: a charter of liberties of free Englishmen in the right line of Magna Carta, the Confirmatio Cartarum and the Petition of Right. (in Stone 1965b: 39)

This relates to his identification of 'country magnates' as the core of the Country party. Trevor-Roper offers no doubt unintentional support for this anchoring of Country aspirations in a distinctively national political culture when he characterizes Country's favoured foreign policy as 'a privateering war with Spain as in the days of "Queen Elizabeth of famous memory", in which a gentleman could "get a ship and judiciously manage her"' (1953). We should, of course, be equally mindful of just who Hexter's 'free Englishmen' were, what kind of 'liberties' they had in mind, and for whom. The forms were those of a national culture, the substance increasingly – in the sense we have drawn from Zagorin – bourgeois (and, it goes without saying, enduringly masculine).

One does not need to swallow the historical myth wholesale in order to recognize its contemporary force. The point is that the 'Good Old Cause' was amongst other things – but centrally – embodied in and given social expression through notions of Englishness. And the England in question was both a realm governed by King-in-Parliament and due process, and, by 1640, a Protestant nation. Religion was not, in the seventeenth century, a disposable set of rationalizations, it was a vital element in the framework within which people thought: including thinking their politics. Protestantism, like the place of Parliament or the rule of law, was an integral part of a political culture which was by this time both coherent and distinctively (and proudly) English. That culture, moreover, was firmly embedded in sometimes ancient institutions, ways of doing things, in which Hexter's 'country magnates' had their being. It cannot be comprehended other than against the backdrop of state formation and regulation we have so far sketched in this book.

That culture, finally, was by 1640 sufficiently national in its scope – and again only the antecedent history we have outlined, particularly in the Tudor period, can explain this – to extend beyond the governing classes, and to be capable of radical inflexion, both political and religious. As Aylmer testifies:

The best authorities tell us that there were two main sources of Leveller thinking . . . the radical, iconoclastic Calvinism of the protestant reformation [and] the more rationalistic, optimistic temper of the renaissance. . . . The indigenous English contribution to Leveller ideas is both more particular and more elusive: it owed a great deal to the notion and to the partial practice of self-government, locally if not nationally, and to the tradition, even if it were partly a hollow one, of the individual's rights at law. The attitude of the Levellers towards the common law, indeed towards the whole English legal system, was highly ambivalent. On the one hand, they were emphatic and persistent in claiming their full rights under Magna Carta and other statutes and legal traditions: not to have to answer to interrogation by which accused persons might incriminate themselves; and not to be arrested except on a magistrate's warrant, and then not to be tried save before a jury of their peers. Yet at the same time they subscribed to the historical myth of the Norman Yoke. (1975: 12–13)

The Levellers' ambivalence tells us much about English political culture. Christopher Hill has further investigated radical ideas in the seventeenth century, and their roots – including in Coke's *Institutes* (1958, 1965, 1975); Edward Thompson extends the story to the eighteenth and nineteenth centuries and the making of the English working class, in whose formative period 'the liberty tree' and supposed rights of 'freeborn Englishmen' loom large (1968). On the other side, this anchorage of English radicalisms within a long-standing national culture – and one easily bent, moreover, to national chauvinism – may be one reason why they have been more prone to take 'reformist' than 'revolutionary' form.

With these points in mind, let us now turn to the outcome of the revolutionary decades. The Restoration of Charles II in 1660 confirmed the defeat of the radical elements in the revolution; the propertied classes had coalesced against the threat of 'anarchy'. And in appearance much was as it had been, especially with the institutions of state. Back with the king, his reign postdated to 1649, came the bishops and the House of Lords. Aylmer suggests that if anything the Restoration gave the 'old administrative system' a new lease of life, prolonging it beyond what might otherwise have been the case (1961: 467). Innovations in government tried under the Commonwealth – for instance the beginnings of a professional, salaried civil service – were (with some exceptions) not pursued (see Aylmer 1961: 435ff.; 1957). Notwithstanding how much did not change, the period between 1660 and 1702 was to see some important administrative developments, notably in fields related to economy; 'the rise of the Treasury, the birth of the Board of Trade, the enlargement and subsequent division of the Secretary of State's departments, appointment of new officers to regulate and oversee . . . all this constituted a considerable achievement' (Aylmer 1973: 437). There were, nonetheless, some more decisive shifts, which were both demonstrated by and consolidated in the 'Glorious Revolution' of 1688–9.

The independent power of the Crown was effectively broken, never to be regained; and this breaking marked a further stage, indeed a watershed, in the long making of 'the State' as an impersonal body, a transcendent object representing 'society', the Leviathan theorized by Hobbes in these years as 'Mortall God'. Abolition of the Crown's powerful equity jurisdiction left it with no independent judicial authority. Common law triumphed, both over reforming demands from below, and over royal interference from above. Hill sees it as a law well adapted by Coke – whose *Institutes*, as Blackstone drily put it, 'had an intrinsic authority in courts of justice, and do not entirely depend on the strength of his quotations from old authorities' (quoted in Hill 1980b: 118; cf. his 1965: ch. 5) – to the needs of burgeoning capitalist society. Common law provided both stability (as against royal arbitrariness) – stressed by Weber as a key precondition for rational capitalism – and substantial liberty, for men of property. With the possible exception of the Netherlands, late-seventeenth-century England was in the bourgeois sense probably the freest country in Europe; though we should register both the measures against non-conformists, the so-called Clarendon Code, and, in the 1660s and 1670s, stricter press censorship than had prevailed before 1640, by way of qualification.

Such legal reforms as followed the Restoration pushed in the same direction of extending liberties for the propertied. New uses of the writs of *certiorari* and *mandamus* developed remedies for citizens against arbitrary government; the 1679 Habeas Corpus Act offered protection (to those with money to use the writ) against arbitrary arrest; juries ceased to be accountable for their verdicts, and after 1701 judges were independent of the executive. One important indication of the shift to bourgeois mores in the legal field is the selection of juries on grounds of their ignorance, rather than knowledge, of the facts at issue: 'a trial ceased to be a communal indictment and became a case between parties' (one of whom, in criminal trials, was the Crown) (Hill 1964: 481). A property qualification for jurors – of freehold land worth at least £20 per annum, ten times the Parliamentary franchise – was introduced in 1665.

Such liberty could and did coexist with what was, by the eighteenth century, one of the bloodiest penal codes in Europe, with capital offences, largely for crimes against property, multiplying by the year.[6] It is a mistake to see 'repressive' and 'restitutive' law as mutually exclusive, or 'repressive' law simply as a feudal hangover. As regards the lower orders, the Restoration both increased the power of landowners as JPs – leaving them freer of Privy Council control and delegating to them many of the powers formerly belonging to Church courts – and put them, as MPs, in a stronger position to pass statutes in their own class interest. They did. There was no 'alliance' of Crown and peasantry against the aristocracy in England, of the kind Brenner detects (and sees as a barrier to capitalism) in France (1976). As Christopher Hill remarks, 'the unfettered sovereignty of JPs drawn from the employing classes was hardly liberty for their employees' (1969a: 145). 'As JPs the gentry put down the riots of their labourers, and as MPs they passed the statutes which allowed them to do so' (Harding, quoted in Hill 1969a: 141).

The bishops returned, but without High Commission the ecclesiastical courts lost their teeth – at least as regards the powerful – though at local level the parson continued to buttress the squire (whose nominee he often was). High Commission had been hearing 80–120 cases a day in the 1630s (Hill 1964: 297). By the 1680s the lower ecclesiastical courts were finding it impossible to get their sentences enforced. It is to be noted, however, that Church courts retained jurisdiction over marriage and divorce until 1857. The Crown could no longer use the Church, as had been attempted in the 1630s, as an apparatus of propaganda independently of Parliament. In the long run this further Erastianization contributed to the privatization of religion, its dissociation from the public sphere, typical of bourgeois societies: the recognized existence of dissent dates from the Restoration. Notwithstanding 'intermittent but severe persecution' and the Clarendon Code, licences for dissenting chapels were issued from 1672. Other, more secular – and more specifically bourgeois – forms of legitimation and modes of discipline were increasingly to take over in the 'public' sphere. Christina Larner, speaking more generally, calls this '"the political dethronement of God". The Kingdom of God on earth ceased to be a political objective and was replaced by the defence of property, nationalism, and liberty' (1982: 56). This partial displacement of religion as a dominant legitimating code for and within the state, towards solid bourgeois values of law, property, 'liberty' and civility was a major cultural legacy of the revolutionary decades.

This does not deny our earlier points concerning the importance of religion in the seventeenth century, or for a considerable time afterwards. Religion continued to be a major instrument and vocabulary of moral regulation. There is an extensive literature on the affinity between Protestant values – individualism, sobriety, abstinence, labour – and the moral relations of capitalism, which we will not rehearse here.[7] Suffice it to say that what we are witnessing is less the demise of religion as a 'moral technology' than a shift in its forms, from the visible coercion of Church courts and public penances to internalized disciplines of conscience and sect; a shift thoroughly consonant with a wider embourgeoisement of social relations and identities. But some of the ethos of Puritan discipline is caught in short-lived statutes of the revolutionary decades, when the Kingdom of God was still sought in earthly polities: the Blasphemy Act of 1648 made denial of the Trinity, scriptural authority, bodily resurrection or the last judgement capital offences; actors and popular musicians were to be whipped as rogues. We also see a characteristic family discipline: in 1650 adultery and fornication (on second offence) were made capital crimes (Baker 1979: 185; cf. Hill 1964, chs 6, 13; 1978a; Thomas 1978). Hill quotes Calamy, urging MPs in 1641: 'First reform your own families, and then you will be the fitter to reform the family of God. Let the master reform his servant, the father his child, the husband his wife' (1964: 430). Hill's important study (1964: ch. 12) traces this discipline back to the Reformation and shows how, in his words, 'the household was almost part of the constitution of the state' (p. 434). Henry VIII (34 and 35, cap. 1) permitted merchants, as well as noblemen and gentlemen, to read the Bible in their families whilst prohibiting this to artificers, journeymen, husbandmen, labourers – and women; under Elizabeth householders could be fined £10 if their children and apprentices failed to attend church (35 Eliz. cap. 1). 'Before 1640 the preachers had proclaimed the rights and duties of men, but they were manifestly thinking almost exclusively of householders' (p. 455): both women and 'the poor' were excluded. Gregory King's estimate of the English population in 1696 took as its unit the household rather than the individual. This patriarchal dimension of the 'Protestant ethic' has usually been neglected in sociological discussion (but see Thomas 1958, 1959, 1977; Thompson 1977b; Rowbotham 1977; Rapp 1983; Stone 1977; as well as Hill), but it was crucial, not least in its implications for state formation. We will see later that similar 'household' paradigms continued to structure, for instance, nineteenth-century franchise reform.

The Crown was financially subordinated to Parliament. Legislation against non-Parliamentary taxation was confirmed in 1660; so was legislation against royal monopolies, hitherto an important source of revenue and patronage. Abolition of the Court of Wards, and of feudal tenures (1646, confirmed 1660), deprived the Crown of feudal revenues. Compensation for wardships by excise further increased royal dependence on Parliament. Excise, a form of tax based on consumption rather than status, from which unconsumed wealth – in other words, capital – was exempt, also has a deeper cultural significance:

Acceptance of this principle marks the transition from a hierarchical, functional, estates conception of society, in which the duty of the poor is to labour rather than to pay taxes, to a theory of society as composed of individual atoms, with rights to be recognised by the state which must be paid for: a Ritz Hotel view of society. Equality before the law and excise are expressions of the same mode of thought. (Hill 1969a: 182)

After 1660 the king could no longer 'live off his own'; 'henceforth [he] became dependent on a Parliamentary civil list, a salaried official, the first civil servant' (Hill 1955: 59). Anti-monopoly legislation also removed the Crown's ability to regulate economic activity independently of Parliament. Whatever the economic role of royal monopolies, patents and licences may have been under the Tudors, in the changed economic conditions of the late seventeenth century their curbing almost certainly benefited the growth of capitalist enterprise. Again, the shift in the balance – and forms – of power was consolidated by the events of 1688–9.

Two other enduring regulative legacies of the revolutionary years are worthy of particular note. Hill has powerfully argued that abolition of feudal tenures provided a major boost to capitalist agriculture (1969a: Pt 2, ch. 3). This measure effectively gave landlords absolute, modern, property rights:[8] their land became a commodity which could be freely bought, sold, mortgaged. It was also freed from the constraints of wardship and arbitrary death duties. Blackstone thought this 'a greater acquisition to the civil properties of this kingdom than even Magna Carta itself' (quoted in Milsom 1981: 3). The allied device of strict settlement, Hill argues, facilitated capital accumulation and the consolidation of property which formed the basis for the eighteenth-century Whig oligarchy; younger sons, meanwhile, were impelled to careers in Army, Navy, the civil service, and the colonies. The stabilization of landed property in certain families into the nineteenth century – we shall trace some of the continuing power that went with that in later chapters – has recently been demonstrated by Lawrence and Jeanne Stone (1984), in a study which unfortunately appeared too late for detailed discussion here. At the same time, importantly, smaller landholders did not achieve the same rights. Copyhold was specifically excluded from the 1660 law, while in 1667 legislation did the same for small freeholders without written title (a bourgeois Quo Warranto?). This facilitated rack-renting, evictions and enclosure, and thus the creation of a landless proletariat. Perkin sees abolition of feudal tenures as 'the decisive change in English history, which made it different from the continent' (quoted in Hill 1980b: 116); Robert Brenner considers the English peasants' failure to win security of tenure a major factor in the rapidity, by comparison with France, of the development of capitalism in England (1976).

The second revolution/Restoration continuity worth highlighting is of economic policies and instruments. The Navigation Acts (1650, 1651, confirmed and revised 1660, 1661) made possible the closed colonial system: they provided for colonies to be subordinate to Parliament, and all colonial trade to be carried in English ships. Adam Smith thought them 'perhaps the wisest of all the commercial regulations of England' (quoted in Hill 1969a: 155). Hill sees them as marking 'a transition from an organisation based on monopoly companies to a total integration of the country's trade based on national monopoly, with the state playing a leading role. . . . The Navigation Acts created a monopoly big enough to be open to the whole merchant class.' They represented 'a Baconian vision towards which men had long been groping: that state control and direction could stimulate material progress' (ibid.: 157). Braudel's observations, quoted above (p. ix), are worth recalling here. The Dutch War of 1552–4 was 'the first state-backed imperialist venture in English history', the Spanish war which followed it England's 'first state-backed grab for colonies in the New World' (Hill 1980b: 117). The capture of Jamaica in 1655 gave England the basis for the slave trade; the second and third Dutch wars broke the Netherlands' hold on the tobacco, sugar, fur and slave trades. The Portuguese alliance of 1654 – consolidated by Charles II's politic marriage to Catherine of Braganza – brought England Bombay, and entry to the Portuguese West African and Brazilian trades. All this anticipates the aggressive commercial foreign policy and wars waged by the English state in the eighteenth century. Ireland, conquered by Cromwell, remained an English colony. In the 1660s imports of Irish sheep, cattle and dairy products to England were prohibited. After 1689–91 indigenous Irish trade and industry was heavily controlled – not to say, in some cases, destroyed – to England's advantage.

More detailed arguments on the contribution of the seventeenth-century revolutions to the development of capitalism can be found in Hill's writings. But perhaps – as Hill himself sometimes suggests (see especially his 1980a) – the really crucial consequences were cultural. After the experience of regicide and republic, the abolition of bishops and House of Lords, the 'wild, revolutionary ferment' of the 1640s 'in which every heresy under the sun was printed and preached' (Hill 1980b: 122), the boundaries of the conceivable had irrevocably altered and the world could never be the same again, whatever the apparent 'restorations' of form.

The ferment of discussion which Milton had welcomed in *Areopagitica* . . . bubbled on for eight years or so before the conservatives managed to get the lid back on again. The memory of it faded – more slowly and less completely perhaps than the books usually suggest. Blake remembered it, and so did Catherine Macaulay and the Wilkesites, Paine and the American rebels, Thomas Spence, William Godwin, the Corresponding Society, and the Chartists. The young Wordsworth recalled Milton the libertarian, Shelley recalled Milton the defender of regicide. The Revolution had shown that the old order was not eternal: the possibility of establishing God's kingdom on earth had been envisaged, especially by those normally excluded from politics. The Long Parliament itself had argued that 'reason hath no precedent, for reason is the fountain of all just precedents'; Levellers, Hobbes, Locke, and many others evolved systems of rational and utilitarian politics. By 1742 David Hume could assume that no one took claims to divine right seriously. (ibid.: 133)

The revolution, Hill argues, did much to liberate science (now under the patronage of the Royal Society). In the arts, too, it had long-term consequences: the novel, that 'bourgeois literary form *par excellence*' (ibid.: 135), had its roots in the spiritual autobiographies of the sectaries and Bunyan's epics of the poor. Milton wrote the last great epics of English literature: the distance between Spenser, say, and Defoe, Fielding and Richardson (and the modern world) is immense. Holdsworth notes a much increased discussion of 'public affairs' and a veritable explosion of political theory (1972: vol. 6, 273ff.). We have pointed, also, to enduring shifts in both rhetorics of state legitimation and modalities of social discipline which have their roots in these years. In many ways – to return to the paradox with which we began this chapter – it can be argued that the new social relations, of production, of social discipline, were so articulated that they profoundly changed the *meaning* of a state system which seems otherwise to have so little changed, the culture of politics.

Does all this, then, amount to a 'bourgeois revolution'? The question is a difficult one to answer. Yes, if by this we mean – and in itself this is a lot – that the events of 1640 through 1688–9 deserve to be called revolutionary, and facilitated the development of capitalism and a wider embourgeoisement of culture and society; on either point there can really be little dispute (see Hill 1955, 1959, 1969a, 1980b). But the appropriateness of the concept, whether as description or explanation, may in other respects be doubted. The notion of a 'bourgeois revolution' popularly conveys the idea of a set-piece struggle between clearly defined class groupings, with the victorious bourgeoisie emerging in secure possession of political power. This clearly was not the situation in seventeenth-century England. It encourages overly neat identification of political actors with conflicting social and economic class interests. The evidence militates against any such conclusion here. Finally, and from our point of view most seriously, the very notion of *a* bourgeois revolution suggests a momentary rupture, a defined and dated event, in which political power visibly changes class hands. Not only is this an implausible description of the events that culminated in the Restoration of 1660 and the 'readjustment' of 1688–9. It also seriously obscures, and massively oversimplifies, the complex and protracted history of state formation and transformation through which capitalist classes did come finally to achieve political dominance in England.

When all is said and done, the English revolution is difficult to fit into such precast models. Though 'the middling sort' were increasingly drawn into its turmoils, and genuinely radical demands and programmes did emerge – with enduring consequences for later oppositional politics – such institutional and legal legacies of the revolution as survived 1660 for the most part stemmed from initiatives of the 'natural rulers' of the country, the traditional core of the political nation itself. And the basis of these initiatives – in some ways a very conservative one – lay in a national political culture centred on institutions rooted in the long history of medieval and Tudor state formation. Certainly by the mid-seventeenth century this culture was being inflected in a bourgeois direction, as the economic character of the dominant classes, in particular the landed classes, itself changed. Equally, the institutions and culture of English polity were to prove exceedingly suitable vehicles of embourgeoisement. But they were not themselves bourgeois in origin. And it is their adaptability to bourgeois purposes that is, from our point of view, their most interesting feature; the whole burden of our argument is to suggest that – for no doubt contingent reasons, in terms of any supposed 'logic' of capitalist development – exactly the singularity of English state formation and state forms (together, certainly, with other peculiarities for the most part not addressed in this book) go far towards explaining why it was specifically in England that modern capitalism was so spectacularly to triumph.

So it is, in our view, ultimately unhelpful to try and press the English revolution into the procrustean mould of '*the* bourgeois revolution' – having only then to qualify it, as one must, as 'incomplete', a revolution that 'stopped half-way'. The theoretical schemata obscure more than they illuminate. The revolutions of the seventeenth century were one moment – without doubt, a seminal one – in the making of Thompson's Great Arch. They reformed the

English state, in some ways dramatically, not for the first or the last time. But the *longue durée* is equally pertinent both to explanation of the English revolution – what made it possible, and why it assumed the forms it did – and to its long-term consequences. Loades's judicious summary seems to us to make exactly the right emphases:

it would be a mistake to underestimate the significance of the King's defeat and death at the hands of his rebellious subjects. . . . Not only had the ultimate proof of accountability been given, but constitutional limitations of a tangible kind unthinkable a century before had been fastened upon the King's authority. Consequently, although much of the Tudor achievement survived, the Tudor monarchy as it had been wielded by Elizabeth and adapted by James I and Charles I perished in the Civil War. . . .

In theory and in practice the propertied classes were the great gainers by the revolution, which in spite of its alarms ended by entrenching them in political power. At the same time, the aristocracy had received a sharp lesson . . . [in] the dangers which could follow if the 'lower orders' were called in to settle quarrels within the ruling class. The experience was never to be forgotten . . .

In 1660 no less than in 1450, the aristocracy were in command of the political situation. But whereas the feudal magnates of the fifteenth century had been individuals whose power lay in their own resources, the squires and politicians of the Restoration were masters of a sophisticated constitutional and administrative machine. That machine was primarily the creation of the Tudor monarchy, which, by a long slow process of unification and centralisation had made England the governable entity it was by the late seventeenth century. That civil order and political obedience to which all the monarchs had contributed from Edward IV onwards had been shaken by the Civil War and its aftermath, but was ultimately strengthened rather than destroyed by the shock. The political system which was to emerge in England between 1660 and 1689 bore little resemblance to the Tudor monarchy in any of its more obvious features, but it was nonetheless firmly rooted in the successes and limitations of the government which they had created. (1977: 460–1)

5

From Theatre to Machine: 'Old Corruption'

Thine, Freedom, thine the blessings pictur'd here,
Thine are the charms that dazzle and endear. . . .
That independence Britons prize too high,
Keeps man from man, and breaks the social tie;
The self-dependent lordlings stand alone,
All claims that bind and sweeten life unknown. . . .
Nor this the worst. As Nature's ties decay,
As duty, love and honour fail to sway,
Fictitious bonds, the bonds of wealth and law,
Still gather strength, and force unwilling awe.
Hence all obedience bows to these alone,
And talent sinks, and merit weeps unknown;
Till time may come, when stripped of all her charms,
The land of scholars, and the nurse of arms . . .
One level sink of avarice shall lie. . . .
O then how blind to all that truth requires,
Who think it freedom when a part aspires!
Calm is my soul, nor apt to rise in arms,
Except when fast-approaching danger warms:
But when contending chiefs blockade the throne,
Contracting regal power to stretch their own,
When I behold a factious band agree
To call it freedom when themselves are free;
Each wanton judge new penal statutes draw,
Laws grind the poor, and rich men rule the law;
The wealth of climes, where savage nations roam,
Pillag'd from slaves to purchase slaves at home. . . .
Have we not seen, round Britain's peopled shore,
Her useful sons exchanged for useless ore?
Seen all her triumphs but destruction haste,
Like flaring tapers brightening as they waste;
Seen opulence, her grandeur to maintain,

Lead stern depopulation in her train,
And over field where scatter'd hamlets rose,
In barren solitary pomp repose?

Oliver Goldsmith, 'The Traveller; or,
A Prospect of Society' (1764–5)

In the history of English state formation, the century from the 'Glorious Revolution' of 1688–9 to the Economical Reforms movement of the 1780s is, in some ways, extraordinarily difficult to deal with. (In others, Goldsmith's poem, like his 'The deserted village' (1770), says it all.) In terms of our overall long-waves argument, some parallels can be drawn with the century after the 1530s. The (partially) reconstructed state forms left by the seventeenth-century 'settlement' undoubtedly did in many ways facilitate ongoing social and economic transformations; the eighteenth century saw the triumph of agrarian and commercial capitalism, and the beginnings of industrial revolution. The seventeenth-century reconstruction is most significant for what it 'allowed', the 'liberty' it opened up for men of property in ways we have adumbrated in our last chapter. But beyond this, state activities actively fostered both capitalist enterprise and the consolidation of a bourgeois ruling class – and its rule – in a variety of more specific ways which we will examine.

Yet at the same time, state forms themselves remained largely 'unrationalized', and were in no way a simple instrument of the capitalist classes as a whole who thus benefited from their activities. This was a more particular – a very particular – political formation, known later as 'Old Corruption'. As in the later sixteenth and early seventeenth centuries, there was an ossification, a stalling, in state formation; gaps were to open between 'Old Corruption' and sectors of the dominant and rising classes; a relatively narrow elite, the 'Whig oligarchy', monopolized key positions; and demands for reform arose as the century wore on. The historiographic problem is to relate 'Old Corruption' to the manifest embourgeoisement of society that did take place during the eighteenth century, in ways that do not, teleologically, deny or marginalize those very features that made Old Corruption what it was.

E. P. Thompson elaborates on these themes. The settlement of 1688, he argues,

inaugurated a hundred years of comparative social stasis, so far as overt class conflict or the maturation of class consciousness was concerned. The main beneficiaries were those vigorous agrarian capitalists, the gentry. But this does not mean that the governing institutions represented, in an unqualified manner, the gentry as a 'ruling–class'. At a local level (the magistracy) they did so in an astonishingly naked manner. At a national level (desuetude of the old restrictions on marketing, the facilitation of enclosures, the expansion of empire) they furthered their interests. But at the same time a prolonged period of social stasis is commonly one in which ruling institutions degenerate, corruptions enter, channels of influence silt up, an elite entrenches itself in positions of power. A distance opened up between the majority of the middle and lesser gentry (and associated groups) and certain great agrarian magnates, privileged merchant capitalists, and their hangers-on, who manipulated the organs of the state in their own private interest. (Thompson 1965: 322; all references to Thompson hereafter (in text, citations and notes) are to E. P. Thompson unless otherwise indicated)

Thompson sees 'Old Corruption' as a specific, historically particular parasitism; a political formation *sui generis* whose networks of place, pelf and patronage have been well documented by historians of the period.[1] Taking contemporaries' descriptions seriously, he considers 'Old Corruption' to be

a more serious term of political analysis than is often supposed; for political power throughout most of the eighteenth century may best be understood, not as a direct organ of any class or interest, but as a secondary political formation, a purchasing-point from which other kinds of social and economic power were gained or enhanced. (1978b: 141)

Notwithstanding certain developments in state formation after the Restoration noted already – the rise of the Treasury, the birth of the Board of Trade, and so on – Aylmer argues that 'a great deal did not change' with the 1688 settlement; offices were still treated 'much like other pieces of property and most offices continued to rely for payment on fees, gratuities and perquisites' (1973: 437). This, and an unreformed Parliament, was the territory on which Old Corruption could install itself. For much of the century, 'the State' was, not to put too fine a point on it, a racket, run by particular groups within the ruling classes largely for their own benefit. But it is not enough to dismiss it with this observation, and see capitalist development as something that occurred entirely independently of this 'parasitism'. Old Corruption was conducive to capitalism, if in complex and contradictory ways.

Although we agree with the general emphasis, of contemporaries as well as later historians, on the patronage–clientage, place-men and fee-plunder features of state employment in the eighteenth century, two qualifications need to be made. First, financial and administrative support of military and naval forces (and for war), as well as for trade, is central. We will say more on this below. Second, although the 'unique formation' of Old Corruption (Aylmer's 'extraordinary patchwork – of old and new, useless and efficient, corrupt and honest') was just that, there are some features which deserve mention. Holmes (1982: ch. 8; cf. Finer 1952b, Parris 1968, Aylmer 1974, 1980c) finds he can support estimates of 'public servants' of some 10,000 in 1688 (Gregory King), 12,000 in the mid-1720s (his own estimate) and 16,000 in 1759 (Joseph Massie). This compares with the severe underestimate of 1797 of 16,267 reported in an official return of 1828 (quoted in Gretton 1913: 111; Cohen 1941: 23). Equally significant is Holmes's demonstration of a number of individual, familial and inter-generational 'official careers' over decades and his discussion of the stratification within the 'public officials': the overwhelming majority earned between £40 and £80 a year. For 506 posts in 1727, he has found 301 with between £100 and £190 (mostly at the bottom end), a further 121 cases of between £200 and £450 a year, with only 84 being paid £500 a year or more and only 24 of these receiving more than £1,000 (Holmes 1982: 256–7). As he goes on to stress (and to demonstrate with many examples) 'some of the most prosperous civil servants were in offices where the rewards lay entirely in fees and commission' and others were allowed to boost their income by fees. Of course this hierarchization was previously and still remains a persistent feature of state employment: William Farr's inquiry of 1846 found of 13,540 'Assessed Posts', 8,704 with salaries not exceeding £100 p.a. (being paid a total of £18,791 p.a.) and 4,836 with salaries above £100 (being paid a total of £1,278,806) (Farr 1848: 113). Between 1947 and 1968 the administrative class of the civil service was never more than 1 per cent of all civil servants, that is never more than 3,100 individuals in a total non-industrial civil service which (excluding the Post Office) was always around 500,000 people or more (Fulton Report 1966: vol. 4; cf. Kelsall 1966; Chapman 1970; Kellner and Crowther-Hunt 1980). *Plus ça change....*

A number of commentators stress the importance of what is portrayed – misleadingly, in our view – as the 'weakness' of English state formation at this point in its history, the implied comparison being with strongly centralized and bureaucratized European absolutisms. Thus Aylmer emphasizes that office-holding was not 'so fatally attractive as to draw too many of the ablest people away from other pursuits'; the burden of the state on society, though greater than previously, was not 'economically crippling' (1974: 259).[2] (Porter (1982: 391, after Peter Mathias) reckons state expenditure as increasing from £6.1m in the first decade of the century to over £20m in the ninth, over £33m in the last, and over £60m in the first decade of the nineteenth century.) Thompson argues that it was land that remained central in the theatrical circuits land–money–politics–office–honours–title:

It was both the jumping-off point for power and office, and the point to which power and office returned. . . . This was the predatory phase of agrarian and commercial capitalism, and the state itself was the prime object of prey. (Thompson 1978b: 139)

In this context, he considers, Old Corruption's 'greatest source of strength lay in precisely the weakness of the state itself: in the desuetude of its paternal, bureaucratic and protectionist powers; in the licence it afforded to agrarian, mercantile and manufacturing capitalism to get on with their own self-reproduction; in the fertile soil which it afforded to laissez-faire' (ibid.: 141). Braudel makes a similar point, on a more general level:

the modern state, which did not create capitalism but only inherited it, sometimes acts in its favour and at other times acts against it; it sometimes allows capitalism to expand and at other times destroys its mainspring. Capitalism only triumphs when it becomes identified with the state, when it is the state.

In England, he thinks, this happened after 1688 (1977: 64–5). But, he adds, the growth and success of capitalism require 'certain social conditions. They require a certain tranquility in the social order and a certain neutrality, or weakness, or permissiveness by the state' (ibid.: 74), and England was relatively singular in this latter respect. All this suggests that where Old Corruption was most important was in its 'non-intervention' in 'civil society', its leaving 'private business' alone; that the significance of the seventeenth-century settlement was the largely negative one of removing constraints which had previously impeded capitalist development.

In one important sense this is true. As Lipson argued (1946: 165) the eighteenth century saw the triumph of *laissez-faire*; capitalist enterprise, whether agrarian, commercial or manufacturing, was certainly less hamstrung by state regulation than at any time previously. But this should not be taken to imply an absence of state regulation as such. We would argue that 'weakness' is the wrong term; permissiveness is closer – with the proviso that what was permitted for some was experienced as imposition for most. What appears as the 'weakness' of the eighteenth-century 'state system', glancing over our shoulders at European absolutisms, was in fact its openness to men of different kinds of property; and this openness was precisely its strength. Exactly the 'archaic', unbureaucratized, flexibilities of English state forms were practically and representationally far more conducive to capitalist transformation than any absolutism, fostering and rewarding (certain kinds of) privateering 'initiative' and 'enterprise'.

In part, what we are witnessing here is the construction of the 'typical' state/economy relation of bourgeois societies, whereby the former secures the conditions in which the latter can 'freely' operate, *through* the inflection of older forms. This needs qualifying, however, in two ways (both for this period and in general). First, to create and sustain those conditions entails extensive state activity, by a state which is strong enough to do the job. One index of states' success here is precisely their ability to naturalize such conditions – constituting, for instance, certain forms of property as 'natural rights of man' – in such a way that their agency is 'forgotten'; much eighteenth-century struggle was around precisely this sort of moral regulation. Second, notwithstanding the general paradigm of *laissez-faire*, specific state policies aided definite capitalist interests in ways that are not always sufficiently acknowledged. Thompson is clear on both points:

Indeed, that state, weak as it was in its bureaucratic and rationalizing functions, was immensely strong and effective as an auxiliary instrument of production in its own right: in breaking open the paths for commercial imperialism, in imposing enclosure upon the countryside, and in facilitating the accumulation and movement of capital, both through its banking and funding functions and, more bluntly, through the parasitic extractions of its own officers. It is this specific combination of weakness and strength which provides the 'general illumination' in which all colours of that century are plunged. (1978b: 162)

Finally, we would argue that this particular state formation, in its institutions and its imagery, was one focus or embodiment – and itself an almost theatrical representation – of the actual moral relations through which, in England, capitalist transformation historically proceeded. Sociological models can sometimes encourage overly neat notions of transition from *Gemeinschaft* to *Gesellschaft*, 'community' to 'cash nexus'. The reality is more complicated. Notions of propriety and deference materialized in the seemingly arcane state relations of Old Corruption – as well as the moral worth of money so evidently paraded there – were means through which eighteenth-century English social relations were reconstructed along capitalist lines, cementing the ruling class and hegemonizing the ruled. Again we stress our general theme of state formation as cultural revolution: in the eighteenth century, we can very clearly see the latter as organized forms of cultural production, and the products are within and around us still, we use and exchange them every day. As so often in England, revolutionary transformations were accomplished (and concealed) through new uses of old forms and the tracing of a thousand lineages from the past.

J. H. Shennan concludes his book *The origins of the modern European state, 1450–1725* (1974) with the following quotation from Hobbes:

This is the Generation of the great LEVIATHAN, or rather (to speak more reverently) of that *Mortall God*, to which we owe under the *Immortall God*, our peace and defence.

In England by the beginning of the eighteenth century, this impersonal body – mutated from the 'second body' theory of Tudor rule, the king's 'body politic', via the English revolution[3] – entailed a particular theory of Parliamentary sovereignty. Parliament, as we saw in the last chapter, was both freer of royal control than ever before and securely representative of the landed classes. The active peerage numbered about 130, a body small enough, as Plumb comments (1950: 34), to know all about one another. As regards the Commons, an Act of 1711 established a landed qualification of £600 p.a. for a knight of the shire and £300 for a burgess. The Septennial Act of 1716 raised the price of a seat in the Commons; by the end of the century, a borough seat was estimated to cost some £5,000. County elections were effectively decided by country gentlemen; their power over those of their tenants who could vote (on what was anyway a narrow franchise) was such that Namier thought that 'not more than one in twenty voters at county elections could exercise his statutory rights' (quoted in Hill 1969a: 218). After 1720 most borough elections were not contested. For much of the century Parliament was run by the Whig oligarchy: 'for all practical purposes England was a one-party state' (ibid.).

The Privy Council was no longer the central organ of government (though it remains important, to the present day, as a legitimating and enabling form); the core of administration, in the eighteenth century, lay with an 'inner cabinet' of the Secretaries of State, the Lord Chancellor, the Lord Privy Seal, the Lord President of the Council, and the Chancellor of the Exchequer (Plumb 1950: 49ff.). These and other ministers were appointed and dismissed by the king, and dependent for their powers largely on the royal prerogative, but they were answerable in the final analysis to Parliament, which thus had an effective veto over ministerial appointments. The king's pardon was no plea to any act his ministers might have committed. It is worth noting, here, as part of the 'extraordinary patchwork', just how unbureaucratized much in the functioning of central state forms remained for most of the eighteenth century: Roman numerals, courthand and tallies continued to be used in the Exchequer.

Precisely because of the state forms we have analysed in earlier chapters this theory and practice of sovereignty inflected what might have become a specific personalized absolutism into forms of rule which, employing the same rhetoric of 'reasons of state', legitimized the rights of the political nation. These 'reasons' had already been codified in England, and simultaneously made features of the sinews of impersonal power. Milsom (1981: 4) argues that 'private law supposes an economy based upon the exercise of private rights, as opposed to the management of resources understood to be ultimately at the disposal of authority.' For Coke, 'The Common Law is the absolute perfection of reason itself' (quoted in Hill 1965: 250). But, as Hill brilliantly argues,

Rationality is a social concept, and social divisions in England (and elsewhere) were producing conceptions of what was 'rational' which were so different that in the last resort only force could decide between them. The 'reasonable-ness' of the sanctity of private property was imposed by the pikes of the New Model Army and confirmed by Dutch William's mercenaries. (Hill 1965: 254; cf. Hill 1967, 1969b)

The key question – then as now – as Hobbes and others realized, was 'Who is to interpret?' (Hill 1965: 254).

The period from the 'settlement' of the late seventeenth century until the economical reforms of the 1780s can best be understood, for our purposes, as that of a double consolidation of certain relations of production simultaneously involving property and labour. The con-firmation of the enforced legitimacy of certain property forms carried with it dramatic consequences for the labour regimes of the majority of the population. If we crudely characterize the social relations of feudalism as defined by land and service, the long transformation continues by their redefinition, through existing state forms, as landed property and labour discipline. This redefinition was materialized through a range of theatrical representations as social propriety and deference; it is important to understand the latter not as mere 'feudal relics', but as integral to the moral relations of eighteenth-century agrarian capitalism. Old Corruption was one such theatre, another was the 'gallows tree' at Tyburn. Here more than ever, as Christopher Hill's work on the period from the 1530s and Thompson's from the early eighteenth century taken together demonstrate, we have to understand the meaning of state forms through their materialization in the historical experience of different social groups.[4] Later one form of this discipline will be theorized as political economy (and used against Old Corruption), as more 'archetypally' capitalist – urban and contractual – forms of labour relation emerge. But for much of the eighteenth century the constitution of a capitalist ethos is expressed in other terms, drawing on paternalist paradigms of master and servant;

even if this was often more a matter of style than substance, and under increasing strain from the growth of free and mobile labour. As Thompson emphasizes,

This was not an easy or quick transition. Hill has reminded us of the long resistance made by the free-born Englishman against the pottage of free wage labour (in his 1967). One should note equally the long resistance made by their masters against some of its consequences. These wished devoutly to have the best of both the old world and the new, without the disadvantages of either. They clung to the image of the labourer as an *un*free man, a 'servant': a servant in husbandry, in the workshop, in the house. (They clung simultaneously to the image of the free or masterless man as a vagabond, to be disciplined, whipped and compelled to work.) (1974: 382–3)

Recent studies of dominant notions of 'property' in this period – along with their necessary complement, studies of crime and protest[5] – have tended to confirm Hill's definition of the 'bourgeois conception of liberty: the right to be left alone, to work, to make money, to trade freely' (1977: 263). As John Commons concluded his classic study *Legal foundations of capitalism*:

Economic theory, like legal theory, started with Liberty rather than Purpose. Liberty is the individual's absence of physical coercion . . . especially in England after the Act of Settlement [1701] . . . the rights which it afforded came to be looked upon as a natural right of man, in the sense, not of an ideal that man ought to have by the aid of government, but in the sense of something which he previously had by nature and was deprived of by government. (1924: 385)

The 'other side' of such liberty – social discipline – is well illustrated by a passage from Blackstone's *Commentaries* (1765) with which Sir Basil Thomson begins his illuminating *The story of Scotland Yard*. This draws attention to that wider meaning of policing (and police) so central to the two hundred years of state formation from the 1680s onwards:

By public police and economy I mean the due regulation and domestic order of the Kingdom, whereby the individuals of the state, like members of a well-governed family, are bound to conform their general behaviour to the rule of propriety, good neighbourhood and good manners; to be decent, industrious in their respective stations. (Thomson 1935: 3)[6]

That, in many ways, is what this book as a whole is about. It was, we should interject, the natural rights of *men* that were being formed and confirmed during this period: Blackstone's 'well-governed family' was patriarchal. But the crucial point that emerges from both these quotes is the way liberty and property were – simply – *there* for some men: gentry, governors, rulers, regulators; and the 'rule of propriety' takes this 'natural order' for granted.[7] We are not the first to observe that property ('owning, being owned') and propriety ('correctness of behaviour or morals') have the same etymological root. State activities were central to the naturalization of both.

Property extended and protected by law is the key to the puzzle of natural rights (for some men) *within* the 'old administrative system' (Aylmer 1961: 467; Plumb 1963: ch. 6; 1967: ch. 4). The prime force of the state was law, 'the strongest limb of the body politic' (Brewer and Styles 1980: 13), and the law was 'elevated during this century to a role more prominent than at any other period of our history' (Thompson 1978b: 144). The problem was twofold: to legitimate the rights of property (the natural rights, much discussed, in fact applied only to some forms as we shall see) and to police the labouring poor into the habituation of their stations. The freeing of production forms and relations entails consistent state activity (Polanyi 1945: ch. 5; Hill 1969a: pt 4) enshrined in legal enactment, in a code. Conventional historiography has been much concerned to show how this 'century of stability' demonstrates what Holdsworth considers 'adaptation' (1924: 6) and Lord Justice Scarman calls the 'superb flexibility' (quoted in Griffith 1975: 38; cf. Griffith 1977b, 1978) of English law.[8] Weber, commenting on the 'less rational and less bureaucratic judicature' of England is more perceptive:

Capitalism in England, however, could quite easily come to terms with this, especially because the nature of the court constitution and of the trial procedure up to the modern period amounted to a far-going denial of justice to the economically weak groups. (1914b: 218)

Property rights were experienced as negative legal regulation by the general population in terms of the Poor Law, apprenticeship, hours and wages of work and a more diffuse moral regulation. But the great catastrophe which above all pervades the eighteenth century is the acceleration of that great 'freeing' of labour (and thus making of labour-power) that divides wage-labouring from generalized poverty; the long movement from service to employment, from provision to production/consumption, from political theatre to the individualism (and special associationism) of the vote: enclosures.[9] John Clare (describing his own experience in 1809) sums it up well:

> Enclosure came, and trampled on the grave
> Of labour's rights, and left the poor a slave
> (quoted in Harrison 1984: 230)

By 1809 it was indeed the grave of 'labour's rights' that were being trampled upon, since enclosures can now be seen as part of a wider transformation.

Enclosures are widely understood to relate to two phases (and two forms) in English historical experience: first, that of the nobility in the Tudor and early Stuart period, accomplished by personalized plunder,[10] second that of the eighteenth century, favouring the capitalist gentry/tenant farmer group, and accomplished by statute law. For Marx the specific novelty of the eighteenth century is that 'the law itself becomes now the instrument of the theft of the people's land' (1867: 724). This grasps important truths, both as to the periodization (the last Act against depopulation consequent on enclosure was passed in 1597, all anti-enclosure statutes repealed in 1624) and forms of enclosure, and as to the class character of eighteenth century Parliament and law. But we would want to qualify it in two ways, consonant with our general emphases. First, some of the activity of king/Crown (and the sovereign Parliament) is clearly of a similar form to enclosures, both for earlier periods (Quo Warranto, Valor Ecclesiasticus, distribution of confiscated or forfeit lands, within England and beyond), and during and later than the eighteenth century (after the 1715 and 1745 in Scotland, plantations in Ireland, land companies in Africa, Canada, Australia). This underlines our general stress on the uniqueness of royal, then state, power and its enabling consequences for definition of property forms. Second, for the dispossessed and cleared the differences between these forms and periods may have been slight indeed both as to the magnitude of the loss and as to their conceptions of law, politics and state legitimacy. Enclosure and engrossing can be traced from the thirteenth until the late twentieth century.

Hoskins (1977: 185)[11] estimates that before 1760 some 400,000 acres of open field had been enclosed by 250 Acts, between 1761 and 1844 some 2,500 Acts dealt with more than four million acres of open field, and after the General Enclosure Act of 1845 there were a further 164 Acts covering some two million more acres of open field. That is, after 1700 almost half the arable land of England was converted from one system to the other; as late as 1794, according to Mantoux (1928: 148) the open-field system still prevailed in 4,500 out of 8,500 English parishes. As to 'waste lands', some 1,800 Acts after 1760 covered about two million acres. Taking both together we are talking of over six million acres and over 4,000 Acts, largely between 1760 and 1845. Mantoux estimates that some 40,000 to 50,000 small farms also disappeared through engrossing during the eighteenth century. These Acts of Parliament operate within wider fields of force which effectively naturalize and legitimize some material interests as proper (hence 'moral') whilst simultaneously making others 'unnatural', criminal, illegitimate and immoral – even heathen and infidel. The disciplinary significance of enclosures is not an invention of latter-day historians:

Enclosure of commons was praised by contemporaries because it forced labourers to 'work every day in the year'; 'their children will be put out to labour early'. By depriving the lower orders of any chance of economic independence, the 'subordination of the lower ranks of society . . . would be thereby considerably secured'. (These illuminating phrases come from official Board of Agriculture reports.) (Hill 1969a: 269–70)

The law was used not only to privatize as property what had been commonly enjoyed, but also – and inseparably – to render as crimes what had been customary rights, and to execute, transport or condemn to the hulks those subsequently criminalized.[12] Between 1688 and 1820 the number of capital statutes grew from around 50 to over 200; the vast bulk of the additions concerned offences against property (Hay 1977: 18). By 1740 it was a capital offence to steal property worth one shilling. Food rioters and machine-breakers faced the death sentence and enclosure rioters transportation; a mass of capital statutes were passed by Parliament to protect specific kinds of property, often without debate; with the development of banking similar protection was given against forgeries and frauds. Many eighteenth-century statutes removed the right of benefit of clergy from particular kinds of larceny. The Black Act of 1723, studied in detail by Thompson, created some 50 new capital offences at a stroke. According to Radzinowicz, 'it is very doubtful whether any other country possessed a criminal *code* with anything like so many capital provisions as there were in this single statute' (quoted in Thompson 1977a: 23, emphasis added); but what is of equal interest is the casualness with which it passed Parliament, *nem. con.*, without a division or serious debate. Locke's view that 'government has no other end but the preservation of property' (quoted in Hay 1977: 18) was the common sense of the governing classes. By an Act of 1726 use of violence in labour disputes carried a sentence of 14 years' transportation; workers' combinations were statutorily outlawed in tailoring in 1720, weaving and wool-combing in 1726, silk, linen, cotton, fustian, iron, leather and other industries in 1749, and hat-making in 1777 (Hill 1969a: 266–7).

As to enforcement, at local level much remained in the hands of JPs, acting singly, in pairs or in quarter sessions; at this period they nakedly represented gentry interests, at least in the countryside. Assizes – the only point of contact for most people with the central state – were, as we have noted for previous centuries, occasions of great pomp and ceremonial. Blackstone was aware of how 'the novelty and very parade of ... their appearance have no small influence upon the multitude' (quoted in Hay 1977: 27). The awesome centrepiece of the assizes was the ritual surrounding pronouncement of the death sentence. Executions were public spectacles, and (in Thompson's words) 'the ritual of public execution was a necessary concomitant of a system of social discipline where a great deal depended upon theatre' (1974: 390). Until 1790 women found guilty of high and petty treason could be burned with fire until dead; the last such burning took place in 1789 (Baker 1977: 307, n. 161). Men found guilty of high treason were hung, drawn and quartered; for petty treason 'merely' hung and drawn; for a felony 'simply' hung. The last public hanging was in 1868 (Best 1971: 273). For petty crimes and misdemeanours branding, whipping (not fully abolished until 1948), fines and the pillory (used until the 1830s) were common. Transportation was 'on offer' instead of both death and branding from the early decades of the eighteenth century, along with work in the hulks and penitentiaries from the 1770s. Proven suicides could be buried at crossroads with a stake through their hearts until 1823 (Westermarck 1917: 256). Ritualized terror was central to the rhetoric and the rule of law.

But it was not the only element in the drama. Douglas Hay, in an extremely sensitive essay, draws out a number of other important points. First, he emphasizes the majesty of the law. Its rituals, in his judgement, 'echoed many of the most powerful psychic components of religion' (on which in some cases – assize sermons, priests attending on the scaffold – they drew), underlining the law's transcendent quality: 'execution was a fate decreed not by men, but by God and Justice' (1977: 29). The strict (which is not to say 'fair') procedural rules of trial strengthened the illusion that the law was The Law, before which all were equal and all equally powerless, the judges its creatures rather than the law the creature of their class. This was buttressed by:

an extremely pervasive rhetorical tradition, with deep historical roots. . . . The law was held to be the guardian of Englishmen, of all Englishmen. Gentlemen held this as an unquestionable belief: that belief, too, gave the ideology of justice an integrity which no self-conscious manipulation could alone sustain. (ibid.: 35)

We have commented sufficiently on these 'deep historical roots' and the ideologies they sustained in previous chapters. Celebrated cases, whether the execution (for murdering his steward) of Lord Ferrers in

1760, 'like a common felon', at Tyburn, or the acquittal of the leaders of the London Corresponding Society by a Middlesex jury in 1794 were frequently invoked to confirm the law's dispassionate quality.

Second, Hay draws attention to the dispensation of mercy integral to eighteenth-century law. JPs had great latitude acting out of formal sessions. Juries, and to a lesser extent judges, were often 'lenient'. Suicides were often found to be of 'unsound mind'. Baker estimates only 10–20 per cent of those convicted of capital offences were sentenced to death, and of those only some 50 per cent (30 per cent by the later eighteenth century) were actually executed. Critics of the Warwick school make much of this. Hay's argument, however, is that such mercy does nothing to qualify power, it is itself a mode of control, and one central to the patriarchal imagery of order in eighteenth century England. Since in England (unlike France) prosecutions were mainly private, gentlemen could decide not to prosecute; their word, as character witnesses, could influence juries not to convict, or judges to recommend pardons (which were very common). Such acts 'bridged great vertical distances in the social order'; but they did so, Hay argues, in a way that 'helped create the mental structure of paternalism' (ibid.: 42), cementing dependence with gratitude and qualifying the impersonal transcendent rigour of the law with personalized intercession. We have here something far stronger than coercion alone. What was substantially a class justice was reified and legitimized in impersonal, majestic and terrible forms; where it was personalized, it was personalized as patrician benevolence and merciful dispensation. As Hay summarizes it,

A ruling class organises its power in the state. The sanction of the state is force, but it is force that is legitimised, however imperfectly, and therefore the state deals also in ideologies. Loyalties do not grow simply in complex societies: they are twisted, invoked and often consciously created. Eighteenth-century England was not a free market of patronage relations. It was a society with a bloody penal code, an astute ruling class who manipulated it to their advantage, and a people schooled in the lessons of Justice, Terror and Mercy. The benevolence of rich men to poor, and all the ramifications of patronage, were upheld by the sanction of the gallows and the rhetoric of the death sentence. (ibid.: 62–3; cf. Linebaugh 1968; Thompson 1974; 1977a; 1978b)

Along with this normalized surveillance, regulation and ritualized punishment, there were the larger events such as the defeated 1715 and 1745 revolutionary risings in Scotland. After the '45 Prebble (1961: 233) estimates there to have been 3,470 prisoners. Of those whose fate is known (2,786), 120 were publicly and ritually executed (ibid.:

261ff.), 936 transported, 222 banished and 1,287 released or exchanged. Scotland and England had been unified in 1707 (in the process increasing 'what was already the largest free trade area in the world' (Hill 1969a: 224)). The 'defeat of the '45 brought an extension of London influence over the Highlands of Scotland similar to that which the outcome of the Civil War had brought to the dark corners of northern and western England a century earlier' (ibid.: 225).[13]

London itself had a population of around half a million in 1700, compared with around 200,000 in 1600, and nearly a million by 1800.[14] In contrast no other city had more than 30,000 people; most towns had populations of 5,000 or less. Although urbanization is a phenomenon of the nineteenth century, we might register here that concern with the specifically urban features of 'Improvement' is not absent from the eighteenth. Falkus[15] instances specific improvement commissioners for London and Westminster from 1662 and for other towns from 1725. Noting that the *Annual Register* for 1761 had argued 'several great cities, and we might add many poor country towns, seem to be universally inspired with the ambition of becoming little *Londons*' (1976: 259), he goes on to argue:

after 1762 the granting of Improvement Acts becomes a regular feature of most Parliamentry sessions. In total more than 100 separate bodies of improvement commissioners were set up in towns throughout Britain between 1750 and 1800. (p. 264)

Town improvement was a marked feature, rather neglected by historians, of urban growth in the eighteenth century; it affected towns of all kinds and sizes. (p. 270)

Alongside this formal, state-supported 'Improvement', another facet of the 'moral revolution of 1688' (Bahlman 1957) was the Societies for the Reformation of Manners, partially revived within Methodism in the 1750s and again in the form of the Society for the Suppression of Vice and Immorality (1802 onwards).[16] Specific features of the making of this bourgeois ethos can be traced through various sources; whether that of the 'first great apologist' (as G. D. H. Cole considered Defoe (1928: x)) of the entrepreneurial class, Mantoux's surveys (1928: pt 3, ch. 2), or more recent detailed work, such as that of Nicholas Rogers on eighteenth-century London (1978, 1979) which finds 'distinct but overlapping fractions of the capitalist class' evident by the early eighteenth century, and 'the dominant ethos of the society . . . bourgeois and plutocratic' (1979: 453–4).

A brief word ought also to be said here on direct state fostering of commerce. Walpole removed all export duties on British manufactures and corn, and some duties on imported raw materials for manufacture. An Act of 1719 forbade workmen from taking their skills abroad; it was at one time an offence to shear sheep within four miles of the coast in case their fleeces should be smuggled overseas. Both exemplify a widespread attitude of national protectionism. Foreign policy through the century was not consistent: Hill (1969a: pt 4, ch. 3) shows the interplay of war and peace lobbies, and their respective connections with commercial and landed interests. But English wars led to the capture of new territories and markets. The War of Spanish Succession gave England the *Asiento*, the monopoly of carrying slaves to the Spanish Americas. England became the world's leading slave-trading nation. After 1730 Parliament granted £10,000 p.a. for the building of forts, to protect slaving interests, on the Gold Coast. Recapture of Canada from the French in the Seven Years War opened up new markets for English manufacturers, and access to fish and fur trades. Exports to North America grew appreciably over the century; from 1699 onwards colonial manufactures and exports from there were heavily regulated and at times suppressed (see Hill 1969a: 235–6) where they conflicted with English interests. Clive's conquest in India stimulated more direct state intervention in the affairs of the East India Company (empowered to tax and wage war by charter in 1661) from 1766 onwards (cf. Misra 1959). Contemporaries were blind neither to the importance of commerce, nor to the role the state could play in promoting it, whatever their disagreements on how this should best be done. The Duke of Newcastle, who effectively controlled government patronage for 40 years after he became Secretary of State in 1724, 'was "bred up to think that the trade of this nation is the sole support of it", and endeavoured always "to contribute all that was in my power to the encouragement and extension of the trade and commerce of these kingdoms"' (Hill 1969a: 226–7). Old Corruption was a funnel through which mercantile wealth and colonial plunder found its way into politics – Clive, for instance, buying himself first a Parliamentary seat and then a peerage – cementing the ruling class.

Before we leave this particular, unique form of state – Old Corruption – a more general emphasis, implicit in much of the above, is called for. We thoroughly endorse the arguments of those who have pointed to the peculiarly ritualized, theatrical qualities of eighteenth-century rule. The theatre of law was one part of this, the rituals of conspicuous display and ornamentation, the much remarked 'civilized' tone of eighteenth-century upper-class life – fenced-off parks, elegant mansions with their 'classical' façades and formal gardens, the hunt, the reserved pews (and late entries) at church, coaches, footmen, wigs and powder – another. This social style effortlessly blended the rural–paternal and urban–sophisticated; integral to it were the London season, the stately provincial watering-places, the 'rites of passage' of Oxford and Cambridge and the Inns of Court (Thompson 1965: 42–4; or any of Jane Austen's novels). For Thompson (1974; cf. Speck 1977: 53ff.; Money 1979) there was a 'complex theatrical reciprocity between patrician society and plebeian culture' during this period; 'a studied and elaborate hegemonic style, a theatrical role in which the great were schooled in infancy and which they maintained until death' intersecting uneasily with a robust and profane popular culture, such as, quintessentially, at Tyburn – a performance of highly differential significance (see Linebaugh 1975). These representational – i.e. performed and visible – features of power pervade written and visual images of the time. Both the visibility of success and power, and the rituals of punishment carry forward crucial symbols of legitimacy which are not absent from English state forms in the twentieth century, however much a different language (of system, bureaucracy and efficiency) may seem apposite. Hogarth plays brilliantly with this difference between those who behold (whom he often satirizes without mercy), and those who are spectacles, whether objects of pity or objects of menace. For Goldsmith ('The deserted village'):

> Here, while the proud their long-drawn pomps display,
> There the black gibbet glooms beside the way.

But we think the theatrical, ritualized, performed (Bagehot's 'dignified') features of these state forms must be emphasized for two further reasons. First, and most importantly, in providing a repertoire of collective representations – and Durkheim's concept is a very literal one here – a particular moral order is being made. This moral order is a material constituent of the consolidation of men of (different kinds of) property, and provides the code for the subsequent moralization of others. The eighteenth-century Old Corruption rituals and theatre (and the continuities – real and constructed – on which they were built) provided an ethos and imagery for 'the State' which did not disappear with the rational system built from the 1830s onwards. The dignified, 'irrational', 'pomp and circumstance' features – such a sore trial to the systematizing mind, and so constantly bemoaned as 'feudal relics' – enabled the sponsored unification of the ruling classes, old and new, as a historic bloc, establishing a particular form of civilization, politics, culture, nationality – Englishness, in short. And this was in turn later to facilitate an extended, sponsored admission of the non-propertied into the 'political nation' (from 1867), allowing a peculiar constitutional recognition of 'labour'. This perspective is drawn from Durkheim, not the Durkheim misused in discussions of the death of Queen Victoria, the coronation of Elizabeth II, or the wedding of Charles Windsor to Diana Spencer as collective celebrations of solidarity, but the Durkheim superbly drawn upon by Lukes:

the ritual of elections, alongside that within legislatures, law courts and the administration . . . plays a significant role in legitimating and perpetuating the political paradigms or *representations collectives* which contribute to the stability of the political system. (1975: 305)[17]

Our second reason for emphasizing this theatricality is because it was a pervasive metaphor in the crucial civic philosophy and sociological theorizing of the Scottish Moral Philosophers,[18] to which we now turn. Their work is doubly significant for our purposes: first, in the way it (for the first time) theorizes much of what we have tried to describe – the Scottish philosophers were, in many ways, the first sociologists of capitalist civilization; and second, as a watershed, a turning-point, in which many of the motifs of the nineteenth-century revolution in government are prefigured. For these reasons this work is worth discussing in some detail. Frederic Jameson has written:

philosophical thinking, if pursued far enough, turns into historical thinking, and the understanding of abstract thought ultimately resolves itself back into an awareness of the content of that thought, which is to say, of the basic historical situation in which it took place. (1971: 345; cf. Clarke 1927: 23)

The 'social situation' of the Scottish Enlightenment was the enormous Great Leap Forward in Scotland 'after the Forty-five' (Youngson 1973),[19] especially in the Scottish universities and intellectual life generally. This was much fostered by a 'classic instance' of English state formation as cultural revolution:

The clans were disarmed, hereditary jurisdictions and military service were abolished. Estates were confiscated and sold to monied lowlanders. New roads and bridges were built, judges went on circuit, Highlanders were forcibly educated in English. Dr Johnson noted the social consequences. 'When the power of birth and station ceases, no hope remains but from the prevalence of money. . . . The chiefs, divested of their prerogatives, turned their thoughts to the improvement of their revenues, and expect more rent as they have less homage.' The evictions and depopulation which followed were the work of the chiefs themselves, 'degenerated from patriarchal rulers to rapacious landlords.' (Hill 1969a: 224–5)

Later tartans were to become 'acceptable', even fashionable, within a radically changed set of relations and significances. The present English queen (Elizabeth I of Scotland, it might be said) annually does her time at Balmoral, while the Prince of Wales can be seen reading self-penned stories set in the Highlands, on BBC children's television, attired in kilt and sporran. The show must go on.

Smith, Hume, Kames, Ferguson, Millar (and their key later popularizer, Dugald Stewart)[20] were as much historians – better, perhaps, sociological historians – as they were philosophers. But – and this is not simply word-play – we might also reverse the opening of Jameson's comment, since their historical thinking was 'pursued far enough' to eventuate in a philosophical vocabulary, a moral code, no less, without which the forms, timbre and practices of the 1830s' 'revolution in government' (which we examine in our next chapter) cannot be understood. Speaking crudely, and mobilizing the recognition of differential moral codes so central to the work of Thompson and others, we should understand what later became celebrated and dominant as 'political economy' to be simultaneously the discovery of economy (and 'the economy' argued for as a self-sufficing 'private' realm governed by the laws of the market) and a politicization of a moral code (entailing specific forms of 'policing') which makes that possible. The theories of the Scottish moralists entailed a doubling of their theoretical reflections upon history (which was comparative sociology, we should note; a major instance of that 'learning from abroad' often crucial to state formation): if one side of their flag is emblazoned with 'Commerce', the other says 'Civilization'. The fabric of the flag is Liberty which if we peer closely at the stitching turns out to be Law. The 'market' is *made*, some men must be free(d) to constrain other men and almost all women, thereby to construct progress.

Somewhere between the 1740s and 1850 (and it would be foolish to be more precise) history changes gear; where it had been a moving on from, it became a rushing forward towards: 'Improvement' (of that which exists) becomes 'Progress' (towards an end-state). Since 1945 there has been the much remarked ending of this onrushing history-as-progress, to fracture, splinter and divide as either 'one damn thing after another'/'not having done too badly; said with a smile, but nonetheless sadly' or futurology. The triumph of monetarism (along with radically restructured state forms and new kinds of cultural formation) seals this as securely as any kingly seal. The 'enchantment' of monetarism (as Wilhelm Reich so perceptively noted of fascism) is oriented to the past, to securing the old verities, the old standards; it is a social equivalent of that world-wide 'back-to-basics' movement in state-provided educational systems. But in between times, from the 1760s until the 1960s (being crude again in order to be clear) political economy provided a moral rhetoric, a theatrical repertoire, a secular equivalent for religion that linked the facts of commerce to the promise of liberty. Progress, it was frequently said, would deliver the goods. Now fiscal policing and a language of necessity reign supreme. But we anticipate too much.

Smith, drawing like Hume (1754; cf. Forbes 1970) on the historical experience of *The making of the English ruling class* – that yet to be written multi-volume work which this book attempts to annotate – relates commerce and liberty: where the former is widely developed and institutionally secured, then the latter flourishes. In 90 per cent of later interpretations of Smith it is simply the achieved and accomplished phenomena that are taken to be his theoretical and prescriptive centrepiece. But Smith (and the others) read – that is to say, construct – their histories to demonstrate how a set of intervening variables link the causal primacy of commerce to a certain liberty; taken together this is the civilization they seek to prescribe and celebrate. Central to it is a theory of human nature; but as central is an understanding of state forms, that 'optimal institutional structure' (Rosenberg 1960, Forbes 1975, Winch 1978) which makes it possible for the fiction of the 'self-regulating market' to operate as if it were possible naturally. The market is a regulated social relation policed by force and moralized by a 'willing' discipline; that specific dialectic of force and will, coercion and consent – and how much would we learn by reading the Moral Philosophers and Philosophical Radicals as if they were Gramsci! – has to be sustained, reconstructed, extended and generally kept up to date. Cultural politics since the 1760s[21] can be taken to register the dangerous degree to which the principles at the heart of this justifying rhetoric can be imbibed in their necessary abstraction and then applied back to the real social situation of coercive disadvantage: if labour is the source of all value, why are those who labour poor and powerless? If education is necessary to elevate the mind and culture the skill of the person, why does that education not include the principles of social structuring, the division of the fruits of labour, the tyranny of men over women?

But something else, of equal import, is also going on in the Scottish Enlightenment: the recognition of 'civil society' and the announcement of a new-reality *society* as such. Elias (1939) has persuasively argued the radical division within feudal and early modern civilizations between 'Society' (equivalent to the French *'Le Monde'* as in, of course, the World of Paris) and the rest, *les autres*, those without. This 'Society' equates with what we have called 'the political nation'. Following the earlier reconceptualization of 'the population' as part creation, part object of state activity, what the Scottish philosophers announce is the recognition of labouring as having to be brought within society. This recognizes, at the same time, that part extension, part upward incorporation of different ruling groups into an historic bloc (those whose property and activities had to be freed) as 'The People', or – to anticipate a later clarification – 'The Public'. This bloc is essentially bourgeois, largely capitalist, forming a 'natural aristocracy' of talent and achievement, and fitted thereby to govern, that is to make – in alliance with the older aristocracy (not of talent, one presumes!) – rules for the rest, the populace, those who labour. The poor turn out to be necessary. The rituals of rule – that extensive theatricality of state repertoire – are central to this, and involve two forms of spectatorship. Internally to the ruling historic bloc there are orders of status and etiquette, those acting observe one another closely. Externally, for the ruled, there are the spectacles of terror and patronage, punishment and benevolence, along with that form of localized 'natural policing' that allowed the surveillance of this social audience from those on the stage.

Smith's *Wealth of nations* (1776)[22] involves all of this, as a reading of his *Theory of moral sentiments* (1759)[23] or his *Lectures on jurisprudence* (delivered in the 1760s)[24] shows. These involve a dual orientation towards the law and government. First, they contain a theory of legislation (which Bentham was to make his own territory): laws must simultaneously clear away obstructions to the path of commercial progress for those with profitable property – the possessive individualism thesis – and these appetites must be further fed by ensuring that those same laws preserve and strengthen property rights against any counterclaims. The freeing of capital entails the imprisonment of labour ('free labour' now, of course). Second, because of this contradiction – that social progress (for some men) involves socialized pain (for other men and most women) – they contain a theory of education (which was to be central to the 1830s' revolution as we will see). State forms must be created which provide or regulate appropriate cultural forms as a system of instruction and moral training for the young. The state thereby becomes conceptualized as legislator and educator, the latter being necessary to guard against erroneous, dangerous interpretations of the former, for example as to law's systematic class and patriarchal bias. Sometimes this is explicit (and the words will ring oddly to those tuned to the pulpits of Thatcher, Reagan, Mulroney or Professor Milton Friedman,[25] who find all of this 'voluntary co-operation'). In the 1760s Adam Smith lectured that:

Laws and governments may be considered in this and indeed in every case as a combination of the rich to oppress the poor and preserve to themselves the inequality of the goods which would otherwise be soon destroyed by the attacks of the poor, who if not hindered by the government would soon reduce the others to an equality with themselves by open violence.[26]

Smith was equally candid about where the wealth of the nation comes from. In an early draft of *Wealth of nations*, he wrote:

In a Society [NB] of a hundred thousand families, there will be perhaps a hundred who don't labour at all, and yet, either by violence, or by the orderly oppression of the law, employ a greater part of the labour of the Society than any other ten thousand in it. The division of what remains after this enormous defalcation, is by no means made in proportion to the labour of each individual. On the contrary those who labour most get least. (quoted in Winch 1978: 88–9)

The terms here are worthy of an essay in themselves. 'Combinations of the rich', as we shall exemplify, morally sanctioned and legally supported, complement anti-combination legislation against the labouring poor/working class – the same groups 'hindered by government' and subjected to 'the orderly oppression of law', in ways we have discussed above. No wonder Marx congratulated Garnier (the French translator of Smith) for using the word 'Society' 'for capital, landed property and their state' (1867: 363). How classical are these writings of Smith, Bentham or Ricardo compared with the 'toadying to the bourgeoisie' (as Marx, again, put it) of the Mills, Nassau Senior and the later technicization of economics as 'merely calculation' (see Marx 1873; 1863: vol. 3, 499ff.).

In 1776 – the year Smith's *Wealth of nations* was published, fateful also for George III's infamous 'loss' of the American colonies – there appeared the anonymous *Fragment on government* by Jeremy Bentham (1748–1832). With his typical manic modesty – he penned around ten million words at a conservative estimate – Bentham thought this *Fragment* 'the very first publication by which men at large were invited to break loose from the trammels of authority and ancestor-worship on the field of law' (quoted in Harrison 1948: xxxvi, n. 3). The *Fragment* was a commentry on Blackstone (whom Bentham had returned to Oxford to hear lecture), but reflected also Bentham's voracious reading of Beccaria, Helvetius, Hartley, Priestley, Hume, Smith and so on. It enshrines his 1768 'Great Discovery – *Legislation*', and begins his elaboration of a science of it, a theory with its own practices:

Correspondent to *discovery* and *improvement* in the natural world, is *reformation* in the moral . . . if there be room for making, and if there be use in publishing, *discoveries* in the natural world, surely there is not much less room for making, nor much less use in proposing, *reformation* in the *moral*. (1776: 3)

Representing here, as always – which is why the curious lineages from Bentham through Whig-Liberalism to Fabianism[28] are so important to unravel – the edge of radicalism that is progressive (in human terms), Bentham argues against any justifications of social institutions by 'age', 'divine laws', or 'laws of nature'. They can only be measured by the *'principle* of UTILITY': *'it is the greatest happiness of the greatest number that is the measure of right and wrong'* (1776: 56, 3).[29] Despite later scholarship Halevy's classic study of 1934 (as indeed his history of the nineteenth-century state generally) remains the principle resource for studying this new moment. It is from Halevy that we gain the insight about Bentham's necessary obsession with legislation. Bentham himself declared:

Law alone has accomplished what all the natural feelings were not able to do; Law alone has been able to create a fixed and durable possession which deserves the name of Property. (quoted in Halevy 1934: 503; cf. James 1973)

In our view Bentham's texts, as such, are less significant than his enthusing of a group of significant persons, notably James and John Stuart Mill and Chadwick, which we shall consider below. But central to our purposes here is to draw out how Bentham (along with his epigones and disciples) theorized a specifically political society complementing and making possible the self-regulating market. It was from this – his theorization of what 'Society' could do for society – that his theorization of 'the State' develops: 'the establishment of legislation as the primary means of reform, and of central control and inspection as means for the direction of administration' (Harrison 1948: xi; cf. Finer 1959, Henriques 1974, Corrigan 1977a).

When a number of persons (whom we style *subjects*) are supposed to be in the *habit* of paying *obedience* to a person, or assemblage of persons, of a known and certain description (whom we may call *governor* or *governors*) such persons altogether (*subjects* and *governors*) are said to be in a state of *political* SOCIETY. (Bentham 1776: 38)

The division, by Bentham and others, of society (by 'Society') into two classes – 'the one governing, the other governed' (Halevy 1934: 405) – is the key accomplishment to accompany the great discoveries of capital and labour. The 'revolution in government' of the 1830s operated by fusing both through utilizing the existing moral repertoire, institutional practices and – above all – theatrical representations of achieved, legitimate (and legitimating) rituals of English Erastian political culture. By then, however, the question of questions has a different name. It is 'the Working Class question', which we shall address in our next chapter.

In 1980 Gerald Aylmer discussed the 'old administrative system' as the set of practices from which the modern, permanent civil service

(Parris 1968, 1969) 'emerged' (1980c). He illustrates the slowness of reform and rationalization with the example of the inquiries into the Chancery courts: there were extensive investigations in the 1730s, but a table of permitted fees was not drawn up until 1740 and *not published until 1815*. In most cases even this 'follow through' did not exist. There is an almost total gap in inquiries (apart from those concerning the East India Company) between 1740 and 1780, and he suggests that it was not until the 'spectre of Jacobin revolution began to haunt the minds and imaginations of the British ruling class' that 'efficient government' (as opposed to the 'bogey of an uncontrolled, and seemingly uncontrollable National Debt') was placed on the agenda. But before the Economical Reforms debate of the 1780s, we must be careful not to understand Old Corruption merely as a static, cyclically reproductive formation. It was productive and reproductive of a certain political nation (with internal divisions as sharp as those dividing it from the rest) which was open (to some). Spectators could cross from the audience of deferential onlookers and shout their wares and shares from the stage itself. Whilst we should note the work of both Namierites (wealth, influence, patronage, and so on) and Beer's chilling statistic (1957: 623) that 'fully three-quarters' of the 5,034 MPs from 1734 to 1832 had 'their principal economic interest in land', we also have to see the opening toward 'new men', by marriage (D. N. Thomas 1969, 1972; Clay 1968), by purchase of place or office, and by legitimized combination. Mantoux, typically, captures this theme ably:

In spite of its recent origin, of the dissimilar elements which had gone to its making and of the unequal moral value of its members, the manufacturing class soon became conscious of its own existence. Such class-consciousness, which is based on common interest, can make its appearance only where it is able to find expression. In this respect conditions in England were more favourable than in any other country. The freedom of the political system, and above all the collective habit of petitioning, gave ample scope for advancing collective demands. (1928: 388–9; cf. Rogers 1978, 1979)

This needs major qualification in its silence regarding precisely the legal and other constraints which attempted to prevent the labouring classes, very conscious of their existence, from finding relevant forms of expression (and combination); or, if finding them by hard struggle, being disempowered from their political, cultural and social publication, demonstration and effective utilization (see Polanyi 1945: pt II; Thompson 1965, 1967, 1968, 1971; and – to be fair – Mantoux 1928: 399–477).

Some of these 'new men' – their novelty residing more in their representation of certain non-aristocratic, non-landed, non-London, non-Court interests than their lack of a wealthy lineage – formed the basis for the movement for Economical Reforms of the 1780s. However little they actually achieved, they have been taken as a bench-mark and rallying-cry of the bourgeoisie/radical reformers ever since. Of the available extensive literature,[30] we find Torrance's 1978 paper the most significant for our purposes. But what almost all commentary 'misses' is how in the very period during which the 'permanent civil service' (Parris 1968) was being created, 1780–1830, the most comprehensive battery of legislative, practical and other regulatory devices against the emerging working class is also established. A recognizably modern 'democratic' nation state steps onto the stage with the partly self-made, partly 'Society'-made working class (Thompson 1968: 887).

Finally, 'something else' is also present during this formation of what are recognizably modern structures of thought and practice. We speak here, as we have previously, of the simultaneous making of nation and state. Through the eighteenth century there were innumerable occasions to ensure that Englishness was a constituent feature of loyalty to the state. The foreignness of enemies could be shown through their externality to this culture in a variety of ways. The Scots revolutions of 1715 and 1745 (Hill 1969a: 213; Rogers 1975) were seen to involve an 'alien creed'. How happy is a language that can elide 'Jacobite' and 'Jacobin' to stitch together varieties of Englishness to oppose so many enemies: Spanish, Catholics, French, Dutch! This important relating of nationalism (the making of nations) to nationalization (the making of states) has been much studied; of that extensive literature we wish to emphasize the work of Kiernan (1965, 1978). Nationalism, he argues, is best understood as a construction, as 'class resentment artificially diverted into xenophobia' (1965: 35). Warfare – of which the eighteenth century saw plenty – is always central to making and reconstructing state forms,[31] not least because:

Frontiers are more than lines on a map: they frequently define quite distinctive systems of thought and action. The state is, of course, pre-eminently such a system; and it is therefore through a history of nations that we must begin any empirical study of the role of the state in that international phenomenon which we call the Industrial Revolution. (Supple 1971: 301)

Linking to Loades's and Hill's discussion of Protestant, anti-Spanish English nationalism in earlier periods is Newman's characterization of the nationalist features of 'British middle-class consciousness in the early 19th century': 'an aggressive and specifically "anti-French" sort of nationalism, empirical, constructive, earnest, moral, comfortably pseudo-religious as well as Evangelical' (1975: 418). The fear of

French Revolution remains an element of bourgeois consciousness until 1917, when Bolshevism supplies the new enemy. Let us quote from a latterday '18th century Whig' here, John Le Carré: 'Our present war began in 1917, with the Bolshevik Revolution. It hasn't changed yet' (1978: 116).

The nexus we have briefly sketched – the 'settlement' of 1688, extending through the unique and contradictory forms of Old Corruption to the Economical Reforms and the 'Revolution in Government' (which we will consider below) – allowed the ruling classes of Old and New England (the double meaning is intended) to make themselves. Roy Porter, concluding his admirable *English society in the 18th century*, brings out the enabling qualities of Old Corruption very well, and sums up much of what we have tried to argue here. He emphasizes:

three main aspects of eighteenth-century English society. First, the fundamental strength and resilience of the social hierarchy. It was presided over by a super-confident oligarchy, swimming with the tide, without an exposed Achilles' heel, whose dominion was consolidated early in the century and never – at least until the 1790s – seriously challenged, let alone jeopardised . . . The English ruling class knitted itself together. . . .

second . . . though the social hierarchy was inegalitarian and oozing privilege (some of it hereditary), it was not rigid and brittle. There was continual adaptiveness . . . . Money was a passport through more frontiers than in other nations. English society was not frozen into immobilized, distended and archaic forms. . . . Men could not be parted from their property, capital was allowed to ferret where it would, and new riches could be manicured into respectability. . . .

third . . . their [the ruling order's] attempts to secure consensus within this acquisitive, restless society. . . . The hope was to win acquiescence and endorsement by influence and persuasion – bluster, grandeur, liberality, promises, show and swank, the open door held just ajar. Those in power and their media mouthpieces dangled before people's eyes ambition, self-respect, new enjoyments, polite values, and fashionable life styles. (1982: 358f.)

They also dangled, we should perhaps recall, those other 'promises' of transportation and the gallows tree, equally in pursuit of 'consensus' and 'acquiescence' – though this is not intended to nullify Porter's third, important point.

But it is ironic (if the word is not too 'light') to write this as we stand on the other side, indeed at some distance, from the Great Arch of state formation. For, as Finer (1952a) brilliantly shows, this same nexus also always contained a variety of possibilities. Now we write in the midst of continents being ravaged by that once subordinate (but now so hegemonic) strand: individualized 'pure' political economy.

One writer kept that subordinate theme alive during his long life (1820–1903), Herbert Spencer. From his 1842 letters 'The proper sphere of government' through to his final works, as part of a project to secularize morals, Spencer had argued the 'traditional defences of the individual'. A hundred years ago, in his *The man and the state* (1884) Spencer neatly explained what had happened since 1780 and what we can now see around us today:

The question of questions for the politican should be – 'What type of social state am I tending to produce?' (p. 91)

Noting how particular policies and their practices had confirmed, made dominant, certain ideas – and how a 'small body of officials' has 'and immense advantage over an incoherent public' (pp. 93, 94) – he argues against society as 'a manufacture . . . it is a growth' (p. 147).

The great political superstition of the past was the divine right of Kings. The great political superstition of the present is the divine right of Parliaments. (p. 151)

That 'minority' view from one side – of 'the State' doing too much – is matched by another and much less attended to 'anti-state' view, this time of the majority, and from below. We think that the deep roots for the support (contradictory as that might be) given by that 'majority' in our own times to that previously marginalized, minority view that is now so dominant can be found in the ways through which 'the State' was formed. But 'monetarism' (Spencer revived) no more addresses that majority's needs than did the liberal/social democratic forms so rapidly attenuated (if not actually demolished) since the 1960s. A routeway to those needs is to be found from different historical experiences, a different perspective and organization of anti-state and anti-Parliament (Parssinen 1973; Yeo 1979, 1980):

The time may not be far off when the phrase 'national interest' acquires the same adverse connotations as its predecessor 'the Divine Right of Kings'. (Rapaport 1967)

6

'The Working Class Question':
'Society' and society

The Working Class Question is the real question, and that is the
thing that demands to be settled.
> Disraeli to John Bright, March 1867;
> quoted in Tholfsen 1961: 226

In England it became the unwritten law of the Constitution that
the working class must be denied the vote. The Chartist leaders
were jailed; their adherents, numbered in millions, were derided
by a legislature representing a bare fraction of the population, and
the mere demand for the ballot was often treated as a criminal act
by the authorities. Of the spirit of compromise allegedly characteristic of the British system – a later invention – there was no
sign. . . . The Chartists had fought to stop the mill of the market
which ground the lives of the people. But the people were granted
rights only when that awful adjustment had been made. Inside
and outside England, from Macaulay to Mises, from Spencer to
Sumner, there was not a militant liberal who did not express his
conviction that popular democracy was a danger to capitalism.
> Polanyi 1945: 221

'Capitalism' – or the market – lives by recognising and rewarding
inequalities, and depends on them to provide the motive force
that makes it work. . . . Democracy, one might say, legitimised
inequality (since you do not tax stolen goods), with the help of
the trade unions.
> Marshall 1972: 9; cf. Mannheim 1936: 249f.

One citizen, one vote, combines political fairness and equality;
but one citizen, one income, would be unjust to the talented,
enterprising or hard working as it would be over fair to the lazy.
> Maudling 1974

State formation and cultural regulation (the two quite inextricably
connected) reach a frenzy during the years of what we can without

exaggeration call the English terror, when the working class was hammered and machined into acceptable relations (Thompson 1968; Prothero 1979; Goodwin 1979). Here are some brief indications (no more) of what we mean by the latter. The notorious Combination Acts, outlawing workers' combinations, were passed in 1799 and 1800, five years after the trial (and acquittal) of the leaders of the London Corresponding Society on a charge of high treason. What was new in these laws was their inclusiveness, and the empowerment of JPs to convict summarily. Combinations had been forbidden for specific industries throughout the eighteenth century, as we have seen. As importantly, workers were prosecuted at common law for conspiracy and breach of contract, and (in the case of strikes) under those clauses of the Elizabethan Statute of Artificers relating to 'work left unfinished'. Here they could be dealt with summarily, the fact of a strike being treated as sufficient evidence of crime. This repertoire of powers was cumulatively regulative: 'the effectiveness of the legislation is not to be judged by the number of prosecutions, but by its general deterrent effect' (Thompson 1968: 554), though many people were prosecuted. By an Act of 1797, 'unlawful oaths' carried the penalty of seven years' transportation (it was for this that the Tolpuddle Martyrs were transported in 1834). The Peterloo Massacre of 1819 was followed by the 'Six Acts' restricting rights of public assembly and demonstration. In the same period, vestiges of paternalist and protective legislation were swept away, as for the woollen trade in 1809. The clauses of the Statute of Artificers relating to apprentices were repealed in 1813, and those allowing JPs to fix minimum wages in the following year; the clauses regarding 'unfinished work' remained, of course, on the statute book.

In 1824 the Combination Acts were repealed, and the law further changed in 1825. The form of repeal is indicative of much subsequent state regulation. Combination as such was no longer a crime; but both the legitimate objects of combination (wages, hours of work) and allowed forms of organization and activity were very narrowly circumscribed. The same continues to be true of trade union legislation, not least that enacted by the present British government. The story we wish to be trace, then, is not only one of violent repression, there is more 'subtlety' than that. Equally to be witnessed is a concerted moral revolution, an attempted organization of consent and incorporation, which culminates in a certain kind of admission – sponsored, protracted, conditional and profoundly disruptive of labour's own forms of social organization and expression – of labour into society. Both sides of the handling of 'the working-class question' are equally important, but the latter has had less attention than the former and will be our prime focus here, in both its forms and its ethos. The modern, democratic, nation state, we shall argue, has its origins in this double 'handling'.

The theory and practice of Improvement changes gear in the fifty years 1780–1830 as the working-class question comes on the agenda for old, reformed and novel state institutions. Government comes to be understood as guaranteeing the rights and freedoms of men of property against, above all, the claims of labour: the new working class being made and seeking to make itself during those years. The immediate response is repression of the sort we have exemplified, at its peak between 1780 and 1830, energized by the *grande peur* wafting from over the Channel. In the eventual course of handling these contradictions, state powers are immensely augmented, new 'instruments' come into being, old resources are modernized, and – centrally – a new theory of representation is put into practice. This theory eventually – much later – permits the sponsored admission of labour itself into the re-formed polity. In this period, not land but more abstract forms of property come to be what is represented politically, enshrined in law, culturally articulated and, above all, normalized as a new moral code of individualized character. This specifically moral revolution informs all the institutional innovations we will consider in this chapter.

This revolution is in fact a struggle – material, categorial, moral – of possessive individualism with displaced collectives which attempts centrally to individualize the latter as if they had, or could someday possess, bourgeois properties individually without possessing profitable property. This contradiction will never go away, it is universal to capitalism. Labour – wage-slavery, dependency-relations of alienation, exploitation and oppression – remains a collective and collectivizing category (and experience): there is a shareable sense (across differences) of subordination, there is a tendency toward unity within difference. Capital is not like this, capital is an individual and individualizing possession and capitalists tend to be singular and aggregate, i.e. fissiparous. Competition always leads to engrossing and enclosure of some capitalists by others. Raymond Williams, from *The long revolution* (1961) to *Towards 2000* (1983) is wholly correct in his sustained attention to labour's tendency to represent its moral order through significations, forms and practices of a collective and co-operative kind. Founded as this is in shared and daily reproduced experience, it remains irrepressible while capitalism lasts.

As capitalism is made in England, older theories and symbologies have to come to terms with this central contradiction; increasingly so, by the later eighteenth century, as the growth of fluidity – mobile property, and masterless, unservile labour – undermines older integrative mechanisms and representations. One result is the doubling orientation we have already touched on, in our account of the Scottish Moral Philosophers, within bourgeois theories. On the one hand, there is a formation of collectivities of and from labour within production, a recognition of the facts of capitalist life. It is because of this recognition that Marx dubs political economy from Petty to Ricardo as 'scientific', in contrast to the vulgar and philistine apologetics which followed (1873). Labour is increasingly nakedly theorized as what it is in capitalism, a form of property and a factor of production, and imagized, in much of the literature of the time, as 'animals' or 'machine'. E. P. Thompson quotes a telling exchange in relation to the 1832 Reform Act:

Q. Are the working classes better satisfied with the institutions of the country since the change has taken place?
A. I do not think they are. They viewed the Reform Bill as a measure calculated to join the middle and upper classes to Government, and leave them as a sort of machine to work according to the pleasure of Government. (1835 Select Committee; quoted in Thompson 1968: 915)[1]

And so it was: 'The wealth of the nation being nearly synonymous with its health, it is evident that the labouring poor of the British people is a machine which it is the duty as well as the interest of the state to protect' (Review of the Report on the Sanitary Condition of the Labouring Classes' in *Quarterly Review* 11, 1842, p. 441)[2]. This backhandedly acknowledges difference: labour as a distinctive, collective historical experience of the unpropertied.

On the other hand, there is a parallel project of forming moral individuals of and from labouring persons, in the bourgeois image, denying this same difference and collectivity. Political economy speaks towards the former: labour as property, factor of production, 'animals', 'machine'. Moral philosophy speaks towards the latter: persons who labour as individuals, with rights to be granted (by whom?) liberty. What needs remarking is the simultaneity here: labour is homogenized within production as, within society, the extensive theorization of persons (in general) as possessive individuals proceeds apace. The overdetermination of the latter is very clear in the great texts of 'the Atlantic Revolution', with all their talk – which could mean more, if translated into the language of real communities and their material and coercive disadvantages – of 'Man' and 'his Rights'. 'Society' in discovering society tries to find a place for *les autres*, labour, to conceptualize them as more than objects of pity and mercy, or terror and punishment, or, importantly, as simply unknown, at exactly the same time as that same 'Society' was massifying, classifying as means of production, objectifying those very same people as labour – as a form, an extension, of their social power, their property.

This contradiction illuminates how it was possible for exactly the same years to be marked by a state formation of a greater extent than at any period previously, and to be celebrated as *laissez-faire*. State intervention (though the term is almost unusable if we are to understand what took place) enabled, accomplished, stabilized, regulated into dominance that market on which *laissez-faire* theory depends. The government could be oriented to the rights of property, the laws of the market – in other words, 'non-interventionist' – whilst 'the State' was actively and very extensively engaged in stabilizing that form of and those relations of society without which capitalist production could not be realized. 'The State' as fiction, as illusory unity – the author of its own representations, the stage-director of all political theatre, investing every belief and act with moral signification – is formed in the struggle to make this violent 'awful adjustment' happen again and again. 'The State' as happening (we echo, deliberately, Edward Thompson's famous remarks on class as also a happening (1965: 85)) is of course in one way far too spontaneous an image: its rich symbology, its majestic *mise-en-scène*, its thumping Rule-Britannia, pomp-and-circumstance Englishness draws on and draws together everything we have sketched previously. These were the bricks out of which the Great Arch was made.

'Society', then, turns improvement on its new possession, labour. Formally and then really subordinating labour within production, it then catches up those same bodies, hearts and minds in their 'idle time' to thread together the fabric of the nation. As labour in production it had to be free(d) to be exploited; as labour in society it had to be moralized, normalized, individualized. It had to be simultaneously 'freed' and 'regulated'; forced and yet (positively) willed into new 'stations'; coerced and yet, gradually, to be sure, consensed into democracy. Of course Marxist theory spent almost fifty years focusing on 'bodies of armed men, prisons, etc.' as if that was all we could think, say, or feel about the state. That *was* what it was like, that is how it felt – from below. Only after the epistemic and ontological victory of a certain democracy was it possible to begin, carefully, to recognize also there, the consensual, the willingness, that 'the State' was an organizational form, handling the contradiction these few terse pages have attempted to indicate. 'The State' has to be open to new forms, open in exactly the same way that 'Society' was open to new men and new forms of mobile property (Pocock 1972; 1980a, b, c). That is why 'the working-class question' is the question of questions:

No political structure will remain stable once it has ceased to correspond to the social structure of the nation, and no social structure is stable which does not correspond to the economic structure, that is the organization of production. That is the simple, if Marxist, truth of politics. (*The Times*, editorial, 8 July 1975)

These years see a triple making, which taken together cements a distinctively new kind of civilization. First, 'Society' – comprising men of property – is extended, reformed, kept flexibly 'open'; it enlarges itself, shifts and inflects its voice, founds and celebrates a 'middle class'.[3] Second, the working class is resistingly involved in its own being made. Third, forms of rule – features of state formation – are equally made and making. We see a further 'revolution in government', centring on the 1830s, comparable in magnitude with those we have examined previously. It is impossible to think away, or to think separately, this third making. We say this not simply because it was a central means for the other two, which it was, but also because the end-product – *the* (modern, democratic, nation) 'State' – was differentially experienced and had a different meaning for the propertied whom it protected and the labouring whom it machined and moralized. This is not mere rhetoric. There is probably as much cultural ferment and struggle in the years from 1780 through to the 1840s and beyond as there was between 1640 and 1660, with an equally enduring legacy. But unlike the earlier period, the later was marked by an enormously augmented and nationally organized system of regulation.[4]

In these years, the Great Arch is finally finished, many of the bricks marked by the graffiti of the vanquished, and much blood – most of it foreign – mixed with the cement. What else was the Great Exhibition of 1851 unveiling to the world? It is worth remarking (not entirely in passing) that there were, of course, many examples of actual arches around; the history of the social architecture of bourgeois triumph and discipline has yet to be written, but nobody who wanders the civic/public social landscape of London and the provincial cities can fail to be struck by these real architectonics of their revolutionary victory. Noticing this we can again see the doubling discussed above: the visible power of the market materialized as its 'private' buildings, urban mansions, department stores, company headquarters, chambers of commerce, and the equivalent moral powers standing out grimly in those 'objects of terror', the union workhouses after 1834, through the central police stations from the later 1830s and especially the 1850s, on to the schools after 1870. We have always been equally struck by the central public buildings: town halls, museums, art galleries, public libraries, constructed from the later 1830s right through the nineteenth century. These graphically materialize another facet of the moral revolution, a particular civic culture, confidence, consciousness, pride: civil society as civic institutions. Nor should the evocations of Victorian 'Gothic' be overlooked (any more than those of eighteenth-century architectural 'classicism').

This revolution in government required its instrument to handle its Improvement, but it made use of all that had come before, including the instrument of the first Cromwell, statute law – the legislative programme of the 1830s exceeding that of the 1530s. But we must not expect to find here any clean, totalizing, codifying 'breaks'. The 1830s' revolution makes use of the rich repertoire of powers, devices created over the preceding centuries, above all that of the legitimacy of Parliament. Older forms continued to be 'useful'. If we are to use terms like constitutional monarchy, constitutional bureaucracy, then we have to understand that adjective (and its reference, 'the' constitution) in terms of all we have sketched in this book. We thus agree with Otto Hintze who found, in 1908,

in the English Cabinet all the combined historical elements that have formed the ministries of today: the great offices of Court; the Secretaries of State, and the collegiate Privy Council. (1908: 22)[5]

As we would wish to do, he roots all three in the twelfth century. Thus, although as we have noted Plumb finds an 'inner Cabinet' meeting regularly by the 1720s (above, p. 93; Plumb 1967: 179; Holdsworth 1972: vol. 10; 466ff.), innovation and regulation by Orders-in-Council (that is, the continuing power of the Privy Council) remains important, sometimes prospectively or retrospectively legitimated by statute. For example, the new Board of Trade (replacing that abolished in 1782) develops from a Committee of (Privy) Council on trade and plantations formed in 1784, reorganized by an Order-in-Council of 1786. Until the 1960s this was its 'fundamental instrument'. But its officers (1817, vice-president; 1826, president; 1867, parliamentary secretary replacing the vice-president) and its responsibilities (shipping, 1854 and later; weights and measures, 1866; and – given, taken away, and returned 1842, 1846, 1851 – railways) were established by statute law.[6] Education from 1839 until 1899 (not 1870) was 'organized' by a committee on Education (from 1870 'the Education Department') of the Privy Council, but its single officer (Vice-President, 1856) and some of its responsibilities, together with a certain regulation of its finances, were established by statute law (Holdsworth 1972: vol. 14, 123ff.).[7]

The crucial shifts in Treasury control (a history with deep roots in the wider formations we have outlined) are similarly 'peculiar',[8] importantly so given the links between changes there and 'control' of 'the civil service', which we shall briefly examine later. According to Holdsworth,

Just as the Exchequer was the heart and centre of the government in the days of the Norman and Angevin Kings, so the Treasury is the heart and centre of our modern machinery of executive government. (Holdsworth 1972: vol. 14, 108; whom we follow below)

The key statutes (much foreshadowed in the Economical Reform debates) mark a formal – if not final – going 'out of court'. These are: 1833 – Commissioners for Auditing the Public Accounts, and the Receiver-General; much more significant, 1834 – the Comptroller-General, the Treasury clerks (holding office on the same terms as judges), and the centralizing of funds within the Bank of England, the ending of fees; 1835 – Paymaster-General for the Army, Navy and other government departments; 1849 – Boards of Commissioners of Inland Revenue, with their own Receiver- and Accountant-General. But most accounts name as *the* key change the Exchequer and Audit Act of 1866 (the Commons had formed a Public Accounts Committee from 1861). The 1866 Act created a Comptroller and Auditor General. Holdsworth quotes from Anson's standard account (*The Crown*) the significant point that this official's duties are 'as regards issue, ministerial; as regards expenditure, judicial' (vol. 14, 111), but a substantial measure of independence from the Treasury was not secured until 1912.[9] None of this fully altered, i.e. modernized and rationalized, the 'system'. The Treasury still means the commissioners – a collective Lord Treasurer (of which the First Lord is often the Prime Minister) – and the relevant Cabinet post is still designated Chancellor of the Exchequer, who annually (or often more frequently) presents a Budget. Orders-in-Council were and are used to supplement and extend (or go beyond and around) Treasury powers-by-statute. There remains, after all, a Bank of England, with a Governor.

Finally, from '1688 there were two main Secretaryships [of State]; one for the Northern Department [the northern part of Europe], one for the Southern . . . [which dealt] with Southern Europe and with Irish and Colonial Affairs' (Cohen 1941: 23, n. 2). In 1782 the Home and Foreign Offices were created, with the former becoming *the* Secretary of State heading an Office with enormously extended powers-by-statute.[10] À propos centre/locality relations – a theme we have several times returned to in this book – Carolyn Steedman makes the important point that 'between 1856 and 1886 there were only two short periods when neither the Home Secretary nor the Parliamentary Under-Secretary had a *practical* understanding of the nature of local government . . . it was county experience that was represented most firmly at the Home Office' (1984: 29). Of the 18 men who were Home Secretaries or Parliamentary Under-Secretaries during this period, four were deputy lieutenants and two were chairmen of county quarter sessions; of the remainder, one was Lord Belmore, another the Earl of Rosebery, and a further four were JPs.

The Foreign Office[11] remains far more 'peculiar' than any of the others. We need to attend as much to its empowerment by prerogative and by privilege (in all senses of the term) as to powers-by-statute vested in the Secretary of State. Surrounded by secrecy, permeated with patronage,[12] saturated with senior staff,[13] the links are obviously with defence.[14] Our own largely 'internal' focus in this book (shared by so many who have studied state formation – even, curiously, those who emphasize the 'bodies of armed men, prisons, etc.' approach) does not do enough to grasp this extensive organization of 'the State' as *nation*, and the degree to which that external form is, in turn, a content for political and cultural determination 'at home'. Englishness – as nationalism at home, imperialism abroad – permeates the social power of the state, nuancing and enormously enhancing its legitimacy through a systematic practice of identification. At times, as we have indicated all too briefly in our book, this is very evident. As a necessary anticipation of our central discussion of democracy we cite the brilliant article by Harcourt (1980) examining the complex nexus of the Great Reform Act of 1867, which brings these themes together:

Reform, public order, economic recession, integration of the classes, concern about defence, and the challenge to Britain's international standing, were all components of the same crisis, and whether by chance or ingenuity it was the same power groups which had to handle them within the confines of time and circumstance. (p. 87)

In the midst of her complex argument she quotes from Disraeli (in 1866) the theme of greatness through imperial power:

There is no Power, indeed, that interferes more than England. She interferes in Asia, because she is really more of an Asiatic Power than a European. She interferes in Australia, in Africa, in New Zealand. (*The Times*, 14 July 1866, p. 10; quoted in Harcourt 1980: 96)

Long before other powers[15] – and with some remarkable echoes in events in the last few years! – English expeditions, usually by gunboats, but sometimes by 'expeditionary forces', in the words of Disraeli again (speaking of the Abyssinia expedition of 1867), elevated the military and moral 'character of England throughout the world'. For *The Times*, of course, it was the inevitable outcome of a conflict between 'civilization and barbarism', but more important – a key thesis in Harcourt's work – is the transmission of these views to working-class audiences.

The crucial way in which Harcourt weaves together knowledge/ power relations is in fact what, for us, brings to focus *the* instrument of the 1830s' revolution. From this time on we can sensibly talk about the machinery of government. The mode of regulating that machinery was part of the same moral revolution we have sketched above: some values, norms and qualities (appropriate to the life situation of some social groups) were elevated to become value, normality, the quality of life itself. This is no latter-day Foucauldian emphasis imposed by us, it permeates the writings of those revolutionary vanguard bourgeois intellectuals who made the revolution of the 1830s. To them we shall return shortly, but first some broad brush strokes of clarification.

Internal to the wider revolution we have described – how 'Society' discovered and attempted to moralize, in a special sense, socialize, society, how it turned its desire for Improvement on its new possession, labour, and how this turns on an antagonistic contradiction – was a change in orientation to 'the State'. This was, in part, a stabilizing of that set of structured relations of social power, of politically organized subjection, as if it were a thing. In the course of that long struggle (however many battles have been won, the war is not quite over yet) some concepts are 'brought forward' from that rich repertoire we have described thus far, others are transformed – that policing of Blackstone, for example, becomes a definite agency, the blue locusts of Mr Peel – and yet others are created anew. But even in the case of the latter, state forms are moralized and legitimated by virtue of a wider endeavour central to this period: there is a concerted attempt to disentangle 'the State' from interests, from clientage, from its previously more overt class and patriarchal register. In this, what drops below the political horizon (Bagehot's efficient parts of the state) are above all debates over form, understood to be the representational locus of favouring and disfavouring practices. 'The State' comes to represent a neutral, natural, obvious set of institutionalized routine practices which successfully claim the legitimate monopoly of national means of adminstration.[16] Simultaneously lifted above the horizon, to the very heavens, are the dignified aspects of the constitution. There are, of course, internal relations which link efficiency to dignity through the central sociological 'ether' of rituals of ruling. It matters what is done in the name of the Crown, by authority of Parliament, by virtue of stated powers. It equally matters how those further routinizations of charisma – rituals of bureaucratic administration – are conducted and legitimized, by what they are authorized. What this revolution accomplishes is the legitimation as forms of regulation, coercive and consensual controls – as, in a word, forms of state – of the powers of the propertied: 'Democracy legitimises stolen goods,' as Marshall sharply observed.

Central to this is a transformation (within continuities, like the commission-form) of a relation we have discussed throughout this book: the forms of agency that handle centre/locality relations.[17] As E. P. Hennock has recently summarized,

> I propose to approach the changing relations between local and central government in the first place by looking at the provision of common minimum standards. From that point of view this first period is characterised by the prevalence of local standards at the discretion of local rulers. I shall argue that the changes in central/local government relations were in the first instance largely due to a feature of the mid-nineteenth century that I have called the centralisation of knowledge.... From the 1830s onwards inspectors, travelling the country on behalf of central government departments, were able to assemble standardised information about different localities. (1982: 40)

The centralization of knowledge requires *facts* – and the legitimization of some facts, and the methods used to collect them, against other facts – to justify features and forms of *policy*. The facts relate to what we may call the statistical idea, and the policies to what we may call the educational idea. Those thousands of volumes of Blue Books (Parliamentary publications) which fill the rooms of what used to be called the State Paper Room of the British Museum (now the Official Publications Library of the British Library) need to be reconceptualized as key instruments of the moral revolution of the nineteenth century. They are the English disciplines of state formation in this period. Commissions of inquiry rapidly increase after 1800, energized in part by the Economical Reforms movement, in part by the needs of war – the short-lived Board of Agriculture and its reports are transitional but significant here – and in part by the urgency simply to understand what is happening. Between 1832 and 1846 alone there were over 100 royal commissions established (Finer 1952a: 39).

Chadwick, as always, was quite clear as to their purposes, and his (like Bentham's) impatience with democratic party politics is evidenced. In a section of his two-volume collected papers (Chadwick 1887: II) – entitled 'The development of statesmanship as a science by the investigation of State necessities' – there are a number of texts which exemplify this. In 1859, for example, in a speech to the Society for the Amendment of the Law, Chadwick declared that he had never known one such 'investigation':

which did not reverse every main principle and almost every assumed chief elementary fact [NB] on which the general public, Parliamentary committees, politicians of high position, and often the commissioners themselves, were prepared to base legislation. (Chadwick 1859a: 127; emphases removed)

In the same year, in a paper to the Statistical Society of London, the remedy for any number of social problems (including 'bad morality, anti-social feelings and painful sense of individual insecurity, pervading and corrupting all society, and extending to the Commons House itself') is argued to be 'well-examined and complete collections of facts as to past experience on which to found safe practical rules for future guidance' (Chadwick 1859b; cf. 1857, 1862, 1871, and Finer 1952a).

There is a parallel structuring for the centralization (and legitimation) of certain facts (that become knowledge) between the operation of, on the one hand, commissions and committees of inquiry – set agenda, controlled membership, definite form of inquiry, relationship between gathered evidence and final facts forming the basis for reports and recommendations – and, on the other, the various inspectorates – central office, terms of reference, controlled membership/appointments, definite forms of inquiry and regular report forming the basis of facts and knowledge at the centre. These are of immense moral and material significance for three reasons. As facts they magnetized definite forms of agency, provision and regulation as effective, appropriate and necessary. As procedures and facts, plus policies, they solidified as the neutral practices of administration, problem-solving. And as modes of seemingly empirical argument they simultaneously handled and concealed the contradictions discussed earlier in this chapter.

State inspectors (sometimes called assistant commissioners, for example in relation to the Poor Law from 1834 until 1847) spread like a contagion: factory inspectors from 1833; inspectors of prisons from 1835; Her Majesty's inspectors of schools from 1839; for the mining population from 1842, for mines from 1850.[18] They were charged with inspecting and reporting upon the implementation of Acts, the legitimate operation of institutions, the suitability – above all the 'efficiency' – of agencies in receipt of central funds, and so on, but they all report on far more than their specific duties demand. They operated as a vanguard in two distinct senses. First, as agents for that national system of Improvement which the more radical of them recognized was needed, they sought to secure not simply, in their different 'fields', a national minimum standard provision across the country, but to ensure that they would be a 'transmission belt' between the best examples (in their localities, and nationally) and the rest of the relevant institutions. Second, they acted to establish and standardize a range of civic institutions which would concretely symbolize the extension of 'Society' as society beyond the efforts (if any) of either individual paternalist capitalists or local groupings of the same. These civic institutions could be either 'objects of terror' – the union workhouse, the police station – or they could be those new public institutions (including ornamental parks and gardens) which celebrated civic character, demonstrated provincial pride, and characterized cultural citizenship.

Some contemporaries recognized this strategy, and knew to what it was oriented. Manchester (a frequent site in these changes as we shall see) was the location of a private committee – the Manchester Board of Health – founded in 1796, which called for state intervention on behalf of apprentices. Sir Robert Peel (*the* Peel's father) inspected his own factories and supported what became in 1802 'an Act for the preservation of the Health and Morals of Apprentices and Others'.[19] This was a 'perfectly transitional' attempt to combine features of the Statute of Apprentices (abolished in 1813) and modern Factory (local inspectors were to be appointed) and Education (curriculum, place and personnel of instruction were stated) Acts. But what it did was to register, however weakly, that – in Bentham's words, and also from 1802 – the 'most neglected class must become the principal object of care. The less parents are able to discharge their duty, the more necessary it is for government to fulfil it' (quoted in Montmorency 1902: 217). That is, as the same source recognizes, education is 'an indirect mode for preventing offences'. This is the great rallying call of the bourgeois radicals throughout the next 30 (or, come to that, the next 180) years. In 1832 Kay, in his classic commentary on the cotton operatives in Manchester, closes by arguing that 'morality is worthy of the attention of the economist' (1832: 82) and the 'ignorant are, therefore, properly, the care of the state' (ibid.: 93). By 1853 Kay (then Kay-Shuttleworth) is much more assured. Arguing that a 'Christian state has collective duties', he cites the 1834 Poor Law as an example of how the state does interfere on behalf of some moral values and ends by quoting from Dr Vaughan (*British Quarterly Review*, August 1847): 'Government MAY be a moral teacher to the extent that it MUST be a moral administrator' (Kay 1853: 282).

But it is Chadwick who brings the points together so neatly, and in a relevant commentary on precisely one of the new disciplinary texts we discussed above. H. S. Tremenheere had sent a draft of his first report as newly appointed Commissioner for the Mining Districts. On 4 September 1844 Chadwick replied in a letter which is worth quoting fairly fully:

Such investigations are a new element in Government, and it is important that the public, the Houses of Parliament, and the Government itself should on every opportunity be impressed with the importance of a special agency [he means inspectors generally] and with the respect for it in tracing out principles of social and political economy which otherwise would have been unattended to, and in arresting popular delusions and suppressing the power of mere shouts and mere shouters.

Finer's excellent study (1952a) shows that the latter were not exclusively socialists, but included a number of powerful groups – precisely those who celebrated St Chad's double demise when *The Times* thundered about how they would not be bullied into health by Mr Chadwick. But Chadwick continues in his letter to Tremenheere:

The observations as to the want of civil organisation for the new districts are important. . . . I think however you give undue prominence to church extensions. The remedies first in order are: infant schools; juvenile schools for the young; police force better organised . . .; restrictions on the sale of fermented liquors; remedies against strikes . . . and lastly better appointed religious teachers, after the preventing of immorality by the prevention of overcrowding for which see the Health of Towns evidence. (Chadwick MSS 2181/4: 23) [20]

This *is* the modern world. The strategic, informing features – so lost on studies of 'the State' through individual bureaux, in the misty realms of ideology, through Parliamentary politics, or in those Marxists for whom 'the State' is simply a class reflex of power and interests held by capitalists, or worse, by capital – are palpable. Chadwick did more than ensure that the sewage flowed smoothly out of London, but he did that too.

As has been well said, 'Chadwick was Chadwick' (Cullen 1975: 187, n. 56), by which is meant his exceptionality – but hardly anyone since Finer has recognized the strategic genius involved here – has dominated the actual study of inspection. It is similar to that tedious game of *cherchez* Bentham (Burn 1963: 140; Thomas 1974: 53, n. 4; Cullen 1975: 181, n. 56). Roberts (1960: ch. 6) and Perkin (1969: 268) classify as Benthamites Leonard Horner, H. S. Tremenheere, J. P. Kay-Shuttleworth and Edwin Chadwick, when the first three in explicit publications (severally) take their distance from the character-ization of Bentham employed by Roberts and Perkin, and the last demonstrated his practical distance. In fact Chadwick donated to us a precise understanding of what he was about, writing – in some remarkable 'Notes on political economy' of 1852 – that 'the govern-ment has to solve an almost insoluble problem' in relation to the triad of (economic) *laissez-faire*, liberty, and morality.[21]

The generality of inspectors are best classified as middle class. Roberts (1960: 152ff.) finds 'few examples of really self-made men'; normally they were 'sons of country gentlemen or members of the professional classes or businessmen. Their families . . . had wealth and position.' They are better considered as state servants than civil servants because of their backgrounds, their self-definition as reporting directly to ministers (many of whom they knew and met socially), and because – for the first generation, at least, in each inspectoral realm – they worked more individually. In realm after realm we can see the slowness with which inspectoral norms were routinized and how long it took for the victory of the central office over the circuits of the inspectors. Looking back over the first few years of inspection, one HMI remarked in 1851:

the instrument of Inspection, while it is one of which the public will never stand in awe, because it is so easy to remove a misbehaving inspector, is of sufficient power to accomplish all that the State can desire. (Fletcher 1851: 33)

Kay-Shuttleworth, two years later:

Their labours have also spread among the humbler classes a general sense of the vigilant care of the Government for their well-being, and thus, among other concurrent causes, have promoted that political repose which has characterised the English poor, while the whole of Europe has been threatened with a socialist rebellion, has suffered the confusion of democratic revolutions, and the revulsion of military despotism. (1853: 88)

Harris (1955) – the fullest study of inspection thus far – offers as the first of his seven 'convincing reasons' for inspection 'one of the major purposes of central control is to secure the enforcement of a national minimum standard' (p. 9). We must stress how this had to be enforced amongst the ruling and middle classes as well as, in this manner as in so many others, 'shoving civilization downwards' to and at the propertyless. E. C. Tufnell made this point clear when he wrote, in 1837, to the Poor Law commissioners how 'far more can be done through indoctrinating the [Poor Law guardians] through the agency of the assistant Commissioner'.[22]

A central 'problem' to be handled by state formation in this period was the factory system, which must be understood as far, far more than particular relations in production, buildings and steam power. The tremendous surge in basic industries (coal-mining, iron-smelting) and machine production also 'colonized' (the term is happily used for 50 years) the 'new districts' with new social forms that lacked both the old forms of moral or natural policing (the oversight of *les autres* by men of 'Society') and the newer civic institutions. Some of the shifts need simply to be registered. Manchester – to start with that social setting which provided so many images for the period – had 27,000 people in 1773 and 'not a single cotton mill; by 1802 the population was 95,000 and there were fifty-two cotton mills' (Harrison 1984: 217). Between 1801 and 1850 Manchester grew to 303,000; Bradford to 104,000 (from 13,000). In 1801 London was the only city with more than 100,000 people, by 1851 there were nine such cities. Moreover, whilst in 1851 half (but note that!) the population of Leeds, Sheffield and Norwich had been born in those places, for Manchester, Glasgow and Bradford it was just over a quarter, and for Liverpool even less (ibid.: 227). The three great 'ideas' which energized the system of national improvement that was state formation in this period – the twin faces of 'the statistical idea' and 'the educational idea', and the much more subordinated (for it too much challenged local powers) 'sanitary idea' – faced a very different 'population' to the theorizations of any earlier period.

Those who formed 'the State' and propounded a system faced three enemies: the great aristocratic families and their patronage–clientage hold on central and local apparatuses of power; individual capitalists and entrepreneurs, often grouped into local power bases representing, quite explicitly, fractions of capital; and the working classes. The ethos of state formation is best understood through Nettl's fruitful concept of normlessness, where politics is about '*establishing norms* in the first place', and groups promote 'norms that they competitively offer as legitimate for the whole society' (1968: 588). This is what James Mill meant in his lucid survey 'The state of the nation' in 1826:

every class of combination of men have a strong propensity to get up a system of morality for themselves, that is, conformable to their own interests; in other words, to urge upon other men, as good, such lines of conduct as are good for them, whether good or evil to other people. (James Mill 1826; 225; the male reference should be noted)

If certain machineries of routinization can be established (or reformed from older rituals of rule) then 'what is essentially an *evaluative* matter can be transformed into an apparently *factual* one' (Parkin 1971: 83). Parkin follows Lockwood here: 'A dominant class has never existed which did not seek to make its position legitimate by placing highest value on those qualities and activities which come closest to its own' (1958: 209).

But the issue here is more complex. The group and their system were not 'a' or 'the' dominant class, they were happy to take on the term middle class and to see that class as the one 'which gives the nation its character' (*Westminster Review*, 1824).[23] Sir James Graham, in the same year, indicates how this class had taken over certain gentry notions (as explicated by Morrill (1979) for the early seventeenth century, and themselves involving an even older classsical reference):

The seat of public opinion is in the middle ranks of life – in that numerous class, removed from the wants of labour and the cravings of ambition, enjoying the advantages of leisure, and possessing intelligence sufficient for the formation of sound judgement, neither warped by interest nor obscured by passion. (quoted in Briggs 1956: 69)

Notice the fourth and fifth words: public opinion. We have to read these carefully. For Burke in 1795 (and contrast his notion of 'the swinish multitude'), 'the people are of adult age, not declining in life, of tolerable leisure . . . and some means of information, above menial dependence: i.e. about 400,000' (quoted in White 1957: 48). James Mill, in 1826, celebrated the 'value of the middle classes of this country, their growing numbers and importance, are acknowledged by all' (1826: 269). Brougham in 1831: 'By the People, I mean the middle classes, the wealth and intelligence of the country, the glory of the British name' (quoted in Briggs 1956: 69, n. 2). W. H. Mackinnon defined 'public opinion' (i.e. the opinion of *these* 'people') in 1828 as:

that sentiment on any given subject which is entertained by the best informed, most intelligent and most moral persons in the community, which is gradually spread and adopted by nearly all persons of any education or proper feeling in a civilised state. (quoted in Peel 1971: 70)

With Briggs (1956; 1959a: 114) we may date this from the 1790s – at the same time as a specific notion of 'the provinces' (Read 1964; cf. Hoskins 1965) is employed.

It is time – and the brevity of our remarks immediately above may not help here – to clear away the chessboard model of the nineteenth century (actually it is that masculinist power model which is at its base) which sees 'new classes' sweeping away the old – an analogue for that search for English 'equivalent' of 1789 which so befogs the rationalist mind. There was no simply 'triumphant' middle class, it was capitalism – profitable forms of property – that ruled, but the forms of that rule were reconstructed through some features of the ethos and system of the middle-class, authentically bourgeois radicals we have been discussing. Equally, as we have stressed throughout, it drew on older forms and symbologies, notably in its legitimating and 'dignified' aspects. The radicals won sufficiently for their purposes (if not sufficiently for their successors in the late 1960s and early 1970s). At the same time it is as well to recall the continuing enormous power of the landed aristocracy (however much their wealth came now from other sources). No Cabinet between 1830 and 1900 had less than 41 per cent 'aristocratic element', the only two below 50 per cent were Gladstone's 1868 and 1892 Cabinets; the average for the period was 71 per cent (Arnstein 1972: 210).[24] We shall discuss continuing landed (and military) power in relation to Parliament and the locality below; the greater and the lesser landed aristocracy and gentry continue to be rulers of central and local state institutions until the 1880s or later, but the forms of their rule were not the same. The 'gentleman ideal', 'public opinion', and state forms are a set of signs for the 'dance' (cf. Brebner 1948) of ruling-class ideas in this period, endlessly twirling around the figures of Revolution, Restoration/Reformation, and Improvement; a dance which gives this period its obdurate density, its refusal to fit itself 'willingly' to any theoretical model *a priori*. King William IV, offering a definition of the 'natural influence' of the peers of the realm in 1831 could equally have been quoting half a dozen state servants on the need for a middle class to be 'as natural' as this:

It is natural that they should possess influence over those to whom their property enables them to give employment and subsistence; and it is desirable that a useful union should thus be promoted between the upper and the lower classes of society. (quoted in Davis 1974: 80)

The 'link', of course, cementing old and new rulers and forms of rule, varieties of 'natural influence' of a reconstructed 'Society' in and over society, is possession of profitable property. George Nicholls, in 1846, speaking as a Poor Law commissioner discusses the 'promotion of well-being' by 'possessors of property' (1846). For Tremenheere (writing of the mining districts) 'proper' schools, 'proper' churches, 'proper' shops all establish a middle class:

precisely in those localities where their valuable influence and instrumentality are most wanting, as the connecting link between those who gain their living by the work of their hands and those who accumulate vast fortunes by the skilful direction of that labour. (PP 1852 (1525) XXI: 12–13: cf. PP 1844 (592) XVI: 26–8, for almost similar words)

Indeed, as we have mentioned, several state servants saw their task as amongst other things adequately to educate the propertied as to their responsibilities. Not infrequently they relate character to national character, and see that as permeating from above. Samuel Smiles's notion of character was related to 'The True Gentleman' (1859: ch. 13).

Smiles's 'gentleman' reference also alerts us to another dimension of the state formation of this period. 'Society' sought to mould and

civilize society, to individualize and moralize its members, differentially, in ways appropriate to their respective 'stations'. We have seen
how 'the public' was explicitly construed in class terms. An equally
central axis of state practices is – once more – gender. The 'same'
procedures of state – ostensibly neutral: 'gender-blind', as also class-
blind or colour-blind – operate differently on different groups. From
Alice Clark's 1919 study, through Kelsall's examination of wage
regulation (1938: 70ff.), to the more recent work of Hill (1958: ch.
14), Keith Thomas (1958, 1959, 1971, 1977), Rowbotham (1977: chs
1–4) and Hamilton (1978), we can see how a variety of gendered
categories, relations and practices began to be formed in the seventeenth century, which cumulatively worked to describe and prescribe
difference as disadvantage. The Restoration was as much patriarchal
and paternal as it was anything else; so, as we have indicated (p. 81
above) were Puritan ethics of 'family discipline'. Other work, which
we have cited, shows how a much longer history is entailed in the
repertoires through which this naming (and silencing) of gender is
legitimated, taken for granted, and organized. We have discussed the
subordination/exclusion of women in the major 'public' domains of
law (and rights therein) and political representation over the centuries
at various points in this book. Diana Barker's study of the regulation
of the marriage form (1978) registers just what relations of reponsibil-
ity and subordination were being recorded when marriages and births
began to be listed by order of 'the State' (by the Marriage Act, and
Births and Deaths Registration Act, of 1836, following Thomas
Cromwell's precedent of three centuries previously). Such notions of
legitimacy and respectability were enormously augmented within the
wider civilizing project of the 1830s, as Henriques (1967) shows in
relation to bastardy, or Hall (1979) in relation to domestic ideology.

Hakim (1980) has demonstrated how that most technical and
seemingly neutral of 'administrative' instruments, the census, involves
in its very enumeration (and in explicit announcement in its sociological prefaces) debates which have an extraordinarily modern resonance:
for instance, is domestic labour a productive occupational category?
This 'statistical' example – concerning definitions of 'the population'
and 'who are our subjects?' – reminds us exactly what is being
discussed here: the formation of social identities. The latter is now
ably attended to in the extensive literature that relates state formation
and sexuality (notably O'Brien 1981, Weeks 1981, Coward 1982,
Snitnow 1983) and re-examines familial forms within this pattern
(Rapp et al. 1983; Olsen 1983 – excellent on legal regulation; for
reviews see Thompson 1977b, Hill 1978a). Other recent works shows,
from the 1830s, gendered features of schooling for pupils (Purvis

1981, Davin 1978, 1979) and gender differentiation in teaching (Purvis 1980, Widowson 1983).

Here we wish only to remind (or inform) readers of both the longevity of the conceptualization and organization of gender differences through state forms, and the intensity and comprehensiveness of their reconstruction around and within the wider 'socializing' project of this period. Because women were successfully claimed (documented, enumerated, legitimated) to belong within the household, to have a domestic identity – such well-ordered families, of course, reflecting and upholding a well-ordered society – they could not be thought of as having a public existence. As Hakim shows clearly (cf. Corrigan 1977b, 1982a), this does not simply deny their significance or productiveness so much as locate their 'true place' within the family, subordinated within relations of dependency to men who were responsible for them, as for children. As such they were no more to represent themselves publicly than were that other class of 'dependants' within the patriarchal household, 'servants', to represent themselves as employees, until the 1930s and the 1920s respectively. Neither category could be properly contracting individuals. As Diana Barker comments,

The dominant interpretation of Individualist philosophy in the nineteenth century itself would be better named Familialism – or simply Patriarchy. It envisaged full legal citizenship extended to all heads of households and 'individual obligation' as being between household heads. The possibility of dependents (married women and children – and at an earlier date, servants) being seen as rational, contract-making, independent individuals was not considered in most political thought of Maine's day. (1978: 256; see also her note 21, on Spencer)

R. Barker, discussing 'the pale of the constitution', makes it clear that 'women were not envisaged when "people" or "English men" were thought of,' observing that 'as ever, the commonplace was the greatest defence against change – not what was considered essential, but what was considered obvious' (1978: 112–13, cf. Harrison 1978). Women thus continue to exist, schizophrenically, both within and without the law. Within it, they exist as persons who (if above the age of responsibility) are capable of intentional acts and thus of committing crimes. But they are without it – in both senses of the word – because as specifically subordinated persons they cannot use it to name or change that subordination, to express *their* social experience.

English law, and state policies and practices mere generally, find it 'difficult' to conceive or allow a relating of women and property (above, pp. 36–7; cf. Holcombe 1977). For property is a prerogative of 'free', independent individuals, fully human beings, and – consistently over the centuries, even as definitions of property shift – it is thereby a defining quality of those morally fitted to be citizens, the real public. While the class reference of 'the public' is overt in the contemporary usages we have quoted, the exclusion of females goes so deep as not to be thought worth indicating at all. It is taken for granted, part of the deep structures of thought. Conversely, time and again – and through to the 1980s – it is found eminently possible to understand women as property, personally in relation to specific men (fathers, brothers, husbands) and more generally as social property (cf. Robertshaw and Curtin 1977, Harrison and Mort 1980). This has been the legitimated, approved, public expression of the social identity of some 52 per cent of the population. There is no language to register the enormity of what was done, though a term like social schizophrenia catches some its horror. Masculine dominance is constitutive of the cultural revolution which is English state formation. It should not therefore surprise us that as the centuries of denied, derided, deranged and deformed historical experience are rediscovered, named and celebrated, feminism has compelled a recognition of all theories of and practices oriented toward 'the State'. The consistency and totality, over centuries, of the exclusion/subordination of women has no real parallel in the experience of any other social group, and nowhere is it clearer how central a problem 'the State' remains if human capacities are ever to be fully realized.

The 'statistical idea' (cf. Cullen 1975) was one form of educating in both directions: gently upwards and horizontally, and coercively downwards. In 1798 Sir John Sinclair prefaced his *Statistical account of Scotland* with a definition of statistics as 'the Population, the Political Circumstances, the productions of a country and other matters of State' (quoted in ibid. 10). In 1833 – the year of the founding of the Manchester Statistical Society,[26] a Statistical Committee of the British Association for the Advancement of Science, and a Department of Statistics (under G. R. Porter) at the Board of Trade – the *Penny Cyclopaedia* defined statistics as 'that department of political science which is concerned in collecting and arranging facts illustrative of the conditions and resources of a State' (quoted in ibid.: 11). Concerning the Board of Trade, Brown (1958: 80ff.) has noted that statistics were 'taken to mean the collection of facts descriptive of a state: its geographical features, climate, population, resources, scale of trade and habits'. G. R. Porter was Ricardo's brother-in-law, and his *Progress of the nation* (3 vols, 1836; 3rd edn 1851) is symptomatic. In 1834 the London Statistical Society was founded. In 1837, as a consequence of the Registration Act of 1836 – which must be compared with Thomas Cromwell's introduction of parish registers three centuries earlier (1538), and the points we made about that apply equally here – Dr William Farr was appointed sub-Registrar-General (the top post going to Lord John Russell's brother-in-law R.H. Lister); within two years 2,193 local registrars had been appointed.

William Guy defends a definition of statistics as a 'science of States' as late as 1870 (p. 440). Skeat's *Etymological Dictionary of the English Language* derives the word 'statistics' from state (statist-ic). Just as Guy argues that the British Association 'grew from' (i.e. in part against) the Royal Society in 1831, so did the National Association for the Promotion of Social Science 'grow from' the London Statistical Society in 1856. The membership of all these societies was small, but their personnel significant. Guy (p. 441) claims that the NAPSS had a membership in 1869 of 1,500, and the London Statistical Society and the Institute of Actuaries together had 608 – but the latter includes 51 peers and 31 MPs. Thomas Malthus was chairman of the British Association Statistical Committee; Kay was active in the founding of the Manchester Society; Horner was a member of the British Association Committee from 1834. Chadwick was everywhere: his bibliography indicates the fusion of these sites for 'broadcasting', his addresses to the BAAS or the NAPSS appear in the *Journal* of the (London) Statistical Society, as do papers by Tremenheere and Kay, who also published in the *Transactions NAPSS*. G. W. Hastings, the first secretary of the NAPSS[27] – founded to relate 'the improvement of the people' and 'social economics as a whole' – shows the moral classificatory/regulatory framework clearly:

do we not find that each one of the social problems we have been in any way at pains to unravel strikes its roots into the substance of the nation, ramifying through a hundred secret crevices into classes apparently the most removed from its influence? (1856; quoted in Mitchell 1968: 1–2)

Of course by about that time, or within that decade, 'the State' had successfully secured a monopoly over the legitimate right to collect a range of statistical information, and over the next 25 years statistics would fracture into descriptive gathering of 'the facts' and 'higher statistics' as a branch of mathematical reasoning and calculation. Hakim (1980) as we have mentioned shows how significant were the prefaces to the census.

If 'the statistical idea' provided the 'facts', what was the solution? Education. But again, and immediately, we have to shake this term loose from its connotations this side of the state formation we are describing. Halevy (1923b) suggests that it is only through a focus like educational transformation – as project and method – that we can understand the thematic unity of the changes of the 1830s. In 1837 the Central Society for Education was formed to discuss this question:

to show how all the social relations, the tone, the strength, of the national character, are dependent upon it; how civilisation varies as its quality changes; how, in a short time, manners may be modelled by it. (Duppa 1837: 26)

Echoing Chadwick's remarks on commissions of inquiry and inspectors' reports, Duppa had argued that the 'appreciation of Statistical information is gradually gaining ground . . . vague generalities should be quitted, and the exact quantity of particulars of which a general assessment is made should be shown' (p. 24). This is a methodology. For Duppa it is a matter of:

heaping fact upon fact, and argument upon argument, classifying and opposing, and, in the instances in which it can be done with safety, drawing a conclusion; and thus attempting to give to the theory of education a more scientific character than it has yet assumed. (1837: 2)

Which facts? Whose scientific character? The Philosophical Radicals knew very well what they wanted:

We advocate, both for England and Ireland, the necessity of a national provision for the training of the young. In the old we cannot hope for much improvement. But the new generation springing up might be modelled to our will. (*Westminster Review*, January 1837; quoted in Halevy 1923b: 105–6, n. 5)

It is crucial that the major legislative enactments involving forms of inspection be reconceptualized to accord with the view that contemporaries had of them – as educational measures. This is true of the initial Factory Act and the numerous extensions (Horner 1834, 1837; Tremenheere 1861, 1865a); it is also true of the Poor Law (Kay 1838a, b, e; 1839b; 1840a, b; 1841a; cf. 1839a and generally). If Kay is taken to be unrepresentative, consider the closing section of the 1834 Poor Law Report (written by Chadwick and Nassau Senior):

We are perfectly aware that for the general diffusion of right principles and habits we are to look, not so much for any economic arrangements and regulations as to the influence of a moral and religious education. . . . [What we propose will] remove the obstacles which now impede the progress of instruction, and intercept its results; and will afford a freer scope to the operation of every instrument which may be employed, for elevating the intellectual and moral condition of the poorer classes. We believe that if the funds now destined to the purposes of education, many of which are applied in a manner unsuited to the present wants of society, were wisely and economically employed, they would be sufficient to give all the assistance which can be prudently afforded by the state (Poor Law Report 1834: 496–7).

Here we have a formula which echoes down the years: spending on education will lead to saving on other costs. Thirty-four years before its supposed invention by T. H. Green, as a part-defence, part-definition of 'Liberal legislation', the Rev. W. J. E. Bennett argued 'a just expenditure on education would relieve us of the overwhelming burden under which we now labour in these three evils', poor laws, police, prisons (1846: 43).

But it is Kay (Kay-Shuttleworth) who brings so many of these points together, as both prescription – the first text was circulated 'by authority' after all – and description (the reflections of a 'local squire', as he liked to define himself after retirement). Kay had already noted in 1832 'evils everywhere requiring the immediate interference of legislative authority' (1832: 112). The answer was state formation:

The authority of government, especially in a representative system, embodies the national will. There are certain objects too vast, or too complicated, or too important to be intrusted [sic] to voluntary associations; they need the assertion of power. (1846 in 1862a reprint: 451)

This is why 'moral obligation' through state and law and in its domination over merely 'economic laws' is a major part of the answer to the question Kay-Shuttleworth asked himself in 1860: 'Why did capitalism develop so well in England?' (1860: 89ff.). Notice the exact terms here:

It is impossible either to limit the pernicious influence of pauperism or crime to the wealth and productive power of the country, or to combat them effectually without employing moral transformatory as well as economical repressive forces for their extirpation ... sanitary measures reach even the moral nature of man. They are part of civilisation. (1860: 92)

In the face of this – quotations that could have been multiplied tenfold (cf. Corrigan 1977a) – it may seem otiose to quote later historians to clarify our argument further; for such it remains, and there is much that would significantly strengthen our case that has been omitted for reasons of space. Each chapter here in the end demands the thousand pages Edward Thompson gave to the *Making* that responds to and refuses that which we depict. But we want to do so, having first suggested a reversal of terms that have been employed in recent discussions. On the one hand, we would argue that we should see this national system of Improvement as class expression in precisely the sense which structuralist and post-structuralist thought has delineated: the establishing (coercively and consensually, and over a century or more) of the approved, public, legitimated, 'correct' forms of expression for the organization of historical experience of older and newer groups within the ruling class. Historians old (Feiling, quoted in Holdsworth 1972: vol. 13, pp. 153–4 n.) and new (Hennock 1982: 39) are not afraid of using the term historical experience, or of recognizing that a certain ethos, some key ideas, need not be seized by the masses for them to be, nevertheless, a material force. Social control, on the other hand, we would like to wrench from its normal top–downward, manipulation-of-the-subordinated mode of employment, and to see it as exactly what was being argued for by socialists, Chartists and others against the national system. This is as clear in Marx (who uses this term explicitly against 'the political economy of the middle class', cf. his 1864) as it is in Morris.

Tholfsen has offered two superb articles which do much to capture the ethical features of the whole moral revolution, thereby widening, back to its early nineteenth-century referent, the terms, energy and project of 'the educational idea':

Both in politics and in social life there was the same tendency to describe goals in moral and idealistic terms. In both spheres to be reasonable meant accepting the arguments of social superiors. Liberalism was not a narrowly political doctrine, but an expression of the mid-Victorian ethos. As such it was extremely effective in attenuating conflict and fostering co-operation (1961: 246)

Noting, ten years later, how a 'salient feature of' this cohesive 'culture was the tendency to invest ordinary activities with the highest moral significance' (1971: 61), he identified the extensive material range of the 'ethic of improvement':

elementary schools, Sunday schools, Mechanics Institutes, mutual improvement societies, reading rooms, libraries, temperance societies, friendly societies, co-operatives, savings banks, churches and chapels. To a striking degree, implicitly and explicitly, in ritual and litany, these institutions celebrated the ideal of improvement in all its forms. (ibid.: 63)

Supple, in his interesting essay 'Legislation and virtue', notes how 'in the last resort the welfare of the poor *as a class* was assumed to lie in changes in the values and habits and priorities of individuals. . . . Put crudely, the working class was expected to adopt the cardinal middle-class socio-economic virtues' (1974: 213; cf. Harrison, 1974). For all his qualifications, in a recent review essay F. M. L. Thompson states:

It can be accepted that that social order [nineteenth-century England], or indeed any social order, was not developed and sustained exclusively 'by legal systems, police forces, and prisons', although the edifice of legal and administrative rules and sanctions is clearly not unimportant in the shaping of personal and group conduct. Authority and the legalised force on which it ultimately rested were, as always, exercised in ways of intended to uphold a social fabric congenial to holders of power, and they were concerned to induce the people to accept as legitimate the ways in which authority was exercised. (1981: 207)

This is just a trifle bland, a little too easy. If state formation is intra-class struggle, part of the making of a coherent, confident and secure ruling class in England, then we have to attend to the social schizophrenia it produces in those upon whose lives it is visited. The Philosophic Radicals spoke of modelling a whole generation to their will – that is not a dinner party! Nassau Senior, Chadwick and Kay were quite clear about the violence that the 1834 Poor Law Amendment entailed. Out-relief was ended or drastically reduced in what were severely depressed areas. Within the workhouses 'a discipline so severe and repulsive as to make them a terror to the poor' was enforced (the words are those of an assistant commissioner (quoted in Thompson 1968: 295)): reduction in diet, silence during meals, 'prompt obedience', religious exercises, segregation of the sexes, separation of familes even where of the same sex, labour, total confinement. Kay writes of his visit to one workhouse (Cosford Union) that he observed:

that the custom of permitting paupers to retain [in] their possession, while residing within the walls of the workhouse, boxes, china, articles of clothing, &c., had been perpetuated. . . . I therefore directed these articles to be taken into the possession of the various Governors. (quoted in ibid.: 296)

Different forms of property, clearly! Kay is similarly plain in so many of his discussions as an assistant Poor Law commissioner; after all in East Anglia, the place from which he writes his first full report (1836), there had been small but armed risings. Later he saw the 1834 system as 'essentially a measure of police . . . to increase public order, and with it the security of property' (1859: 135). For Beales what the 1834 system attempted to establish:

beside economy, was a system of social police which would open up the labour market and render the labour factor of production mobile and docile, that is, disciplined and as nearly rational and predictable as may be. (Beales 1948: 315; cf. Thompson 1968: 295ff.; Inglis 1971: 372ff.; Coats 1972a: 165)

Trades unions were identified as 'criminal' (Kay 1839a, 1846, 1866a, 1868 follow the theme through; Tremenheere in 1893 is very antagonistic) even when not actually criminalized. For Robert Lowe all trades unions contain 'the germs and elements of crime' (quoted in

Briggs 1954: 258). Bagehot thought 'a political combination of the lower classes as such and for their own objects, an evil of the first magnitude' (1872: 277). When trades unions finally were legalized, the required forms of organization (and accompanying legislation) restricted them, and their orientation toward 'the State' had changed from the first 50 years of the nineteenth century. Anyway, their legal rights were and are hardly the most secure in the face of either judge-made or statute law. Notwithstanding repeal of the Combination Acts, the dominant legal framework for most workers, until 1875, was the master and servant legislation (cf. Simon 1954; Corrigan 1977b), which laid down totally different rights/duties for masters and servants.

But these overtly violent and coercive forms of regulation should not be overemphasized compared with the forcefulness with which certain social and moral classifications were materialized, strengthened, broadcasted and repeated. These marked people, and demonstrate how the modern democratic (we will come to that in a moment) nation state continues 'to deal in ideologies', to be 'interested' in all forms of moral regulation, including – centrally – establishing forms of approved, acceptable social identity. The Poor Law considerably strengthened the older classification between the deserving and undeserving poor – between the orphaned, old, sick and damaged on the one hand, and the sturdy beggars, rogues and vagabonds on the other. This modernizes the eighteenth-century contrasts between pity and punishment, benevolence and the 'Bastilles'. It also 'encouraged' the self-formation of a 'respectable' working class. Likewise the Vagrancy Act of 1824 (and its many extensions – 1850s, 1868, 1872 – the latter adding 'destitute children' to its categories, and the whole corpus only repealed with the Criminal Justice Act of 1982). Recalling Lamparde's 'flying beggars' – this history is a very long one! – 'William Cartwright believed in "vagrant crime", and from his appointment as Chairman of Brackley Poor Law Union in 1835 sought to separate the "criminal tramper" from the respectable working man tramping in search of work' (Steedman 1984: 57). George Grey defended the 1856 Act by saying 'whatever would give protection to property must give increased value to property' (quoted in ibid.: 62).

From the 1833 Factory Act onwards – and subsequent legislation extends the reach of regulation by defining more and more places of work as 'factories' within the meaning of the 1833 Act – a major classification of age and gender categories is enshrined, with enormous consequences. The labour force is henceforth split between: children; young persons and women; and adult men. The first category have to be protected (their definition, in turn, relates increasingly to the statutorily defined school-leaving age); the second category have to be regulated; only the third group are capable of making 'free' contracts. We have commented on one wider context for this, the general disabilities of married women regarding property ownership and contractual rights through to the twentieth century (chapter 1). This gender classification is also woven into the very first form of state-provided education, in Poor Law schools, and extends through the advice provided by HMIs in relation to grants-in-aid for other schools after 1839. With the specific exception of textiles (and even here the divisions around 'skill' are important) women were effectively driven from a wide variety of waged employments, at precisely the same time as a dominant domestic ideology was being established for bourgeois ladies and respectable, responsible working-class wives.[28] The massive employment category for single women was domestic service (on the general continuities of unfree labour categories cf. Corrigan 1977b). As late as 1881 'servants of both sexes represented one in 22 of the whole population. . . . They were 34 per cent of all women employed in 1891 and still 23 per cent in 1930' (Davidoff 1974: 310; cf. her 1973). Much of what became known (and is still known) as 'women's work' extends the 'caring' and 'support-ing' practices seen as central to domesticity and housewifery: nursing, elementary school teaching, clerical grades within the civil service, catering and, of course, secretarial work. Since women were not 'given' the vote until 1918 (and then only if over 30) their effective seclusion from social life is severely marked. Whatever the (complex) origins of this dual structuring – of both 'work' and 'home' – by gender, it is difficult to underestimate the (continuing) role of state regulation, through such enshrined classifications, in routinely con-certing it. This is cultural revolution: we are talking not just of 'ideologies', but of the regulated formation of identities and subjecti-vities (male as much as female).

This is an appropriate note on which to move to that theory and practice of representation we first drew from Helen Cam in relation to what was specific to the Parliament of the English, and its novel (and yet not so) inflection in the nineteenth century. Two preliminary emphases are in order. Speaking crudely, socialist (and sociological) theories of 'the State' have tended to move between two poles: state as force, state as consent. Both have been at one time or another violently abstracted: 'hegemony' is now used as a noun and sails through time, much as 'bodies of armed men, prisons, etc.' had done for too long before. The roots of the 'force' theory, we suggest, lie in the thoroughly correct repudiation of states' own consensual-authority claims: the project of defining, mapping, naming 'reality' –

the state's statements – we have argued is fundamental to state formation. Beneath the 'appearance' of consent, it is argued – in a favourite and fatal dichotomizing figure – the state 'really' rules by force. So it does: 'hegemony' is not self-securing, it is constructed, sustained, reconstructed, by particular agents and agencies, in part by violence. But force and will, coercion and consent, cannot thus be separated either. Whilst we should reject states' claims as description – they are, precisely, claims – we need equally to recognize them as material empowerments, as emphases which cartographize and condition the relations they help organize. Here, as elsewhere, to adapt an old sociological maxim, what is defined as real (which is not to say the definitions are uncontested) is real in its consequences.

Which brings us to the substantive point: the grand claims of Englishness – slipping into Britishness, with the emphasis on 'Greater' (in all senses) from the 1850s and beyond – and the minutiae of a thousand skirmishes around habits and mentalities, which seek to define what it is to *be* (properly) English/British, are part of the energy of power. Central to such conceptualizations, as we have indicated all too briefly, are evaluative comparisons. These may be 'internal': well-ordered nations are like well-ordered families, political economy is to the former like domestic economy is to the latter (hence talk of 'the nation's purse'). Or they may be 'external' (and more or less stridently chauvinistic): 'We English' excel at this or that obvious virtue. 'Character' and 'duty' are key notions which sinew together on the one hand the personal forms of conduct and belief (the premium always being on the former) and on the other the ethical ideas established as institutions, which achieves its final philosophizing in the latter part of the nineteenth century. (Certain) personal modes of conduct, orientations to action in Weber's terms, are sanctified as national characteristics. Twenty years ago Philip Abrams acknowledged this:

It is impossible not to see how decisively political life is conditioned by national character.
    I use the term national character deliberately.
    . . . much of what political sociologists are doing is little more than an attempt to explain systematically what an older generation had in mind when they spoke of national character or used terms like 'not ready for democracy' (1964: 54)

This latter term – 'democracy' – is of the greatest significance since more than any other it has enabled a particular discourse to become the medium of discussion. What could, after all, be more just than 'one man, one vote'? Well – and this is our second preliminary point – we could pay serious attention to how all such terms ignore the degree to which society is organized through gendered relations and how these neutralizing terms, the more general ethos in which they are embedded, and the eventual materialization of this ethos in institutions all orient themselves towards a social figure in dominance who is *a man*. Here, at least, it is explicit: 'one man, one vote' meant just that (see Harrison 1978). This man of the practical sociology of the franchise – and what a sociology it was! – is at one, of course, with the 'Man' of the famous Declarations. Masculinity here is not 'merely' a matter of 'linguistics': we are talking of *His*tory and Hu*man*ity, not because of the etymology of the words, but because of what they have come to signify, their practical cognitive and evaluative connotations. Women may have been subsequently 'admitted' into these grand abstractions, so that the latter can appear as generic categories (or more accurately, generics are now seen as having to 'include' the other half of the human race – an advance of sorts). But this 'admission' (analogous to that in which labour was allowed into 'representative democracy') was ever partial – recalling the Declarations, we should also recall that in 1983, over two hundred years after 'We hold these truths to be self-evident, that every man has . . .', the Equal Rights Amendment to the US Constitution (outlawing sexual discrimination in any form, i.e. seeking to make 'Man' and 'His Rights' genuinely generic) failed to pass Congress. And such 'admission', as importantly, came after these social classifications had been pre-formed, organized, given their meaning, made 'obvious' in their reference and signification, stabilized and solidified, through a longer making of regulated gender identities.

Central to this making has been, as we have tried to indicate (again too briefly) at various points in this book, multiple forms and theatres of doctrinal, political and administrative power and regulation from 'time out of mind'. The representative state is, in its very constitution, a male institution, reflecting and regulating that wider structuring of and by gender which is one major constituent defining what (and who, and on what terms) enters into 'public life'. We are not talking here simply of the numbers of women in Parliament or other 'public' institutions (though that is itself significant) but of the very meaning – intrinsically gendered – that 'public life' has. The 'Mortall God' is sexed (just as He is classed, raced, tongued, penned, styled, dressed). If He – to adapt both Durkheim and Hobbes – represents society, it is a very particular form of 'Society' that is held up as an object of worship and emulation.

To return to our narrative. Democracy arises precisely in that complex 'moment' when 'Society' recognizes society and in that recognition attempts the dis- and re-organization of the latter. It marks a transition from 'the political nation' to 'the nation'. The grand metaphor of 'the constitution' serves to handle this transition and the resulting theory and practice of representation handles the more massive contradiction surrounding the moral individualization of labour with which we began this chapter. That England produced a Labour Party (formed, in part, from a Labour Representation Committee based within the Trades Union Congress) is one product of this handling, as we will indicate in our next chapter.

In Helen Cam's depiction of the theory and practice of representation at the time of Parliament's initial stabilization as a set of political forms, there is no space for the organized expression of interests that are below the horizon of 'the national' or above the ceiling of the locally represented collectives (geographically defined) within the represented. Burke, who was no fool, could have been writing then when he argued in 1774 that Parliament should be seen as:

a *deliberative* assembly of *one* nation, with *one* interest, that of the whole – where not local purposes, not local prejudices, ought to guide but the general good, resulting from the general reason of the whole. (quoted in Beer 1957: 615)

There are some remarkable manuscript annotations on these and other speeches of Burke by Jeremy Bentham and it was against Orator Burke (among others) that Bentham was happy to be called 'Leveller' and 'Jacobin' in his 1817 articles in the *Pamphleteer*. That contrast, written out in terms of many others, has formed a complete false historiography of Radicalism in general, and its approach to franchise reform in particular.[29]

Buried within the principle of utility is a contradiction and a concealment. The concealment is one we have remarked on previously: who is the judge of what 'the greatest good' might be? But the contradiction is part and parcel of that. It was first highlighted by Halevy in 1934 (a study completed after his brilliant sketches of state formation from the 1780s through to the early 1840s). As rapidly as Bentham attacked any natural-law basis for law, for social relations, Smith's followers demonstrated a natural-law basis for social relations; as Bentham smashed fictions in the social realm, Smith's followers established them. Two points seem insufficiently to have been taken up in the ensuing puzzlement. First, all radical bourgeois theorists articulated three projects (summed up, of course as one – Progress): firstly, against the existing philosophies and practices governing social arrangements where forms of landed property (and the Crown and aristocracy) held power, secondly against forms of labour's property (in part protected by paternalistic legislation), and thirdly for a society which would be really open (for them). In this, Benthamite radicalism and Smithian radicalism had different targets. But they were part of this shared project, only applied to different features of social relations: crudely, Bentham's critique applied to those features of existing social order and its legitimations which were obstacles to that which Smith's followers sanctified as natural law in the 'economic' realm. We are suggesting that this has the greatest possible significance for the novel and continuing aspects of state formation *and* the content and justifying rhetorics of its culturally revolutionary features. Second, these are not, our argument suggests, 'merely' contradictions of texts, of communications, of intellect. They register correctly the contradictions entailed in the project itself.

Two commentators catch the point exactly. Halevy stresses the fictional illusion at the heart of Benthamism:

the Radical State as defined by Bentham's Utilitarianism is a state which confers sovereignty on the people; after which the people finds itself constrained to delegate a certain number of political functions to a minority of individuals, elected directly or indirectly. (1934: 409)

Both he (ibid.: 414ff.) and Coates suggest the doubling of this strategy we have often remarked upon in this chapter. For the latter the desired reforms:

would sweep away obstacles to the spontaneous activities of the middle class in whose virtues he [Bentham] believed; they would release energies in the economic sphere where the identity of interests was conceived as natural. (1950: 360)

But it is James Mill's work, from the 1808 *Commerce defended* through the 1817 *History of British India* (with its focus on the 'machinery of government'; cf. Halevy 1934: 271; W. Thomas 1969: 258), to the famous *Essay on government*, that spells out this new theory and practice most clearly. And it is to the work of D. C. Moore and W. Thomas that we owe its clarification. We need to place the discovery of a particular form of political democracy, entailing a stabilization of the forms of proper politics, within not only the wider contexts of social formation, but specifically inside the contours of the constructed 'public' we briefly discussed above. Halevy (1934: 419) and W. Thomas (1969: 254; cf. Carr 1971, 1972; W. Thomas 1971b, 1974) stress how James Mill's *Essay on government* (1820) simultaneously discusses universal representation and a limited suffrage. Thomas and D. C. Moore (1969: 12) also clarify how the *Essay* involves a sociological understanding of the ballot. In sum, democracy will allow representation whilst flexibly stabilizing (the first term as important as the second) bases and forms of power: what Mill called 'the grand discovery of modern times, the system of representation' will accomplish both. The secret ballot was required because of 'diseased habits' (quoted in W. Thomas 1969: 280; cf. Halevy 1934: 405), and because the means of the ballot would 'moralize' the effective influences in society (Moore 1969:12).

Kinzer (1982) however shows how complex the question of the secret ballot actually was. When finally adopted the Ballot Act of 1872 ran for eight years only. It was annually renewed from 1880, only being enacted without term from 1918. Kinzer argues the secret ballot was the price Gladstone paid for having Bright in his Cabinet. But of most interest to our argument is the case that was put against it. Secret voting was loudly proclaimed to be very un-English. Voting, it was argued, should be public because those who possessed the franchise 'spoke for' those who did not. John Stuart Mill, *opposing* the ballot, argued that how a vote was cast was additionally of legitimate concern to other electors because it was an exercise of power. The continuing resonance of both the theatricality of political ritual which we drew attention to in the eighteenth century (and in Adam Smith), and very much older English notions of representation, are well illustrated here.

James Mill once defined universal suffrage as 'collecting the public opinion' (recall how that was defined in 1828, as we indicated above) 'in the most perfect possible manner . . . upon one particular point, not abstract, not complicated – Who are the fittest men to administer the affairs of government?' (quoted in W. Thomas 1969: 273). One of the key passages in the *Essay* carries this further:

if the whole mass of people who have some property would make a good choice, it will hardly be pretended that, added to them, the comparatively small number who have none, *and whose minds are naturally and almost necessarily governed by the minds of those who have*, would be able to make the choice a bad one. (quoted in ibid.: 253; Moore 1969: 10; and by Halevy 1934: 423 with the emphasized passage missing)

The man who proceeds to the scene of an election with the reverence in his heart, which the moral influence of property implies, will not be deserted of that moral impulse, when he places his vote in secrecy. (quoted in W. Thomas 1969: 281)

J. S. Mill – the well-known Radical – defined a natural state of society as being attained when:

those whose opinions the people follow, whose feelings they imbibe, and who practically and by common consent, perform, no matter under what original title, the office of thinking for the people, are persons better qualified than any other. (quoted in Moore 1969: 15)

We might remember what for Durkheim 'defines the state' here. Moore goes on to quote (ibid.: 29) J. S. Mill's argument against a wider suffrage in 1854, while W. Thomas argues (1971a) that by the 1830s J. S. Mill was pledged to an 'Aristocracy of Talent'.

We have to read these texts properly, and not through 'twentieth-century' eyes. First, in discussing the people they are discussing men, of property. Second, they are arguing a series of connections between property and morality and a hierarchy of worth within the ranks of the morally worthy men who possess property. We need in this context to reinterpret the connection between philosophical radicalism (and more generally reform) and the Whigs (cf. Beales 1974). This is the central argument of D. C. Moore, collected in his book *Politics of deference* (1976) but traceable in his articles from 1961 onwards, which have had much influence on our general argument about state-formation-as-cultural-revolution in this chapter. In brief, Moore is arguing that the movements of reform sought to perpetuate certain 'communities' – hierarchies of power centring on admixture of moral worth and ideological leadership – whilst allowing the rapid spread of new relations in production. Such perspectives typically conflate two separate 'justifications': why forms of government are needed at all (where individualism and self-interest are used) and why certain people govern in certain ways (where the social and moral influence of property and talent justify class rule).

Halevy in the 1920s (1923b: 63; supported by modern work, such as that of D. C. Moore, Nossiter 1970a, b, c; 1976; Aydelotte, 1962 onwards) showed how little the elected Commons after 1832 differed from that before the Reform Act:

the first Reformed Parliament, returned by a middle class electorate, was like its predecessors a Parliament the overwhelming majority of whose members were country gentlemen and members of the aristocracy.

Sir George Young argued in 1867, in his 'The House of Commons in 1833', that the 'Aristocratic Element' was 326 members. A contemporary opinion strikes us as accurate:

The promoters of the Reform Bill projected it, not with a view to subvert, or even remodel our aristocratic institutions, but to consolidate them by a reinforcement of sub-aristocracy from the middle classes. (*Poor Man's Guardian*, 25 October 1832; quoted in Thompson 1968: 893)

The Reform struggles were essentially a struggle for public opinion (in that nineteenth-century sense we have severally clarified): a resisting 'aristocracy' had to be persuaded – including by a threatening 'mob' (Hamburger 1963) – to give a little in order to save a lot. The actual minute extension of the franchise was largely symbolic (the complementary reduction in propertyless voters was not). Recent historiography has found a considerable degree of 'willingness' (we are thinking of Gramsci's use of this term) on the part of Whig and some Tory aristocrats, including some evidence of their initiating activity in relation to administrative reform. As important is an older view which sees the 1830s changes as confirming and strengthening the sovereignty of Parliament. J. S. Mill, once again, clarifies the strategic orientation of:

Radicalism: That the essentials of it are not only reconcilable, but naturally allied, with all that was venerable or deserving of attachment in the doctrine and practices handed down to us from those ancestors, and those great teachers, whom they [the Conservatives] delight to honour; That it is the pretended apostles of those traditional opinions and institutions who dishonour them; That the low objects to which they prostitute them, and the low grounds on which they defend them, are loosening the hold which those old ideas had on the intellects and on the affections of mankind, and sinking what is good and noble in them, along with what is effete or despicable, into a common contempt; that it is the Radical view of them alone which can save them; That to be ever again objects of veneration in this New World, these Old Things must be seen with the eyes of radicals; That they must reconcile themselves with Radicalism, must fill themselves to overflowing with its spirit; That Conservatives must adopt the radical creed into their own creed – and discard all with which that creed is essentially incompatible, if they would save that in their own which is true and precious, from being lost to the world, overwhelmed in an unequal contest. (1838b: 502)

Similar arguments as we have advanced here apply to the reorganization of municipal government from the 1830s onwards. The 1835 Municipal Reform Act established a standard form of borough council, empowered (amongst other things) to control police and make by-laws. The councils had some financial autonomy (through rates) but in other matters (e.g. raising of loans) required Treasury authorization. The electoral qualification was householders of three years' standing who paid the poor rate; this was a narrower franchise than that established for Parliamentary elections by the 1832 Reform Act, but 'was wide enough to let into the municipal electorate most of the wealthier merchants and industrialists of the large towns' (Thomson 1950: 73). This is less an erosion of traditional oligarchies than their selective, sponsored augmentation. A similar 'logic' is at work in the shift of administrative responsibility under the 1834 Poor Law

Amendment Act from parishes to (restrictively elected) Boards of Poor Law Guardians, on which, however, JPs had the right to sit *ex officio*.

The cultural revolution which we see state formation as entailing is, then, well illustrated in the forms of state regulation and provision centring upon the slow, protracted, complex acculturation which franchise reform, party formation, and all of official politics involve. Older sociologies such as Miall's *The franchise as the means of a people's education* (1851; cf. Peel 1971: 71ff.), from a different perspective, James Hole's 'Light, more light!' (1860; cf. J. F. C. Harrison 1954), or Monkton Milne's 'On the admission of the working classes as part of our social system' (along with other texts in the 1867 *Essays on reform*), and recent work such as Herrick (1948), D. C. Moore, and Davis (1974), have shown how in public debate, newspaper discussion and private correspondence 'Society' very, very carefully calibrated the extensions of the 1830s democracy–representation system. Questions of 'worthiness' remained central. A transformation of the notion of property from profitable property to fixed properties (and hence the establishment of a rating qualification that introduced men without property in the Smithian/Benthamite sense) makes sense within this project. So does the continued total ignoring of women, fitting with their general subordination, their invisible 'status' in the discourses of politics and law. The shift to the household-head encapsulates both, and broadcasts a new, wider, notion of propriety. It was clearly understood through the late 1840s to the late 1860s that this would add to the electorate working-class men, but – and the degree of agonizing sociologically here over the specifics is very instructive – it was felt, in the end, that this (mild) representation of labour would be unlikely to damage the 'true interests of property' because those who had the vote would be respectable men.

An adequate account of all this would have to work carefully forward to describe, document and delineate the significantly new dialectic at work in all periods after the 1830s. There is no longer only the continuing significance of ruling perspectives and philosophies to take seriously. In addition the categorial frameworks and substantive evidence provided by state forms of identifying and collecting facts have to be properly integrated.[30] The complexity of cumulating bodies of argument needs also to be stressed. Moving through Spencer's 'Proper sphere of government' (1842), through *Social statics* (1851), to his later work, like *The man and the state* (1884), quoted earlier, one finds (as Spencer's own 'Filiation of ideas' (1899) makes clear) a set of emphases which cannot be read and understood simply as they stand. Spencer's work with Sturge and Miall, for the Complete Suffrage Union, only makes sense if we understand the kind of state (his life's theme as he explains himself, part and parcel of the secularization of morals) he thought was necessary. Equally J. S. Mill's work, over a similar time-span – he and Spencer corresponded about franchise reform in the 1860s in an instructive way – needs to be interpreted with a similar stress on complexity and contradiction from the 1838 and 1840 essays on Bentham and Coleridge through the *Principles of political economy* of 1848 to the famous *Representative government* of 1861, and beyond. J. S. Mill is always discussing the paradigm we drew from his work above. Just as the 'general law' of *laissez-faire* has clearly indicated exceptions – notably education and more generally law itself – so too does the ability of individuals in relation to voting have to be seen as specified in terms of their moral worth and their rationality. (Recall Hill's comment on the latter, quoted above.) In 1848, J. S. Mill had argued that the future depended on the degree to which the working classes could be *made* rational beings; Roach (1957), Ryan (1974) and – crucially – Wolfe (1975) show how *Representative government* (the words of the title are extremely important, of course) registers some doubts (1861: ch. 5) about whether this is in fact possible. Wolfe makes much of the essay 'Centralisation' by J. S. Mill in the *Edinburgh Review* (published anonymously, as was typical, and excluded from Mill's *Collected Works*) in 1862. Here Mill makes clear that there are different problems as between the authority of law and the authority of office and it is always 'the mode of State interference' which is 'crucial'. But a different side of the recognition is provided in Mill's 'chapters on socialism' which, although written in 1869, were first published by Harriet Taylor in the *Fortnightly Review* in 1879. There J. S. Mill, implicitly at least, answers exactly what his father had argued in 'The state of the nation' in 1826:

The classes, which the system of society makes subordinate, have little reason to put faith in any of the maxims which the same system of society may have established as principles. (quoted in Briggs 1978: 69)[31]

The whole debate around the franchise (cf. Blewett 1965; and R. Barker 1978 for the post-1885 situation, which more properly belongs in our next chapter) needs to be informed by these wider perspectives which while seen as context for us, this side of the instrumentality of their moral project, were part of the *content* of that supreme moral act: the vote. We have already indicated how protracted was the making of the nation of citizens: the end of plural voting based on property rights came with the elections of 1950 (like many of its predecessors, but for the first time with *some* justification, the relevant statute was called The Representation of the People Act). This still left those far from ⁱⁿconsequential 'residues', the House of Lords (with that forgotten 'third element' the Crown – and the Privy Council – actually constituting two-thirds of what we too rapidly misrecognize as Parliamentary democracy) and the City of London. This is not to mention judges appointed for life (until 1959, when 75 was fixed as the age of retirement) or the host of other features of the remaining nomination-patronage system which complements that permanent civil service which the 1830s made possible, or at least began. It should however be said with some emphasis that before 1918 the national electorate was 'only about 60 per cent of adult males', with, of course, no women voters at all. 1832, 1867, 1884 extended the votes to men of property, certain householders in urban constituencies, and their brothers-in-patriarchy in the counties, respectively (Clarke 1982: 51). This is because this 'corresponded to widely accepted notions of what was fit and proper':

The head of household exemplified a well-formed concept of citizenship . . . [which] gave a coherent social logic to the ground of qualification for the vote. (ibid.)

This concept of citizenship is not unrelated to the 'social logic' of the 'family wage' policy that had also gathered ground from the 1830s on, and which was integral to the gendering of employment discussed earlier, nor to the wider exclusion of women from the discourses of politics and law. It is also as well to recall how any involvement with the Poor Law, including for some years medical treatment, led to the loss of the franchise (matched, perfectly, by JPs' right to sit *ex officio* on Boards of the Poor Law Guardians).

By 1886, when Gladstone told a Liverpool crowd how 'all the world over' he would 'back the masses against the classes' (quoted in Briggs 1978: 71), we are in a new territory. But nothing could confirm better what we have been arguing than the same Gladstone describing how the 1867 Reform needs to be understood as entailing a reconceptualization of the new voters as 'fellow Christians, our own flesh and blood', and the remarks of, fittingly, the Chancellor of the Exchequer arguing for the 1867 Act:

I believe those persons whom we ask you to enfranchise ought rather to be welcomed as you would recruits to your army or children to your family. (quoted in Lazonick 1978: 23)[32]

We have already discussed the imperial context of these changes (following Harcourt 1980). The registration of (some) working-class men as soldiers/children extends that rich set of terms and signs through which the subordinated are welcomed into the political nation – The Nation now – firmly placed under the Law of the Father, all the better that these, the last of 'new men', can constrain and culture as patriarchs and non-commissioned officers within the army of labour and their 'own' households. Such imagery endures: in that last imperial fling, the Falklands war, for Mrs Thatcher – Mother to the Nation? – the troops were never anything but 'our boys'.

Two final points in this area are of some importance. First – to repeat an earlier general emphasis – what we have been saying applies very much to the English state 'at home' (which alas includes within the statistics and reach of the thinking the whole of Wales). The orientation to franchise extensions, as much in the local (Keith-Lucas 1977; Dunbabin 1977; Dearlove 1979) as in the national/central focus, was always mediated by a clear sense that it was English ideas, institutions, forms and, not infrequently, people that should rule. Franchise extension before 1918 was always statistically less in Scotland and Ireland than in England (and we suspect the same applies to Wales, but the figures do not most of the time allow this separation). The vast empire beyond 'the United Kingdom of Great Britain and Ireland' (later 'and Northern Ireland') had no representation at Westminster at all. The Mother of Parliaments never quite got around to furthering those procedures, instead – and oriented very specifically to some parts of the empire (those now 'White Dominions' because of the genocide of the indigenous peoples) – some limited sovereignty was granted. In subsequent work (Corrigan) we shall show just how limited – and how formed from London – that sovereignty was. While on the subject of empire, we might wryly note that despite centuries of resistance within England to reform movements which sought clarification of the law in the interests of access and limitation of its 'superb flexibility', 'much of the common law was codified between 1830 and the 1860s for use in India' (Baker 1979: 190).

Secondly, the Chancellor's reference to the Army is pertinent in this connection for three further reasons. First, there is the slaughter of non-English people in defence of the English nation state (cf. Hanham 1973, Bond 1974, Lloyd 1974). Second, it relates to a general claim – then as now – that the appropriate model of factory, farm, office or school discipline was military (cf. Weber 1920c: 261, which anticipates Gorz, Braverman, Beynon and others). Third, officer-peers in the House of Lords extend through the nineteenth century as follows: 1837, 10 per cent; 1853, 15 per cent; 1855, 27 per cent; 1898, 35 per cent (Harries-Jenkins 1973). Young's 1867 analysis of the 1833 Parliament gives 271 military and naval personnel (which he, significantly, includes within the wider 326 'Aristocratical Element') of a total of 652 MPs. To this day, and not only in its self-imagery, the male English ruling class significantly centres on 'officers and gentlemen'. There remains a significant permeation of these ex-Army, ex-Naval (latterly ex-RAF) 'types' through the political and adminis-trative elite, centrally and sometimes far more powerfully locally (not least in relation to regional seats of government, emergency service officers, and the whole panoply of a Gauleiter state which repeated struggles have shown to be waiting in the depths to inherit the earth).

So much for how 'our' Members of Parliament came to be able to claim to represent all of us, and how we by marking a piece of paper (correctly marking it, that is) are joined together in the magic religious ceremonial of virtual representation. How simple it once was, moving cardboard figures across a chessboard, to see 'the aristocracy' defeated by 1832 and the 'bourgeoisie' defeated by 1867 and 1884 (and patriarchy by 1918 and 1929?); certainly that is what Fabian history (the Fabian Society being formed in January 1884) would like us to think. Despite certain claims – centrally those of the middle class themselves – it is time we returned to Marx's recognition (echoing that of the *Poor Man's Guardian* which we quoted above) in 1855 that 1832 was equally a victory for the old regime. Althorp, the man who introduced the Poor Law Amendment Act, said that 1832 was 'the most aristocratic act ever offered to the nation' (quoted in Marx 1855: 452). For Lord John Russell 'the object of the Reform Bill was to increase the predominance of the landed interest' (quoted in ibid.: 454). Nassau Senior could argue, in a letter to de Tocqueville in the 1860s,

The Poor Law Amendment Act was a heavier blow to the aristocracy than the Reform Act. The Reform Act principally affected the aristocracy of wealth. . . . The Poor Law Act dethroned the country gentlemen. (quoted in Beales 1931)

But, apart from the general studies we cited above (principally Arnstein and D.C. Moore), Brundage and others have shown the enormous continuing power of the landed interest and the country gentlemen (Brundage 1972, 1974, 1975, 1978; Digby 1975, 1976, 1977, 1978) throughout the nineteenth century.

If Parliament has been one major thread running through this book, 'the law' has been another, and some brief observations on changes – and continuities – after 1780 are called for here. Agents and agencies of law remain major forms of rule. We should record, to begin with, a thread of argument – of justifying rhetoric which bears little relation to actual practice – which concurs with Dugald Stewart's quotation from a manuscript of Adam Smith in 1755 that the only activities of government should be 'peace, easy taxes, and a tolerable administration of justice' (quoted in Paul 1979: 31). In 1842 Spencer argued, 'if it be conceded that the administration of justice is the only duty of the state, we are at once relieved of one of the greatest objections to the enfranchisement of the working class' (1842, quoted in Peel 1971: 281, n. 74). That's fine, providing we forget (as it encourages us to) the property qualification for jury service – from 1665 to 1972[33] – the nomination–patronage system for judges (Griffith 1975, 1977a, b), and the (continuing) power of the House of Lords as the highest judicial court in the land (Stevens 1979, Jowell 1979).[34] John Griffith reproduces data from an unpublished doctorate (1977b: 25) on the social class origins of the senior judiciary from 1820 to 1968, which, with data he examines for this same period and beyond it until the 1970s, he summarizes as showing that 'in broad terms, four out of five full-time professional judges are products of public schools, and of Oxford and Cambridge' (1977a: 633). Between 1820 and 1968 an average of 15.3 per cent came from the traditional landed upper class and a further 12.7 per cent from the professional, commercial and administrative class (that is numerically, 59 and 49 respectively), and 47.4 per cent from the wider upper-middle class (that is, 183). Taking these three categories together we have 75.4 per cent (or 291 members) of the senior judiciary from 1820 to 1968. These were all men.

Judges are of course appointed, by the Prime Minister on the advice of the Lord Chancellor. As a mild empirical aside, we might remark that the Lord Chancellor always received a higher salary than the Prime Minister and sits on a Woolsack 'chairing' the House of Lords quite differently from the way a Prime Minister organizes the business of the House of Commons, which is chaired by 'the Speaker' – the latter office being continuous from the reign of Richard II. One Lord Chancellor, Lord Halsbury – the editor and founder of the famous *Statutes* series[35] – held office for three periods totalling 17 years between 1885 and 1905. The present incumbent of the office, Lord Hailsham, alias Mr Q. M. Hogg, then again Lord Hailsham of St Marylebone, has had a very good run for our money, his theses on 'elective dictatorship' (*The Times*, 15 October 1976; cf. Griffith 1975) apparently having lapsed from his memory since 1979.

We should note augmentation of judicial powers – as more and more procedures are regulated by law – and specifically how Acts of 1840 (for Chancery) and 1875 (generally) empowered the judiciary to make and alter rules of procedure. The Common Law Procedure Act of 1854, which allowed the possibility (in civil cases) of trial of facts by judge alone, led to the gradual disappearance of the civil jury (and arguably, through a parallel erosion of the boundaries between issues of fact and issues of law, encouraged a revival of 'judge-made law' (cf. Baker 1979: 81–2)). This is 'capped off' by the law lords being empowered since 1966, through a Practice Statement (3 All ER 77), to overrule their own precedents. Conversely we should register, from the 1830s, a certain Erastianization. Abolition of the old writs of summons, and their replacement by uniform writ in 1832, led in Baker's view to a closure in 'the categories of legal thought . . . where once the law might have developed through the recognition of new writs it is now left at the mercy of commissions and an overworked Parliament' (ibid.: 61). In 1875 the old courts were merged in a single High Court of Justice, initially (to avoid compulsorily retiring the Chief Justice of Common Pleas and the Chief Baron of the Exchequer, which would have been 'unconstitutional') with five divisions, reduced to three by Order-in-Council after their deaths in 1880.

The period from the 1780s onward also saw other, interlinked changes in the pattern of eighteenth-century 'moral policing'. There is an extensive literature on this which we do not have space to reproduce here.[36] The major developments we would highlight are as follows. In the 1820s and 1830s there was, first, a marked shift in kinds of punishment. The 'bloody code' of eighteenth-century England was substantially repealed: where there had been over 200 capital offences on the stature book in 1800, by 1841 there were only eight. Transportation to America had ceased to be an option after 1776; transportation to Australia was suspended in 1853. From the 1830s imprisonment increasingly became the usual form of punishment for most crimes, and prisons – 'penitentiaries' – a very visible part of the urban landscape of England, joining those other 'objects of terror', the workhouses. Older historiography (up to and including Radzinowicz 1948/68) sees here only enlightenment, humanism and the inexorable march of progress. Recent work (inspired by Foucault 1977) interprets the change rather as a shift in *forms* of discipline, from the theatrical repertoire of the eighteenth century – the doctines of maximum penalties selectively (and publicly) applied, ably defended by Archdeacon Paley – to a more 'rationalized' (and specifically bourgeois) system of graduated punishments applied uniformly, and mainly behind prison walls, with a view to reforming the mind and character of the individual offender. It is as likely that the impetus came from a diversity of factors, ranging from the reluctance of juries to convict felons when death was the main penalty on offer, through fears of public disorder on 'hanging days', to the perennial dread of typhus spreading from the hulks moored in the Thames (themselves introduced as a 'temporary' expedient when transportation to the

American colonies became unavailable as a punishment after 1776). Conrad's characterization of penal evolution as a story of 'witless drift' has a ring of truth about it.

There are new 'scientific' penologies – Bentham's Panopticon (adapted, incidentally, from a scheme Jeremy's brother Samuel had pioneered for surveillance of labour, while supervising the dockyards of Prince Potemkin in Russia), the 'separate system' of secluding offenders, regimes of silence (Henriques 1972, Tomlinson 1978, 1981, DeLacy 1981, Evans 1981) – together with a specifically moral, reformatory focus consonant with the wider educational ethos of the Radicals. These had some impact on policy, as in the design and discipline of Pentonville. To this extent, Foucauldian arguments are pertinent. But they need qualification, considered as an account of what actually occurred. Bentham's Panopticon was never built in England; and 'the penitentiary, which had been introduced in the 1840s as an instrument for remaking human character, survived into the late 19th century by virtue of its penal features' (Ignatieff 1978: 204). It is as well to recall also that the last hanging, drawing and quartering in England took place at Derby in 1817, and the last public hanging in 1868, whilst as late as 1900 9 per cent of adult offenders found guilty of indictable offences were whipped (Halsey 1972). In the case of juveniles, the comparable figure is 14.4 percent in 1910, and 9.9 per cent in 1920, betraying the differential age classification we have remarked before. It remains, of course, a 'peculiarity' of the English that Britain is one of the last countries in Europe where schoolchildren can legally be beaten.

In the same period, recognizably modern – professional, bureaucratic – police forces were established, under the control of stipendiary magistrates (a new development; JPs were unpaid), initially in London. Early attempts at this were the Middlesex Justices Act of 1792 and the setting up of the Thames Police Office in 1800; after this date there were nine 'police magistrates' in the metropolitan area, controlling seven small police forces, who were responsible to the Home Secretary. These magistrates had enhanced powers of arrest and summary conviction, notably under the Vagrancy Act of 1744; legislation of the 1820s further strengthened these powers. Stipendiary magistrates spread: Salford in 1805, Manchester 1813, Merthyr Tydfil 1829, and many other conurbations in the 1830s and 1840s. The big shift to a 'modern' police force came however with Peel's Metropolitan Police Act of 1829. It is noteworthy that Peel drew extensively, in framing this Act, on his experience as Chief Secretary for Ireland (where he had pioneered such a force) in 1814. Further legislation (1835, 1839) allowed for the pattern to be extended elsewhere, but only after 1856 was establishment of constabularies mandatory. A related change concerned prosecution: Acts of 1778 and (particularly) 1826 allowed prosecution costs to be reimbursed. Philips (1980: 180) gives figures for 1805 onwards showing (for England and Wales) a sharp upward trend in committals for trial on indictment: for 1805, 4,605; for 1820, 13,710; for 1830, 18,107. These are less likely to reflect a rising 'crime wave' (though reformers portrayed them as such) than the shift in methods of law enforcement. The wider moral context of all this, however, is what most needs to be remembered. Blackstone's notion of policing was not dead, only the forms had changed. The objective is ably expressed by Colquhoun, disciple of Bentham, police magistrate himself, and a tireless exponent of the 'new police':

And it is no inconsiderable feature in the science of Police to encourage, protect, and control such as tend to innocent recreation, to preserve the good humour of the Public, and to *give the minds of the People a right bias*. . . . Since recreation is necessary to Civilized Society, all Public Exhibitions should be rendered subservient to the improvement of morals, and to the means of infusing into the mind a love of the Constitution, and a reverence and respect for the Laws. . . . How superior this to the odious practice of besotting themselves in Ale-houses, hatching seditious and treasonable designs, or engaging in pursuits of the vilest profligacy, destructive to health and morals. (quoted in Philips 1980: 177)

It needs again to be emphasized that here, as elsewhere, there are no clean breaks. These reforms, in particular the establishment of the 'new police', were trenchantly resisted, both from below and from within the ranks of 'Society'. The innovations spread very slowly; and certain continuities from the eighteenth century and before were very marked. A number of commentators grasp this (on the pattern more generally, see Darvall 1934: ch. 12; Mather 1959):

the landlords are . . . the true rulers of the English provinces. From among them according to long-established custom, was chosen the body of justices of the peace. (Halevy 1912: 37)

This is said of 1815. As one writer observed in 1862, 'At the first whisper of duty, magistrates act, county magistrates assemble and volunteers turn out' (quoted in Spring 1963: 275). Magistrates continued to be, in large measure, 'the State' until the later nineteenth century (Marshall 1974). General (Zangerl 1971) and specific studies (Warwickshire, Quinault 1974; Lancashire, D. Foster 1974; Buckinghamshire, Lubenow 1977) stress two features. First, magistrates as agents of order, a particular order mixing their local status/power and a more general regulation of themselves by changing patterns in the laws protecting and legitimating certain forms of property; second, the extremely gradual, complex, slow transformation between country-gentry rule and the arrival of a different category of 'social leaders' (Lee 1963: 5; Lubenow 1977: 251). Slowly, very, very slowly, country gentry become social leaders who in turn become professional experts; in fact, we would want to argue, the class and gender backgrounds of the third group differ only slightly from the first.

This slowness of 'rationalization' is well illustrated by the spread of the 'new' police. Steedman (1984) shows a continuing mixture of forms, old and new, an 'extraordinary patchwork' to recall Aylmer's depiction of the previous century, for long after the initiating reforms of 1829 and beyond. For instance the permissive Rural Police Act of 1839 had resulted in a pattern by the 1850s: 18 counties had established constabularies, 7 further counties only for some districts, but 13 had made use of later legislation (1842, 1850) to sustain and strengthen the ancient system of parish constables. Thirteen boroughs had not changed from the old system as late as 1856, despite the mandatory 1835 Act. And after 1856 'Additional Constables' paid by private owners 'permanently stationed to protect specific pieces of property' numbered up to 25 per cent of Northern County and Borough Forces (p. 46). The median relationship of police to people was as follows: 1858, 1:1,406; 1868, 1:1,275; 1878, 1:1,221; but these figures (p. 50) include all those working for the police as if they were 'on the beat'. Steedman brings out clearly the dialectic of making power regular in the relation of centre and locality, yet another side of the ruling-class dance of the period. Centrally, officers – authorized, regularized, legitimated and inspected; locally, representatives – locally empowered and sometimes elected. This is the 'old, old' sheriff problem again! The traditional 'political nation' is alive and well in the localities and fighting to keep its traditional forms of moral policing and surveillance.

Apart from the general studies of local government (Dearlove, 1979; for county councils especially, Dunbabin 1963, 1977) – in which the reconceptualizations of D. C. Moore, Spring (1963: 275 ff.), Arnstein (1972, 1975) and Brundage are very important – a very full survey of the composition of the magistracy is provided by Zangerl (1971). This shows that for the boroughs the gentry continued to provide 45 per cent of magistrates in 1841; for the counties the figures are 1841, 77.1 per cent; 1885, 68.1 per cent. Equally important is the filiations of the nomination–patronage system. Lords lieutenant (not infrequently, the relevant dukes and earls) were *the* 'local' representatives consulted when it came to constructing that list (which exists more generally in the 1980s) of 'the Great and the Good' from which reliable men (and, now, a few women) might be selected for these

Great Duties of State. Zangerl also (and several of the local studies endorse this) shows how a certain necessary change-within-continuities is 'handled' over the century:

Assimilation, rather than disturbing the established order of social relationships, reinforced the value system of the landed classes. The circle of landed allies on the county bench merely expanded to include bourgeois individuals as well as Anglican clergymen, doctors, barristers and military officers. (1971: 125)

It is striking – to move to another scenario of rule and other 'significant persons', whose study should not be (as it too often is) isolated from this wider context of who ruled – that this listing corresponds exactly with Corrigan's as yet uncompleted study of the 50 or so key state servants who dominate the period after 1832, with the second (Dr Kay, Dr Southwood Smith, Dr William Farr) and third (Chadwick, Tremenheere, E. C. Tufnell) being the most important of the latter four groups at the national level.

And what of that national group of state servants and the famous reforms of Northcote–Trevelyan? The bourgeoisie love exact dates. So many official and general accounts date 'the civil service today' from 23 November 1853: the Fulton Report, chapter 1; the historical chapter in the 1912–14 Royal (MacDonnell) Commission on the Civil Service; Thornhill 1975: 2; Kellner and Crowther-Hunt 1980: 23; etc., etc., etc. In fact George Trevelyan[37] told the Playfair Commission of 1875, 'The revolutionary period of 1848 gave us a shake, and created a disposition to put our house in order, and one of the consequences was a remarkable series of investigations' (quoted in Hart 1960: 42; cf. McGregor 1951: 156ff; Cohen 1941: 92, n. 2. Hughes 1942: 23 suggests 1846 might have been 'a shock' too). Trevelyan and others (Northcote's 'equal billing' hardly seems deserved)[38] investigated over a dozen Offices and Departments from 1848 to 1857 – those regarding the Home Office, the Foreign Office, and the Military and Naval Offices were never published (Hughes 1942: 61; Hart 1960: 103ff. Cohen 1941: 92 is incorrect). Hughes argues that it was these special reports that form the basis of what are normally dated the '1853 reforms'. Note further, that although a Civil Service Commission was established by an Order-in-Council on 21 May 1855, open competition (we shall see both how 'open' and how limited was its operation shortly) was not established until 4 June 1870, when once again the instrument was an Order-in-Council.

Like anything of significance this whole area is one of debate, much of it mystifying. Like most areas we discuss in this book, the best course is to return to the documents and/or to the fullest administrative histories. Here the work Hughes (1942, 1949) is a prime source. Centrally involved in so-called open competition are certain moral and political values extending from the radical critique of both the Philosophical Radicals and the Economical Reformers. There is also the practical recognition that employees and officers of state are increasingly divided between policy-making administrators and clerically routine operatives.

George Trevelyan argued in a letter to the editor of *The Times* ('Not for publication') that 'our high Aristocracy have been accustomed to employ the Civil Establishments as a means of providing for the Waifs and Strays of their families' (quoted in Hughes 1949: 85). The famous Northcote-Trevelyan report was commissioned by Gladstone in March 1853, Gladstone having earlier placed Northcote on the enquiry in progress into the Board of Trade. On 31 January 1854 Trevelyan wrote to Gladstone urging publication of the report in part, stressing its educational effects in relation to the second, subordinated level of the civil service: '*in its application to the lower ranks of society* it is likely to be productive of very beneficial effects by promoting education, and impressing the rising generation with the value of character' (Hughes 1949: 82; cf. there, pp. 210ff., 217, and Hughes 1942: 51 for similar arguments). This focus is admirably displayed in the Dean of Hereford's pamphlet (Dawes 1854). On 27 February 1854 Trevelyan wrote to Gladstone arguing that:

The old established Political Families habitually batten on the Public Patronage. Their sons, legitimate and illegitimate, their Relatives and Dependents of every degree are provided for by the score. (quoted in Hughes 1949: 210)

Of course, as an instance of a trend that continues from 900 to 1984 AD, both Northcote and Trevelyan (like Chadwick, Kay-Shuttleworth, Tremenheere, Fletcher, Horner, Tufnell, Farr) also wanted to use these areas of public patronage for their own kith and kin. One could rewrite English history in terms of these 'jobs for the boys'. Gladstone wrote to Lord John Russell in 1854 that he sought to effect a reform which would 'strengthen and multiply the ties between the higher classes and the possession of administrative power' (quoted in Hughes 1942: 28; cf. Hart 1969). He, like Queen Victoria and Sir James Graham, sees the utility of both the aristocracy's 'insensible education' and the 'highly educated classes'. On this kind of evidence – let alone the history since 1854 – Hughes is correct that the reforms sought to raise 'the social standing of the service, not to lower or "democratise" it' (Hughes 1942: 33). For Graham Wallas (1858–1932), according to a remarkable chapter (both Chadwickian and Foucauldian) entitled 'Official thought' in his famous book, the 'permanent Civil Service' is the 'real "Second Chamber", the real "constitutional check" in England' (1908: 249; cf. Wiener 1971; Collini 1972; Wolfe 1975: 228ff.). For J. S. Mill open competition by examinations 'appears to me one of those great public improvements, the adoption of which would form an era in history . . . a great and salutary moral revolution' (quoted in Hughes 1942: 35).

An external context for all these 'moral revolutions' within state formation, routines and personnel was the contemporary existence of the Financial and Administrative Reform Associations which first raised slogans whose currency is now quite efficacious: ability begins to be identified with commercial experience, administrative efficiency, and profitability (cf. O. Anderson 1965, 1974). McGregor links the ARAs to the Fabian Society a generation later (McGregor 1957: 151), and Chadwick and Dickens were both involved. Two judgements by recent historians seem to us to capture the continuities entailed in these changes. First a formulation in terms of what was later discussed as the 'brains and numbers' controversy: for Lord Annan the aristocracy of talent had their Bill of Rights in the Report of 1853, their Glorious Revolution in the Order-in-Council of 1870 – 'no formal obstacle then remained to prevent the man of brains from becoming a gentleman' (Annan 1955: 257). For Richard Johnson, patronage 'was now being exercised through the educational institutions of the mid-Victorian intelligentsia . . . this change of patronage, of course, redefined in subtle ways what it was to be a civil servant in both a social and political sense' (1969: 12). Parris hits the target: 'The Administrative Class type was not created by open competition. Open competition served to perpetuate a type which had already come to the top' (1969: 159).

Fry (1969) demonstrates that the 1853 report and 1870 Order were implemented cautiously, noting special resistance in the Home Office, the Education Department (cf. Johnson 1969; Sutherland 1969b, 1973) and the Foreign Office, whose 'peculiarities' we have remarked on before. Emphatically, neither the report, nor the Civil Service Commission, nor open competition killed patronage. For a start – and it is an important starting point – it was Cornewall-Lewis's notion of 'limited open competition' among already selected candidates, rather than fully open competition among all comers, which was dominant. Of the 1920s (for the earlier period see the admirable account of Preston-Thomas, who added the word 'work-shy' to the English language) Lord Bridges described the civil service as a 'University with separate colleges' (quoted in Fry 1969: 35) and Harold Scott reported from the Home Office how 'Office life was still influenced by the rhythm of the London season' (quoted in ibid.: 44, n. 1).

Departmental sectionalism remained strong; it was only in 1936 that promotion by examination across the classes was established. Russell-Smith (1974: 19ff.) reports both on how the Oxford syllabi dominated the open competition of the 1920s and on the degree of 'missionary zeal' amongst her generation of state servants. The 'country-house test' flows through into the so-called Method II appointments of the post-Fulton reforms (for this pattern see Kelsall 1966; Chapman 1970). Allen (1975) shows Oxbridge entrants into the top grades of the civil service to be 85 per cent in 1960 and 57 per cent in 1970, while later studies have consistently found a male Oxbridge bias factor of some 20 percent in those areas amenable to statistical checking. But our own favourite quotations come not from the academic or official literature, but from that significant burst of populist rhetoric in the lower-middle-class press. First, the *Daily Mail*:

The plain fact is: We're being run by a secret elite that has lost its nerve. (17 June 1976)

Our rulers seem both blind and deaf. The dwell in a land of their own living off a diet of Civil Service briefs and party propaganda. *They make pretentious speeches about the British disease. But the truth is that THEY are the British disease. They are the slowcoaches holding back the class.* (18 October 1976)

The London *Evening News* of 26 October 1976 editorialized as follows:

So Easy
We have often wondered what it takes to get to the top in Whitehall.
    This is Lord Crowther-Hunt's view, as expounded to a Commons committee investigating the Civil Service.
    'Be born in classes one or two, go to public school, read classics at Oxford . . .'
    Simple, isn't it? As simple, indeed, as being born with a silver spoon in your mouth.

Subsequently, Peter Kellner and Lord Crowther-Hunt produced their book *The civil servants: an inquiry into Britain's ruling class* (1980) which had been preceded by a number of crucial revelations, notably in the Crossman *Diaries* and other journals and writings of senior Cabinet ministers, along with the very important analyses and interviews of Peter Hennessy in *The Times* (from 1976). Much of this was complemented if not initiated by the findings of the late Maurice Edelman (1975a, b, c, d) about the availability of patronage involving hundreds of organizations, tens of thousands of 'places', and funds of upwards of £2.5 billion a year. But earlier documentation was available. Thus the MacDonnell Commission (1912–14) found a growth of patronage from 1880: in 1881 there were 4,142 nominated posts, in 1900 5,947; in their own ten-year survey (1901–10) they found that nomination filled 62,568 posts, open competition 27,369 and limited competition 7,669 (Appendix: Q.325 and Annex 1). And this 30 years after the 1870 Order-in-Council!

Enough has been said here, we hope, to show a made national system of Improvement by the 1870s. One comprehensive theme needs to be stated finally. We have focused upon the 'philosophy' that legitimates the 'machinery of government' and *really makes it work*. The people we have quoted, partly prescriptive, partly descriptive, show throughout the otherwise differentiated ruling groups not simply a sharing of ideas and values, but an increasingly strong grasp of how certain moral values inform what politics should or must be in terms of legitimated practices conducted by ordered, measured rituals. The procedures of politics are held to be constituted as a body of many parts, currently discovered and correctly described by Great Men, sustained and sedimented from 'time immemorial' (the common law, Magna Carta, Parliament, the constitution, 'We English . . .') and capable of being modulated to incorporate and represent all. The rationality of these forms of representation is to be found in the same nexus of rationality presented in making the law; indeed without this 'law' such forms are inconceivable. Politics, in essence, becomes sacralized: 'the constitution' becomes worshipped like 'the Trinity' or the 'Body of God'. Each momentary involvement in procedures of representation is like the partaking of the Host – the theological disputes are similar. Is the Body of the Constitution actually there when some chairman (as empirically it normally was) calls a meeting 'to order', when Bills 'are read' – the first, second and third times – and then become Acts which go to 'the Other House' and are eventually signed by the monarch (that most tired of all the arms of government!)? They then enter into the law of the land, the Heavenly Host. Or is all this merely symbolic and metaphorical? Because then, 'the law' (and the procedures for orderly meetings) are subject to interpretation and there is an organized clerisy (judges, statutory officials) and administrators (local and central 'servants' of this clerisy, or so the fable runs), who clarify and implement. All of this engages, cumulatively and comprehensively, in the most definite kind of regulation there is; representing persons as individuals. A person can of course be anybody, but only as a citizen does he (and after 1918, she) vote, enter the body politic, and then only in a minutely prescribed routine/ritual which requires prior approval and authorization (electoral rolls, marking the ballot paper in the prescribed fashion). All the time the incense-strewn murmuring: are the procedures being followed?

Ronald Butt is correct (*The Times*, 7 February 1974), there *was* a revolutionary victory entailed in the successful claim to the legitimacy of certain forms – and their required monopolization – as official politics, in short as politics full stop, empowering all other forms of regulation. It was a victory not simply of negativity, of imposition, of constraint – though those were amongst its means, to a degree we have not been able sufficiently to discuss here – but one also of positivity, of willingness, of joined construction; and this latter is, consequentially, its most important side. But this remaking of Parliament sovereign is only understandable in terms of the more general legitimation of a certain routinization, and in England a specific ritualization, of rule, in all the areas examined in this chapter and beyond.

Conspiracy theories (and explorations of social change on the basis of intentions of powerful actors) are currently and correctly subject to much criticism. More ludicrous, but equally powerful, is the notion that if any social fact can be found to be irreducible to the organization of belief and activity involved, therefore all theories of connection or determination or agency are invalidated. This has opened the door to a form of 'discourse analysis' entirely congruent with sociobiology or cybernetics (the working class return as animals or machines, once again). We remain mindful of forms of social struggle and their unintended consequences. We wish to argue, nonetheless, that the limited semi-sacralization of 'the State' is a revolutionary victory, of particular socially powerful groups, and it cannot be understood without understanding their situation, perspectives and objectives. These animate the forms established, the ways of proceeding, the taken-for-granted rules of order from the tiniest social exchange through to the full-blown rituals of rule. They make evident for us the rules of order internal to the neutral, natural, universal and obvious procedures – summating as 'the State', Philip Abrams's 'distinctive collective misrepresentation of capitalist societies' – we have taken for granted for too long.

Since the splitting and fragmentation of the 1880s it has taken almost a hundred years to find the object that was common to so many discourses of the years from 1780 onwards. In a curious way what makes it visible now are the real changes from the 1960s that mark an ending, a decoration as if for a monument, of the Great Arch. In one way, such concrete metaphors ignore one consistent theme: state formation, because it is cultural revolution, donates the terms through which 'the State' may be worshipped, criticized, grasped, reformed, reconstructed, denied, held together, affirmed and carried onwards. As Coleridge put it, at the end of his Ninth Philosophical Lecture, at the Crown and Anchor Tavern in the Strand, on 8 March 1819:

the influences of philosophy must not be sought for either in the lives of philosophers themselves or in the immediate effect of their writings upon the students of speculative knowledge. No! We must look for it everywhere, only not in their own shape, for it becomes active only by being diluted. It combines itself as a colour, as it were, lying on the public mind, as a sort of preparation for receiving thought in a particular way, and excluding particular views.

This is the supreme achievement of state formation: what George Eliot called 'the images that are habitually associated with abstract or collective terms' – 'the picture-writing of the mind' (quoted in Briggs 1978: 76).

But the architectural metaphor returns. It is difficult to avoid, given the actuality of Whitehall/town hall. But now, we suggest (as, in another way, the Falklands campaign does) it returns as farce. For Burrow in his admirable study of those Whig historians in his *The Liberal Descent*,

The great Victorian histories now seem like the triumphal arches of a past empire, their vaunting inscriptions increasingly unintelligible to the modern inhabitants: visited occasionally, it may be, as a pissoir, a species of visit necessarily brief. (quoted in Kenyon 1981: 1408, col. V)

7

Epilogue: 'There Is, Above All, an Agency'

> There is, above all, an agency upon which we are all tending to become increasingly dependent, that is the State.
>
> Durkheim 1902: 227

Somewhere we cross a line, step over a threshold, but we have tried to show that it is extraordinarily difficult to say when. 'The State' is first referred to impersonally in the 1530s, in the 1640s there are years when the 'impersonal body' is all there is, henceforth the 'Mortall God' rules if it does not reign, and then from the 1780s a national state is frequently discussed. But that national state, as we tried to show, was recognized for what it was, the crucial means through which 'the population' were modelled, 'socialized' in that special sense. By the 1880s something had changed: a curious 'Socialism' could be named, as we shall see, and the orientations of 'some people' to the state had changed. Briggs (1961: 239) quotes Bland in the first edition of the *Fabian Essays* (1889), who remarks:

the sort of unconscious or semi-conscious recognition of the fact that the word 'state' had taken to itself new and diverse connotations – that the state idea has changed its content.

Briggs shows that Bland 'argued that working people had themselves changed from fearing it as an enemy to regarding it as a "potential saviour"'. R. Barker argues that 'extensions of state power which would have previously been controversial were now pursued as little more than practical necessities' (1978: 127).[1]

For Ernest Barker, by 1880 there is 'economic Socialism' (compared to the political Radicalism of 1848) and the 'idea of social readjustment by the state' (compared to *laissez-faire*). That contrast donates the title – *From radicalism to socialism* – of Wolfe's important study

(1975). A number of commentators, then and since, have found in the late 1870s and early 1880s 'Socialism' or 'Collectivism'. This 'Socialism' is very peculiar – or is it? We think there is something very similar in this 'Socialism' (and its specific socialization, here not through the vote but through 'social legislation') and that earlier moment when 'Society' discovered and sought to model society. There is first, a point we shall return to, Webb's linkage in the *Fabian Essays* of 1889 of socialism brought about by scientific sociology (and/or the 'irresistible sweep of social tendencies'). There is second (and Webb shares this fascination; cf. his 1888 lecture to the Hampstead Society for the Study of Socialism, quoted in Wolfe 1975: 282) the 'learning from abroad', oriented particularly to Germany, especially the linkage of the anti-socialist laws of 1878 and the 'positive legislation' of 1881 (Dawson 1891; Davidson 1969: 256ff.; for the later moment of state insurance see Braithwaite 1957). Third, as we have already noted, the franchise after 1884 only included 58 per cent of adult males (28 per cent of all adults); the respectable male strata remained thin. Fourth, if, as Hennock (1976) has shown, orientations to poverty were changing – it was becoming recognizable as what a different Chadwick (W.E.) called 'a social disease' which 'like sickness must be treated differently' (1905: 22; note how he called to his aid social science – ibid.: p. 18) – socialization of the poor remained the project.

If Pelling (1965: 11) is right and it was changes in the pattern and extent of state activity which led Sir William Harcourt to declare in 1889 'We are all socialists now', then – we suggest – something of the huge hydra of state formation and cultural revolution which we have depicted *prior* to the 1870s has much to contribute to understanding this generalized change in discourse and evaluation amongst different classes. In 1840 J. S. Mill had extended an argument (in relation to Coleridge) that the government should promote 'public welfare' by suggesting that 'a State ought to be considered as a great benefit society, or mutual insurance company' (1840: 157). In the 1860s there was discussion of a 'State Friendly Society' linked to the new Post Office, as in the plans of the Rev. J. Y. Stratton, whose 1868 scheme was appended by Tremenheere and Tufnell to their *Enquiry* (PP 1867–8 (4068–1) XVII). In 1880 Tremenheere, discussing his own scheme for compulsory health insurance, refers to a memorial submitted to the Royal Commission on Friendly Societies (1872–4) which had amongst the signatories two archbishops, six bishops, 17 lay peers, 35 MPs, 37 chairmen and 8 deputy chairmen of Boards of Guardians, 52 JPs and nearly 90 clergymen (1880: 276; cf. his 1881). In his 'Reform of the Poor Law', Webb argued that:

it seems desirable to promote in every way the feeling that 'the Government' is no entity outside of ourselves, but merely ourselves organised for collective purposes. . . . Regarding the State as a vast benefit society, of which the whole body of citizens are necessarily members. (1890: 104)

This is the context for the famous 'clarifications' of A. J. Balfour, who was influenced by both Webb (Young 1973) and T. H. Green (Pelling 1965: 11):

Socialism will never get possession of the great body of public opinion . . . among the working class or any other class if those who wield the collective forces of the community show themselves desirous to ameliorate every legitimate grievance and to put Society on a proper and more solid basis. (quoted in Fraser 1973: 123)

Social legislation is not merely to be distinguished from Socialist legislation, but is its most direct opposite and its most effective antidote. (quoted in Miliband 1960: 37, n. 1; Fraser 1973: 129; Hay 1975: 3)

John Rae shows the shifts very clearly in 1890 when he establishes and distinguishes the 'English doctrine of social politics' from both an anterior 'practice of *laissez-faire*' and 'the modern German theory of State socialism' (1890: 435). Social politics also differentiates 'Socialistic legislation from sound and wholesome Social Reform . . . if we are all socialists now . . . it is not because we have undergone any change of principles on social legislation, but only a public awakening to our social miseries' (ibid.: 439). Let an old Whig–Liberal explain to us 'what was going on'. Tremenheere closes his last pamphlet – *How good government grew up and how to preserve it* (1893: 24) – with this quotation from William Lilly's *Century of revolution* (1890). A well-regulated democracy, says Lilly, is:

a state of organic growth, a state of society issuing from the history of the world and the nature of things; a political fact, the result of long continued development; the latest term in a movement that has been in progress since the beginning of European civilisation. It reminds the wealthy of their responsibilities; it recognises the value of man as man; an individuality in which is implanted the germ of progress, and the right of all possible freedom in his efforts to attain it. . . .
   This is a democracy which will not allow itself to be led away by the discounters and jugglers of universal suffrage, but which is schooled and governed by the strong and wise.

A sharply different perspective is interjected by Philip Abrams:

In the thirty years before 1914 many British intellectuals came to see the new sociology and the new Liberalism – the Liberalism of free education, unemployment insurance, town-planning, old-age pensions, guaranteed minimum wages, and a managed labour-market – as theory and practice of a last stand against socialism (1968: 60)

A whole range of work – especially by Stefan Collini, Peter Clarke, Michael Freeden[2] – has now established the validity of that statement. Rather than duplicate it (even if we had the space) let us try to interpret it, and other material, in the light of our overall argument thus far.

First, what was the object (and/or changes) around which this theoretical shift was organized? In contrast, as we shall shortly illustrate, to the continuities from the 1830s – themselves energized far earlier – and compared with the famous Liberal reforms of 1906 onwards (let alone the changes after 1916), the novelty of *new* state forms around 1884 is difficult to detect, despite conventional historiography wishing to start its fables of the 'modern state' from this period (calling this 'the' interventionist state, compared with the 'minimal', 'nightwatchman' or, ludicrously, *'laissez-faire'* state before). Of course the legislation of the 1870s and, less so, the 1880s is significant, but much of it is consolidation and administrative formalization of legitimated structured social relations long in being.

Three modes of consolidation are worth exemplifying. First, consolidation by extending a definition to embrace more and more examples of what are claimed to be 'the same' social relations: the best example of this is the Factory Acts of 1867 and 1871, then the Factory and Workshop Acts of 1878 and 1901.[3] Second, consolidation and extension by adding to the functions of formerly more narrowly defined groups of authorized agents: this is well illustrated by additions to the work of Poor Law Guardians, responsibilities which continued long after the Local Government Board was established in 1871. Third, consolidation by singular 'idea' or 'method': this is traceable, for instance, in the work of Sir John Simon, from his appointment as medical officer to the City of London in 1848 through his medical officership with the Privy Council from 1858 to his appointment as chief medical officer to the Local Government Board in 1871. In the same way the principles and system of the 1848 Act became the powers and system of the 1866 Sanitation Act and the Public Health Act of 1875. But still the 'patchwork' persists. Certain rights of men of property change very slowly (if at all) – patriarchal social relations are a central example, another would be housing (Tarn 1973, Gauldie 1974, Wohl 1968, 1977). A third would be the zigzag criminalization/legalization regarding trades unions. What is particularly significant here we have already mentioned (and shown in the making earlier): the 'social' recognition of labouring men. This is extended through the simultaneous ending of master and servant legislation for some categories of employee (forms of limitation for others continued for many long years); the legalization of a certain form of regulated trades union; forms of new association of previously unorganized and partly organized workers; and a focusing on the need to represent the labour interest. At the same time certain forms of practical trade unionism were criminalized. Thus, while the Trade Union Act and the Criminal Law Amendment Act of 1871, and the Conspiracy and Protection of Property Act and Employers and Workmen Act of 1875 ostensibly legalized peaceful picketing and protected union funds from damages in cases of tort, legal judgements in *Lyon* v. *Wilkins* (1896–8) effectively outlawed the former, and in *Temperton* v. *Russell* (1893), the action of Trollope & Sons against the London Building Trades Federation (1896), and – of course – the Taff Vale case (1901) did away with the latter protection (see Pelling 1976: ch. 6).

We have noted continuities in reforms of the judicial system (consolidation of the courts in the 1870s and 1880s); the establishment of county councils in 1888 followed the pattern of borough councils set up in 1835. Permanent boards, modelled on the Board of Trade, were set up to deal with various Privy Council and Home Office functions: The Local Government Board in 1871, the Board of Agriculture 1889 (and Fisheries, 1903), the Board of Education 1899. But none of this was unprecedented, any more than was the practice, after 1870, of 'delegated legislation', the roots lying in procedures of 'scientific' policy formulation and execution discussed in the last chapter. It is probably of equal significance that, at the same time and in a number of areas, state regulation slightly recedes, having created a legitimate space and relatively available market for commercial provision of commoditized cultural forms: from cheap mass newspapers (relevant taxes having been removed between 1865 and 1870), through brand-name goods available in more extensive shops linked to distribution chains, to commercially provided leisure activities.

This period is often depicted to be that of 'the masses'. But Briggs's admirable survey (which should be complemented by the work of Raymond Williams and Stephen Yeo) quotes a much earlier 'recognition', from the *Westminster Review*'s 1833 review of J. P. Kay's *Moral and physical condition of the working classes in Manchester* (1832): 'The rapid progress of our manufactures and commerce has accumulated great masses of population, in which society has assumed new relations among its several classes' (Briggs 1978: 66). Apart from illustrating neatly once again our thesis about 'Society' discovering and modelling (or desiring to model) society, this alerts us to something we think important. 'The State' was enormously augmented through the 1830s/1870s period. In myriad different civic institutions it became a visible part of urban social architecture, it was felt across the whole range of social relations. The period depicted by Philip Abrams, 1884–1914, is one which bears, we would argue, certain striking parallels to that around and after 1776 in the previous century (or represents, to put it differently, another turn of the same screw). Then, through a descriptive historical sociology – recognizing the new object, society – political economy/moral philosophy conjointly establish the theory and legitimation for new state forms which urge on Improvement by men of property to all their possessions. For the subsequent century Improvement becomes progress, and this 'progress' takes as its object national society. The Radicals of the 1830s wanted a *national* system of Improvement.

Building on this 'system', by the later nineteenth century 'national society' could be considered through various metaphors, notably those of Social Darwinism; and it becomes possible to talk about 'national efficiency' and to be concerned that 'the disease of poverty' is, amongst other things, 'an ailment of the body politic' (John Burns, preface to Preston-Thomas 1909: viii). The specific crisis recognized in the 1880s is a crisis of modelling, that is, a crisis in the wider project of that specific 'socialization' we have traced through the nineteenth century (and rooted yet earlier). It is now recognized that the moralization of the working class cannot be extended far enough, civilization cannot be 'forced downwards' fast enough because poverty is not simply a character defect. Furthermore the impoverishment of large groupings within the working class leads to the physical deterioration of 'the stock' – future generations, of workers! of soldiers!, are endangered. But the project remains the same. Certain of its forms – acceptance of the need for a limited recognition of labour (and regulated legitimation of some of its distinctive organizations, like trades unions), acknowledgement of poverty as a social problem – depart from the previously dominant 'pure' individualizing moralism (though today's monetarist myths amply testify to the latter's continuing resonance), that is all. There is a specific novelty, but there are no radical breaks.

What the work cited earlier in support of Philip Abrams has shown is that conventional dichotomizations of personnel and politics in that 30 years have obscured strong connections and elective affinities, both within this period itself and with that which preceded it: we see a generalized moralism (on the one hand, duty; on the other, a sniffing distance from the 'wretched' poor) and a commitment to science. These characteristics should not strike us as new. Moral philosophy becomes a certain moral sociology; political economy fractures into the social sciences in their recognizable modern forms. But none of this makes sense – how, now, 'the State' could be seen from a variety of perspectives as a set of available, legitimated, neutral resources – without that practical history, also involving its own sociological theorizing and methodologies, of state formation from the 1830s (Abrams 1968). That practical history made the 'peculiar' state-centred Social-ism of the 1870s and beyond thinkable. We find that the double targets of so much of this new Liberalism, ethical Socialism, and Progressivism, are the entrenched *ancien régime* (especially around land reform) and working-class self-organized socialism. This is familiar territory.

Recent work has made clear the filiations between Benthamism and Fabianism (the inter-textual link frequently being J. S. Mill; cf. Wolfe 1975; Mack 1955; Abrams 1968; Collini 1977, 1980b). Their methods were strikingly similar (cf. Finer 1959):

'Nothing in England is done', Webb wrote to Edward Pease in October 1886, 'without the consent of a small intellectual yet practical class in London not 2,000 in number. We alone could get at that class. . . .' This was, and in some ways remains, the Fabian purpose. (MacKenzie 1976: 10; cf. Walker 1976)

Like Chadwick's 'Friends in Council' group, or Spencer's 'the X club', the Fabians intersected with numerous such clubs – permeation was the name of their game after all – such as the Progressives' Rainbow Circle which met from 1894 to 1920. We might, in this connection, extend J. R. Hay's emphasis (1975: 69) on Dangerfield's *Strange death of Liberal England* (1935) by noting L. T. Hobhouse's 1920s estimation that 'moderate Labour – Labour in office – has on the whole represented essential liberalism' (quoted in Clarke 1974: 178), that is ' "Ordinary Labour" = "Good Liberal" ' (quoted in Nicholls 1962: 127). Fabianism, gradualism, elitism, hierarchy, patriarchy and a semi-worship of 'the State' are key features which form labourism and the Labour Party.[4] They are typified most exactly by the twin themes hegemonic in relation to education (whose definition 'officially' as state-provided schooling was accepted): *access* (for larger numbers; as in the slogan of 1944 'Secondary Education for All') and *control* (by councillors from Our Party). The Labour Party never was, and whilst any of these ideas and forms are prescriptively dominant never will be, a revolutionary party, although as focus and above all as hope it has been and remains a locus for the struggles of the labour movement to revolutionize society. It had two MPs in 1900, 30 in 1906 and after the miners affiliated 'their' MPs it had 40 in 1909. As Clarke (1982: 52) shows – with reference to J. A. Hobson's account of the 1910 election, published in *The Sociological Review* of 1910 – this above all suggests a complex of groupings of support within what was then considered 'the Progressive alliance'.[5] Recall that Sidney Webb lived from 1859 to 1947 (Graham Wallas 1858–1932, L. T. Hobhouse 1864–1929). Webb was 42 when Queen Victoria died; Wallas was 50 when his *Human nature in politics* (1908) was published, and 67 when he acclaimed 'Bentham as a political inventor' (1925). Webb was a civil servant from the age of 19 to 32, and from the age of 33 to 41 LCC councillor for Deptford. Wallas sat on the Royal Commission on the Civil Service, 1912–14 (the MacDonnell Commission).

We have not the space to trace out the contours, of contradictions and continuities. We want though to indicate how progressivism registers a thematic unity, partly descriptive of a state system long in being before its theorization, partly prescriptive of further ways in which that system – and the opportunities it offered for a certain expert-in-employment – should be extended. This thematic unity was shared far more widely than can be seen by those who make heroes of the Fabians (or misread Bosanquet and others of the Charity Organization Society as purely Spencerians), or, the larger number by far, who search here, there and everywhere in the late 1870s and early 1880s for 'the modern state'. Not 'the State' but 'the idea of the State' is what had changed. Above all there was this sacred object recognized as there to be worshipped, worked, used and consolidated. Some of the practices, as we indicated earlier with regard to patronage (which is merely the vertical version of the horizontal practice of permeation that so links Benthamism and Fabianism), strike us as modernized, but still recognizable versions of that parasitism of the eighteenth century and earlier. There were careers open to men with talents (and the right connections); but their project remained one of *social*ization, extending that earlier attempt to model society in the self-image of 'Society'. Sociology and social work originate in this same nexus. Hence the salience of the London School of Economics, explicitly 'open' – from the start – for servicing capital (the railway magnates) and the state (Sidney's chum, Lord Haldane, put some defence work their way). By the 1930s the impact of Rockefeller funding was shaping up whole programmes of study and research.

We cannot leave this 'Happy Band' without quoting Halevy's sharp observations (which later work has nuanced but not negated; cf. Winter 1974, Weeks 1976) based on meetings with the Fabians. His work brilliantly recognizes the object of the 1830s/1880s search in terms of the 'policy of social peace' (1919, 1921, 1922): a series of attempts to find the institutional equivalent of Parliament to contain the class struggle (1919: 121–2; cf. Goldthorpe 1962, 1969; Meacher 1974a, b. Ronald Butt, *The Times*, 7 February 1974, is partial answer to these latter, but should be read with both Braudel and Halevy in mind). Halevy quotes the 'happy formula' (his description) of the Fabians:

Our goal, as socialists, is the elimination of capitalism, but not of the wage system. Far from wanting to abolish the wage system, we want to universalise it. We want all men [NB], instead of being divided into wage-earners and profiteers, to be equally, *if not with the same rank*, paid functionaries of the State. (Halevy 1921: 125; emphasis added)

What the Fabians – and all the other members of the Progressive alliance – signify is a general crisis of that grossly uneasy class of intellectuals: the aristocracy of talent. These lusted after their right to become a new clerisy, to orient their vocation more nearly (loving it more dearly) to the state. In general terms the shifts in franchise and other reforms of the late 1860s onwards had not provided (from official politics) what they had hoped for. Exactly in step with that certain social-ism (and its key instrument: social legislation) which we sketched above, we find a fracturing of disciplines and a new set of emphases from the same period (Abrams 1968: ch. 6). Significantly, periodical literature (Annan 1952, Mowat 1969, Freeden 1972, Clarke 1974) is central to these shifts in 'vocation' (and all the play in that term is deliberate). There is, we might note in passing, another textual history to be traced here, the form of the periodical of information, opinion, 'facts' and permeation is part of the history of the making and remaking of the English ruling class. A number of the major books which are now taken as markers in this period originate as essays, in the *Fortnightly Review* (1865 onwards), *The Nineteenth Century* (later *The Nineteenth Century and After*, and then *The Twentieth Century*), and *The Progressive Review* (1896 onwards).[6] These, with the continuing journals of an earlier formation, and the newspapers like the *Daily Chronicle*[7] and the *Manchester Guardian*,[8] were places to permeate and place in exactly the manner of an earlier period (and of course it still continues) (Clarke 1974; cf. Preston-Thomas 1909).

This crisis is too multiform to be traced here. It is also very much alive. Neither the problem in which it is rooted – that contradiction we outlined at the beginning of the last chapter, the ultimate unassimilability of labour – nor the project of 'the State' as its solution have gone away. Alfred Marshall was appointed college lecturer in 'Moral Sciences' at St John's Cambridge in 1868 (and it was not until 1867/8 that T. H. Green, in Oxford, began to lecture on philosophy; his notable lectures were in the early 1880s). According to Routh (1976: 20; cf. Kennedy 1957) Marshall was still debating 'in his thirtieth year' (that is during 1871–2) 'whether to give his life to economics or psychology': this from a founding father of technical economics. Another, W. S. Jevons, spelled out a different wording of the same truth in his *The state in relation to labour* (1882; Stigler 1975:

196). A wider context can be gained by taking seriously the *Essays in reform* (1867), and the founding of the Fabian Society (1884) plus the Fabian Essays (1889),[9] as contextualized prescriptions. Between the first and the second – i.e. between the first and second significant extensions of the male franchise – political economy is fractured into economics and what is recognizably sociology (Abrams 1968, Cairnes 1870, Ingram 1878, Lowe 1878, Spencer 1884). This is, in turn, part of the fracturing of Whig-Liberalism before the break over Irish Home Rule. Sir Henry Maine's *Popular government* (1885, six editions by 1909) was an extension of *his* historical sociology (cf. Burrow 1971, Bock 1974, 1976). Roach (1957) shows major Liberals – Robert Lowe, Henry Maine, Selbourne, Goschen, Stephen and A. V. Dicey – critical at dates earlier than the start of the Gadarene rush towards the Conservative and Unionist Party as a mark of patriotism.[10] Liberal imperialism can be rooted here also (Matthew 1973; Emy 1973).

There is a nice 'moment' for lovers of the historical curiosity in Robert Lowe's statement in 1878, 'The future is all for the sociologists, and I am included to think it will long remain so,' and Sir Keith Joseph's rhetorical question, 'Is Beckerman amongst the sociologists?' in 1975. Sir Keith moved to declare sociology a potentially inappropriate subject to take if the person concerned wished to receive mandatory grants for postgraduate teacher training, and to send 'his' inspectors to investigate 'bias' in sociology and applied social studies at the Polytechnic of North London in 1983. The latter specifics should not be overly distinguished from the philosophy which provides the context, ably established by Joseph himself (1975, 1976).

W. J. Linton editorialized in the fifth issue of *The Cause of the People* (17th June 1848) 'Three things are wanted that our cause may triumph: understanding, energy and organisation.' In a remarkable lecture (which we would have liked to reproduce in full, it says so much) entitled 'Communism' (1893), William Morris implicitly recalls Linton's 'trinity formula':

Intelligence enough to conceive, courage enough to will, power enough to compel. If our ideas of a new Society are anything more than a dream, these three qualities must animate the due effective majority of the working people; and then, I say, the thing will be done. (1893: 8; cf. Thompson 1976: 729)

But this is exactly what the understanding of state formation as cultural revolution has also to comprehend. In its final form, for example with H. M. Hyndman (1881: ch. 4), the ontological and epistemological dominance of 'the State' is such that even the Poor

Law is 'communistic in principle' (four years later Chamberlain too could find 'the Poor Law as Socialism', quoted in Wolfe 1975: 217), and every extension of 'State rule' was 'a stepping stone to socialism'. Understanding/Intelligence, Energy/Will, Organization/Power – these are the inner trinity of the state itself. As Bacon said of the law, we might say of the state, its claim to rule is total and we argue within it every day. Its understanding is its power, its energy and will are its legitimacy whose 900-year making we have tried to trace.

Marx and Engels described the whole trajectory of 'Conservative, or bourgeois socialism' in 1848 as aiming at:

administrative reforms, based on the continued existence of those relations; reforms, therefore, that in no respect affect the relations between capital and labour, but, at the best, lessen the cost, and simplify the administrative work, of bourgeois government. (1848: 514)

Four years later Marx himself noted how:

The peculiar character of the Social-Democracy is epitomised in the fact that democratic-republic institutions are demanded as a means, not of doing away with two extremes, capital and wage-labour, but of weakening their antagonism and transforming it into harmony. (1852: 121)

The *Grundrisse* and *Capital* (all four volumes) need to be read in the light of this perspective; it is reiterated, forcefully, by Marx in his 'late' writings of the 1870s and 1880s precisely in regard to 'the State' (Sayer and Corrigan 1983, 1985; Sayer 1983b, 1985). William Morris considered what was being formed in the 1880s to be social democracy. This, 'the State' of which so many now speak, hurts more than it helps.

If that is the ethos – a highly material concept in terms of its implications for conduct – what is the eidos? What shape and weight did the axle of discipline have? Two brief illustrations. First, that abiding concern, 'idle time'. Here as elsewhere the shapefulness was designed (Abrams 1982a: ch. 6). Amidst the manic papers of 1875 of the National Association for the Promotion of Social Science (they include, for instance, proposals for total nationalization of railways in India and a line from London to Calcutta, to be paid for by taxation of India through until 1976! Thereby revenging 1776?) there is the little gem of Francis Fuller: 'How to elevate the people – physically, socially, and morally; avert social dangers, and strengthen the ties of Society, Law and Order, by encouraging and enabling the masses to pass their leisure hours beneficially'. Here he writes,

It is a point of self-interest and self-protection *for us* to exert ourselves to improve the tone of popular amusements to induce *men* to cultivate the 'leisure hour' for the good of mind and body. *Our* safety, *the security of society*, of *our* homes and families, in the long run, are concerned with *the form* in which they take their recreation. (1875: 717; emphasis added)

By then, and it is of the greatest possible significance, entertainment – in proper acceptable forms – had become the normalized ingredient of culture for the masses. As *The Times* editorialized on 17 January 1980:

The notion that politics is something apart, a specialised area of life which concerns politicians but is irrelevant to ordinary people and their activities, is very widespread but quite illusory. All organised human life is by definition political.

Second, that one area of regulation which all general theories of the minimal state except specifically and by name: education. The statistics here register both the continuities, and the specific forms of Erastianization – consolidation rather than novelty – that characterize the 1870s and 1880s more generally. From 1870 there is state provision for, and from 1880 state compulsion of, a defined cohort (all persons of a particular age range whose parents cannot prove that they are obtaining 'as efficient an education' from other provisions) to attend in total institutions – major organizers of social and biographical space and time – called schools. Although many echo the then Minister of Education of Ontario (Ross 1894: 28)[11] and consider the Education Act of 1870 'the Magna Charta of English Education', according to Kay-Shuttleworth the Act of 1870 had been able to build on a system which in 1869 had over one million pupils in 13,644 inspected schools with 25,342 teachers and pupil teachers (1876). By 1874/5 the same source, quoting official data, is able to record 2,250,000 pupils in about 27,000 schools. Since the 1870 Act nearly 2,000 Board Schools had been built, plus about 2,700 voluntary schools. By 1875 there were 40 teacher-training colleges, by 1892 43. Of these, 17 were for men, 26 for women (Ross 1894: 56; his subsequent statistics, e.g. for London, p. 52, or nationally, p. 68, show this gender division to be quite general).

For 1892, Ross shows 4,609,240 children (2,300,377 of them in voluntary schools) and 19,515 schools (14,684 of them voluntary) with 48,772 teachers, 23,558 assistant teachers and 20,961 pupil teachers (ibid.: 36). Sutherland (1973) provides all the national statistics from 1870 to 1895 (Appendix A) and notes how state support expands from £760,561 in 1870, to £6,661,640 in 1895

(Appendix B). But these figures of pupils – one million-plus in 1869, 2,250,000 in 1875, 4,609,240 in 1892 – say a lot. What sort of state forms can double in six years, and more than double again in the next seventeen, the number of human beings under its paternal gaze? There is an undoubted leap forward here; it does not come *de novo*. Both points matter equally.

Additionally, like all statistics of the state, these facts tell but a part of the story. H. S. Tremenheere (1865: 12–13) estimated that the number of children covered by one other feature of state educational provision in 1865 were:

Under the Factory Acts in 1862:	573,000
Under the extension Act in 1864:	30,000
Covered by the Commission thus far:	1,200,000

i.e. some 1,800,000 children. Adding this to Kay-Shuttleworth's statement about 1869 we have some 2,800,000 children being educated, excluding those in Poor Law Union schools, military and naval schools, and, of course, those in the schools for that real 'public', the children of the middle and upper classes. In 1871[12] the total population of the United Kingdom was 27,400,000. On this crude analysis, more than 10 per cent of the population – legally defined children – were under a condition of compulsory moral surveillance by 1870.[13] The development of childhood itself as a regulated socio-legal category can be traced through from 1833. Incidentally significant numbers of children continued to experience factory and Poor Law education until 1918.

Finally (and fittingly) we might record one more cyclical continuity – indicative of the problem (capitalism) which 'the State' attempts to 'manage' – as evidenced in figures for pauperism. Officially defined paupers rose from 8.1 per cent of the population in 1801 to 10.2 per cent in 1831 (hitting 12.7 per cent in 1813); by 1841 (i.e. after the 1834 Act) the figure was 5.9 per cent; by the end of the century, 2.4 per cent. State expenditure per capita on poor relief dropped from 8/11 in 1803 (12/8 in 1813) to 7/3 in 1900. In 1975, claimants and dependants were 8.3 per cent of the UK population – reaching, again, pre-1834 Poor Law levels – and social security expenditure 20.2 per cent of all central government expenditure. In 1984 the latter figure (that is, to use the more explicit language of the nineteenth century, poor relief) had risen to 30.4 per cent of public expenditure.[14] As we have remarked before, *plus ça change*.

It is time to conclude. We cease our narrative, quite deliberately, where so many 'pick up the baton' and run: from the 1870s and 1880s.

To trace the story from then on would require many more pages. But it could not be told at all without the centuries-long historical experience of differential empowerment and denial we have essayed here. By the 1880s the recognizably 'modern' democratic nation state – 'the State' – can be named. This last chapter has attempted no more than to register this, particularly in its relation to social democracy, and to suggest two kinds of question about the 'modern' features of 'the State' after the 1870s and 1880s. First, we have sought to show, here and in the previous chapter, that the 'patchwork' persists, distinctively unmodernized features are carried forward, and it would be a foolish strategical analysis that saw them as mere archaic residuals. They embody powers. They continue to confer legitimacy on what is new. Second, we have argued that there is a novelty, but that it resides in ways persisting practices (rituals, routines, rationalizations) were articulated, consolidated, and made ethical institutions. To change the idea of 'the State' – to make it, in fact, visible *as* 'the State' – was an enormous accomplishment, and one which much legitimation work has to labour to sustain. But it is not an accomplishment which can solely be dated from the 1870s and 1880s: a better starting point would be in the twelfth century. There are moments when this dominant 'idea of the state' is challenged – around 1911–14 and again 1918–19, around 1926, during the 1939–45 period and beyond. But, in general terms, 'it' holds, and in this 900-year making such 'general terms' are what count. The current language of necessity governing England – which has structurally done more harm to more people there than the 1930s – shows, more graphically (and more tragically) than any words of ours could do, the enormous legitimacy, flexibility and continuing resilience of this set of state forms.

Part of the reason for this is the very considerable extent to which we, now, after those 900 years, inhabit those forms, or better, they inform and colonize us. If our book has pointed to the anatomy of this state of England's green and pleasant land, then is it far-fetched to ask after the physiology of the citizenry within that enveloping state? Does not their identity, in part, partake of this multi-century making? Is there not a strong sense in which part of what it means to be born English is to have some of all we have sketched in the blood? We hope this will not be read as an 'incorporation thesis' – we have said enough by now to indicate both the necessary partiality of the 'inclusion' of the endless categories of *les autres*, and the stubborn facticity of the contradictions on which the project of 'the State' is founded. These contradictions will not go away. The presence of 'the idea of the state' within us, in the multiple ways it totalizes and individualizes us, remains for most people a problem: in a thousand ways popular cultural forms register a profound ambivalence, a contradictoriness, toward 'the State's' statements and their legitimacy. Edward Thompson's analysis of certain eighteenth-century anonymous letters (1975; cf. Corrigan and Willis 1980) brings this out well. There are cries from below: they cannot be taken simply to negate the ritualized deference and rationalized democracy. Both are true, that is the point, and it is almost impossible for historiography to grasp. As Engels once remarked in another context, what is needed here is a little dialectic (1890).

We point, rather, to the sinews of power, the modalities of rule. In a justly famous quotation Marx once said of capital that it 'is not a thing, but rather a definite social production relation, belonging to a definite historical formation of society, which is manifested in a thing and lends this thing a specific social character' (1865: 814–15; cf. Wells 1981, Sayer 1983a: ch. 2). A similar fetishism attends 'the State'. 'It' is not a thing, out there, to be used, captured, or come to that smashed, much as the whole trajectory of state formation and its theorizations from Fortescue to the Fabians has been to represent it as such, as impersonal power, as Mortall God. What is made to appear as 'the State' are regulated forms of social relationship; forms, as we quoted Philip Abrams at the start, of politically organized subjection. The enormous power of 'the State' is not only external and objective; it is in equal part internal and subjective, it works through us. It works above all through the myriad ways it collectively and individually (mis)represents us and variously 'encourages', cajoles, and in the final analysis forces us to (mis)represent ourselves. Over the centuries the compass of this regulation has ever widened, and such regulation is (partly) constitutive of 'available' modes of being human. To say it again, state formation is cultural revolution; that is its supreme (if never final) achievement, and the essence of its power.

We will explore these points more fully in the Afterthoughts which follow. But it seems appropriate to end our narrative here with another comment on what has been 'going on', as seen from another of those breathtakingly long-lived ruling-class English institutions. We refer of course to *The Times*, published since 1785. Again the masculinity of the analysis might be noted:

The differences so stubbornly insisted upon in Ulster concern the most fundamental of all political issues: allegiance, national identity, the legitimacy of the state, matters which Englishmen had settled for themselves by the end of the seventeenth century. These are issues which are usually disposed of only when one side prevails decisively over the other. (21 November 1979, editorial)

In Britain, certainly since the time of Elizabeth I, our geographical boundaries have never been big enough to contain the fundamental British character and British spirit.

> Margaret Thatcher, interview, *Daily Telegraph*,
> 19 September 1984

Mrs Thatcher said it [The Falklands war] made us realise we are all really one family.

> BBC News Broadcast, 21 May 1982,
> quoted in Broadbent 1984

You know about our country and how all the grandest young lads go to Eton and Harrow and get it banged into their heads that they are the leading class and they must keep it that way. Well our young lads are getting good lessons on the [picket] line too.

They're learning what free enterprise is all about, and who makes the laws and why they are made and what the police are for. They learn this on their own from experience and they don't need any undisciplined smart ass from London to tell them how things are.

> Jack Acheson, official, National Union of Mineworkers Lodge,
> Dalkeith, quoted Toronto *Globe and Mail*, 15 August 1984

Afterthoughts

We remarked at the beginning of this book that 'classical' social theory has much to offer to an understanding of state formation as cultural revolution. It will be helpful briefly to review some major themes in this literature, before offering some general observations of our own arising out of the foregoing study. Important discussions of the relation of state formation to capitalism are to be found in both Marx and Weber.[1] Weber is adamant that it is 'the nation state alone within which modern capitalism can flourish' (1920b: 250). To understand this, one has to understand his concept of capitalism. What he – carefully – called modern, Western, rational capitalism, a historically unique phenomenon distinct from money-making activity in general, was for him characterized above all by its rationality. This is not a value-judgement; Weber in fact thought both accumulation for its own sake and capitalism's moralization of work as such substantively irrational. He was pointing, rather, to the degree of calculation that distinguishes modern Western capitalism. Capitalism for Weber is rational to the extent that 'it is organized around capital calculations. That is, if it is ordered in such a way as to make planned use of material goods and personal services as a means of acquisition, so that, when the final balance-sheet is drawn, the final revenue . . . should exceed the "capital"' (1920a: 334). To us it is 'second nature' that productive enterprises should operate thus – a measure precisely of the success of capitalism's cultural revolution! One of the myriad examples would be Sir Henry Plumb's declaration that 'Without profits there can be no production' (BBC News broadcast, 25 September 1975). But, Weber would argue, both the technical devices making such rationalism possible, like double-entry book-keeping, and the appropriate institutional framework and cultural ethos, are of relatively recent origin.

Such 'sober bourgeois capitalism', based on the permanent enterprise oriented to constantly renewed profit (rather than pursuit of spectacular *ad hoc* killings) has definite preconditions. Like Marx, Weber regards as crucial 'the appropriation of all physical means of production ... as the disposable property of autonomous private industrial enterprises' and the presence of 'persons ... who are not only legally in the position, but are also economically compelled, to sell their labour on the market without restriction' (1920b: 208). He also cites, amongst other things, rational technology, freedom of the market, general commercialization of economic life, and separation of household and enterprise.[2] Though, characteristically of classical sociologies, Weber himself does not elaborate on this, the latter separation is centrally organized through the social regulation of familial forms, gender relations, and sexual division of labour – not least by state activities, as we have exemplified. Of particular importance for us, Weber further argues that modern capitalism demands a framework of rational law, administered by the national state:

If this development [rational capitalism] took place only in the occident the reason is to be found in the special features of its general cultural evolution which are peculiar to it. Only the occident knows the state in the modern sense, with a professional administration, specialised officialdom, and law based on the concept of citizenship. ... Only the occident knows rational law, made by jurists and rationally interpreted and applied, and only in the occident is found the concept of citizen. (1920b: 232; cf. his 1920a)

We would of course say: the cultural revolution peculiar to it. Rational, calculating capitalism, for Weber, 'needs ... law which can be counted upon, like a machine' (1920b: 252). Stability and predictability of the legal environment are essential to it. This can be achieved only in the centralized and standardized jurisdiction of the modern state, with its monopoly of the legitimate use of force, and its bureaucratic apparatuses of enforcement. States are also environments within which other forms – too easily taken for granted – of standardization which facilitate calculation, for instance of currency or weights and measures, can most readily be achieved.

Both modern law and modern polity rest on the concept of the citizen, the autonomous free individual with specified rights and duties. In a pregnant phrase Weber describes 'the bourgeoisie in the modern sense of the word' as 'the national citizen class' (ibid.: 249). He defines 'citizenship in the political sense' as signifying 'membership in the state, with its connotation as the holder of certain political rights', and 'citizens in the class sense' as 'those strata which are drawn together, in contrast with ... the proletariat and others outside their circle, as "persons of property and culture"' adding that the latter sense is 'a specifically western and modern concept, like that of the bourgeoisie' (ibid.: 233–4). Marx drily observes of the notion of 'citizenship': 'it should read: domination of the bourgeoisie' (Marx and Engels 1846: 215).

Finally Weber, perhaps more than any other classical sociologist, stresses also that modern capitalism requires a specific and novel practical ethos. He summates this as 'the rational spirit, the rationalisation of the conduct of life in general, and a rationalistic economic ethic' (1920b: 260); 'the origins of economic rationalism depend, not only on rational technology and rational law, but also in general on the capacity which men have for certain kinds of practical rationality in the conduct of their lives' (1920a: 340). For Weber this rationalization of conduct is a seminal feature of occidental culture in general and modern western civilization in particular. Its compass is very broad, and the concept a key one in his sociology. 'Practical rationality' comprehends both the capitalist's rational pursuit of profit and the development of labour discipline in its multiple forms: punctuality, regularization (and extension) of hours of work, payment by the hour or by the piece are expressions of the same cultural revolution. So is a wider instrumentalization of social relationships, evident in wholesale bureaucratization of organizations of all kinds; Weber extends the analysis even to cover art and music. Without getting involved in the 'Protestant ethic' debate we can endorse Weber's crucial insight here. We would stress, however, that this cultural rationalization cannot be dissociated from state formation, or analysed as a merely ideational matter. We have amply exemplified the role state formation has played in enforcing this new discipline: whether the self-discipline of the bourgeoisie, the labour discipline imposed on the working class, or – crucially, for it informs the society which provides the wider context and condition for discipline *in* production – the broader social discipline, the habituation of the meanings given to particular social orders and activities, of the sort encapsulated in Blackstone's notion of policing or nineteenth-century notions of 'respectable men'.

Marx's analysis of the connection between state formation and capitalism, as we might expect, has different emphases (though more is complementary in the two traditions than is often realized). Marxist analyses of the state as a form of organization of class power are sufficiently familiar not to require elaboration here. But in the context of this book, we can usefully note Marx's keen appreciation of the early role of the English state in facilitating capitalist relations. In *Grundrisse* he observes that '*governments*, e.g. of Henry VII, VIII etc. appear as conditions for the historic dissolution process [of feudal relations] and as makers for the conditions of existence of capital' (1858: 507). In Part 8 of *Capital I*, he details the various state or state-aided activities he has in mind. These range from 'spoliation' of church property, alienation of state lands, abolition of feudal tenures, and facilitation of enclosure and clearances, through anti-vagrancy legislation, wage regulation, and criminalization of workers' combinations, to colonial policy, protectionism, modern methods of taxation, and the national debt. By the end of the seventeenth century, he considers, these 'different momenta of primitive accumulation' arrive at 'a systematical combination'. The point he chooses to emphasize is that:

These methods . . . all employ the power of the State, the concentrated and organised force of society, to hasten, hothouse fashion, the process of transition of the feudal mode of production into the capitalist mode, and to shorten the transition. Force is the midwife of every old society pregnant with a new one. It is itself an economic power. (1867: 751)

We ought also to be aware that notwithstanding any general claims about state and class, Marx did not, in his empirical studies, unproblematically treat states as the obedient tools or creatures of a monolithic ruling class. This is abundantly clear in his studies of French politics, both in the 1850s and the 1870s.[3] But to take English examples, he saw the history of factory legislation in terms of struggles, within the arena of official politics, in which the working class carried victories against capital; the Ten Hours Bill was 'a working men's measure' (1864: 346). He likewise viewed the 'British constitution' as a 'compromise between the bourgeoisie, which *rules not officially* but in fact in all decisive spheres of civil society, and the landed aristocracy, which *governs officially*' (1855: 221). We would in fact want to qualify both judgements – precisely on grounds of historical inquiry – but we cite them illustratively.

A second theme in Marx's analysis is perhaps less familiar; it is also, unfortunately, less easy to summarize in the space available here – we have elaborated elsewhere.[4] Marx argues, in brief, that not only is the modern state (with all due caveats) an instrument of bourgeois rule, but also that the state *form* as such is distinctively bourgeois, both in the sense that this form reaches its apotheosis in capitalist society, and in the sense that it is an essential relation of that society. He clearly does not mean that coercive governance did not predate capitalism, nor would he deny that many of the institutions of the modern state had precapitalist origins. What he is saying is perhaps easiest approached through an (idealized – we stress) contrast with feudal society.[5]

For Marx, an abstract universalization of politics (as the sphere of the 'general interest') and formal depoliticization of 'civil society' (all

being construed as equal citizens, whatever their substantive inequalities) are two sides of the same historical process, equally constitutive
of capitalist civilization:

The *establishment of the political state* and the dissolution of civil society into
independent *individuals* – whose relations with one another depend on *law*,
just as the relations of men in the medieval system of estates and guilds
depended upon *privilege* . . . is accomplished by *one and the same act*.
(1843b: 167; cf. 1843a: 32)

The key point here is that the conditions under which economic
activity can take capitalist forms – can be organized, in other words,
predominantly through the production and exchange of commodities
(including of labour-power as a commodity) – are for Marx those of
this two-sided transformation of social relations. The hierarchical,
personalized, localized relationships of feudal society are doubly
fractured. From one side, the process is one of increasing individualization, the 'freeing' of individuals from feudal bonds to
become the formally equal, abstractly human subjects of the
bourgeois world-view. If the rituals of homage are a symbol of feudal
relationships, contract is the master-symbol of this brave new world.
And it goes to the heart of the matter. For Marx, the 'freeing' of
individuals is condition and corollary of the privatization of property,
its conversion into a commodity, unencumbered by 'its former
political and social embellishments and associations' (1865: 618).
Objects – above all land, means of production, labour-power – can
become disposable private property only insofar as their owners are
free to dispose of them. Behind the citizen stands the bourgeois. From
the other side, this process is integrally one of state formation.
Commodity relations – Marx's 'cash nexus'[6] – are not sufficient unto
themselves. State regulation is required to secure conditions under
which individuals can thus freely pursue their 'private' transactions,
and to equalize these conditions for all. Minimally the state must
ensure physical security and (a particular) social order. But beyond
this, as Durkheim brilliantly demonstrated in his analysis of the
'precontractual' conditions presupposed in any contract – a devastat-
ing critique of Spencer and the Utilitarians – extensive moral
regulation, the organization of consent, is required.[7] The 'anarchy' of
capitalist 'civil society' is predicated upon regulation by the state;
contrary to appearances – and *laissez-faire* ideologies – it is organized.
Law, before which all are deemed equal and to which all are
considered subject, is the paradigmatic – though not the exclusive –
regulatory framework appropriate to this society. Other sociologies
besides Marx's have picked up on this dual transformation,

individualization *and* state formation: for Tönnies the transition is from *Gemeinschaft* (community) to *Gesellschaft* (society), for Weber from patrimonial to rational–bureaucratic authority, for Durkheim from mechanical to organic solidarity. Durkheim once again is particularly interesting for his grasp both of the centrality of what he calls 'moral individualism' – putting a supreme value on the abstract human individual as such – to the bourgeois order, and of the state to its articulation. In his own words 'it is only through the state that individualism is possible' (1904: 64).

This transformation of the social geography – ultimately of social identities – is itself a cultural revolution of profound dimensions, with major consequences for negotiating (that is, finding one's way around) the world in general, and recognizing the value of our differences specifically. Marx is clear that core values of bourgeois political discourse – liberty, equality, democracy, rights – suppose the historical individual of 'civil society', *bürgerliche Gesellschaft*, and have as their reference point the polity constituted on its basis (see his 1843a, b; Marx and Engels 1846: pt 2, passim; Sayer 1985). Indeed, one way of seeing what he is getting at is to trace the shift, over centuries, in the connotation of 'liberties'. The very notion of human rights – rights which attach to the individual as such, without consideration for social status or material circumstance – would have been well-nigh incomprehensible in the feudal context. Such values are, typically, abstract and formal in their reference; this is a corollary of their very universalism. They are not defined in material or particularistic terms. This is, in one way, their strength. For the materially subordinated – in other words, the majority – this is also their limitation: not just in the negative sense of their ideality, their unrealizability, for most people most of the time (in the way, to use Christopher Hill's wry illustration, we are all 'free' to stay at the Ritz Hotel), but in the strongly positive sense that construction of social identity in these terms actively denies the possibility of expressing the real experience of difference, of material subordination, politically, as anything other than 'personal' and 'private' misfortune. All are equal in the illusory community. In a materially unequal society assertion of formal equality can be violently oppressive, it is itself a form of rule. But this is not our major point for the moment; we will elaborate on these themes below. At this stage in the argument we wish to register, simply, the centrality within the social theories we have considered of state formation and its associated cultural revolution to ordering a society in which capitalist economy is possible: to invert the 'standard' Marxist dogma. For Marx, as much as for any other theorist considered here, these transformations can by no stretch of the imagination be considered 'superstructural'. They are integral to the making of a bourgeois social order, a civilization. Capitalism is not just an economy, it is a regulated set of social forms of life.

These theoretical models are undoubtedly illuminating – providing they are read as critique, not putative historical description, orientations to historical inquiry, not substitutes for it.[8] They grasp significant and far from obvious generic features of capitalist society, and point to their interrelatedness. But regarded from a historical viewpoint, as depictions of any particular capitalism or the processes of its formation, such ideal-types are obviously inadequate; this is not their analytic function. Construction of commodity relations and formation of the political state was nowhere, empirically speaking, 'one and the same act'. The existence of commodity production and exchange – as Marx was well aware – long predated the emergence of capitalism as a dominant mode of production. They were present as subsidiary but important forms of economy throughout most of feudal Europe, extensively so from the eleventh century. The political state – 'the State' in the modern sense – was also, as we have seen, very long in the making. This is true in two senses. First, those agencies and institutions which ultimately came to be identifiable as 'the' state in many cases had a long – in England, an extremely long – precapitalist pedigree. Second, the organization of these agencies into the kind of polity Weber describes as 'rational–bureaucratic' or Marx contrasts with feudal forms of rule was protracted, and indeed in many instances remains – in terms of the models' expectations – no more than partial.

In England this is particularly apparent. It was the uncodified common law, not 'rational' Roman law, which provided the legal framework within which capitalism developed in England. The English state lacked any elaborate professionalized bureaucracy, in Weber's sense, until well into the nineteenth century (and even then, as we have severally indicated, it was and is far from being free of 'patrimonial', nomination/patronage features). England remains a monarchy, and – we insist – not merely cosmetically so. English sovereigns long ago lost significant personal power, but monarchic forms remain central not only to the legitimacy but also to a significant extent to the machinery of English state power. The government is 'Her Majesty's', symbolically delivered to her at the 'State' opening of Parliament in elaborate ceremonial which includes kissing of hands. In any society, something conveys authority on forms of rule, legitimates power. Royalty – the centrepiece of the 'dignified' parts of the constitution – epitomizes a claim to legitimacy based, *inter alia*, on antiquity, tradition, continuity, a self-conscious and carefully constructed Englishness. It is an emblem of what is held to set 'us' apart from other countries, with their *parvenu* monarchs or their vulgarly elected heads of state. This is not 'merely' a matter of ideology, it is, practically, enabling. States of emergency are declared (legitimated, authorized) by Queen-in-Council. When, in 1984, Her Majesty's government sought to ban trades unions at GCHQ (by Order-in-Council), they argued in the courts that their action could not properly be subject to judicial scrutiny because it concerned national security and thus came within the province of the royal prerogative. Information given to opposition leaders on Privy Coun-cillor terms (such as Tam Dalyell alleges was done concerning the Falklands task force) is subject to total secrecy in the interests of national security. In England, too, a hereditary upper chamber, a House of Lords, retained extensive legislative powers well into the twentieth century and is still far from toothless, as is indicated by its 1984 quashing of the 'paving bill' for abolishing the Greater London Council. The Lords remains, as we have noted, the highest court in the land. We have exemplified many more such 'unmodernized' features of the 'modern' English state in our text. Nor is this failure to conform to the models merely an English eccentricity; we have seen the failure in 1983 of the Equal Rights Amendment (outlawing sexual discrimination) to pass the US Congress. Half the population, at least, it seems, have still fully to enter the political nation of 'equal' citizens in that supposed 'home' of bourgeois democracy. The long struggle of Afro-Americans for civil and political rights tells the same story.

It is wrong, we believe – profoundly wrong – to see in this kind of 'deviation' an 'incomplete bourgeois revolution', or the survival out of time of 'feudal relics'. This is a dominant perception of English experience, both from the left (Anderson and Nairn) and the right (Sir Keith Joseph); Engels anticipated them in finding the 'logical incongruities' of the British state 'a sore trial to the reasoning mind'.[9] The correct conclusion to draw is otherwise. Societies are not like 'reasoning minds'. It is the expectations – of 'social formations' like cybernetic systems, of 'revolutions' that are clean breaks – which are at fault. The sociological pictures, then, need shading; at times, indeed, they need to be comprehensively rethought.

What needs first to be added to the sociological realization that capitalism is never 'merely' an economy is the historical realization that empirically we are only ever talking about historically particular capitalisms. Outside theoreticians' models, there is no such thing as capitalism 'in general'; real capitalisms only ever exist as particular, historical forms of civilization. These do not, as Marx put it, fall from the sky. They are actively constructed through the transformation of pre-existing social forms. This historical legacy both constrains and provides the (only) resources for capitalist construction, 'in-forming' it, giving it its particular shape and weight. Thus although, for instance, one might be able 'in theory' to imagine a non-patriarchal capitalism – patriarchy cannot be inferred from the concept of capital, and attempts to do so are invariably reductionist (and dismissive of the subordination of women as women) – all real capitalisms have in practice been constructed through patriarchal forms of social relationship, which have a history independent of that of capitalism itself.

This dialectic of constraint and construction is central to historical understanding; it is also, in many ways, the most difficult thing to grasp. Both Whig interpretations of English history and many varieties of Marxism fail to grasp it, the former seeing only continuities without understanding how they have been transformed to make something qualitatively new, the latter searching for definitive revolutionary breaks without sufficiently appreciating the nature of the raw materials out of which capitalist civilizations are built and the constraints and continuities these impose. The 'logical incongruities', in short, must serve as the starting-point for reconstructing the history of capitalist civilization in England – or anywhere else, since in the real world all cases are in their own ways 'peculiar'. They should not be dismissed as a set of irritating disturbances to be put on one side.

England was 'peculiar' in a number of ways. Macfarlane stresses the long heritage of English 'individualism', perhaps overly so. Marxist historians have done valuable work on 'differentiation' among medieval peasants and craftsmen. Brenner seeks a master-explanation for the emergence of capitalism in England in contrasts of the lord/peasant relation there with both Eastern Europe (where a 'second serfdom' could be imposed) and France (where peasants gained greater property rights). We have drawn attention to the peculiarities of the aristocracy in medieval and early modern England, making for a more commercial spirit. But without wanting to deny the importance of any of this, where England was most visibly 'peculiar' – with implications for all these more evidently 'economic' issues – was in the central terrain covered by this book: state formation, and its accompanying cultural revolution. Here, we believe, there is a lot to be added to the theories we have discussed; specifically on the basis of English experience, but of more general relevance also.

In terms of those theories themselves, we would expect England's early national unification around a state capable of exercising governance internally and – at least by the mid-seventeenth century – defending 'national interests' externally to have provided capitalism with a uniquely favourable environment in which to grow. Braudel acknowledges this in his identification of late-seventeenth-century

England as the first truly national market. But at least as important, and much less often remarked, is the cultural significance of this state formation. We trust we have substantiated our thesis that state formation is cultural revolution. The foregoing theories go some way towards recognizing this, in areas we have discussed. What they do not sufficiently address – and this is a direct consequence of their lack of historical specificity, for historical inquiry brings this out very clearly – are the cultural implications of the fact that we are dealing specifically with *nation* states. It is in terms of national polities that state formation reconstructs social relations, internally as well as with 'outsiders' (including 'enemies within'), reshaping identities and loyalties; the 'illusory community' of the bourgeois state is always represented as a national community. If we are to take seriously Marx's argument that the state is the *form* in which the bourgeoisie organize their social power, we cannot ignore the fact that the cultural *content* of that form is integrally national. The state is the major agency through which capitalism's wider cultural revolution is organized, its key material regulative agency. It is both, in Durkheim's words, 'the very organ of social thought' – actively reshaping social classifications and cementing them in its routines, broadcasting (claimed) collective representations and sanctifying them in its rituals – and 'supremely the organ of moral discipline'. Most Marxism has entirely ignored this moral dimension of state activity; the Durkheimian tradition, on the other hand, grasps it in insufficiently historical and material terms. Cultural revolution is not merely an ideational matter, and cannot be considered independently of the materiality of state formation – what state agencies are, how they act, and on whom.

For people to (be encouraged/constrained to) identify themselves predominantly in terms of nationality, rather than either more locally (e.g. subjects of a particular lord) or more widely (as e.g. in the medieval concept of Christendom) is a relatively recent historical phenomenon. How national identity is constructed is of course crucial. In the subordinated lands of the Austro-Hungarian empire in the nineteenth century, for instance, nationhood was largely defined through suppressed cultural forms – above all language itself – and oppositional historical traditions. The operas of Dvořák and Smetana – in a country where opera is not just an elite cultural form – which draw on heroic Czech mythology (Dalibor, Libuše), history (The Brandenburgers in Bohemia), folk tales (Rusalka), or idealizations of popular life (The Bartered Bride), symbolize this construction of a sense of nation though cultural forms of resistance; so does the building of the National Theatre in Prague in 1881, by popular subscription. In the twentieth century, in China, Vietnam or many

African countries, national liberation struggles have been indissolubly bound up with wider social struggles and often led by socialist parties.

The English experience is different. One might, at a pinch, construe Tudor nationalism as a struggle for national independence from papal domination; many contemporaries undoubtedly did. But the content of English nationalism has rarely been popular (as distinct from populist); the revolutions that made England a nation have been (where successful) revolutions from above. England was, in Trevelyan's phrase, 'hammered into a nation', primarily through the machinery of state (1962: 109); the hammer, we might add, falling harder on some than others. In consequence dominant images of national identity and tradition – of, in that significant phrase, national character – are closely bound up with both the culture of the English ruling classes and the (claimed) history of the state forms through which their power is organized. We mean this to apply to those celebrated elements of 'national character', the supposed reasonableness, moderation, pragmatism, hostility to ideology, 'muddling through', quirkiness, eccentricity, and so on, of 'the English', every bit as much as to the more evident patriotic symbols of the rule of law, the 'Mother of Parliaments' and the Royal Family. This very particular set of cultural images was fundamental to the construction of English capitalist civilization, in a number of ways.

First, they were integral to the making of the English ruling class itself – from the mid-sixteenth century, if not before, a class increasingly capitalist in substance, if in some ways distinctively 'aristocratic' in style. This is true in both a material and cultural sense. As JPs, deputy lieutenants, MPs , the 'political nation' met, conferred, deliberated, acted; the institutions of the nation state were the sinews of their power, the instruments giving coherence and continuity to their actions and aspirations. They were material forms of self-organization, on a national scale from an early date. They were also enviably flexible forms within which the enlargement of the political nation, of 'Society', could be 'managed' across the centuries (albeit at times with difficulty). These institutions were the focus for a political culture expressed in self-consciously national forms, of enormous solidity, confidence and depth. The seventeenth-century gentleman JP, the nineteenth-century manufacturer MP, could and did lay claim to, and routinely articulate their aspirations in terms of, national traditions stretching back to Magna Carta and beyond, and a supposedly unbroken history of gradualist evolution. This applies equally to bourgeois (and indeed some non-bourgeois) radicalisms, from the Mills to the Fabians and beyond. There is an important sense in which for instance Burke *and* Paine belong within an English national political culture in a way in which Jacobinism, Bolshevism or today's catch-all demon, 'Marxism', emphatically do not – the latter having been comprehensively regulated out of our 'common' heritage. These already national forms of political culture were means through which bourgeois values, aspirations and images were eventually portrayed as universal, the common good; and deeply rooted means at that. The bourgeoisie in England was in its very formation a class both organized and thinking of itself nationally.

Marx observes that if it is to rule successfully, every bourgeoisie must be able to present itself as the representative of society as a whole. On reading such statements we are habituated immediately to think – as Marx himself was undoubtedly thinking – of eighteenth-century French *philosophes* and those 'quintessentially' bourgeois documents, the Declarations of American Independence and of the Rights of Man: declarations of a new world. But the quintessential bourgeoisie – if England is indeed capitalism's 'classic ground' – did otherwise. The forms through which they claimed to speak for all were bourgeois neither in origin nor, in terms of 'classical' sociological expectations, in character. They were those of this existing national polity and culture, already claiming, with some legitimacy, to be 'above' class and other differences – albeit, importantly, a polity and culture increasingly transformed from the sixteenth century onwards. They were also, arguably, much more solid for that than would be 'classical' bourgeois legitimations, in exactly the way Holdsworth argues that 'lawfulness' in general is a more powerful support for government than specific codified laws. In Weberian terms, in England a (slowly and incompletely) rationalizing state continued (and continues) to be legitimated by primarily traditional forms of authority: the power of symbol, ritual, custom, routine, ways in which things have 'always' been done, in which the very bizarreness and anachronism of the forms is its own legitimation, protecting them from 'rational' scrutiny. The 'puzzle' of eighteenth-century Old Corruption perhaps best exemplifies this, but there were no clean 'breaks' in the nineteenth century either. This is a far deeper, more tenacious, more flexible set of resources for ruling than any more overt (and thus overtly challengeable) political ideology is likely to be. It should also make us wonder whether some standard sociological contrasts of 'tradition' and 'modernity' are not, perhaps, a trifle overdrawn – useful in seeing the wood for the trees but of very little practical help in guiding our way through the undergrowth.

Second, this set of cultural images provided the moral energy for English imperialism: the successive imposition of English civilization on the 'dark corners' of England itself, Wales, Scotland, Ireland and eventually that British empire which covered a quarter of the globe. To say this is far from denying the brutality of conquest (or the rapacity of commerce): Drogheda, Culloden, Amritsar, the slave trade, the Opium Wars are chapters which cannot be excised from the long history of English 'civilization' of less fortunate peoples. Our point is that it took a national culture of extraordinary self-confidence and moral rectitude to construe such imperialism as a 'civilizing mission' (and in fact to rule with surprisingly little use of direct armed force, in comparative terms, from the 'Mother Country'); *and* for long periods, with a fair degree of success, to bedazzle the domestically subordinated with the spectacle of empire. We can trace this through from the heroic myths of the 'elect nation' in the sixteenth and seventeenth centuries to the more philistine, secular and complacent but no less missionary motifs of the nineteenth. Beside the greed and butchery we must put the reading matter on the East India Company ships, the ethos of the district commissioners and the Indian civil service; not in order to write off (or excuse) the former, but rather to understand the cultural forms, the energizing vision, that could animate and legitimate it notwithstanding.[10] Marx's remark about 'making the world in their own image' applies very literally in the case of the English bourgeoisie.

Third, those same cultural forms were key forms of rule as much within 'the nation' as without. Some general observations of Durkheim's and Marx's, concerning the character of moral order, are worth interjecting here. Durkheim sees society (in general) as 'an end that surpasses us and at the same time appears to us to be good and desirable, since it is bound up with the very fibres of our being' (1906: 56). This is what we mean when we talk about social structuring as the creation of social identities, of subjectivities. Moral order accordingly has a dual character, both externally regulative and internally constitutive: it 'must . . . be not only obligatory but desirable and desired' (ibid.: 45). Marx and Engels comprehend this in class terms:

'Vocation, destiny, task, ideal' are . . . the conditions of existence of the ruling class . . . which are ideally expressed in law, morality, etc., are more or less consciously transformed by the ideologists of that class into something that in history exists independently, and which can be conceived in the consciousness of the separate individuals of that class as vocation, etc; and which are set up as a standard of life in opposition to the individuals of the oppressed class, partly as an embellishment or realisation of domination, partly as a moral means for this domination. It is to be noted here, as in general with ideologists, that they inevitably put the thing upside down and regard their ideology both as the creative force and as the aim of all social relations, whereas it is only an expression and symptom of these relations. (1846: 472–3)

What both Durkheim and Marx are talking about is the attempted construction of aspiration, the internalization of bourgeois norms as constitutive of personalities. The concept we have used for this is discipline, which is similarly Janus-faced – recall Milton's comments. What needs to be added to their realization is an appreciation of historical context; we need to talk about particularity and agency. In the bourgeois world, it is precisely as the nation that Durkheim's transcendental 'society' is made palpable; Marx's ruling-class domination, likewise, is nationally organized, bourgeois conditions of existence idealized as national character. Here, as in a hall of mirrors, requisite forms of behaviour, attitude, aspiration, feeling are held to be properly English – providing 'Englishness' with a substantial content – while their claimed Englishness is exactly what gives them their transcendental legitimacy. The Nation, in short, is the master-symbol which sinews capitalism's cultural revolution, displacing earlier vocabularies of legitimation – kinship, the ties of vassalage, Divine Right – though, as in England, these latter may be drawn upon in its construction. The nation epitomizes the fictive community in which we are all citizens, staking out the cognitive territory which that revolution comprehensively re-forms. And 'the State' – the nation made manifest – is the material agency through which this reformulation is concerted; not its source, that lies in relations of production and reproduction, but the central means of its organization.

Particular – bourgeois, patriarchal – conceptions of 'the English way of life' were more or less forcibly imposed on the majority, and this imposition is a major means through which the male English ruling class has legitimated its rule. To speak in the name – and language – of the nation both denies the particularity of what is being said (and who is saying it) and defines alternatives and challenges as sectional, selfish, partial, ultimately treasonable: recall the *Times* editorial with which we began this book. To define 'us' in national terms (as against class, or locality, or ethnic group, or gender, or religion, or any other terms in which social identity might be constructed and historical experience comprehended) has consequences. Such classifications are means for a project of social integration which is also, inseparably, an active *dis*integration of other focuses of identity and conceptions of subjectivity. They provide a basis for construction and organization of collective memory – the writing of history, the manufacture of 'tradition' – which is inseparably an active organization of forgetting.[11] Sociologists have, in general, treated 'integration' far too neutrally, ignoring its differential aspects: who is seeking to integrate whom, to what ends, by what means, and in what forms; and who suffers, which ends are denied, which means declared illegitimate, which forms suppressed, whose histories rewritten, thereby? These points are important, and bear expansion. This will also allow us to elaborate on our criticisms of the predominant idealism of ways in which moral regulation and cultural revolution are conventionally apprehended.

Nation states constitute and regulate a field of social vision which is both unitary (minimizing differences within the nation) and Manichaean (opening up a regulative and rhetorical space for those who are 'alien' to what is claimed to be 'the English way of life'). This is the field within which official politics proceeds, both grounding and bounding it. 'The State' symbolizes, is in Marx's terms the ideal incarnation or embodiment of, the nation; particularly so, we would argue, in the English case, where conceptions of national identity are so closely bound up with the history of state formation. Its symbols and rituals come to stand for, represent, that which demarcates – i.e. in the Manichaean vision, constitutes – us, sets us apart and makes us what we are. Disloyalty conversely is seen to threaten our very subjectivities. It is the linking of the transcendent symbols of nationhood with the humdrum, ordinary and everyday, in such a way that the former can be claimed as representing the latter, that is crucial here. The power of this discourse is enormous: to take a small but revealing example, not the least of General Galtieri's atrocities (and a means through which the notion of English sovereignty over the Falklands/Malvinas was concretized, each echoing back the other) was to make the – for these purposes, English[12] – inhabitants drive on the right hand side of the road. Internally the nation (and its symbolic incarnation, 'the State') is held to transcend differences and hence claims citizens' primary loyalties. The category of those outside the nation, conversely, is an extremely capacious and flexible one. Evidently it includes Argentine generals; but by extension it also embraces all those who are 'disloyal'. Margaret Thatcher was doing nothing new when in 1984 she compared the president of the National Union of Mineworkers to Galtieri (and suddenly discovered the fascist qualities of the latter). Papists, Jacobins, 'Marxists' (not to mention suffragettes, gypsies, trades unionists) have all been apprehended in the past centrally in terms of their supposedly un-English qualities, allegiances (recall the 'Zinoviev letter') or forms of behaviour. In the English case the vocabulary of (more or less racist) xenophobic epithets is particularly rich, this being one cultural legacy of having civilized the world.

The materiality of this project needs far greater emphasis than it has traditionally received. The social classifications of capitalist civilization are actively – often forcibly – regulated by the state, and made palpable in its routine functioning. What counts as a 'real' property right, as between, say, rights in conquest, custom, law, is defined by state practices, legitimating certain forms of claim, outlawing others. A relation between two people is only a marriage if contracted according to certain forms, religious or civil, solemnized in definite, licensed places, and recorded in specific registers. The same is true of what constitutes a household, a trade union, a political organization, a school, a university; we have exemplified this central facet of state formation as cultural revolution, over centuries, in considerable detail and for many areas of social life. The routines of state both materialize and take for granted particular definitions. 'How things are' (allowed to be) is not simply a matter of ideological assertion (and 'consensus' is never merely ideational); it is concretized in laws, judicial decisions (and their compilation as case law), registers, census returns, licences, charters, tax forms, and all the other myriad ways in which the state states and individualities are regulated. It is recorded – concretized in time, linking past and present, and mapping out the shape of the future, in an apparently unbroken chain – in that official documentary system whose longevity and breadth in England we have remarked before. This is how we are collectively (mis)represented – not abstractly, not ideally, but in the very forms in which the rituals and routines of state operate. This is, without doubt, an immensely powerful language, alternative representations appearing fragmentary and insecure in the face of this massively authoritative organization of what is to count as reality. This system of power is inseparably also a system of knowledge, both in terms of quantity (how much the state knows, its 'intelligence' – comprehensive, and remarkably early, in the English case) and quality (the authority claimed for it, other sources of knowledge being less authoritative by the very fact of being unauthorized). Recall the long, long history of surveys, commissions, inquiries, inspections, the establishment of authorized facts, in England, from Domesday to the Blue Books.

But – it is time again to emphasize – social integration within the nation state *is* a project; and one in constant jeopardy from the very facts of material difference – the real relations of bourgeois civilization – whose recognition official discourse seeks to repress. Two things need to be said here. First, acquiescence (to a fact) should not be confused with assent (to an ideal). Compliance is not always consent; we should not too readily presume the 'incorporation' of the working class or any other subordinated group. Difference will always provide the experiential basis for alternative identifications, aspirations, moralities, and this basis will exist so long as capitalism endures. 'Common' cultural symbols, values and heritages will be differentially experienced and interpreted: representations – an instance would be English 'liberties' – may be collective without being unitary in their meaning. Second, and in consequence, bourgeois social integration needs always, as we have said, also to be understood as entailing the active disintegration – dilution, disruption, denial – of such alternatives, and it cannot proceed otherwise, because bourgeois society is factually not the unity it is claimed to be.

Here state regulation is crucial, and the fact of difference – the disjunction between official representations and the reality represented – is why it is so constantly necessary, if bourgeois self-images are to be sustained. What state activities above all regulate into silence are precisely identifications in terms of, and expressions of the experience of, differences – in other words, that which materially (as opposed to ideologically) makes us what we are. These are systematically and concertedly ruled out by the integrative categories of official discourse: the citizen, the voter, the taxpayer, the consumer, the parent, the *'man* in the street'. They are systematically negated by the very procedures of state institutions: we can all cast a vote, we can all write to our MP, we can all sue in the courts, we all have equal opportunities at school, and so on. Material difference cannot be adequately expressed in these forms, while those forms (of speech, of politics, of social organization and practice) through which it could be voiced are actively denied legitimacy, in ways, ranging from outright criminalization to subtler forms of 'encouragement', whose longevity and reach in England we have sufficiently illustrated. Universalizing bourgeois forms and norms is, from one side, the active creation of cultural incompetence; Bernstein's argument on language codes can stand for much here, providing we realize all codes are in their own ways restricted and the privileging of one over another ('standard English') is a matter of power and a means of control. Integration needs to be understood at least as much in terms of rendering the subordinated speechless – striking them dumb – as in terms of the active securing of assent; marginalizing, localizing, parochializing, sectionalizing expressions of the realities of difference in the face of the monolithic idealized unities of official discourse. From the other side the project is one of forcing people to speak in particular ways – as voters, 'respectable' trades unionists, plaintiffs (or more often, for the majority, defendants) in the courts – if they are to be able to say anything at all. Not the least of 'the State's' monopolies is of the means of legitimated political expression.

It is insufficiently appreciated – including by Marxists – just how violent such 'integration' is for the 'integrated' majority. We mean this in two senses. First, it is of itself a massively violent disruption of human personality, a crippling restriction of human capacity. The cruelty lies in defining normality in terms most people are materially prevented from ever aspiring to. The cost of this is written in what is widely perceived, and experienced, as a loss of self-respect when one finds oneself 'unemployed', or – another facet of the same moral order – the sad phrase 'just a housewife'. One of the most bitter ironies of the *Times* editorial with which we began this book is the evocation of 'citizens at their places of work' (to describe scabs) when the miners' strike was precipitated by the National Coal Board's proposal to close pits with a loss of 20,000 jobs. Essential relations of bourgeois order are experienced and expressed as personal inadequacy. Second, overtly violent means have always been and still remain fundamental to the making and sustaining of this order. We should recall the instruments through which the defining forms and images of English 'civilization' were secured; how, for instance, England was made Protestant, or with what violence the rights of private property (for the few) and the habits of wage or domestic unwaged labour (for the many) were instilled and normalized. Or the legalized barbarisms which have throughout the centuries covered by this book enforced domestic subordination on women and made no small contribution to defining culturally dominant images and self-images of 'femininity'.

The general paradigm of regulation, evident in all these cases, is of continuous and more or less violent suppression of alternatives coupled with active 'encouragement' by state agencies and activities of preferred forms: these latter are then typically re-cognized as 'provision', donation into a disordered vacuum. The ordinary procedures of state inflate to become taken-for-granted boundaries of the possible, occupying – in the way an army does a territory – the field of social vision. The same boundaries are massively, powerfully, sanctified in the magnificent rituals of state, catching us up with an emotional force difficult to resist. This latter must be acknowledged, it is central to the energy of rule. The Durkheim/Hobbes parallel with religion goes to the heart of state power. Within 'the State', alternatives become difficult to conceive, in all senses. Our stress throughout this book on the cultural content of state forms and activities is not an argument for 'consensus' versus 'coercion'. Rather it is a question of the violent establishment and continuous regulation of 'consent', orchestrated by that organization which abrogates to itself precisely the monopoly of the legitimate use of physical force in society, 'the State'. Capitalist order has never been sustained (merely) by 'the dull compulsion of economic relations' (*pace* Marx, 1867: 737) and state regulation is not something that can be relegated to the dark ages of 'primitive accumulation'; it was, is and continues to be an essential relation of capitalism, coextensive with bourgeois civilization itself. 'The State' *is* the form in which the bourgeoisie organizes its social power, but that power – and its fundamental violence – is not just the visibly and externally repressive one of 'prisons, bodies of armed men, etc.' The enormous extent of that power cannot be understood unless state forms are understood as cultural forms, state formation as cultural revolution, and cultural images as continually and extensively state-regulated. A central dimension – we are tempted to say, the secret – of state power is the way it works within us.

The final set of observations we would like to make here concerns the implications of our argument for any possible emancipatory historiography, of England in particular, and of social transformations in general. We have argued that state formation is an essential – and, from the left at any rate, generally an understudied – dimension of both how capitalist civilization was made and how it is held together; the central means, to repeat, of its organization. State power is not 'superstructural': it is centrally – which does not mean exclusively – through state formation that the social relations of production and reproduction which underpin a civilization which is bourgeois and patriarchal have been made hegemonic, though 'the State' is not generally the source of such relations. Crucial to this – and equally understudied – we have further argued, is the part played by state formation in capitalism's cultural revolution. 'The State' has orchestrated the unending project of moral regulation. This does not mean that we see state formation as having 'caused' capitalism, any more than that we see the medieval or Tudor English state as in any simple sense 'bourgeois'. We do not seek to replace one either/or dogmatism with another, an economic with a political determinism. But it does mean state formation as cultural revolution plays a far more important role in our conception of both the origins and the nature of capitalist civilization than has normally been the case in historical materialism. This has a number of historiographic consequences.

We have argued that the national character of the nation state is fundamental to capitalism's cultural revolution. Bourgeois classes organize their power, materially and culturally, through specifically national polities. English Marxist historiography has traditionally looked to the upheavals of the mid-seventeenth century as the *locus classicus* of 'the' bourgeois revolution, and its analytic focus has been on the emergence, in those decades, of 'typically' bourgeois forms of polity (which have then to be seen as having been 'incompletely' secured). As we see it, this obsessional search for 'the' English bourgeois revolution has to be doubly qualified.

On the one hand, much more attention needs to be given to the largely antecedent (and non-bourgeois) construction of a *nation* – a set of institutional forms, but also integrally a cultural space – within which more identifiably 'bourgeois' transformations (economic, political, cultural, moral) could operate; to the construction, in other words, of the resources – material, institutional, cultural – out of which the real English bourgeois state was made. This book marks no more than a contribution to this; it is, as we made clear at the outset, precisely an essay. A good deal more research is needed. But to adopt this perspective means that the 'peculiarities' of medieval English polity, and above all the revolution of the 1530s and its consolidation under Elizabeth, need much more consideration than Marxists have generally given them. These are key moments in the making of a nation state; likewise the transformation of the latter into the modern democratic nation state in the nineteenth century also needs re-evaluation in these terms. If forced, we would identify these as the two key moments in the making of the great arch. They have traditionally been left to Whig or otherwise right-wing historians. Though we would not labour the point – for this has not been a comparative study – this book does provide grounds for hazarding that the precocity (and character) of state formation in England may be *one* important reason why England, specifically, became capitalism's 'classic ground'.

Extending the point, we would draw out two historical dialectics which bear on this. The first is a dialectic of continuity and change. Some readers – not least, Marxists – may feel we have strayed dangerously close to Whiggery in our stress on continuities. But Whig historians grasp a truth well expressed by James Campbell et al. Observing that 'no banality could be more secure than that every country and people are the product of their past,' they nonetheless opine that in England the connection – ultimately, in their view, with the Dark Ages – is 'of a different order'. The reason, they think, is 'because of the continuity of the state and its institutions' (1982: 244). We are far from denying the existence of substantial revolutions in English government – the Norman/Angevin, the Tudor, the seventeenth- and nineteenth-century revolutions have been central to our account. But it is equally to the point that these could plausibly be presented as mere evolutions, not least in the implications this has for the legitimation of 'the State' and the order it claimed collectively to represent. In England absolutism was not required to make the nation, nor *philosophes* to hegemonize bourgeois culture.

Related to this first dialectic is the second: of centre and locality. We have traced this throughout the centuries, and need not rehearse it here. But crudely, we would argue that there is to be observed a double contrast with major continental states. In England there was neither 'parcellization of sovereignty' nor 'absolutist' centralization. In mainland Europe the second often succeeded the first. For the 1630s, Aylmer estimates that the total number of salaried state officials for the whole of England was at most some hundreds; for the single French province of Normandy, the comparable figure was over 3,000 (1961: 440). In brief, and related to the 'precocity' of state formation, the English polity worked through the 'collaboration of well-to-do classes in power' from an early date noted by Bloch; and this, we would suggest, allowed the changing ruling-class formations in England *national* political expression – and ultimately power – in a way impossible in most European polities. In other words it was not just the earliness, but equally the peculiar character of English state formation – the peculiar 'openness' of state forms to a changing political nation – that made it so conducive, at the end of the day, to capitalism's wider revolutions. We might follow Edward Thompson (1965) here in criticizing the 'urban bias' (again reflecting dominant and overly schematic sociological paradigms) of many Marxist accounts, seeking here there and everywhere for a 'classical' bourgeoisie, living in towns and struggling against the 'feudal state'. In the English case it is the embourgeoisement of the landed classes (gentry and peers!) themselves – as well as, to be sure, their trading, familial and other ties with urban elites – which should claim primary attention.

On the other hand, what is (mis)construed as the 'incompleteness' of the seventeenth-century revolutions needs similiarly to be rethought, in terms of an understanding of the historically particular cultural and political forms – resources – through which the real English ruling class actually did make itself and organize its rule. We have suggested that exactly the supposed 'anachronisms' of English polity and culture lie at the heart of the security of the bourgeois state in England – to the present day. It is this that Whig historiography grasps, albeit ideologically. None of this is to deny either the reality or the necessity, for capitalist classes, of major transformations of state forms, in the seventeenth century or after. 'The State' was, as we have shown, periodically and comprehensively re-formed; its history is not one of smooth evolution (or teleological unfolding) but of successive 'long waves' of revolution and consolidation. It is a question of the overall conception we have of 'the bourgeois revolution'. It is time the search for *an* English '1789' was buried once and for all. We are speaking of a great arch spanning centuries rather than decades. We hope this book contributes to a rethinking of traditional Marxist historical periodization.

We hope, also, that it contributes to a reassessment of the objects of historical materialist research. These have far too frequently been narrowly 'economic', an effect of the tyranny of base/superstructure models – whether overt or not – which we have criticized elsewhere.[13] There are of course major exceptions to this charge – we are thinking for instance of the life-work of Christopher Hill, that Marxist who insisted on the need to take religious justifications for conduct seriously, or of Edward Thompson, who has rightly savaged 'base/ superstructure' thinking, or of Raymond Williams's 'cultural materialism' – without which this book could not have been written. What we have tried to show is that in the real world 'economies' exist only as historical forms of civilization, and in the case of capitalist economy state formation is crucial to their making and sustaining. Capitalism is not, and never has been, 'self-regulating', ideologies to the contrary notwithstanding. Here, the imagery – it should be said, the exceedingly masculinist imagery – of states as objects or instruments, capable of being 'captured' and 'used' equally by different classes, needs jettisoning as much as the iconography of 'the' momentary revolution to which it is integral. What we have been dealing with, in this book, is the immensely long, complicated, laborious micro-construction and reconstruction of appropriate forms of power; forms fitted to ways in which a particular class, gender, race imposes its 'standards of life' as 'the national interest' and seeks their internalization as 'national character'. The capacity of such groups to rule rests neither on some supposedly 'prior' economic power – it is, on the contrary, above all through state forms and their cultural revolution that such power is made, consolidated, legitimated and normalized – nor simply on their control of some neutral set of state instruments. Their political power resides rather in the routine regulative functioning of state forms themselves, in their day-to-day enforcing, as much by what they are as in any particular policies they carry out, of a particular social order as 'normality', the boundaries of the possible.

This again means certain areas cannot be safely ceded to bourgeois historians. We have in mind particularly legal, 'administrative' and 'constitutional' history. Their minutiae show what 'the State' materially is, as against its 'encouraged' self-images; the nuts and bolts, the very fabric of rule. We have sufficiently argued that the history of cultural forms cannot be severed from this fabric. We are beginning, now, to see studies of key areas and forms of rule, from this perspective: notably of the criminal law and its social classifications, and of the regulation of gender relations and familial forms. But there is room for more. We need equally to examine, from the point of view of their cultural consequences, the more apparently mundane, routine, workaday facets of state activity – private law, taxation, 'administration': the routines of rule. It is in these that the elementary forms of bourgeois civilization are daily established – echoed and authorized – before any 'special apparatus of repression' (which is how, touching only the tip of the iceberg, Engels defined the state) becomes necessary. The magnificent rituals, the 'dignified' parts of 'the State', cry out for equal attention. Analysis of both is central to any truly materialist understanding of the workings of the bourgeois world. History cannot only be written from below.

To conclude. In one sense, this book has been 'about' England; we sought historical specificity to illuminate – nuance, modify, question, sometimes reject – generalities. But its relevance, we hope, does not end there. Nor does it end with capitalism's past. One service the bourgeoisie have done the future is to demonstrate just how transformable the world is.

We took the concept of cultural revolution initially from the historical experience of socialist, not capitalist, construction; and we would like to end by taking it back to those roots, in the struggle for the emancipation of the many, not the domination of the few. Socialist construction was something Mao Tsetung argued would take many centuries, and as many cultural revolutions; transformations, as Marx put it, of people's circumstances and selves. The historical experience of attempted socialist construction has already shown – in often bloodily tragic ways – the paramount necessity fundamentally to rethink what, and how much, is involved in any conceivably emancipatory social transformation. Socialism too needs to rid itself of the 'muck of ages' if it is to be more than a new form of oppression. Nothing shows this more eloquently than the history of women's struggles for self-emancipation, and the multiple blocks which existing socialist forms – of thought, of morality, of political practice, of social and material organization – put in their way. The historical experience of peasants, treated as a 'sea of enemies' and regimented into collective farms, and of workers, denied trade union and other forms in which their specific experiences could be expressed (within what Nikita Khrushchev conceptualized as the 'state of the whole people'), tells other parts of the same story, from Kronstadt and the Committees of the Poor, through Stalin's 'pacification of the villages' in 1929, to Solidarity and the genocidal 'social reconstruction' that followed the (no less genocidal) US bombing of Kampuchea. We have indicated what we think 'actually existing socialism' has achieved, for the majority, elsewhere.[14] But no intellectually or morally serious emancipatory politics can ignore these 'deformations', or their roots in existing forms of socialist theory and practice. They are not, unfortunately, mere aberrations, attributable to the iron logic of circumstance or the personal evil of a Stalin or a Pol Pot. 'Backwardness' and 'betrayal' will not do forever as explanations; for long they have been moral and intellectual evasions.

One only learns through trial, and there is no trial without error. It is only through the struggles of the subordinated that the tyranny of social forms and practices, both those inherited from capitalism and its past, and those created by new forms of social order (planning, parties, unitary ideologies) can be recognized for the fetters on the liberation of human capacities that they are. It is only in such struggles that emancipatory social forms – through which differences can be recognized and celebrated, as ingredients of a collectively human future, rather than regulated and denied – are discovered. These, too, do not fall from the sky. In the past we have argued on the basis of the historical experience of socialist construction that both untransformed capitalist 'techniques' of production and the state 'machine' have in this way been shown to be as much fetters on as resources for emancipatory social transformation, an integral part of what needs to be transformed rather than the means for transformation socialists have so often held them to be. We would now go further, questioning much in the systematic, objectivist, 'scientific' and instrumental – in short, authoritarian and hierarchical – quality of much socialist (social-democratic as well as Marxist) theory[15] and practice more generally, and its relative unconcern with both the 'personal' and the 'moral'. Feminist critique has done *all* emancipatory politics an inestimable service in restructuring political discourse and practice around these issues, though the same concern can be found in (too often, subordinated) strands in the socialist tradition. As Catherine MacKinnon has written, 'because Marxists tend to conceive of powerlessness, first and last, as concrete and externally imposed, they believe that it must be concretely and externally undone to be changed' (1982: 520). There is a revolution in political epistemology here, of profound importance: a timely focus on the exercise of power as residing, at root, in forms of human relationship and the construction of different subjectivities, and emancipation as beginning with the construction of forms and forums within which that experience can be voiced. Studying capitalist construction, capitalism's cultural revolution, leads us only to generalize these points. For there are important parallels to be drawn between these two endeavours, though their aims and objectives – domination and emancipation, exploitation and liberation of people's collective capacities – could not be more fundamentally opposed.

What emerges most forcefully from this study is that capitalist political and cultural forms are precisely that: *forms* – of social practice, identity, organization – which open up some possibilities and close down others, develop some human capacities and under-develop others. They are specifically capitalist forms, means for the ordering of a world in which most people labour ('at home' or 'at work') for the profit of the few. They are social forms which could be otherwise, as they indeed once were, before the bourgeoisie remade the world in its own image. These forms are not contingently but internally related to capitalism, they are means through which it was historically constructed and has ever been regulated. This carries its own lessons, for (to use classical Marxist terminology for a minute) both reformism and revolution, opportunism and voluntarism, as strategies and tactics of emancipatory transformation.

Against reformism and opportunism, it graphically reveals that the political gains of the bourgeois revolution – however humanized by the struggles of the subordinated – cannot simply be used in any emancipatory politics, they need also to be inwardly transformed, as comprehensively as the English bourgeoisie reconstructed their heritage to make it conformable with their needs, if they are to become means of liberation. Parliamentary democracy, the welfare state, the rule of law, and more general bourgeois conceptions of 'right', are profoundly ambiguous resources in their very constitution. Of course bourgeois democracy should be defended against fascism (or the new fiscal discipline in the name of which the present British government is seeking to abolish elected authorities for London and the major conurbations). Of course 'welfare' states should be defended against monetarist barbarism and the cruelty of 'self-help' ideologies, in a world where the means through which people could help themselves are taken away from them. Of course the rule of law should be defended against governmental diktat (and trial by jury against attempts to rid 'justice' of its remaining vestiges of popular participation). Of course human rights should be defended against governmental expediency and *raison d'état*.[16] But it needs equally to be remembered that Parliamentary democracy works on impoverished definitions of what constitutes legitimate 'politics', which themselves 'depoliticize' other arenas and issues (both 'work' and 'home' being officially outwith the 'public' sphere, the fiction of government non-intervention in 'private industry' being perfectly matched by the police force's reluctance to 'interfere' in 'domestic disputes'). Such democracy also embodies highly restricted notions of representation. Welfare states, in their external, donatory operation, reinforce conditions and experiences of powerlessness – hence the popular appeal of much conservative anti-state rhetoric. Law is bourgeois, male and white in most of its content, and profoundly alienating in its forms. 'Rights' are abstract, insubstantial and in their claimed universality devices which legitimate an oppressive and unequal social order. In short, these are not, in themselves and as presently constituted, possible forms of emancipation; they are intrinsic forms of bourgeois order. One always engages on this territory at a cost, and an emancipatory politics needs to redefine what politics is, and how – in what forms – it can be practised in an emancipatory way. This is what Marx recognized (and thought sufficiently important to prompt him to criticize the statist aspects of his own programme in the *Communist manifesto*) in the Paris

Commune of 1871, the first occasion on which the working class broke state power:

the working class cannot simply lay hold on the ready-made state machinery and wield it for their own purpose. The political instrument of their enslavement cannot serve as the political instrument of their emancipation. (1871: 196)[17]

Against voluntarism and traditional conceptions of 'revolution', the history of capitalist construction teaches other – but equally important – lessons. It shows, first, the enormous complexity and longevity of any social transformation that will be 'solid'; 'revolution' cannot be an overnight business if it is to amount to any more than a changing of the guard. Revolutionary transformation, that history graphically demonstrates, is not just about changing deeds of ownership or capturing 'power', but *making* new ways of relating, new social identities – a new moral order, a new kind of civilization, a different socialization. That history underlines, second, the need to start with existing resources; the only ones there are. As Marx put it in the same text, there are no utopias to be introduced *par décret du peuple*; the starting-point for building the new world lies in the struggles of the old. Much of the tragedy of 'actually existing socialism' lies in its 'forgetting' this – both the constraints and the resources – in the eternal utopian search for short-cuts, which legitimates the party that substitutes for the people, the clerisy whose ideology holds the keys to the future, the repression of real emancipatory transformations now for the promise of the New Jerusalem in the future. There are no short cuts (any more than there were for the bourgeoisie), no magical talismans, no ideological keys to Paradise; utopianism – for all its 'progressive' side – is in the end a profoundly repressive mode of thought when it informs political practices. Marx was right to reject it. The bourgeoisie, seeking to regulate and to rule, could adapt existing institutions of rule and regulation: the progenitors of the national state. The resources for liberation of the majority lie elsewhere. Emancipatory political forms are those – and only those – through which the subordinated can emancipate themselves, articulating the differential experiences and aspirations denied and fragmented in the unifying languages of state. Marx's 1871 conclusion remains apposite; the more so, given socialist experience since 1917. This cultural revolution is centrally:

a Revolution not against this or that, legitimate, constitutional, republican or Imperialist form of State Power. It [is] a Revolution against the *State* itself, of this supernaturalist abortion of society, a resumption by the people for the people of its own social life. It [is] not a Revolution to transfer it from one faction of the ruling classes to another, but a Revolution to break down this horrid machinery of class domination itself. (1871: 150–1)

This revolution too has deep roots and long traditions, in all that state formation has organized itself, and sought to organize us, against. There is more to do than look back in anger. Imagine.

Notes

Introduction

1 Weber 1920b: 249; Marx and Engels 1846: 89. Weber discusses the connection between modern capitalism and nation–state formation *inter alia* in his 1920a and (at more length) 1920b: pt 4; see more generally his mammoth (and unfinished) 1978a. Marx attends to the issue in general terms in certain of his early writings (1843a, b), at various points in *The German Ideology* (Marx and Engels 1846), and again in his writings on the Paris Commune (1871 – see further below, note 17 to Afterthoughts). The role of the English state with regard to capitalism is discussed extensively in *Capital* (1867) especially in pt 8 of volume 1, and in the 'precapitalist economic formations' section of *Grundrisse* (1858). His empirical studies of French (1850, 1852, 1871) and English politics (Marx and Engels 1971 is a good anthology of the latter) are also pertinent.

2 We have in mind particularly Weber 1905 and the vast literature it has spawned (see note 7 to chapter 4 below), and the seminal writings of Emile Durkheim, for whom the moral dimensions of social order were an abiding concern, and who explicitly and instructively related state formation and moral individualism, especially in his 1904. See also Elias 1939.

3 English Marxist historiography is particularly strong here, this having been an enduring concern of, in particular, Christopher Hill, Edward Thompson and Raymond Williams. Genovese is similarly sensitive in his discussions of US history, for instance in his painstaking reconstruction of the slaveholders' ethos and their moral critique of northern capitalism in his 1971.

4 Where there has been a revolution in recent years, requiring all social theories of capitalism, including Marxism, to be thought anew. There is now a voluminous literature on gender and state formation and gender and culture. Note, first, the journals *Women's Studies International Quarterly, Feminist Review, m/f*, and *History Workshop Journal* (produced in England); *Feminist Studies* and *Signs* (from the USA); *Atlantis* and *Resources for Feminist Research* (from Canada). Note also the special issue of *Radical History Review* (20) 1979 on 'Sexuality in history'; Weeks 1981; and three highly important articles, McIntosh 1978, MacKinnon 1982 and Burstyn 1983. A useful overview of these issues can be found in Barrett 1980, and the contrasting, historical argument of Brenner and Ramas 1984 (cf. Barrett's reply to the latter, 1984). See further, note 16 to Introduction, below. Of course gender is not the only relation constitutive of capitalist state formation/cultural revolution; other social classifications – ethnicity, class, age, region, religion, occupation, and so on – are 'at work' there also. But the social, historical, material construction of gender differs from all of these in terms of its universal features. Contesting gender oppression uniquely has produced, of the necessity of struggle, a

totalizing social theory and practice that refuses both those customary divisions so much Marxism reproduces – base/superstructure, theory/practice, public politics/ private lives – and the demoralization of socialism, refusal to see it as a different form of living, being.

5 Lenin 1917: 292. We criticize this in Sayer and Corrigan 1985, which relates to the more general arguments in Corrigan, Ramsay and Sayer 1978. Cf. the complementary argument of MacKinnon 1982.

6 We hope to produce a subsequent volume on this at a later date.

7 Marx 1843a: 32; cf. 1843b: 167 and Sayer 1985.

8 In Marx and Engels 1846: 61. 'The ideas of the ruling class are in every epoch the ruling ideas. . . . The ruling ideas are nothing more than the ideal expression of the dominant material relationships, the dominant material relationships grasped as ideas; hence of the relationships which make the one class the ruling one, therefore, the ideas of its dominance.' This passage can easily lend itself to a crude 'ideological manipulation' or reductionist/functionalist reading: one thing we hope to bring out in this book is the struggle involved in establishing and maintaining 'ruling ideas', and the way state formation is inextricably bound up with and in-formed by that project. 'The State', of course, is itself exactly one such 'idea'!

9 Shanin 1983, final essay, discusses this category and brings out how much 'scientific' Marxism reproduces, in its theory and practices, the social classifications in which it is embedded.

10 Abrams 1977. Cf. his 1982a: ch. 6; 1982b.

11 ' "Every state is founded on force", said Trotsky at Brest-Litovsk. That is indeed right . . . a state is a human community that (successfully) claims the monopoly of the legitimate use of physical force within a given territory. . . . Like the political institutions historically preceding it, the state is a relation of men dominating men, a relation supported by means of legitimate (i.e. considered to be legitimate) violence' (Weber 1918: 78).

12 We have polemicized against base/superstructure conceptions over the last decade. See note 13 to Afterthoughts, below, for references.

13 We have in mind particularly such endeavours to reconstruct the picture 'from below' as Morton 1979, Cornforth 1978, Cole and Postgate 1948, Harrison 1984, Hampton 1984, Benn 1984, Rowbotham 1977, and the major contributions made subsequently concerning familial/demographic history, notably Hamilton 1978, Middleton 1979, 1981, and Seccombe 1983 and forthcoming book on familial forms, gender relations and modes of production. This perspective for more specific periods can be sampled, *inter alia*, in the writings of Hilton, Hill, Manning, and E. P. Thompson; more detailed references are given at relevant points in our text.

14 Valuable general resources for an overview of state formation and its contexts in England include: Aylmer 1961: conclusion; Anderson 1974b; pt I, ch. 5; P. Williams 1979; Hill 1969a; Halevy 1924; Hobsbawm 1969; Perkin 1969. More specialized materials are cited below or in the text. Starting-points for a study of the extension of the English state beyond England would include (1) Wales: D. Williams 1977: esp. chs 12–17; G. Williams 1960, 1978, 1979; Jones and Brainbridge. (2) Scotland: *The Edinburgh History of Scotland*; Croft Dickinson 1977; Smout 1972; Johnston 1974; Young 1979; Dickson 1980. (3) Ireland: MacDonagh 1968; Jackson 1971; Beresford Ellis 1972; Crawford and Trainer 1977; Lee 1973; McDowell 1964; Lyon 1971. Pocock 1975 is a brilliant discussion of the relations of 'English' and 'British' history which shows acute awareness of the cultural dimensions and consequences of English state formation. See also, in this context, Bailyn 1982, Linebaugh 1983, Muldoon 1975.

15 Broadbent 1984 demonstrates this superbly with respect to the unifying rhetorics employed on the 'home front' during the Falklands campaign. We are indebted to Lucinda Broadbent for sight of this study, which is based on exhaustive analysis of BBC and ITN news coverage, in draft.

16 Apart from more general materials cited in notes 4 and 13 above, see: Heisch 1974, 1980; D. Barker 1978; Taylor 1983; Harrison and Mort 1980; Shanley 1982; Davidoff and Hall forthcoming; Hall 1979; J. Humphries 1977, 1981; Davin 1978, 1979; Purvis 1981; Bland et al. 1979; Barrett et al. 1979; Olsen 1983; Burman 1979; Gamarnikow et al. 1983; Allat 1981; Vallance 1979; Rodgers 1981; Ardener 1981; Stacey and Price 1981; Muller 1977; Graveson and Crane 1957; Nissel 1980; Rafter and Stanko 1982; Edwards 1981; Thane 1978.

Chapter 1   'A Remarkably Centralized Country': State Formation in
Medieval England

1 Bloch describes the medieval English political nation as 'a class of manorial lords, of warriors or chieftains, of royal officials and of "knights of the shire" – all of them men whose mode of life differed greatly and consciously from that of the common run of free men' (1967: 331). Hilton emphasizes both the cleavage between the political nation and the rest – 'the gentry and nobility regarded peasants as different creatures from themselves, almost as a different race' – and the fact that the feudal ruling class was 'a hierarchy, not a class of equals . . . the members of the upper ranks of the aristocratic hierarchy, few in number, interrelated by family ties and owning immense stretches of landed property, dominated not only the rest of society but also the rest of the aristocracy.' He also draws attention to the immense wealth and power of ecclesiastics (1973: ch. 1). The secular 'rise' over many centuries of the lower ranks of this hierarchy, the gentry, was to be an important (and much debated) factor in English social development. For the late fourteenth century, Cam offers the political nation as clerical and lay magnates, knights of the shire, gentry, merchants and burgesses, judges and common lawyers (1945: 186 ff.). The shifting contours of the political nation over the fifteenth to eighteenth centuries can be traced through the writings of *inter alia* Hoskins, Loades, Elton, P. Williams, Neale, Aylmer, Hill, Naimer (and his followers) and E. P. Thompson. For further references on the gentry see note 2 to chapter 4 below.

2 On all of Ireland see Dunbabin 1977. 'Ireland' existed as a constant anxiety in all franchise discussion.

3 Figures taken from the second *Abstract of British historical statistics* (Cambridge UP, 1971). Raymond Williams (1983) shows some persistent confusions in discussions of 'democracy' in England, the forgetting of two key levels of power/control outside that 'democracy' – the monarch/Council and the House of Lords. Others have pointed to the civil service as a major 'historic bloc', e.g. Kellner and Crowther Hunt 1980. We discuss the latter in chapter 6 below.

4 'Flexibility' is a key authority claim of 'the law' in England. Cf. Holdsworth 1924 to which we will return later; for criticism see the work of J. A. G. Griffith.

5 Apart from more specific references given in the text, what follows relies upon Maitland 1897, Clanchy 1979 and 1983 and Plucknett 1956. Other resources for an examination of state formation in this period include Harriss 1963, and Richardson and Sayles 1934. The latter has accomplished a valuable revolution in historiography, but arguably downgrades the innovatory impact of the conquest. P. Anderson (1974a: 158f.) rightly criticizes ideologies of 'Englishness' and its

supposed 'unbroken continuities' in this and related work; cf. Hobsbawm and Ranger 1983, Colls 1985.

6 To illustrate this, Chancery Rolls date from 1199 including a series of Letters Patent 1201–1920, and Close Rolls 1205–1903. The Pipe Rolls (compiled largely by sheriffs for the Exchequer) extend from 1131 to 1831, including the Black Book of 1166; Feet of Fines (disputes over land ownership) extend from 1194 to 1833; and Common Pleas (disputes between subjects over entitlement) 1194 to 1875. Ecclesiastical records are also important for the proving and disputing of wills (the supreme authority for which was the Prerogative Court at Canterbury, the records for this extending from 1383 to 1857). Erastianization of the parish occurs in the 1530s – christenings, marriages, burials – and occasions specific legislation on the form of entry and even the quality of the book (George Rose's Act of 1812). None of this stress on the longevity of national records suggests any simple notion of continuity, but the frequency with which series begin in the 20 years 1190–1210 (and terminate in the period from the 1830s to the 1870s) is perhaps worth remarking. Our source here is the admirable *Local historians' encyclopedia* (Richardson 1974). See also the very important Clanchy 1979.

Legal records of various kinds – i.e. those descriptive of the procedures of regulation themselves, rather than records which are themselves 'the law' or the records of legal decisions – date from around 1100. Significant use of cases (but not yet in the modern sense) is evident in 'Bracton', and other writings of the 1240s and 1250s. About the same time some records of pleas, evidence and verdicts are found in the *Year Books*. Studies of the law through cases are first printed in the 1490s, with the first printed *Year Books* appearing in the 1520s. Reports of major cases date from the 1530s, the most famous being those of Coke (1572–1616, some not being printed until the English Revolution), who also begins the major summaries of the law with his *Institutes* (1628–44), comparable to Blackstone's *Commentaries* (1765). Note that, in the words of Earl Jowitt, prior to 1865 all law reports remained 'mere private speculation'; in that year *The Law Reports* started (Jowitt, 1977: 1071).

Statutes began to be systematically collected around the 1250s, but as late as the end of the same century there was no single source for all statutes, although by the 1340s a collection of the Statutes of Parliament was being made (Richardson and Sayles 1934). Printed statutes begin to appear from 1481. No official collection of statutes was published until 1822 (these covering only the period down to 1713); even the *Statutes of the Realm* are acknowledged to be incomplete and to contain apocrypha (Baker 1979: 179).

7 Elton 1969 is a succinct summary of the evolution of Parliamant in medieval and Tudor England, which we have followed here – though with some essential qualifications. More specialized studies include Fryde and Miller 1970a, 1970b; Richardson and Sayles 1934; Davies and Denton 1981; Lehmberg 1970; Neale 1976. Against Elton's drift we would emphasize the long time needed to establish 'political' as opposed to personal rule; see Roskell 1964, Williams 1963. Only with the Triennial Act of 1694 is Parliament regularly empowered. We discuss this further in our text below, chapter 4.

8 The social structure of feudal societies was of course a good deal more complex: see Hilton's and Bloch's writings. But the imagery as imagery ·is important, on two levels: for what it condenses into silence (notably gender differences, usefully surveyed by Middleton 1979, but see also Duby 1984, Lucas 1981, O'Faolain and Martines 1973, Stafford 1983, Shahar 1983, Stuard 1976; and structuring within the third estate); and for its contrast with the dominant social classifications (equal citizens/consumers) of modern bourgeois societies. Marx (1843a, b; Marx and Engels 1846; see Sayer 1985) made much of this contrast and related the transition

from the former to the latter to state formation. We take this up in our Afterthoughts, below.

9 The social, political and moral features of 'representation' (and the slowness of extending the franchise) have been the subject of much useful historiography recently. See Herrick 1948, Moore 1976, Gallagher 1984, Dunbabin 1977, Dearlove 1979. We discuss this further in chapter 6 below.

10 We detail the practical and theoretical exclusion of women from rights in law over the centuries in our text below, pp. 36–7. Their dangerous quality for a polity organized by such classifications is amply testified to – see many of the texts referred to in note 16 to Introduction, above – but it is most clearly signified in the 'crime' of witchcraft, an overwhelmingly female offence. We discuss this in chapter 3 below.

11 Marx acknowledged (*pace* 'base/superstructure' models) that transfer of peasant surplus labour/products to feudal lords required 'other than economic pressure' (1865: 790 ff.). Hilton (1976: 16–17) suggests that by the twelfth century surplus as a whole was transferred less as rent (whether labour, kind or cash) than in the forms of seigneurial taxation and profits of jurisdiction; see also his 1973: ch. 1. Jurisdiction was a (arguably it was *the*) key social relation of feudal production.

12 Weber 1920a; 1920b; chs 22, 29; 1978a: 161–4, 333–7, 375–80 and ch. VIII. Weber 1983 is a useful anthology, Löwith 1982 a worthwhile comparative study with Marx.

13 See Corrigan and Sayer 1981a, and fuller bibliography there. Seminal studies of law as ideology in the English context include Hill 1965: ch. 5 (on Coke); Tigar and Levy 1978; Commons 1924; and the two 'Warwick' books, Thompson 1977a and Hay 1977 (especially the first essay). We discuss law and gender on pp. 36–7 in this chapter.

14 It is commonly said that England 'has no written constitution', and the comparison intended is that of modern democratic nation states founded through revolutionary war (like France or the USA) or 'late unification' (like Germany or Italy). As a comparison this has truth; more generally it is misleading. The English constitution is extensively written: directly so, in such compilations as *Statutes of the Realm*; but also in a broader sense in all the texts of its effectivity – proclamations, orders, inquiries, forms, reports, judgements. It was and is a sealed constitutional code, and thus stronger, more obdurate and at the same time more flexible than any open written code would be. See Holdsworth's point, cited in our text below, p. 38.

15 Maitland documents this for JPs (1897). Hoskins argues that from the 1480s there was a centralization involved in what Clark and Slack (1972: 21ff.; cf. Hoskins 1976: 102ff.) call 'the democratic element in town government'. Mayors had increasingly to be aldermen and restrictively chosen only by other councillors. This concern with 'reliable men' is brilliantly traced in Dearlove 1979, esp. chs 4 and 9. We discuss its continuation over later centuries in subsequent chapters.

Chapter 2   'This Realm of England is an Empire':
The Revolution of the 1530s

1 All the work of Elton listed in our bibliography is relevant. His argument on the 1530s is classically stated in his 1953 and summarized in his 1974c; his 1976 is a qualified restatement rather than in any way a recantation. His 1972 is a brilliant reconstruction of the mechanisms of enforcement of the Henrician revolution, while his 1973 discusses the wider programmes and animating philosophies of Cromwell and those around him. The Elton debate can be followed through Williams's (1963) summary, the important refutation of Stone (1951) by Elton

(1952a, 1961b) and the debate between Elton (1956; 1961a: ch. 7; 1973) and Hurstfield (1966; cf. his 1973 essays). See also Harriss 1963, Roskell 1964. For Hill's view see his 1969a: pt I, pt II/1, and his 1956; for P. Anderson's, his 1974b: pt I, ch. 5. Loades 1977 provides an excellent general discussion of the period. Elton 1968 gives key documents; Powell and Cook 1977 is another useful resource.

2 Loades argues that 'By sheer application, Henry [VII] probably came to know more about his subjects, high and low, than any king who had ever occupied the English throne – and knowledge is power' (1977: 12). The latter point is more generally relevant to the history of state formation in England, from Domesday to the inspections of the nineteenth century and beyond.

3 See Skinner 1978: II, 356. The use referred to is by Thomas Starkey, whose relations with Cromwell are discussed in Elton 1973: 46ff. Thomas Cromwell (1485?–1540), Earl of Essex, was the son of a Putney blacksmith, fuller of cloth, and alehouse keeper. He had no formal schooling, but learned to read Latin and Greek, and spoke fluent French and Italian. His immediate circle included Sir Thomas Elyot, Sir Thomas Wyatt and Edward Hall, and his household had the reputation of being something of a salon for leading intellectuals of the day. Elton (1973) discusses this. As a young man Cromwell travelled widely in Flanders and Italy. After returning to England he trained as a lawyer and practised as a solicitor, whilst still retaining some interest in the cloth business. Entered Wolsey's service, becoming Collector of Revenues for the See of York 1514; in the 1520s was a member of a commission which suppressed some small monastic foundations. Entered Parliament 1523. Became member of Gray's Inn, 1524. Sat for Taunton in the Parliament of 1529. Survived Wolsey's fall, and rose rapidly thereafter in the king's service, becoming the most powerful man in the kingdom after Henry himself. Elton convincingly establishes him as the major architect of the 1530s revolution. Privy Councillor, 1531. Master of the Jewels, Clerk of the Hanaper, Master of the King's Wards, 1532. Chancellor of the Exchequer, 1533. King's Secretary and Master of the Rolls, 1534. Vicar-General – Henry's Vice-Regent in Spirituals – Commissioner for Visitation of Churches, Monasteries, and Clergy, and Chancellor of the University of Cambridge, 1535. Lord Privy Seal, 1536; raised to peerage that year as Baron Cromwell of Oakham. Knight of the Garter, 1537, also Dean of Wells, and Warden and Chief Justice Itinerant of the royal forests north of the Trent. Appointed 1539 to oversee printing of English Bible and suppression of unauthorized translations. From dissolution of the monasteries he received the lands of the priories of Lewis and St Osyth, the monasteries of Colchester and Launde, and part of those of the See of Norwich. 1539 Lord Great Chamberlain of England. 1540 Earl of Essex. Attainted, for treason and heresy, in the same year, and executed on 28 July.

4 Elton (1972: 292) implies that the 1530s legislation brought treason entirely within the common law. P. Williams – in a comprehensive and judicious discussion of the treason law – qualifies this (1979: 376ff.). He also shows how in the course of the sixteenth century many offences not specifically directed against the monarch (but nevertheless dangerous to 'the State') came to be construed as treasonous, including insurrection against the Statute of Labourers to increase wages, and protests against enclosures (ibid.: 377–8). Diggers had begun to dig, Levellers to level – that work is still in progress. One day, perhaps, we can bring the Great Arch crashing down and use the materials to construct something completely different – a Stately Pleasure Dome perhaps!

Chapter 3   An Elect Nation: The Elizabethan Consolidation

1 The latter can be traced in Aylmer 1957; 1961: 435ff.; Braddock 1974. Apart from more specific references given in text and notes, this chapter relies generally on Loades 1977 and P. Williams 1979, both of which give excellent overviews; see also Neale 1953/57; 1958.

2 Foxe's *Acts and monuments*, despite costing over £6, sold more than 10,000 copies by 1603 (Palliser 1983: 355). Foxe himself considered that 'The Lord began to work for His Church not with sword and target to subdue his exalted adversary, but with printing, writing and reading' (P. Williams 1979: 274). The East India Company supplied as reading matter to its ships the Bible, Perkins's *Works*, Hakluyt – and Foxe's *Acts and monuments* (Hill 1965: 159). As Hill remarks, 'the combination is significant.' See further note 12 to this chapter, below.

3 See here Strong 1973; Levey 1971; Trevor-Roper 1976; Ormond 1977; Piper 1977, ch.5. More general studies would include Yates 1974 and Haskell 1971.

4 Quoted above, p. 14. See Hill 1977.

5 This is a major theme in the writings of Joel Hurstfield (1973) who stresses *inter alia* (a) how different was a concept like 'consent' in their terms compared to ours (p. 14ff.), (b) how 'a sense of nationalism, already marked in 15th century England ... came to its full flowering in the age of Shakespeare' (p. 55) – a nationalism focused in order and degree; see Hurstfield's discussion of Henry VI, Act IV, scene 1 (p. 59f.), (c) how this nationalism was tinged and inflected by 'welfare legislation', saving England 'from disaster' (pp. 73, 75).

6 Palliser 1983: 28. On this background more generally see Hill 1969a, Hoskins 1976, 1977, Yelling 1977, Wrightson 1977; cf. Marx 1865: pt 6.

7 See the very famous quotation from Max Weber given in note 11 to Introduction, above.

8 On witchcraft see *inter alia* Larner 1980, 1981, 1982; Anderson and Gordon 1978, 1979; Cohn 1975; Kieckhefer 1976; Macfarlane 1970; K. Thomas 1971; Trevor-Roper 1967, 1969. It is worth mentioning that the witch-hunt in England was less severe than in Scotland or many other parts of Europe.

9 See Pound 1971, Corrigan and Corrigan 1979. 'Gypsies' (The Rom) were called 'wily Egyptians' by that key organizer of 'the law', William Lambarde, on whom see Holdsworth 1972: IV; Conyers Read 1962; and Gleason 1969: ch. 2.

10 Detailed references on regulation of vagrancy and the labour market are provided in note 13 to this chapter. On economic regulation more generally in this period, P. Williams 1979: chs 5 and 6 provide an excellent summary; see also Dietz 1920; Hill 1952, 1956a; 1964: chs 7, 12, 13; 1975: ch. 15; Beresford 1957 and Thirsk 1978.

11 Regulation of corn supply is important (a) because of the evident connection with social order, (b) because here government normally succeeded in enforcing a national 'pro-consumer' policy against sectional interests of producers – one index of the maturity of state formation. It is also a good example of the range of controls employed by the Tudor state. Statutes limited the export of corn, either by forbidding export unless its price fell below a given threshold, or by licensing exporters. By a statute of 1552 domestic corn merchants had to be licensed by three JPs; in 1563 this became an annual requirement. Within this statutory framework Privy Council and local commissioners exercised more direct surveillance and control. In 1565 special commissioners for restraint of the grain trade were appointed, authorized to stop shipments and license exporters. Searches were made by commissioners or JPs for grain in bad years. In 1586–7 Council issued a Book of Orders to JPs for controlling the grain market; frequently updated this became 'the

model for the working of the internal market in grain for the next two centuries' (P. Williams 1979: 192).

12 Apart from the work of Christopher Hill from 1940 to the 1980s – his 1965: ch. 4, on Raleigh, expressing all we are trying to say here – see in addition to Rabb and Foster, Wright 1943, Hirschman 1977, Commons 1924.

13 This has been the subject of extensive commentary in recent years. See Woodward and Corrigan and Corrigan 1979 for references, plus Holdsworth 1972: IV, ch. 2, Dunlop 1912, Tawney 1913, Kelsall 1938, Davies 1956, Beresford 1957, Coleman 1976, Hoskins 1976. As the beginnings of the control of 'idle time' we should note that whilst there were 50 Holy Days in the 1530s, and still 35 in 1549, an Act of 1552 reduced these to 27 and clustered them at Easter, Whitsun and Christmas/ New Year. For the wider Erastian philosophy note Elton 1952a, b; 1961b; 1973: 90ff.

14 The points in this paragraph rest on Loades 1977, MacCaffrey 1963, Strayer 1970, Elton 1961a, Gladish 1915.

15 Aylmer finds that from 1626 'royal commissions [of which he counts 86] may well have been more numerous and varied just before the Civil War than at any time until the 19th century' (1957: 231).

16 Published in vol. 1 (pp. 423–43) of Conyers Read 1925; partly extracted in Elton 1968: 124–7.

Chapter 4   Mortall God Enthroned: One Bourgeois Revolution (of Many)

1 R.C. Richardson 1977 summarizes the historiography of the English revolution over several centuries. For our own discussion we have drawn most heavily on the works of Hill and Aylmer. The 'revisionist' historiography of recent years of Conrad Russell (1979) and others should lead us to qualify simplistic views of e.g. the importance of the pre-1640 Commons and its independence from noble patronage, or the existence of a clear 'opposition party' in Parliament. Manipulation of the Commons by peers and the continuing importance of Privy Council are things we have in any case stressed above. But – as with all such revisionisms perhaps – there is a tendency to bend the stick too far. The same applies of some of the work of Everitt and Morrill. The Civil War *did* happen, issues of principle (amongst other things) *were* at stake, and the events cannot wholly be separated from – which is not to say they are straightforwardly reducible to – secular changes in economic and social structure of the kind stressed in older historiography. Recent discussions, putting 'revisionism' in perspective, include Hirst 1978, 1979, 1980, 1981, Hexter 1978, Holmes 1980, Woolrych 1980, Rabb 1981, Hill 1981.

2 The 'gentry controversy' can be followed through Tawney 1941a, b, Stone 1948, Trevor-Roper 1951, 1953, Tawney 1954, Cooper 1956, Zagorin 1959, Hexter 1961, Cooper 1958, Stone 1965a. Stone 1965b extracts most of the relevant articles. See also Zagorin 1970, Simpson 1961, Mingay 1976, and much of the material cited in note 1 to this chapter, above. Everitt 1957, 1960, 1963, 1966, Simpson 1961, Cliffe 1969, Morrill 1974, 1976, 1979, Fletcher 1975 and Clark 1977 are relevant area studies, Holmes 1980 a discussion of this literature. Hill 1981 usefully reviews much of this and related work.

3 The Caroline peerage was in fact 'a more upstart group than at any time in the previous 200 years', most of the incomers being office-holders (Stone 1965b: 66); debasement of honours was one of 'Country's' major complaints. Blurring the stereotypes further, the Crown was a major encloser and financial backer of 'improvements' like draining of the fens (see Manning 1978). Conversely Zagorin

finds no direct association between 'Country' and 'some advanced form of enterprise' (quoted in Stone 1965b: 53).

4 See his 1965b: 63–80 (extracted from his monumental 1965a); both are correctives to his 1948, which followed Tawney in seeing a financial crisis of the aristocracy. Three brief additional points here. (a) 'One term never used for the peerage before 1640 is "aristocracy", a term used to describe a system of government, not a social group' (Morrill 1979: 71n.). (b) One differentiation device that 'reconstructs' peerage and gentry is the move towards the cash-nexus (making brittle and finally snapping certain social relations) versus the retention of social powers organized around a different authority-value system. This tension, however, can be traced well into the nineteenth century, as we shall argue in later chapters; there was no overnight 'transition'. The former was considered by the Duke of Norfolk to be the 'appreciation of income at the expense of following' (Bush 1971; cf. James 1966). (c) Aylmer (1961: 240) argues that the sale of state offices was a 'major factor in redistributing wealth *within* the propertied and governing classes' and his work since 1959 tends to support the recent conclusion of Braddock that 'for officials, no less than most others in Tudor society, land remained the primary source of income' (1974: 35).

5 Significant recent work on the 'civil war' in what is now the United States of America adopts a similar perspective; see Barrington Moore 1969, Bonacich 1975.

6 We discuss this in more detail in our next chapter. But see, in particular, Hay 1977 (esp. ch. 1) and Thompson 1977a.

7 The starting-point must be in Weber's seminal essay *The Protestant ethic and the spirit of capitalism* (1905). His – much less often read – 1920b, final chapter, and 1906 are equally relevant, broadening his argument. Braudel writes (1977: 66) that 'all historians have opposed this tenuous theory'; he is unfortunately representative of most historians in how badly he misunderstands it. Elton's ill-informed attack on Weber (1963: 312–18) is typical of this; whilst some of his historical charges are valid, much of his fire is directed against a caricature of what Weber actually said. Three correctives: (a) *Pace* Braudel, Weber did not claim that Protestantism 'caused' capitalism. (b) Where he did draw causal connections, with the spirit or ethos of capitalism, he cited other formative influences as well as Protestantism. (c) His argument has been greatly oversimplified, focusing on direct connections (moralization of work, taboos on profligate consumption) rather than the [for Weber more important) diffuse contribution of the Protestant ethic to the living of a disciplined life which is in turn conducive to an economic system based on rational calculations. This does not deny that parts of Weber's argument are inadequate and historically dubious. Correctives (which still see some affinity between Protestanism and capitalism) can be found in Tawney 1938 and Hill 1961a (and Hill's work more generally). These stress the individualizing and emancipatory aspects of Protestanism more than does Weber. E. P. Thompson, in his excellent essay on time, work-discipline and industrial capitalism, argues that 'puritanism, in its marriage of convenience with industrial capitalism, was the agent which converted men to new valuations of time; which taught children even in their infancy to improve each shining hour; and which saturated men's minds with the equation, time is money' (1967: 95; cf. his 1968: ch. 11). Household time altered with differential effects for women; see Smith 1974, 1983, Haraven 1977, Kristeva 1982, Rapp et al. 1983, Olsen 1983.

8 The struggle to establish durable private property of course takes longer than this statement might imply, whether in England – where E. P. Thompson's writings show the persistence of a 'moral economy' through the eighteenth century and beyond – or, in particular, in Wales (hill farmers), Scotland (before and after the

Clearances, e.g. around crofting) or Ireland. Two important general discussions of changing conceptions of property should be signalled here: Kiernan 1976, and Aylmer 1980b. As in all our arguments the specific situation within local social structures also needs examining, as is done admirably in Rollinson 1981.

Chapter 5   From Theatre to Machine: 'Old Corruption'

1 For general surveys of the eighteenth century that illuminate significant themes see Halevy 1906, 1912, Mantoux 1928, George 1931, Polanyi 1945, Hill 1969a, Porter 1892. The work of Namier and his followers traces the networks of patronage. On the fiscal pattern see Roseveare 1973, Brooks 1974, Roberts 1977, Linebaugh 1968, Beckett 1977, Gittins 1977. More generally, documenting how theory comes to terms with labour, see Blaug 1964, Coats 1958, 1960, 1967, 1972a, b, and Meek 1973 – plus of course Marx.

2 Note that state office-holders could still take part in politics: separation of 'non-political' office from political party begins in the 1730s (Aylmer 1974: 258; 1979; 1980c; Parris 1968). The judiciary obtained their 'necessary appearance' of independence long after that of 'the law' – from the Crown in 1701, from politics in 1760 (Cockburn 1972). Other typical examples of 'stalling' would be: inquiries that produced nothing, sometimes not even a report; despite Blackstone, the lack of any systematic attention to the common law; and no official statutes of the realm until the nineteenth century. Holdsworth 1972: vol. 10, 453–519 gives a survey of the mature eighteenth-century state system; see also Holmes 1982: chs 8 and 9.

3 We discuss this above, see also Shennan 1974: ch. 5; Quentin Skinner's work, and King 1974.

4 For a sketch towards this see Corrigan 1980a: ch. 2. The central theme is discipline; cf. Hill 1952; 1964: ch. 6; 1977: ch. 20, and all E. P. Thompson's studies of moral order.

5 On property, see Kiernan 1976, Neale 1975, Aylmer 1980b. On crime and protest, E. P. Thompson's work (and that of Hobsbawm and Rude), Hay 1977, 1980, Cockburn 1977, Brewer and Styles 1980, Beattie 1974, 1975, Pearson 1978 Cohen and Scull 1983; on punishment and the criminal law, apart from these latter, Bentham 1791, Foucault 1977, Ignatieff 1978, Radzinowicz 1948/68. See further, this chapter, note 12 below.

6 'Political economy is to the state, what domestic economy is to the family,' said James Mill in his *Elements of political economy* (designed as a school book, influential in its consequences, partly authored by Bentham, Ricardo and J. S. Mill) of 1821, ably criticized by Marx 1844a; 1844b: 319 ff.; 1859: 179ff. The preceding text of Mill – *Commerce defended* (1808) – first drew Mill and Ricardo together.

7 Clark 1919; Hutchins 1915; K. Thomas 1958, 1959, 1971, 1977, 1978; Rowbotham 1977: chs 1–4; Thompson 1977b; Hill 1978a.

8 Holdworth 1972: vol. 6 is a very useful survey of the rich repertoire of state forms in the early eighteenth century. Note also vol. 14, pp. 100ff. where he discusses delegated legislation in a very interesting way, stressing, 'First, in times of emergency the government must be able to act quickly' (p. 100) and the two periods he singles out are 'the Tudor period and the 19th and 20th centuries'. He quotes Lord Chief Justice Caldecote to the effect that even the right (for whom? we must ask) of personal liberty must give way to the safety of the state which is 'far above the liberty of a few people who might be unjustly imprisoned' (quoted in ibid.). Lord Denning could have been quoted with similar effect. Then there is the contemporary claim – used precisely against the 'right' of some people to form associations of workers (those at GCHQ forbidden by Order to join trades

unions) – that the government is above the law when acting in the royal prerogative (a situation of grace defined by that same government).

9 On 'land' see Mantoux 1928; Jones and Mingay 1967, and then F. M. L. Thompson 1963, Spring 1953. On the meaning of 'land' from below see Rose 1961, Thompson 1971, Hill 1967, Wells 1979 – the latter is very useful.

10 See Hoskins 1976, 1977, Yelling 1977 – the latter two books covering both periods, as does Marx 1867, p 8.

11 See also Yelling 1977; Lazonick 1974; Mantoux 1928: ch. 3. Note the latter's focus on Inclosure Commissioners and an Act of 1757 which was oriented to the welfare of the displaced ('the relief of the poor') through transfer grants from the Commissioners to the Poor Law Guardians, related to legislation of 1551 and 1563 – compensation seldom granted. The British Library has two significant versions of the same pamphlet (*Poor rates reduced* ... 1844) which shows one thematic consequence in the nineteenth century: having taken the land away and denied common rights, lo and behold, allotments are introduced! Corrigan 1977b provides further references to this.

12 Apart from material indicated in notes 1 and 5 to this chapter, see Rusche and Kirscheimer 1939, Radzinowicz 1948/68, Beattie 1970, 1974, 1977, Hay 1977, Thompson 1977a. A crucial set of historiographical explanations is to be found in Marx 1842, Linebaugh 1976, Ditton 1977, plus the fundamentally novel work of Rule 1975, 1979. On the game laws: Thompson 1977a, Hay 1977, Munsche 1977. On the Poor Laws: G. Taylor 1969, J. S. Taylor 1969, Corrigan and Corrigan 1979. On the regulation of vagrancy: Slack 1974, Clark 1979. On popular disturbances: all of Thompson (especially 1975), Darvall 1934, Shelton, 1973, Quinault and Stevenson 1974, Stevenson 1979, Tilly 1975. On punishment: Linebaugh 1968, Sheehan 1978, Ignatieff 1978. See several of these texts and note 36 to chapter 6 below, for the post-1780 period.

13 Cf. Haldane 1962, Wills 1972, Youngson 1973.

14 London's significance can be traced through Hoskins 1976, Foster 1977, Pearl 1979, to Rogers 1978, from the sixteenth to the eighteenth centuries. For the early nineteenth century see Williams 1973.

15 Falkus 1976; see also Hennock 1958, Clark and Slack 1976, Corfield 1976.

16 Curtis and Speck 1976; Halevy 1906; Perkin 1969: 280; Malcolmson 1973.

17 We have already illustrated some of these themes from Durkheim (above; cf. our 1981a). This 'Durkheimian' perspective is also very evident in many writings of the radical bourgeoisie from Adam Smith through to the Fabians. Compare for example Durkheim 1904: 45ff. with Bentham 1776: 37ff. and Green 1881: paras 75ff.

18 The work of the Scottish Moral Philosophers should be conceptualized as the first comprehensive theory of 'development' and a neglected constituent of the first sociological theorizing. Note especially here Pascal 1938. Some texts are gathered in Schneider 1967. Without this location their work becomes fractured and/or lost as 'simply' political economy, or 'merely' philosophy. Correctives to this view can be found through, first, the essential work of Forbes (1975) – significantly his reconceptualizations here complement those of W. Thomas and D. C. Moore for the Mills – and, then, the individual studies of Lehman (1930, 1952, 1960, 1971), and for Smith, the essays collected in Skinner and Wilson 1975, as part of the new critical edition of Smith's work (Oxford, Clarendon Press, 1975 onwards). Two texts on Smith are outstanding: Rosenberg 1960 and Winch 1978. For Bentham, see Rosenblum 1973, 1978, Steintrager 1977 – but older essays, e.g. of Wallas 1925, 1928, or Everett 1966 are still very useful.

19 Smout 1964, Richards 1973a, b, Hechter 1973, 1975.

20 Dugald Stewart (1753–1828). Dugald's father, Matthew (1717–85) was Professor of
   Mathematics and FRS. For a time, 1775–85, Dugald held this Chair with his father
   plus his own Chair of Natural Philosophy; there was one session, 1787–8, when he
   held three Chairs and gave his lectures in Greek and Sanscrit at times. Chitnis
   (1968), in his admirable doctoral thesis, quotes a remark of Dugald in this session:
   'employed in preparing two lectures – the one on the Air-Pump, the other on the
   Immortality of the Soul'. According to the *DNB*, Dugald often started work at
   3 a.m.
21 The four key texts here are Hill 1954, Williams 1958, 1961, and Thompson 1968.
   See also our chapter 6 below and the extensive listing in Corrigan and Gillespie
   1974. More generally see Graff 1981, Febvre and Martin 1976, Eisenstein 1979,
   Cressy 1980, Bisseret 1979, Cohen 1977. On 'social literacy' see Stone 1969,
   Schofield 1973, Cressy 1977 – but above all Webb 1955b, Spufford 1974, Vincent
   1981, Morley and Worpole 1982. On state regulation of 'idle time' and
   commercial provision of 'leisure activities' see Hollis 1970, 1973, Plumb 1973,
   Malcolmson 1973, Reid 1976, Bailey 1977, 1978, Cunningham 1980, E. and S. Yeo
   1981 and all the issues of *History Workshop Journal*. Three contrasting arguments
   can be found in Wright 1881, Jones 1977 (cf. his 1974) and Lazonick 1978.
22 The full title – *An Inquiry into the Nature and Causes of the Wealth of Nations* – is
   important because Smith argued in the earlier *Moral Sentiments* (Anspach 1972)
   that his project entailed a search for the general principles which would contribute
   to a science of statesmanship and legislation (cf. sections of Chadwick's *Health of
   Nations* epitome). Equally Smith's lectures argued that 'Property and government
   very much depend upon one another' (quoted in Paul 1979: 21; cf. Meek 1976).
   Generally see Hamowy 1968, Paul 1979.
23 See the major excursion of Marshall 1984. At last work on 'representation' (or the
   theory of the Polis) has come to take seriously its double reference, e.g. Jung 1983,
   Gallagher 1984. Holquist 1983 moves the debate significantly.
24 These are now provided in a modern, critical edition, see A. Brown, 'Adam Smith
   verbatim', *Times Literary Supplement*, 23 November 1979, p. 46. Note that John
   Millar was lecturing on the 'principles of Government' including 'the present state
   of Engish government' in the 1760s.
25 See M. Friedman, 'Free to choose?', *Listener*, 21 February 1980, and P. Corrigan,
   'Free to choose?', *Listener*, 6 March 1980.
26 Quote from A. Brown, op. cit. note 24 above.
27 Some references to Bentham are given above, note 18, this chapter. He regularly
   wrote 15 folio pages every day. Jeremy's younger brother, Samuel (1757–1831) was
   Inspector-General of Naval Works in England 1796–1805. Everett (1966: 76ff.)
   suggests that Samuel's work there was directly influential on Jeremy, but we must
   also note Jeremy's 1785 visit to Samuel when the latter was assisting Prince
   Potemkin in establishing a model labour colony in the Ukraine, and Jeremy's
   admiration for Samuel's invention there of the industrial version of the Panopticon:
   the one supervisor being able to survey many workers/worktasks at once (see
   Wallas 1928: 52). That the Millbank site (sight?) proposed for the Panopticon
   prison/manufactory is now the Tate Gallery is a matter for some amusement.
   Holdsworth evaluates Bentham in his 1972: vol. 13, 132ff. and in his 1940;
   centrally Bentham aimed at 'giving a better security to liberty and property'
   (p. 571) through a perception of 'the average man of his own day', not here on the
   Clapham omnibus, but 'the qualities obvious to an inhabitant of Queen's Square
   about the year 1800' (Stephens, quoted in Holdsworth 1940: 574; cf. Halevy 1934:
   63, 297, etc.)
28 The Benthamite/Philosophical Radical/Whig/Liberal/Fabian routeways are now
   being charted: Halevy 1965, Beales 1974, Mack 1955; Wolfe 1975; Collini 1977,
   1980b. The locus classicus for us is Abrams 1968.

29 Cf. Bentham's *Book of fallacies*, 1824, quoted Everett 1966: 166–94.
30 Farr 1848: 102 ff.; Halevy 1912: 20ff.; Gretton 1913: 85ff.; Barker 1930: 34ff.;
   Cohen 1941: chs 2–4; Finer 1952b: 347ff.; Parris 1968: 151ff.; Roseveare 1973:
   Document 14; Torrance 1978. Note: (a) the importance of Sir George Harrison
   (Torrance 1968) and Sir Henry Taylor (1831; cf. Shaeffer 1957: 66ff.) in terms of
   the links between 1780s and 1830, plus the changes documented by Stern (1950)
   like the Consolidated Fund, 1787, the Exchequer Loans Commission, 1793, and
   the funding of the short-lived but significant Board of Agriculture (Halevy 1912:
   224ff.; Gretton 1913: 136ff.). On the Poor Employment Act 1817, from which the
   Public Works Loan Board of 1875 developed, see Flinn 1961, 1971; on a state
   policy toward emigration see Johnston 1972. (b) The Administrative Reform
   Associations or Financial and Administrative Reform Associations from 1848 are
   continuations of some of the themes of the Economical Reforms movement
   (McGregor 1957, O. Anderson 1965, 1974; more generally see Wootton 1975 and
   Hollis 1974). Chadwick linked their work to civilization itself (Lewis 1950: 199;
   Wallas 1908: 249ff.), and Dickens was involved, his 1855 'Speech' (well set in
   context by the editor of his collected speeches) links the ARA to the 1780s reforms.
   Anderson (and Marx) note the sustained opposition of Chartists to the ARAs, and
   the support of Christian Socialists.
31 See Weber generally, Hintze 1906, Briggs 1961, Bean 1973, Finer 1975. For studies
   of Englishness and patriotism, aside from Kiernan 1965, 1978, 1982, note
   Cunningham 1981, 1982, and a magnificent complementary essay to our own,
   Stephen Yeo 1984. Aside from Hechter's general work, note for Wales specifically
   Williams 1978 and Morgan's chapter in Hobsbawm and Ranger 1983.

Chapter 6   'The Working Class Question': 'Society' and society

1 See also *Poor Man's Guardian*, 25 October 1832, quoted in Thompson 1968: 893.
2 Responding to reports on diet, *Economist*, 8 October 1864, speaks of the 'increase
   in power to be obtained from the human machine when you give him enough oil'.
   Women are again absent – or are they 'less mechanical'?
3 We discuss the self-definitional celebration of the middle class later. The key text is
   Briggs 1956, but we should attend to that 'sectarianism of English respectability'
   which J. W. Burrow draws out as characteristic of Whig historians in the
   nineteenth century in his brilliant *Liberal descent* (1981).
4 This is exhaustively studied and documented in Corrigan 1977a, which is
   complemented by Richards 1975 (see also his 1979a, b, c) and draws much
   sustenance from R. Johnson 1968 (see his work listed in our bibliography) and
   Abrams 1968. Since 1945 there has been an extensive debate on the 'nature' of 'the
   State' in the period from the 1780s to 1850, summarized and referenced in Taylor
   1972, Stansky 1973, Cromwell 1977. O. MacDonagh (cf. 1958) has recently offered
   a summary (1977); for contexts see also Parris 1960, 1968, 1969. The 1830s remain a
   decade of great fascination; we are arguing this is misplaced. There is more in the
   Sainty series (1972–81) than personnel and note Sutherland 1972. A crucial
   complement to all this work is Thompson 1968, J. Foster 1974 and studies in the
   contrasting traditions which they founded (note especially Jones 1974).
5 On the personnel of the Cabinet 1801–1924 see Laski 1928 and Arnstein 1972. On
   ministerial control see Schaeffer 1957; Fraser 1960; Parris 1969: chs 3–4, 7; Fry
   1969: ch. 1.
6 See also Prouty 1957; for structure and personnel see Sainty 1972–81: vol. 3.
7 For education see R. Johnson 1968 and later work, Bishop 1971, and for the post-
   1870 period the work of Sutherland. For a difference approach to our focus on the

two crucial issues of legitimating authority and forms, see Willson 1955 and Sir Norman Chester's *The English administrative system 1780–1870* (1981). Many of the eighteenth-century terms still apply – a patchwork of the old and new is, after all, recognizable in the daily rituals and momentary routines of state forms in 1984!

8   Roseveare 1973; Gretton 1913: 122ff.; Parris 1969: 203ff. and ch. 8; plus Wright 1969, 1970. For the personnel see Sainty 1972–81: vol. 1; on Sir George Harrison (first Permanent Secretary) see Torrance 1968; on Sir Charles Trevelyan see Torrance, Parris 1969 and Hart 1960, 1969.

9   See also Hennock 1982 for the implications for the regulation of local government; Schulz 1948 on grants and Hennock 1963 on finance are important; more generally see Finlayson 1966 on 1835, Dunbabin 1963 on county councils, and for general overviews Keith-Lucas 1977, Dunbabin 1977, and the very important Dearlove 1979.

10 For structure and personnel see Sainty 1972–81: vols 2 and 5.

11 See Holdsworth 1972: vol. 14, 113ff.; Cromwell and Steiner 1969; for personnel see Sainty 1972-81: vols 2 and 6.

12 The nomination/patronage system survives, of course, in 1984; civil service examinations were implemented last in this site of the most dignified, most pomp-and-circumstance surviving theatre of state.

13 Rarely having more than 50 staff in the Office through the nineteenth century, in 1973 the Foreign and Commonwealth Office had 187 staff of under-secretary and upwards, and a total staff of 12,600 of whom 4,600 were in central administration. For comparison the other departments with more than 50 staff of under-secretary and above in April 1973 are set out in table 1 (with the Foreign Office they are the big six departments after the 1960s reforms). Note that the comparable figures for some other departments are: Scotland – 38 senior staff of a total of 11,300 of whom 4,300 work in central administration; Wales – 8 senior staff of 1,000 (900 of whom are in central administration); Cabinet Office – 25 senior staff of 600 total staff, all working in central administration. But adding up the big six senior staff gives a total of only 670, the size of a small selective secondary school.

TABLE 1   Numbers of staff in five of six largest government departments, 1973

Departments	Senior staff	Total staff	Central administration
Defence	121	272,700	16,800
Trade & industry	106	20,400	5,700
Treasury[a]	94	111,600	5,800
Environment	92	74,700	6,100
Health & social security	70	81,300	7,300

[a]Includes Inland Revenue and Customs and Excise.
Source: Clarke 1975.

14 Holdsworth 1972: vol. 14, 114ff.; Barnett 1970; Strachan 1980 (a contribution to the 'revolution in government debate', rather innocent of considerations of state power!).

15 For the pattern of imperialism see Cain and Hopkins 1980.

16 Weber's 1918 speech 'Politics as a vocation' stresses not only how (as we would put it) part of the self-organizing claim to authority of 'the State' is its successful use of the monopoly of legitimated violence, but also how this is extended through other successful claims to monopolize: 'In the end, the modern state controls the total means of political organisation' (p. 62). Note also Poulantzas's stress in the highly relevant first part of his 1978 book on 'The institutional materiality of the state'.

17 Halevy 1912: pt 2, ch. 1; Mingay 1975; Mitchinson 1962; Gazley 1973; Biebner 1948. One important area of regulation we do not have space to discuss here is organized religion: see Machin 1977, Bentley 1978.

18 On inspection, see Harris 1955, Henriques 1970, 1974, and Hennock 1982, plus the much less useful Roberts 1960. 'Four who made the Inspectoral Revolution' were: Leonard Horner (1785–1864), factory inspector from November 1833 to December 1859, receiving £1,000 per year. Dr J. P. Kay, later Kay-Shuttleworth (1804–77), successively assistant Poor Law commissioner July 1835 to 1842 and (overlapping) assistant secretary to the Committee of the Privy Council on Education from July 1839 to 1849. His salary for the Poor Law work was £700 per year (less after 1839), but the expenses paid him were large (e.g. £1,315 in 1839); for the Education Committee he was paid £1,000 a year until 1842, and £1,200 a year thereafter. H. S. Tremenheere (1804–93), HM inspector for 'British and Foreign' schools December 1839 to November 1843, during which time he also did occasional work as an assistant Poor Law Commissioner; then Commissioner of Enquiry on the state of the Mining Population November 1843 to 1859, during which time he also worked as HM inspector of schools, assistant Poor Law commissioner, and special commissioner for particular inquiries. He then became a Special Commissioner for Lace Manufacture, Journeymen Bakers, and (concurrently with the latter) for Children's Employment, Bakehouses, and Agricultural Employment, 1860 to 1870. During this decade he also inquired into Printworks, Dyeing and Bleaching Works. As inspector of schools his salary varied considerably (it continued to be paid until 1844); at its highest it was £600 per year. As Commissioner for the Mining Districts it was £700 per year; as commissioner-at-large the payment seems to have averaged £50 a month, plus, here and in all the previous examples, expenses. Edwin Chadwick (1800–90), secretary to the Poor Law Commissioners 1834–47; Commissioner on Sanitary Conditions 1846–1848; secretary to the General Board of Health 1848–1854; state pensioner 1854–90. In the first post he received £1,200 a year; in the second, c.£1,000 a year; in the third, £1,500 a year, and his pension was £1,000 a year (contrast Horner whose pension, 1860–4, was £550 a year under the new Superannuation Act of 1859). All these are investigated in detail in Corrigan 1977a, which displays their other familial and social connectivity (they all, for example, knew one another, frequently corresponded, and discussed – explicitly – state formation). Nobody who wants to understand this revolution should read anything until they have read Finer 1952a and Webb 1955a, and then move straightaway to the Blue Books (each of the first three wrote thousands of folio pages) and the other State Papers in the PRO *plus* – and it is a crucial plus – their non-state publications and correspondence. Others who need to be studied would include E. C. Tufnell (1806–86), assistant Poor Law commissioner 1835–47, HMI for Poor Law schools 1847–61, commissioner-at-large (with Tremenheere) 1862–71, and a friend of Horner and Kay; J. Fletcher, secretary to both Royal Commissions on Handloom Weavers and that of 1842 on Children's Employment, one of the secretaries of the London Statistical Society, HMI for British and Foreign Schools until 1852, etc.; Dr William Farr, Dr Southwood Smith, etc. Starting with any one name on this list would lead to their social and political connectedness – the precisely private nexus of discussion and formation which administrative history 'overlooks'.

19 Montmorency 1902: 210ff.; Mantoux 1928: 468ff.; Sanderson 1967:107ff. For the Factory Inspectorate see Djang 1942 but note also Henriques 1971, Robson 1934, Thomas 1948, Ward 1962, 1970a,c. Some excellent work has been done recently on the routinization of inspectoral norms and practices, e.g. Carson 1970a, b; 1979; Bartrip 1979, Bartrip and Penn 1980. In our view the older relating of factory

legislation to changes in capitalist production (cf. Marx 1867, Kuczynski 1945, J. Foster 1969) should not be forgotten precisely because it *is* a part of the routinized practices of inspectors.

20　The Chadwick Manuscripts are housed in the D. M. S. Watson Library of University College, London University. There is a valuable typescript held by this library: J. Percival, *Papers of Sir Edwin Chadwick 1800–1890* (1975). In this collection there are five letters from Horner to Chadwick, five from Kay to Chadwick, thirty-five from Tremenheere to Chadwick, plus the very important letter from Chadwick to Tremenheere on the latter's first report as Commissioner for the Mining Districts which we quote here. There are also 78 letters from Chadwick to Lord John Russell, 1833–72, the first two of which on Poor Law policy are key texts. The D. M. S. Watson Library also contains the Brougham papers and some of the Bentham papers.

21　Chadwick MSS, 85, a bundle of notes and drafts.

22　Public Record Office (Kew, England) MH 32/69, 6 February 1837.

23　Quoted in Simon 1960: 78. On the crucial broadcasting agencies of the day, the *Edinburgh Review* (1802 onwards) and the *Westminster Review* (1824 onwards) see Fetter 1953, 1965. On the more general issue of the diffusion of political economy as framework of discourse see Checkland 1949, Gilmour 1967 and Clements 1955, 1961.

24　On the aristocracy's continuing power see also Arnstein 1975 and Guttsman 1968, 1969, plus R. W. Johnson 1972 and Boyd 1974. Note that in the 1873 *New Domesday survey* 7,000 people were shown to own four-fifths of the land (Massey and Catalano 1978: 68; see subsequent pages for changes since then). The relevance to the Lords is brought out in Pumphrey 1959 and Clarke 1982: 42ff., both for the late nineteenth century. More generally, on wealth, see Rubinstein 1976 and the subsequent debate. We might also note that the average 'aristocratical element' in Cabinets 1895–1970 (when the average size was around twenty) was five (that is, 25 per cent). As to that overlapping other 'aristocracy' – of talent – Cabinet members from Eton also average five, with Oxbridge averaging eleven throughout the same period (Halsey, 1972: 247; see also pp. 233–4 which reveals that Oxford outnumbers Cambridge three to one, and that there has only been one Cabinet that did not contain someone educated at Cambridge, Wilson's in 1964). Oliver Cromwell's Council of State contained fewer aristocrats, as a percentage, than any Cabinet before 1906.

25　Apart from references in previous note, see Spring 1960, 1963, Wilkinson 1974, Coleman 1974, Simon and Bradley 1975, and for Oxbridge Roach 1959, Stone 1975 and Rothblatt 1975.

26　See Wilkinson 1975, Ashton 1934, Elesh 1972, Cullen 1975: ch. 8. Pons 1978 has put 'Manchester' in a wider perspective.

27　On the NAPSS see Rodgers 1952; more generally on such organizations see McGregor 1957, Abrams 1968 and of course Cullen 1975.

28　See here centrally J. Humphries 1977, 1981, Barrett and McIntosh 1981, Hall 1979, and more generally Scott and Tilly 1980, Alexander 1976, Lewenhak 1978, Pinchbeck 1930, Barron and Norris 1976, Beechey 1978, Brueghel 1979, Anthias 1980.

29　Particularly important here are the filiations from Radicalism to Fabianism (and the Fabians' celebration of a particular 'democracy' and competitive examinations into the civil service). We take this up in our next chapter.

30　The implications of this – moral and material classification – have been extensively examined in Corrigan 1977a, 1977b, 1981b, 1982a, 1983e. One important emphasis, on the consequential exclusivity regarding gender categories, is brought out in J. Humphries 1981. More generally it is important to see how shifts in 'machinery' fit into changes in political economy: see Berg 1980; equally important is her collection of documents on working practices (Berg 1979; for a discussion regarding cotton production see Lazonick 1979). Finally another kind of machinery/morality classification is involved in the regulation of the freedoms of capital and the rights of labour internationally: for useful starting-points in the contradictory ways in which 'Britain' became 'the workshop of the world' see Tann and Breckin 1978, and Tann 1978 read with Berg 1980, ch. 9, and the more general Jeremy 1977, Malchow 1976, which also take up encouragement-and-restriction relating to labour. It is equally important to take seriously the located sociology developed and used by key state servants, not least because it pervades the state's official documentary system, both the published State Papers and the manuscript documents in the archival resources.

31 This study by Briggs complements his earlier work on the languages of class (1960), on which we should also stress the value of Bestor 1948. Attention to the shifting meaning of words *over* time (like 'industry' or 'enterprise' – terms for moral qualities becoming descriptive of certain social forms/institutions) and their differential, contested meaning at any *one* time, has been central to the historical materialism of Raymond Williams.

32 'Democracy is much more powerful than aristocracy because the latter cannot arm the people for fear they should seize upon the government' – Henry Newall, quoted in Hill 1980a: 27. Some other points on 'Parliamentary democracy' in this period and after: (a) The Representation of the People Act 1918 introduced the £150 deposit (now to be raised to £1,000) and the idea of lost deposits. Total candidate (not party) expenditure runs from a low of £654,000 in 1931 (all previous figures after 1900 are higher) to £2,155,790 in 1974; note that in 1910 £1,295,000 was spent, a figure not surpassed until 1970 (£1,392,796). (b) University seats (Oxford and Cambridge) were not abolished until 1948. (c) The first woman took her seat in Parliament in 1922. Until 1929 (and again in the period 1935–45) the number of women MPs was in single figures; it was 14 and 15 in 1929 and 1931, it first exceeds 20 after 1945, falling to 17 in 1951. It is never more than 28 (in 1964). At the 1979 election it fell again to 19. This in a legislature, currently of 650 seats, which has never during this period had less than 615 seats. (d) The highest participation in voting this century was 86.6 per cent in 1910 (restricted male franchise), the next highest is 84 per cent in 1950. All others are less than 80 per cent, the lowest figure between 1945 and 1983 is 72 per cent in 1970. (e) Until 1962 the dates of Acts of Parliament are given in terms of regnal years, e.g. 11 & 12 Geo. VI, c.65 is the Statute denoted chapter 65 of the eleventh and twelfth year of the reign of George VI, i.e. 1948. See further Craig 1976, 1978, Butler and Sloman 1975, Halsey 1972. Butler and Sloman is a useful complement to Sainty 1972–81 for earlier periods.

33 See E. P. Thompson's recent writings (particularly those collected in his 1980) and Kettle 1979. It seems entirely to the point that within years of the ending of any property qualification for jury service – itself introduced as part of the bourgeoisification of justice and 'enjoying' (for some) a three-century run until its abolition in 1972 – attempts were made to alter the rules of the game away from juries. For the shifts see Geoff Robertson, *New Statesman*, 10 December 1976, and Harman and Griffith 1978.

34 Jowell's useful review (1979) of Stevens (1979) begins by stressing how frequently he finds law students unaware that the House of Lords is the highest court in the land, or even that it has a judicial function. He also stresses the value of Stevens's book in locating these judicial functions in a political context. The latter draws from his own research and that of Jowell how each law lord tends to believe in a different 'legal ether' (our term, not his): Radcliffe, natural law; Devlin, *Volkgeist*;

Denning, Christian morality; Reid, common sense. Further Jowell notes, 'They are a homogeneous lot, educated . . . almost to a man (and there are no women) at Oxbridge, born of fathers who were almost inevitably clergymen or lawyers (except for Lord Shaw, the son of a baker)'.

35 *Halsbury's Laws of England* has had four editions: 1st, 1907–17, 31 vols; 2nd, 1931–42, 37 vols; 3rd, 1952–64, 43 vols; 4th, 1973 onwards. All four editions were sponsored by Lord Chancellors. It is not a code, 'it is an encyclopedia,' as Lord Hailsham explains in introducing the present edition. There are also *Halsbury's Statutes of England* (3rd edn, 1969–72, 39 vols) and *Halsbury's Statutory Instruments* (1979, 24 vols). All of these are now updated and amended by supplementary volumes, looseleaf services, etc. They should be contrasted with *The Statutes*, 32 vols, updated, since 1948, by the annual volumes *Public General Acts and Measures*. Previous editions include the various editions of *Statutes of the Realm* (see above, chapter 1, note 6) and *The Statutes Revised* (statute law as at 1878, 17 vols, series finished in 1885; as at 1920, 24 vols, series finished in 1929 with 33 supplementary vols). *The Statutes* is thus the third edition. Legal inflation is very evident in the twentieth century. Between 1930 and 1948 there were over 1,000 Public General Acts and related measures passed; in the next 20 years a further 1,200. In 1973 2,300 new pages of statute law were created, in 1975, 3,000. The complexity of the system is well illustated by the Act 'to relax controls over local government' published on 4 December 1979, which contained 246 sections, repealed three whole Acts and parts of 59 others, removing around 300 'controls' but proposing 'changes that will impose tighter control over local authority spending' (*The Times*, 5 December 1979, p. 1). We should not incidentally fix this upon 'Thatcherism': Horace Cutler, then leader of the GLC, reported how in 1978 there were 'over 500 mechanisms available to the government for exercising detailed administrative control'; during the then Labour government's four years (1974–8) the Department of the Environment had issued 'about 600 circulars with the force of law' (*The Times*, 10 November 1978).

36 Some key texts for us are Silver 1967, Storch 1975, 1976, Spitzer 1975, Steedman 1984; cf. Cohen and Scull 1983. We have discussed some of the major issues and provide further references in our 1981a. It is crucial not to lose the sense and sight of the continuing wider reference (as illustrated by Blackstone in the mid-eighteenth century, and Colquhoun in our text below). Thus in a properly sociological theory of policing the Poor Law Unions (several of which employed police officers as relieving officers, just as school boards used police to apprehend truants) and asylums need attention as well as the 'new police'. On asylums see Scull's exemplary text (1979: chs 3, 6, 8) and for some key documents Skultans 1975.

37 Charles Edward Trevelyan (1807–86) entered the Indian civil service in 1826 and served there until 1838. From January 1840 to January 1859 he was assistant secretary to the Treasury (being paid £2,000 p.a. until early 1845, and £2,500 thereafter, plus a further £2,500 p.a. when serving as commissioner for Relief in Ireland). He was knighted on 27 April 1848 and in 1859 became Governor of Madras. On the Trevelyan family as part of the aristocracy of talent see Annan 1955 – a useful essay on Whig–Liberal–Radical–Fabian continuities and connections.

38 Stafford Henry Northcote (1818–87) was private secretary to W. E. Gladstone 1842–5; legal assistant to the Board of Trade 1845–50 (although not qualified at law until 1848); and one of the secretaries for the Great Exhibition from January 1850. Succeeded to the baronetcy in 1851, he was MP for Wigan 1855, Stamford 1866, North Devon 1866, Financial Secretary to the Treasury 1859, President of the Board of Trade 1866–7, Chancellor of the Exchequer 1874. Created Earl of Iddesleigh in 1885 (Sainty 1972–81: vols 1 and 3).

Chapter 7   Epilogue: 'There Is, Above All, An Agency'

1 R. Barker's book is also to be recommended for its stress on the continuing peculiarities of the term 'social' (e.g. 'social insurance') and thus Social-ism, well beyond 1945. As important is the way he illustrates the 'dance' to which we have alluded before: when, as a subordinate theme, the state was attacked as a despotism, it was done through and with Parliament and the law (e.g. by the Lord Chief Justice in 1929, quoted in Barker 1978: 134), those twin pillars of the Erastianization we have traced from the twelfth century onwards. Note however how 'precocious' (restorative?) was Hayek's *Road to Serfdom* (1944) with its demand that liberty, not democracy, was the key political value. Hayek is of course a great hero of monetarists everywhere. But, finally, as important is Barker's clear delineation of just how undemocratic were the procedures through which the sought-for equality of social-ism was being made: expertise and professionalism become dominant. An essential complement to this is Barker 1972.

2 Collini 1972, 1974, 1976, 1977, 1978, 1980a, b, Clarke 1974, 1979, 1982, Freeden 1972, 1978. This revolution in the historiography of the years 1884 onwards has gone almost unremarked. Collini's great superiority (e.g. 1977 and 1980b) is to make connections before the 1880s and beyond the 1920s. He also correctly stresses the value of Philip Abrams's 1968 book which is still almost unknown amongst sociologists and Marxists.

3 Note here (a) it is not until 1871 and 1875 (with the Bank Holiday Acts) that statutory weekday holidays were established; (b) employers' liability dates from 1880 and worker's compensation from 1897, extended to more trades in 1906; (c) it is not until 1908 that the Eight-Hour Day was legally established for (some) male workers (it was the 1853 Act that had regulated the times of work of 'Women and Young Persons', as that of 1848 had done for 'Children'); (d) Trade/Wages Boards began informally in the 1860s and 1870s, with the Statutory Wages Boards (from 1906) based on this earlier history; (e) eventually 'Labour' had its own Department (the Ministry – for a time; it is now the Department of Employment, a somewhat cruel joke) as a 'recognition' by 'the State': see Caldwell 1959, R. Davidson 1969, 1985.

There is now much evidence that suggests that the England of the 1930s was 'closer' to that of the 1830s than Labour, Liberal or Fabian histories would imply. So much of the legislation and administrative reorganization after 1924–6 is consolidating, rationalizing, extending – building on the pattern of the 1870s to 1880s, if not earlier. Furthermore there is clear evidence that much of what is hailed as the 'settlement' (even 'revolution') of 1945 was being discussed, planned for and organized from the early 1930s onwards. We say this to emphasize how for us it is the period from 1964 which now seems decisive, the twin themes being governance (a word chosen by Harold Wilson for his account of the 1964–70 period) and modernization. Curiously it may be the Heath years of 1970–4 which are an interruption of a massive, comprehensive completion of that long revolutionary making we are discussing, although it was during Heath's government that the major restructuration (begun long before) came to its fullest flowering: 17 Departments of State, instead of 26; huge transformations begun in local government, in the legal system, in the organization of social utilities and health provision, in the police and in the nationalized industries – all marked by that double structuring which was so enabling for Thatcher after 1979, de-democratization and engrossing. We cannot think of *any* area of social relations which was not affected by the changes of 1964 through the late 1970s. Then – rather as we see the great arch as a monument – there was intense research activity into centre/locality relations (e.g. the SSRC Panel on Central-Local Government Relations). For some initial accounts see Thornhill 1975, Dearlove 1979, Paul Corrigan 1979a, b.

4 On Labour Party 'theory' see Hobsbawm 1948, Miliband 1960, Bealey 1970, Adelman 1972, Winter 1974, Matthew et al 1976; but a very apposite study is McKibbin 1974. There is everything to be gained from examining three surveys of Labour MPs: *Review of Reviews* (June 1906); *New Society* (13 December 1962 and 2 December 1976).

5 See the materials cited above, this chapter, note 2, especially Clarke 1974.

6 Spencer's *The man and the state* reprints materials from *The Contemporary Review* and *The Fortnightly Review*; D. G. Ritchie's *The principles of state interference* (1902) reprints from the former; F. Harrison's key argument first appears in the latter, etc. etc.

7 William Clarke, the editor *The Progressive Review*, was a journalist with the *Daily Chronicle*.

8 After Hobhouse joined the *Manchester Guardian* in 1889, Beatrice Webb spoke of it as 'practically our organ' (quoted Clarke 1974: 165).

9 The 27,000 copies of this sold in the first 18 months (Wolfe 1975: 293, n. 2) should be compared with the 80,000 copies sold in two years of J. R. Seeley's *The expansion of England* (1883) or the 75,000 copies sold in six months of J. A. Froude's *Oceana* (1886) (Ford and Harrison 1983: 247ff.). In 1882 Henry George's *Progress or poverty?* sold 100,000 copies.

10 H. S. Tremenheere, for example, wrote to E. Chadwick on 13 April 1886 'It rejoices me to see you have joined the patriotic band of iconoclasts in battering that double faced Janus our Premier' (Chadwick MSS, 1888).

11 George Ross, Minister of Education from the Province of Ontario, Canada, made an official visit to England for the 1886 London and Colonial Exhibition and again in 1892. His book (1894) shows how clearly by that time 'the State' was a legitimated object of discourse, something which could be compared and contrasted, studied and learned from. His valuable appendices of curricula for English day and night schools also show the ubiquity of state knowledge/knowledge of the state – e.g. in readers, in English, in geography, and of course in history and in civics. Millions of human beings were 'educated' through such curricula from the 1870s onwards, giving most a distaste for that form of knowledge (and the literature they were compelled to learn). Above all the experience of schooling was the experience of learning to be silent (Corrigan 1983e).

12 The 1891 Census records 39,921 policemen, 97,383 lunatics and 269,000 in the 'Armed Forces of the Crown' from a total population of 34.2 million. More important, 9.3 per cent of the population of Great Britain and Ireland emigrated in the period 1881–1890 – that is, 3,259,000 people – 12.4 per cent to Australia, 10.3 per cent to Canada and 70 per cent to the USA.

13 As important as this kind of information is another set of views: (a) that which indicates the differential consequences of this 'schooling', such as the work of Anna Davin already cited, or the unwritten history regarding Wales, Scotland, Ireland and beyond; (b) that which sketches how this imposition was contested, notably S. Humphries 1980, 1981, Marson 1973.

14 Sources here are for nineteenth-century data, Nicholls, 1898: vol. 2, appx 1; Aschrott 1902, appx XII; Smart 1909; B. and S. Webb 1929b, appx II; Rose 1972, appx A; and Purdy 1860; for the twentieth-century data, Parliamentary answers of 20 October 1976 and 8 November 1976, as reported in *The Times*, 1 November 1976 and 8 November 1976 respectively, and (for the 1984 figure) *The Times*, 13 November 1984.

Afterthoughts

1 See note 1 to Introduction for references.

2 Weber 1920a, 1920b: ch. 22. See further note 7 to chapter 4 above.

3 Marx 1850, 1852, 1871 (text and drafts). On the latter see Sayer and Corrigan 1983, 1985.

4 See Corrigan, Ramsay and Sayer 1980, Corrigan and Sayer 1981a, Sayer and Corrigan 1983, 1985, Sayer 1985.

5 Marx himself develops his argument in these terms in his 1843a and b, and at various points in Marx and Engels 1846. Cf. Sayer 1985, a detailed discussion of Marx's theory of the state in the 1840s; Draper 1977.

6 'The bourgeoisie, wherever it has got the upper hand, has put an end to all feudal, patriarchal, idyllic relations. It has pitilessly torn asunder the motley feudal ties that bound man to his "natural superiors", and has left remaining no other nexus between man and man than naked self-interest, than callous "cash payment"' (Marx and Engels 1848: 486–7). The insightfulness of this at one level needs severely to be qualified by a realization of the extent to which – as our whole argument demonstrates – such market relations depend on others which are not those of the 'cash nexus'. Notably, of course, forms of familial relation which remain, precisely, patriarchal!

7 See Durkheim 1902. His (long out of print in English, and universally neglected) 1904 develops the argument brilliantly in relation to both 'moral individualism' and 'the State'.

8 There is an extensive literature, particularly around E. P. Thompson's 1978a, on this issue; see particularly the discussion in *History Workshop Journal*, 1979 onwards. Our own understanding of Marx's method as critique is outlined in Sayer 1979, and 1983a, the relation of critique and history discussed in detail in the Afterword to the latter.

9 Although Friedrich Engels had thought in 1844 'the history of the social development of the English . . . perfectly clear to me', almost 50 years later some of the exasperation with the resistance to logical schemata of the English comes over in the following manuscript of 1892 'On certain peculiarities of the economic and political development of England' which reads in full: 'By its eternal compromises gradual, peaceful political development such as exists in England brings about a contradictory state of affairs. Because of the superior advantages it affords, the state can within certain limits be tolerated in practice, but its logical incongruities are a sore trial to the reasoning mind. Hence the need felt by all "state-sustaining" parties for theoretical camouflage, even justification, which naturally are feasible only by means of sophisms, distortions, and, finally, underhand tricks. Thus a literature is being reared in the sphere of politics which repeats all the wretched hypocrisy and mendacity of theoretical apologetics and transplants the theological intellectual vices to secular soil. Thus the soil of specifically Liberal hypocrisy is manured, sown and cultivated by the Conservatives themselves. And so the following argument occurs in the mind of the ordinary person in support of theoretical apologetics, an argument that elsewhere it lacks: what if the facts related in the gospels and the dogmas preached in the New Testament in general do contradict each other? Does that mean they are not true? The British Constitution contains many more conflicting statements, constantly contradicts itself, and yet exists, hence it must be true!' (Engels 1892). Corrigan 1977a: ch. 2 discusses Marx and Engels on the 'peculiarities' of English state formation. Cf. Anderson 1963, Nairn 1963a, b, 1964 (and E. P. Thompson's 1965 rejoinder), Anderson 1968, Joseph 1976. We quote Joseph's view of English social development below, note 11.

10 See here the excellent oral histories *Plain tales from the Raj, Tales from the dark continent*, and *Tales from the South China Seas* (Allen 1976, 1980, 1984) – or read Kipling.

11 We take this concept from Milan Kundera. He uses it in connection with Gustav Husak's removal from their posts of Czech historians after 1968. In England the organization of forgetting has usually been more subtly handled, the manufacture or national 'tradition' (see Hobsbawm and Ranger 1983) and the teaching of a particular national history playing its own part. The present Secretary of State for Education and Science, Sir Keith Joseph, has made clear his concern that school history syllabuses should foster 'national pride'. Sir Keith's own view of English social development – oddly congruent with certain Marxist perspectives – is worth quoting at length: 'Unlike some countries in Europe and the New World, e.g. Holland and the U.S., Britain never had a capitalist ruling class or a stable *haute bourgeoisie*. As a result, capitalist or bourgeois values have never shaped thought and institutions as they have in some countries. ... Britain never really internalised capitalist values, if the truth be known. For four centuries, since wealthy commercial classes with political standing began to be thrown up following the supersession of feudalism and the selling off of monastic property, the rich man's aim was to get away from the background of trade – later industry – in which he had made his wealth and power. Rich and powerful people founded landed gentry families; the capitalists's son was educated not in capitalist values but against them, in favour of the older values of army, Church, upper Civil Service, professions and landowning. This avoided the class struggles between middle and upper strata familiar from European history – but at what cost?' (1976: 60–1).

12 At the time of the Argentine invasion, the Falklanders had no automatic right of entry or abode in the UK; their children, if educated in British universities, were liable to foreign-student fees. In connection with the rhetorics through which the Falklands campaign was organized (see Broadbent 1984), we might usefully contrast the way in which Ian Smith's usurpation of British sovereignty in what was then Rhodesia was 'handled' by successive British governments (both Labour and Conservative), and the ease with which the 'rights to self-determination' of its people were 'overlooked' – the majority of the latter, of course, as black people, not being our 'kith and kin'. The contrast provides an excellent example of the way the classifications that unite 'us' as (properly) 'English', sharing in English civility and entitled to 'the State's' protection, are built up out of the organization of difference. See Derek Sayer, letter to *The Times*, 7 May 1982.

13 Sayer 1975, 1977, 1983a; Corrigan, Ramsay and Sayer 1978: ch. 1; 1980; Corrigan and Sayer 1975, 1981a. Cf. Thompson 1965: 79ff., and his work more generally; Williams 1973.

14 Corrigan, Ramsay and Sayer 1978, 1979, 1981; Corrigan and Sayer 1981b, 1982; Corrigan 1975a, 1976; Sayer 1978.

15 See here Teodor Shanin's pertinent paper on 'Marxism and the vernacular revolutionary traditions', in his 1983, together with the other materials in that volume.

16 We further develop this in our 1981a. The recent work of E. P. Thompson (together with other material, see note 33 to chapter 6 above) focuses both on curtailment of rights *in* law and the development of 'the secret state' *beyond* the law, with its increasingly technologized apparatuses of intelligence and surveillance, in England. In addition to Thompson (1980) see here the writings of Duncan Campbell, Tony Bunyan, and the issues of the excellent journal *State Research* (1977 onwards). The only thing substantially new in such buggery, as we might

somewhat impolitely call it, is the electronics. Organized, secret, state 'intelligence' dates from Henry VII if not well before.

From 1919 onwards the UK was divided into 11 regions for co-ordinating police, army and essential services. Although orginally, with explicit reference to colonial administration, the title district commissioner had been used, when formal appointments were made they were civil commissioners (with a Chief Civil Commissioner in London). In the 1930s what were now called Divisions became described as Regions, and in 1939 wartime regional commissioners were appointed in case of invasion. Drawing on previous plans the Conservative government after 1951 established 12 regional seats of governments at an estimated cost of £1,400,000,000! The Spies for Peace blew this cover in 1963 and published all the locations. In 1972 new defence plans drew upon recent colonial/wars-of-independence experience, including that of Ireland – Army manuals included 'Counter-Revolutionary Operations'. These and other documents show a principle of joint command (military and police plus the 'civil' power) as a 'working triumvirate', for national, regional and local levels. But the central control would be a National Defence Council. This was accompanied by renaming the old civil defence apparatus 'Emergency Services' (see the Home Office circular 'Home Defence 1970–1976'). This and later documents demonstrate that in 'an Emergency' (which can be declared by Royal Proclamation or by the Privy Council) the functions of government would be taken over by ten regional commissioners in England and Wales, and one further for Scotland and Northern Ireland (we feel the latter seems rather superfluous in present circumstances!).

All broadcasting and press facilities would be taken over, with the use of telephones graded by classifying user and message in terms of priorities decided by the triumvirate. Post Office exchanges have been adapted to cut off the majority of phones automatically. Naturally there are extensive plans involved in all of this, notably the 'National Security Plan'. Quietly (it was not discovered until 1976) via the neutral sounding Administration of Justice Act 1973, the Home Secretary was given the sole power to order troops into the streets 'in aid of the civil power'. Once again, as all this makes very clear, consensus is not consistently relied upon. What is important is the degree to which these possibilities can be actualized despite the scrutiny of Parliament and within the law through the comprehensive restructuring of state which took place after the mid-1960s. The courage of those within and outside these shadows who have fought – against the Official Secrets Act (passed, hurriedly, in 1911) – to make the truth visible should be remembered.

Middlemas (1979: 19–20) makes a related point, arguing that after 1917 'there was the management of opinion as an unending process, using the full educative and coercive powers of the state.' Established as 'exceptional' because of the 'emergency' conditions of the first world war, 'they were not abandoned. . . . Over the 25 years after 1921, the crude methods of the wartime Ministry of Propaganda developed into the informal (and highly immoral) methods used during the coalition; in due course they were transmuted into an increasingly formal network of information gathering and use essential to the functioning of an interventionist state authority, and grounded increasingly in the assumption that the process was actually neutral – a curious outcome, reinforced by the apparatus of control which ensured secrecy about what government believed the public should not know.' Sarah Tisdall, it should be recalled, was imprisoned in 1984 for leaking 'confidential' information – a memo from the Secretary of State for Defence – not of a military nature, but concerning how the government could best 'sell' the arrival of US Cruise missiles to the British public.

17 These writings of Marx on the Paris Commune – the two long preparatory drafts,

as much as the final (and somewhat more muted) text of *The civil war in France* (1871) – are greatly neglected in the Marxist tradition, Lenin's *The state and revolution* (whose restricted 'reading' we criticize in Sayer and Corrigan 1985) notwithstanding. They are seminal (a) because of the self-criticisms they contain, (b) for the theorization of 'the State' they offer, and the re-evaluation of Marx's 1840s writings (cf. Sayer 1985) which this calls for, and (c) above all for the fact that these theoretical reconceptualizations arise from the experience of social struggle: the first time in human history workers succeeded in taking 'power' into their own hands against 'the State'. Sayer and Corrigan 1983 and 1985 discuss their significance, Sayer 1983b establishes the biographical context.

Bibliography

This is a finding list rather than a full bibliography. Items are listed by author and date; singly authored works are listed continuously before jointly authored works. A few items (e.g. *Dictionary of National Biography, Fabian Essays*) are listed by title; they are also cited thus in text and notes. Publication details are restricted to the minimum necessary to identify the source cited. Place of publication is London unless otherwise stated, except for books published by Edward Arnold (Leeds), Clarendon Press (Oxford) and Harvester Press (Brighton). For journal articles the number given is the volume number except where (as with *Past and Present* or *New Left Review*) issues are numbered consecutively from first publication in a single sequence, when the individual issue number is given.

To save space in what is necessarily a long bibliography we have shortened many titles and abbreviated names of journals, publishers and institutions. The only abbreviation we use in book or article titles is the form C18th, C19th, etc. for the relevant century. Elsewhere we abbreviate as follows:

General

Am	American
Ann	Annual
Assn	Association
Brit	British
Bull	Bulletin
Comp	Comparative
Conf	Conference
Cont	Contemporary
CW	Collected Works
Ec	Economic(s)
Eng	English
Hist	History, Historical
Inst	Institute
Int	International
J	Journal
Mag	Magazine
Mod	Modern
ns	new series
NY	New York
P	Press
Pol	Politics, Political
PP	Parliamentary Papers

Proc	Proceedings
Qu	Quarterly
Rec	Records
repr	reprint(ed)
Rev	Review
rev	revised
Sci	Science
ser	series
Soc	Society, Social
Sociol	Sociology, Sociological
Stat	Statistical, Statistics
Studs	Studies
supp	supplement
Tr	Transactions
U	University

Journals

AES	*Archives Européens de Sociologie*
AHR	*American Historical Review*
BJS	*British Journal of Sociology*
BSSLH	*Bulletin of the Society for the Study of Labour History*
C&C	*Capital and Class*
EHR	*English Historical Review*
EcHR	*Economic History Review*
FR	*Feminist Review*
HWJ	*History Workshop Journal*
IRSH	*International Review of Social History*
JBS	*Journal of British Studies*
JHI	*Journal of the History of Ideas*
JMH	*Journal of Modern History*
JPS	*Journal of Peasant Studies*
NLR	*New Left Review*
NS	*New Society*
NSt	*New Statesman*
NH	*Northern History*
PA	*Public Administration*
P&P	*Past and Present*
RRPE	*Review of Radical Political Economy*
THES	*Times Higher Education Supplement*
TLS	*Times Literary Supplement*
TRHS	*Transactions of the Royal Historical Society*
VS	*Victorian Studies*

Publishers and Institutions

A&U	Allen & Unwin
BAAS	British Association for the Advancement of Science
BSA	British Sociological Association
CCCS	University of Birmingham, Centre for Contemporary Cultural Studies
CSE	Conference of Socialist Economists
CUP	Cambridge University Press

C&W	Chatto & Windus
H&S	Hodder & Stoughton
L&W	Lawrence & Wishart
M&K	MacGibbon & Kee
MRP	Monthly Review Press
NAPSS	National Association for the Promotion of Social Science
NCCL	National Council for Civil Liberties
NLB	New Left Books
OUP	Oxford University Press
RKP	Routledge & Kegan Paul
S&W	Secker & Warburg
T&H	Thames & Hudson
W&N	Weidenfeld & Nicolson

Abrams, P. 1964. The sociology of political life. In T.R. Fyvel (ed.) *The frontiers of sociology*. Cohen & West.
—— 1968. *The origins of British sociology 1834–1914*. Chicago UP.
—— 1977. Notes on the difficulty of studying the state. BSA ann. conf. paper (mimeo).
—— 1982a. *Historical sociology*. Shepton Mallet, Open Books.
—— 1982b. History, sociology, historical sociology. *P&P* 87.
—— and Wrigley, E.A. 1978. *Towns in society*. CUP.
Abstract of British historical statistics. CUP 1971.
Adelman, P. 1972. *The rise of the Labour Party 1880–1945*. Longmans.
Alexander, S. 1976. Women's work in C19th London. In J. Mitchell and A. Oakley (eds) *Rights and wrongs of women*. Penguin.
Allatt, P. 1981. Stereotyping, familism and the law. In Fryer 1981.
Allen, C. 1976. *Plain tales from the Raj*. Futura.
—— 1980. *Tales from the dark continent*. Futura.
—— 1984. *Tales from the South China seas*. Futura.
Allen, P. 1975. The civil service. In Thornhill 1975.
Anderson, A. and Gordon, S. 1978. Witchcraft and the status of women. *BJS*.
—— 1979. The uniqueness of English witchcraft. *BJS*.
Anderson, O. 1965. The Janus-face of mid C19th English radicalism. *VS* 8.
—— 1974. The Administrative Reform Association 1855–1857. In Hollis 1974.
Anderson, P. 1963. Origins of the present crisis. *NLR* 23.
—— 1968. Components of a national culture. *NLR* 50.
—— 1974a. *Passages from antiquity to feudalism*. NLB.
—— 1974b. *Lineages of the absolutist state*. NLB.
—— 1983. *In the tracks of historical materialism*. Verso.
Annan, N. 1952. *Leslie Stephen*. Reissued, W&N, 1984.
—— 1955. Intellectual aristocracy. In J.H. Plumb (ed.) *Studies in social history*. Longmans.
Anspach, R. 1972. Implications of the Theory of Moral Sentiments for Adam Smith's economic thought. *Hist.Pol.Ec.* 4.
Anthias, F. 1980. Women, the reserve army of labour. *C&C* 10.
Appleby, A.B. 1975. Agrarian capitalism or seigneurial reaction? The North-West of England 1500–1710. *AHR* 80.
Archard, P. 1979. Vagrancy: a literature review. In Cook 1979.
Ardener, S. 1975. *Perceiving women*. Dent.
—— 1981. *Women and space: ground rules and social maps*. Croom Helm.
Arnstein, W. 1972. The survival of the Victorian aristocracy. In Jaher 1972.
—— 1975. The myth of the triumphant middle class. *Historian* 19.

Aschrott, P. 1902. *The English Poor Law system.* 2nd edn, Knight.

Ashton, T. 1934. *Economic and social investigations in Manchester 1833–1933.* Repr. Harvester 1976.

Aston, T. 1960. Lollardy and sedition 1381–1431. *P&P* 17.

Aydelotte, W. 1962. The business interests of the gentry in the Parliament of 1841–1847. Appx. to Kitson Clark 1962.

—— 1963. Voting patterns in the British House of Commons in the 1840s. *Comp.Studs.Soc.Hist.* 5.

—— 1965. Parties and issues in early Victorian England. *JBS* 5.

—— 1967a. Conservative and radical interpretations of early Victorian social legislation. *VS* 11.

—— 1967b. The country gentlemen and the repeal of the Corn Laws. *EHR* 82.

Aylmer, G. 1957. Attempts at administrative reform 1624–1640. *EHR* 72.

—— 1959. Office holding as a factor in English history 1625–1642. *History* 44.

—— 1961. *The king's servants.* RKP.

—— 1973. *The state's servants.* RKP.

—— 1974. Office holding, wealth and social structure in England c.1580–c.1720. *Datini Inglesi* 1978.

—— 1975. *The Levellers in the English revolution.* T&H.

—— 1979. Bureaucracy. Ch. 6 in companion vol. to the *New Cambridge Modern History,* vol. 13.

—— 1980a. Crisis and regrouping in the political elites: England from the 1630s to the 1660s. In Pocock 1980a.

—— 1980b. The meaning and definition of 'property' in C17th England. *P&P* 86.

—— 1980c. From office holding to civil service. *TRHS* ser. V vol. 80.

Bagehot, W. 1867. *The English constitution.* Ed. R.H. Crossman Fontana 1965.

—— 1872. Introduction to 2nd edn of his 1867. Idem.

Bahlman, D. 1957. *The moral revolution of 1688.* Yale UP.

Bailey, P. 1977. A mangled mass of perfectly legitimate pleasures. *VS* 21.

—— 1978. *Leisure and class in Victorian Britain.* RKP.

Bailey, V. (ed.) 1981. *Policing and punishment in C19th Britain.* Croom Helm.

Bailyn, B. 1982. Challenge of modern historiography. *AHR* 87 (1).

Baker, J.H. 1977. Criminal courts and procedure at common law 1550–1800. In Cockburn 1977.

—— 1979. *An introduction to English legal history.* 2nd edn, Butterworth.

Barker, D.L. 1978. Regulation of marriage. In G. Littlejohn et al. (eds) *Power and the State.* Croom Helm.

—— and Allen, S. 1976. *Dependence and exploitation in work and marriage.* Longman.

Barker, E. 1930. *A study of the modern state . . .* Repr. as *The development of public services in Western Europe.* OUP 1944; NY Archon Books 1966.

Barker, R. 1972. *Studies in opposition.* A&U.

—— 1978. *Political ideas in modern Britain.* Methuen.

Barker, T. 1975. *The long march of everyman.* BBC/Deutsch.

Barnett, C. 1970. *Britain and her army 1509–1970.* Penguin.

Barrett, M. et al. (eds) 1979. *Ideology and cultural production.* Croom Helm.

—— 1980. *Women's oppression today.* Verso.

—— 1984. Reply to Brenner and Ramas. *NLR* 146.

—— and McIntosh, M. 1981. The family wage. *C&C* 11.

Barron, R. and Norris, G. 1976. Sexual divisions and the dual labour market. In Barker and Allen 1976.

Bartrip, P. 1979. *Safety at work.* Oxford, Wolfson College, Centre for Socio-Legal Studies.

—— and Penn, P. 1980. The administration of safety. *PA.*

Beales, D. 1974. Peel, Russell and reform. *Hist.J* 17.

Beales, H.L. 1931. The new Poor Law. *History* 15.

—— 1948. The passing of the Poor Law. *Pol.Qu.* 9.

Bealey, F. 1970. *The social and political thought of the British Labour Party.* Macmillan.

Bean, R. 1973. War and the birth of the nation state. *J.Ec.Hist.* 33.

Beattie, J.M. 1970. Towards the study of crime in C18th England. In Fitz 1970.

—— 1974. The pattern of crime in England 1600–1800. *P&P* 62.

—— 1975. The criminality of women in C18th England. *J.Soc.Hist.* 8.

—— 1977. Crime and the courts in Surrey 1736–1753. In Cockburn 1977.

Beckett, J. 1977. Local custom and the new taxation in the 17th and 18th centuries. *NH* 12.

Beechey, V. 1978. Women and production. In Kuhn and Wolpe 1978.

Beer, S.H. 1957. The representation of interests in British government. *Am.Pol. Sci.Rev.* 51.

Beier, A.L. 1974. Vagrants and the social order in Elizabethan England. *P&P* 64.

Benn, T. 1984. *Writings on the wall.* Faber.

Bennett, W. 1846. *Crime and education: the duty of the state therein.* Cleeve.

Bentham, J. 1776. *A fragment on government* and *An introduction to the principles of morals and legislation.* Ed. W. Harrison, repr. Oxford, Blackwell 1967.

—— 1791. *Panopticon. CW* (11 vols, Edinburgh, Tait, 1838–48) vol. 4.

—— 1824. Book of fallacies. In Everett 1966: 166–94.

Bentley, J. 1978. *Ritualism and politics in Victorian Britain: the attempt to legislate for belief.* OUP.

Beresford, M. 1957. The common informer, the penal statutes and economic regulation. *Ec.HR* 10.

Beresford Ellis, P. 1972. *A history of the Irish working class.* Gollancz.

Berg, M. (ed.) 1979. *Technology and toil in C19th Britain.* CSE Books.

—— 1980. *The machinery question and the making of political economy 1815–1848.* CUP.

Best, G. 1971. *Mid-Victorian Britain.* W&N.

Bestor, A. 1948. Evolution of the socialist vocabulary. *JHI* 9.

Bezencenet, S. and Corrigan, P. 1985. *Photographic practices: towards a different image.* Comedia.

Bishop, A. 1971. *The rise of a central authority for English education.* CUP.

Bisseret, N. 1979. *Education, class language and ideology.* RKP.

Blackstone, W. 1765. *Commentaries on the laws of England.* 4 vols. Chicago UP 1979.

Bland, L. et al. 1979. Sexuality and reproduction: 3 official instances. In M. Barrett et al. 1979.

Blaug, M. 1958. The classical economists and the Factory Acts. *Qu.JEc.* 72.

—— 1963. The myth of the old Poor Law and the making of the new. *JEc.Hist.* 23.

—— 1964. The Poor Law Report re-examined. *JEc.Hist.* 24.

Blewett, N. 1965. The franchise in the UK. *P&P* 32.

Bloch, M. 1967. *Feudal society.* 2 vols, continuously paginated. RKP. (Completed 1940.)

Bock, K. 1974. Comparison of histories: the contribution of Sir Henry Maine. *Comp.Studs.Soc.Hist.* 16.

—— 1976. The moral philosophy of Sir Henry Maine. *JHI* 37.

Bonacich, E. 1975. Abolition, the extension of slavery, and the position of free blacks. *Am.JSociol.* 81.

Bond, B. 1974. The army. In Barker 1975.

Boyd, D. 1974. The educational background of a selected group of England's leaders. *Sociology* 8.

Braddock, R.C. 1974. The rewards of office holding in Tudor England. *JBS* 13.

Braithwaite, W.J. 1957. *Lloyd George's ambulance wagon.* Faber.

Braudel, F. 1977. *Afterthoughts on material civilisation and capitalism.* Baltimore, Johns Hopkins UP.

Brebner, J.S. 1948. Laissez faire and state intervention in C19 England. *JEc. Hist* . supp 8.

Brenner, J. and Ramas, M. 1984. Rethinking women's oppression. *NLR* 144.

Brenner, R. 1976. Agrarian class structure and economic development in pre-industrial Europe. *P&P* 70.

—— 1977. Origins of capitalist development. *NLR* 104.

Brett, T. et al. 1982 Planned trade, Labour Party Policy and US intervention. *HWJ* 13.

Brewer, J. and Styles, J. (eds) 1980. *An ungovernable people: the English and their law in the 17th and 18th centuries.* Hutchinson.

Briggs, A. 1954. Robert Lowe and the theory of democracy. In his *Victorian People*, rev. edn Penguin 1965.

—— 1956. Middle-class consciousness in English politics 1780–1846. *P&P* 9.

—— 1959a. *The age of improvement.* Longmans.

—— (ed.) 1959b. *Chartist studies.* Macmillan.

—— 1960. The language of 'class' in early C19th England. In Briggs and Saville 1960.

—— 1961. The welfare state in historical perspective. *AES* 2.

—— 1978. The language of 'mass' and 'masses' in C19th England. In *Ideology and the labour movement.* Croom Helm.

—— and Saville, J. (eds) 1960. *Essays in labour history.* Macmillan.

Bright, C. and Skocpol, T. 1984. *Statemaking and social movements.* Ann Arbor, U Michigan P.

Broadbent, L. 1984. The home front. Mimeo. Rev. version to appear in Glasgow University Media Group, *War and Peace News,* Open UP, 1985.

Brooks, C. 1974. Public finance and political stability. *Hist.J* 17.

Brown, L. 1958. *The Board of Trade and the Free Trade Movement 1830–1842.* Clarendon.

Brueghel, I. 1979. Women as a reserve army of labour. *FR* 3.

Brundage, A. 1972. The landed interest and the New Poor Law. *EHR* 87.

—— 1974. The English Poor Law of 1834 and the cohesion of agricultural society. *Agricultural Hist.*

—— 1975. The landed interest and the new Poor Law. *EHR* 90.

—— 1978. *The making of the new Poor Law.* Hutchinson.

Bunyan, T. 1977. *History and practice of the political police in Britain.* Quartet.

Burman, S. (ed.) 1979. *Fit work for women.* Croom Helm.

Burn, W.L. 1963. Review of MacDonagh 1961. *Hist.J* 6.

Burrow, J.W. 1971. 'The village community' and the uses of history in late C19th England. In McKendrick 1974.

—— 1981. *A liberal descent: Victorian historians and the English past.* CUP.

Burstyn, V. 1983. Masculine dominance and the State. *Socialist Register 1983.* Merlin.

Bush, M.L. 1971. The problem of the far North. *NH* 6.

Butler, D. and Sloman, A. 1975. *British political facts 1900–1975.* 4th edn, Macmillan.

Butt, R. 1974. Dangerous doctrines. *The Times,* 7 Feb.

Butterfield, H. 1931. *The Whig interpretation of history.* Penguin 1973.

Cain, P. and Hopkins, A. 1980. The political economy of British expansion overseas 1750–1914. *Ec.HR* 33.

Cairnes, J.E. 1870. Political economy and laissez–faire. In his 1873.

—— 1873. *Essays in political economy.* Macmillan.

Caldwell, J. 1959. Genesis of the Ministry of Labour. *PA* 37.

Cam, H. 1945. The legislators of medieval England. If Fryde and Miller 1970a.

—— 1962. The theory and practice of representation in medieval England. Idem.

Campbell, D. 1980a. Articles in *NSt* 1 Feb., 8 Feb., 15 Feb., 22 Feb., 11 April, 18 July.
—— 1980b. Society under surveillance. In Hain 1980.
—— 1981. Big Brother is listening: phonetappers and the security state. NSt Report 2.
Campbell, J. 1975. Observations on English government from the 10th to the 12th centuries. *TRHS*, 5th ser., 25.
—— 1980. The significance of the Anglo-Norman state in the administrative history of W. Europe. In Institut Historique Allemand de Paris, Beiheft der Francia, t. 9. München.
—— et al. 1982. *The Anglo-Saxons*. Phaidon P.
Carr, W. 1971. James Mill's politics reconsidered. *Hist.J* 14.
—— 1972. James Mill's politics: a final word. Idem. 15.
Carson, W.G. 1970a. White-collar crime and the enforcement of factory legislation. *Brit.JCriminology* 10.
—— 1970b. Some sociological aspects of strict liability and the enforcement of factory legislation. *Mod.Law Rev.* 33.
—— 1979. Conventionalisation of early factory crime. *Int.J for the Sociol. of Law*. 7.
Chadwick, E. 1857. On the economical, social, educational and political influence of competitive examinations . . . in the public service. Paper to BAAS, Aug. 1857. *JStat.Soc.* 21 (1858).
—— 1859a. The development of statesmanship as a science . . . Charles Knight. Repr. in his 1887, I.
—— 1859b. Results of different principles of legislation and administration in Europe; of competition for the field, as compared with competition within the field, of service. *JStat.Soc.* 22.
—— 1862. On the subject matters and methods of competitive examinations for the public service. Paper to BAAS. *JStat.Soc.* 25.
—— 1871. Competitive examinations [address to NAPSS]. In his 1887:I, 327–39.
—— 1887. The Health of Nations: a review [i.e. epitome] of the works of Edwin Chadwick . . . by Benjamin W. Richardson. 2 vols, Longman.
—— Manuscripts. See chapter 6, note 20, above, for details.
Chadwick, W.E. 1905. *Poverty: a social disease*. SPCK.
Chapman, R.A. 1970. *The higher civil service in Great Britain*. Constable.
Charlesworth, M. 1982. *British rule and the Indian economy 1800–1914*. Macmillan.
Checkland, S. 1949. The propagation of Ricardian economics in England. *Economica* 16.
Chester, N. 1981. *The English administrative system 1780–1870*. Clarendon.
Chitnis, R.C. 1968. The Edinburgh professoriate 1790–1826. PhD thesis, U of Edinburgh.
Cipolla, C. 1973a. *The industrial revolution*. Fontana.
—— 1973b. *The emergence of industrial societies*. Idem.
Clanchy, M. 1979. *From memory to written record*. Arnold.
—— 1983. *England and its rulers 1066–1272*. Fontana.
Clark, A. 1919. *Working life of women in the C17th*. Repr. Wakefield, EP 1978.
Clark, J. et al. 1979. *Working-class culture*. Hutchinson.
Clark, P. 1977. *English provincial society from the reformation to the revolution . . . Kent 1500–1640*. Harvester.
—— 1979. Migration in England during the late C17th and early C18th. *P&P* 83.
—— and Slack, P. 1972. *Crisis and order in English towns 1500–1700*. RKP.
—— —— 1976. *Towns in transition 1500–1700*. OUP.
Clarke, J.C. 1927. *Marxism and history*. National Council of Labour Colleges.
Clarke, P. 1974. The progressive movement in England. *TRHS* 24.
—— 1979. *Liberals and social democrats*. CUP.
—— 1982. The Edwardians and the constitution. In Read 1982.

Clarke, R. 1975. The machinery of government. In Thornhill 1975.

Clay, C. 1968. Marriage, inheritance, and the rise of large estates in England 1600–1815. *Ec.HR* 21.

Clements, R. 1955. Trade unions and emigration 1840–1880. *Population Studs.* 9.

—— 1961. British trade unions and popular political economy 1850–1875. *Ec.HR* 14.

Cliffe, J.T. 1969. *The Yorkshire gentry from the reformation to the Civil War. NH.*

Coates, W.H. 1950. Benthamism, laissez-fair and collectivism. *JHI* 11.

Coats, A.W. 1958. Changing attitudes to labour in the mid-C18th. *Ec.HR* 11.

—— 1960. Economic thought and Poor Law policy in the C18th. *Ec.HR* 13.

—— 1967. The classical economists and the labourer. In Jones and Mingay 1967.

—— 1972a. The classical economists, industrialisation, and poverty. In Hartwell 1972.

—— 1972b. Contrary moralities: plebs, paternalists, and political economists. *P&P* 54.

Cockburn, J. 1972. *A history of English assizes 1558–1714.* CUP.

—— (ed.) 1977. *Crime in England 1550–1800.* Methuen.

Cohen, E.W. 1941. *The growth of the British Civil Service 1780–1939.* Repr. Cass 1965.

Cohen, M. 1977. *Sensible words.* Baltimore, Johns Hopkins UP.

Cohen, S. and Scull, A. (eds) 1983. *Social control and the state.* Oxford, Martin Robertson.

Cohn, N. 1975. *Europe's inner demons.* Paladin 1976.

Cole, G.D.H. 1928. Introduction to D. Defoe *A tour through the whole island of Great Britain,* 1726. Everyman.

—— and Postgate, R. 1948. *The Common People, 1746–1946.* Methuen 1965.

Coleman, D.C. 1974. Gentlemen and players. *Ec.HR* 27.

—— 1977. *The economy of England 1450–1750.* OUP.

—— and John, A.H. (eds) 1976. *Trade, government and the economy in pre-industrial England.* W&N.

Coleman, O. 1976. *What figures?* Idem.

Coleridge, S.T. 1819. *Philosophical lectures.* RKP 1949.

—— 1830. On the constitution of the Church and State. 2nd edn, repr. ed. J. Barrell, Dent 1972.

Collini, S. 1972. Review of Wiener 1971. *Hist.J* 15.

—— 1974. Review of A.J. Taylor 1972. *History* 59.

—— 1976. Hobhouse, Bosanquet and the state: philosophical idealism and political argument in England 1880–1918. *P&P* 72.

—— 1977. Liberalism and the legacy of Mill. *Hist.J* 20.

—— 1978. Sociology and idealism in Britain 1880–1920. *AES* 19.

—— 1980a. Golden Gladstoneian days. *TLS* 29 Feb.

—— 1980b. Political theory and the 'science of society' in Victorian Britain. *Hist.J* 23.

Colls, R. (ed.) 1985. *The idea of Englishness.* Croom Helm.

Commons, J. 1924. *Legal foundation of capitalism.* Wisconsin UP 1957.

Conyers Read, T. 1925. *Mr Secretary Walsingham.* 3 vols, Cornell UP.

—— 1962. *William Lambarde and local government.* Ithaca, Free P.

Cook, T. (ed.) 1979. *Vagrancy.* Academic P.

Cooper, J. 1956. The counting of manors. *Ec.HR* 8.

—— 1958. Letter. *Encounter* XI, iii, p. 73.

Corfield, P. 1976. Urban development in England and Wales in the 16th and 17th centuries. In Coleman and John 1976.

Cornforth, M. 1978. *Rebels and their causes.* L&W.

Corrigan, Paul. 1979a. The local state. *Marxism Today,* July.

—— 1979b. Popular consciousness and social democracy. Idem, Dec.

Corrigan, P. 1974. Historical experience of the People's Republic of China. *J.Cont. Asia* 4.

—— 1975a. On the politics of production. *JPS*.

—— 1975b. Dichotomy is contradiction. *Sociol.Rev.*

—— 1976. On socialist construction. *JCont.Asia*.

—— 1977a. State formation and moral regulation in C19th Britain: sociological investigations. PhD thesis, Durham U.

—— 1977b. Feudal relics or capitalist monuments: notes on the sociology of unfree labour. *Sociology* 11.

—— (ed.) 1980a. *Capitalism, state formation and Marxist theory: historical investigations*. Quartet.

—— 1980b. Re-making it new. *Undercut* 1

—— 1980c. Curiouser and curiouser. *BJS* 31.

—— 1981a. The moment of English television. MA thesis, Polytechnic of Central London.

—— 1981b. On moral regulation. *Sociol.Rev.*

—— 1982a. Towards a celebration of difference(s). In D. Robins et al. (eds) *Rethinking social inequality*. Gower P.

—— 1982b. What is the subject of (a) cultural production? *Undercut* 3/4.

—— 1982c. Once again on socialist construction. *Sociol.Rev.* (Aug).

—— 1983a. 'My' body, my 'Self'. *Resources for Feminist Research* 12.

—— 1983b. Hard machines/soft messages. In *Nineteeneightyfour in 1984*. Comedia.

—— 1983c. Film entertainment as ideology and pleasure: towards a history of cinema audiences. In J. Curran and V. Porter (eds) *The British film industry*. W&N.

—— 1983d. Into textuality: timing our words. *Sociol.Rev.*

—— 1983e. In/forming school: space, time and textuality as schooling. Forthcoming.

—— 1984. Doing mythologies. *Border/lines* (Toronto), 1.

—— Forthcoming. The body of intellectuals/the intellectual body.

—— and Corrigan, V. 1979. State formation and social policy before 1871. In Parry 1979.

—— and Gillespie, V. 1974. *Class struggle, social literacy, and idle time*. Brighton, Labour History Monographs, 1978.

—— Ramsay, H. and Sayer, D. 1978. *Socialist construction and Marxist theory*. Macmillan/MRP.

—— —— —— 1979. *For Mao*. Macmillan.

—— —— —— 1980. The state as a relation of production. In Corrigan 1980a.

—— —— —— 1981. Bolshevism and the Soviet Union. *NLR* 125.

—— and Sayer, D. 1975. Moral relations, political economy and class struggle. *Radical Philosophy* 12.

—— —— 1978. Hindess and Hirst. *Socialist Register* 1978.

—— —— 1981a. How the law rules. In Fryer 1981.

—— —— 1981b. 'De-Maoisation' or Bolshevism ... recent events in China. China Policy Study Group *Broadsheet*, Feb. & March.

—— —— 1982. Marxist theory and socialist construction in historical perspective. *Utafiti* (Dar Es Salaam) 1985.

—— —— 1986. *Capitalism's cultural revolution: organising the subject*. Macmillan.

—— and Willis, P. 1980. Cultural forms and class mediations. *Media Culture & Society* 2.

For P. Corrigan see also entries under Bezencenet, Sayer, Spence, Willis.

Coward, R. 1982. *Patriarchal precedents*. RKP.

Craig, F. 1976 (ed.) *British electoral facts 1885–1975*. Macmillan.

—— 1978 (ed.) *British parliamentary election results 1832–1885*. Macmillan.

Crawford, W. and Trainer, B. 1977. *Aspects of Irish social history 1750–1800*. Belfast, HMSO.

Cressy, D. 1977. Levels of illiteracy in England 1530–1730. *Hist.J* 20.
—— 1980. *Literacy and the social order.* CUP.
Croft Dickinson, W. 1977. *Scotland: from earliest times to 1603.* 3rd edn, rev. by A.A.M. Duncan. Clarendon P.
Cromwell, V. 1977. *Revolution or evolution?* Longmans.
—— and Steiner, Z. 1969. The Foreign Office before 1914. In Sutherland 1972.
Crossman, R. 1976. *Diaries.* Cape, 1977 onwards.
Cullen, A.J. 1975. *The statistical movement in early Victorian Britain.* Harvester.
Cunningham, H. 1980. *Leisure and the industrial revolution.* Methuen.
—— 1981. The language of patriotism 1750–1914. *HWJ* 12.
—— 1982. Will the real John Bull stand up please. *THES* 19 Feb.
Curtis, T. and Speck, W. 1976. Societies for the reform of manners. *Literature and Hist.* 3.
Dale, R. et al. (eds) 1981. *Politics, patriarchy and practice.* Vol. 2 of *Education and the state.* Falmer P.
Dangerfield, G. 1935. *Strange death of Liberal England.* Paladin 1970.
Darvall, F. 1934. *Popular disturbances and public order in Regency England.* OUP repr. 1969.
Davidoff, L. 1973. Domestic service. *BSSLH* 26.
—— 1974. Mastered for life. *JSoc.Hist.* 7.
—— and Hall, C. (forthcoming) *The other hidden hand: domestic ideology/family form.*
Davidson, R. 1969. Lewellyn Smith, the Labour Department and government growth 1886–1909. In Sutherland 1972.
—— 1985. *The Labour Department.* Croom Helm.
Davies, M.G. 1956. *The enforcement of English apprenticeship 1567–1642.* Harvard UP.
Davies, R. and Denton J. (eds) 1981. *The English Parliament in the middle ages.* Manchester UP.
Davin, A. 1978. Imperialism and motherhood. *HWJ* 3.
—— 1979. 'Mind you do as you are told'. *FR* 3.
Davis, R.W. 1974. The Whigs and the idea of electoral deference. *Durham UJ* 67.
Dawes, R. 1854. *Remarks on the reorganisation of the civil service and its bearing on educational progress.* Ridgway.
Dawson, W.H. 1891. *Bismarck and state socialism.* Swan.
Dearlove, J. 1979. *The reorganisation of British local government.* CUP.
DeLacy, M. 1981. Grinding men good? Lancashire's prisons in mid-century. In Bailey 1981.
Dickson, T. (ed.) 1980. *Scottish capitalism: class, state and nation from before the Union to the present.* L&W.
Dictionary of National Biography. OUP.
Dietz, F. 1920. *English government finance 1485–1558.* Repr. CUP 1964.
Digby, A. 1975. The labour market and the continuity of social policy after 1834. *Ec.HR* 28.
—— 1976. The rural Poor Law. In Fraser 1976.
—— 1977. Recent developments on the study of the English Poor Law. *Local Hist.* 12.
—— 1978. *Pauper palaces.* RKP.
Ditton, J. 1977. Perks, pilferage and the fiddle. *Theory & Society* 4.
Djang, T. 1942. *Factory inspection in Great Britain.* A&U.
Donajgrodzki, A. (ed.) 1977. *Social control in Great Britain.* Croom Helm.
Draper, H. 1977. *Karl Marx's theory of revolution.* I: *State and bureaucracy.* 2 vols, MRP.

Duby, G. 1984. *The knight, the lady, and the priest.* Allen Lane.

Dunbabin, J. 1963. Politics of the establishment of county councils. *Hist.J* 7.

—— 1977. British local government reform: the C19th and after. *EHR* 92.

Dunlop, O. 1912. *English apprenticeship and child labour.* Fisher Unwin.

Duppa, B. 1837. The central society of education. *CSE Papers* 1.

Durkheim, E. 1902. *The division of labour in society.* NY, Free Press, 1947.

—— 1904. *Professional ethics and civic morals.* RKP 1957.

—— 1906. Determination of moral facts. In his 1974.

—— 1912. *Elementary forms of religious life.* A&U 1915.

—— 1974. *Sociology and philosophy.* NY, Free Press (repr.).

Edelman, M. 1975a. The patronage state. *NSt* 11 April.

—— 1975b. The patronage explosion. *NSt* 11 July.

—— 1975c. How the new system of patronage in government scatters the confetti of privilege. *The Times* 14 Oct.

—— 1975d. Time to stop the public appointments merry-go-round. *The Times* 15 Oct.

Edinburgh History of Scotland. 4 vols, Oliver & Boyd, 1975–.

Edwards, J.G. 1925. The personnel of the Commons in Parliament under Edward I and Edward II. In Fryde and Miller 1970a.

—— 1934. The plena potestas of English parliamentary representatives. Idem.

Edwards, S. 1981. *Female sexuality and the law.* Oxford, Martin Robertson.

Eisenstein, E. 1979. *The printing press as an agent of change.* CUP.

Elesh, D. 1972. The Manchester Statistical Society. *J.Hist. Behavioural Sci.*

Elias, N. 1939. *The civilising process.* 2 vols, Oxford, Blackwell, 1982.

Elton, G.R. 1952a. Parliamentary drafts 1529–1540. In his 1974a

—— 1952b. An early Tudor Poor Law. *Ec.HR* 6.

—— 1953. *The Tudor revolution in government.* CUP.

—— 1956. The political creed of Thomas Cromwell. *TRHS* 6.

—— 1961a. *England under the Tudors.* CUP.

—— 1961b. State planning in early Tudor England. *Ec.HR* 13.

—— 1963. *Reformation Europe.* Fontana.

—— 1968. *The Tudor Constitution: documents.* CUP.

—— 1969. The body of the realm. In his 1974b.

—— 1971. Studying the history of Parliament. Idem.

—— 1972. *Policy and police: the enforcement of the reformation in the age of Thomas Cromwell.* CUP.

—— 1973. *Reform and renewal: Thomas Cromwell and the common weal.* CUP.

—— 1974a. *Studies in Tudor and Stuart politics and government.* 1: *Tudor politics, Tudor government.* CUP.

—— 1974b. Idem. 2: *Parliament, political thought.* CUP.

—— 1974c. *England under the Tudors.* 2nd edn, Methuen.

—— 1976. *Reform and reformation: England 1509–1558.* Arnold.

Emy, H. 1973. *Liberals, radicals and social politics 1892–1914.* CUP.

Engels, F. 1890. Letter to C. Schmidt Oct 27. In Marx/Engels *Selected Letters,* Peking 1977.

—— 1892. On certain peculiarities of the economic and political development of England. In Marx/Engels *On Britain,* Moscow 1962.

Essays on Reform. 1867. Macmillan.

Evans, F. 1923. *The Principal Secretary of State 1558–1660.* Manchester UP.

Evans, R. 1971. Bentham's Panopticon. *Architectural Assn Qu.* 3.

Everett, C. 1966. *Jeremy Bentham.* W&N.

Everitt, A. 1957. *The County Committee of Kent in the Civil War.* Leicester UP.

—— 1960. Suffolk and the Great Rebellion 1640–1660. *Suffolk. Rec.Soc.* iii.

—— 1963. The Community of Kent in 1640. *Genealogists' Mag.* 14.

—— 1966. *The Community of Kent and the Great Rebellion 1640–1660.* Leicester UP.

Fabian Essays. 1889. A&U 1962.

Falkus, M. 1976. Lighting in the dark ages of English economic history. In Coleman and John 1976.

Farr, W. 1848. Statistics of the civil service in England. *J.Stat.Soc.* 11, 1849.

Febvre, L. and Martin, H. 1976. *The coming of the book.* NLB.

Fetter, A. 1953. The authorship of economic articles in the Edinburgh Review 1802–1847. *JPol.Ec.* 56.

—— 1965. Economic controversy in the British reviews 1802–1850. *Economica* 38.

Finer, S. 1952a. *Life and times of Sir Edwin Chadwick.* Methuen.

—— 1952b. Patronage and the public service. *PA* 30.

—— 1959. The transmission of Benthamite ideas 1820–1850. In Sutherland 1972.

—— 1975. State and nation building in Europe: the role of the military. In Tilly 1975.

Finlayson, G. 1966. The politics of municipal reform, 1835. *EHR* 81.

—— 1969. *England in the 1830s: decade of reform.* Arnold.

Finn, G. 1982. Women and the ideology of science. *Our Generation* 15.

Fletcher, A. 1975. *A county community in peace and war: Sussex 1600–1660.* Phillimore 1980.

Fletcher, J. 1851. *Education: national voluntary and free.* Ridgway.

Flinn, M. 1961. The Poor Employment Act 1817. *Ec.HR.* 14.

—— 1971. Policy of public works. *NS* 18 Nov.

Foot, M.R.D. 1973. *War and society.* Elek Books.

Forbes, D. 1970. Introduction to Hume 1754, Penguin.

—— 1975. Sceptical Whiggism, commerce and liberty. In Skinner and Wilson 1975.

Ford, C. and Harrison, B. 1983. *A hundred years ago: Britain in the 1880s.* Allen Lane.

Foster, D. 1974. Class and county government in early C19th Lancashire. *NH* 9.

Foster, F.F. 1977. *The politics of stability: a portrait of Elizabethan London.* Royal Hist. Soc.

Foster, J. 1969. The making of the first six Factory Acts. *BSSLH* 4.

—— 1974. *Class struggle and the industrial revolution.* W&N.

Foucault, M. 1977. *Discipline and punish: the birth of the prison.* Allen Lane.

—— 1982. The subject and power. *Critical Inquiry* 8.

Fraser, D. 1973. *Evolution of the British welfare state.* Macmillan.

—— (ed.) 1976. *The new Poor Law in the C19th.* Macmillan.

Fraser, P. 1960. The growth of ministerial control in the C19th House of Commons. *EHR* 75.

Freeden, M. 1972. English liberal thought . . . 1886–1914. DPhil. thesis, Oxford U.

—— 1978. *The new Liberalism.* Clarendon.

Frisby, D. and Sayer D. 1985. *Society.* Ellis Horwood, forthcoming.

Fritz, P. and Willis, D. 1970. *The triumph of culture.* Toronto, Hakkert.

Fry, G.K. 1969. *Statesmen in disguise: the changing role of the administrative class of the British civil service 1853–1966.* Macmillan.

Fryde, E. and Miller, E. (eds) 1970a. *Historical studies of the English Parliament. 1: Origins to 1399.* CUP.

—— 1970b. Idem, 2: *1399 to 1603.* CUP.

Fryer, B. et al. (eds) 1981. *Law, state and society.* Croom Helm.

Fuller, F. 1875. How to elevate the people. Trans. NAPSS.

Fulton Report. 1966. Committee on the Civil Service. *Report.* Cmnd 3638. HMSO.

Gallagher, C. 1984. The politics of culture and the debate over representation. *Representations* 5.

Gamarnikow, E. et al. (eds) 1983. *The public and the private.* Heinemann.

Gamble, A. 1981. *Britain in decline: economic policy, political strategy and the British state*. Macmillan.

Gardiner, S. 1979. *Constitutional documents of the Puritan revolution 1625–1660*. 3rd edn, Clarendon (first edn 1889).

Gauldie, E. 1974. *Cruel habitations: a history of working-class housing 1780–1918*. A&U.

Gazley, J. 1973. *The life of Arthur Young 1741–1820*. Philadelphia, Am. Philosophical Soc.

Genovese, E. 1971. *The world the slaveholders made*. NY, Vintage.

George, D. 1931. *England in transition*. Penguin 1953.

Gilmour, R. 1967. The Gradgrind school: political economy in the classroom. *VS* 11.

Gittins, L. 1977. Soapmaking and the excise laws 1711–1853. *Industrial Archaeology Rev.* 1.

Gladish, D. 1915. *The Tudor Privy Council*. Retford, Gainsborough and Worksop Times.

Gleason, J. 1969. *Justices of the Peace in England 1558–1640*. Clarendon.

Goldthorpe, J. 1962. The development of social policy in England 1800–1914. Tr. 5th World Congress of Sociol., Washington DC 1964, vol. 4.

——1969. Social inequality and social integration in modern Britain. *Advancement of Sci.*

Goodwin, A. 1979. *Friends of liberty: The English democratic movement in the age of the French revolution*. Hutchinson.

Goody, J. (ed.) 1976. *Family and inheritance: rural society in W. Europe 1200–1800*. CUP.

Graff, H. (ed.) 1981. *Literacy and social development in the West*. CUP.

Graveson, R. and Crane, F. 1957. *A century of family law 1857–1957*. Sweet & Maxwell.

Green, T.H. 1881. *Lectures on the principles of political obligation*. Longman 1937.

Gretton, R. 1913. *The king's government: a study of the growth of central administration*. Bell.

Griffith, J. 1975. Judges and a Bill of Rights. *NSt* 10 June.

—— 1977a. Judges, politics and social class. *NSt* 21 Oct.

—— 1977b. *Politics of the judiciary*. Fontana.

—— 1978. *Administrative law and the judges*. Haldane Society.

See also under Harman.

Guttsman, W. 1968. *The British political elite*. M&K.

—— (ed.) 1969. *The English ruling class*. W&N.

Guy, W. 1870. On the claims of a science to public recognition and support. *JRoyal. Stat.Soc.* 33.

Hain, P. (ed.) 1979. *Policing the police*. Vol.1, Calder.

—— 1980. Idem, vol.2.

Hakim, C. 1980. Census reports. *Sociol.Rev.*

Haldane, A. 1962. *New ways through the glens*. Newton Abbot, David & Charles.

Halevy, E. 1906. *The birth of Methodism in England*. Chicago UP 1971.

—— 1912. *England in 1815*. Benn 1949.

—— 1919. The policy of social peace in England. In his 1965.

—— 1921. The problem of workers control. Idem.

—— 1922. The present state of the social question in England. Idem.

—— 1923a. *The Liberal awakening 1815–1830*. Benn 1949.

—— 1923b. *The triumph of reform 1830–1841*. Benn 1950.

—— 1924. *History of the English people*. 3 vols, Penguin.

—— 1934. *The growth of philosophic radicalism*. Rev. edn Faber 1972.

—— 1965. *The era of tyrannies*. Allen Lane 1967.

Hall, C. 1979. Early formation of Victorian domestic ideology. In Burman 1979. See also under Davidoff.
Halsbury, Lord. *Halsbury's laws of England; Halsbury's statutes of England; Halsbury's statutory instruments.* For publication details see note 35 to chapter 6 above.
Halsey, A. 1972. *Trends in British society since 1900.* Macmillan.
Hamburger, J. 1963. *James Mill and the art of revolution.* Yale UP.
—— 1965. *Intellectuals in politics: J.S. Mill and the philosophic radicals.* Yale UP.
Hamilton, R. 1978. *The liberation of women.* A&U.
Hamowy, R. 1968. Adam Smith, Adam Ferguson and the division of labour. *Economica* 35.
Hampton, C. 1984. *The radical reader: the struggle for change in England 1381–1919.* Penguin.
Hanham, E. 1973. Religion and nationality in the mid-Victorian army. In Foot 1973.
Haraven, T. 1977. Family time and historical time. *Daedelus* 104.
Harcourt, F. 1980. Disraeli's imperialism 1866–1868. *Hist.J* 23.
Harman, H. and Griffith, J. 1978. *Justice deserted.* NCCL.
Harries-Jenkins, G. 1973. Victorian military and the political order. *JPol. & Military Sociol.* 1.
Harris, J.S. 1955. *British government inspection.* Stevens.
Harrison, B. 1974. State intervention and moral reform. In Hollis 1974.
—— 1978. *Separate spheres: the opposition to women's suffrage in Britain.* Croom Helm.
Harrison, J.F.C. 1954. *Social reform in Victorian Leeds: the work of James Hole 1820–1895.* Leeds, Thoresby Soc.
—— 1984. *The common people.* Fontana.
Harrison, R. and Mort, F. 1980. Patriarchal aspects of C19th state formation. In Corrigan 1980a.
Harrison, W. 1948. Introduction to his edn of Bentham 1776.
Harriss, G. 1963. Medieval government and statecraft. *P&P* 25.
Hart, J. 1955. Reform of the Borough Police 1835–1856. *EHR* 70.
—— 1956. The County and Borough Police Act 1856. *PA* 34.
—— 1960. Sir Charles Trevelyan and the Treasury. *EHR* 75.
—— 1969. Genesis of the Northcote-Trevelyan Report. In Sutherland 1972.
Hartwell, R. 1972. *The long debate on poverty.* Inst.Ec.Affairs.
Haskell, F. 1971. Manufacture of the past in C19th painting. *P&P* 53.
Hay, D. et al. 1977. *Albion's fatal tree.* Penguin (1st edn 1975).
Hay, J.R. 1975. *Origin of the Liberal welfare reforms 1906–1914.* Macmillan.
Hearder, H. and Loyn, H. (eds) 1974. *British government and administration.* Cardiff, U. of Wales P.
Hechter, M. 1973. Industrialisation and national development in the British Isles. *JDevelopment Studs.* 8 (1972/3).
—— 1975. *Internal colonialism: the Celtic fringe in British national development 1536–1966.* RKP.
Heisch, A. 1974. Queen Elizabeth I: Parliamentary rhetoric and the exercise of power. *Signs* 1.
—— 1980. Queen Elizabeth I and the persistence of patriarchy. *FR* 4.
Held, D. et al. (eds) 1983. *States and societies.* Oxford, Martin Robertson.
Hennock, E.P. 1958. Urban sanitary reform a generation before Chadwick? *Ec.HR* 10.
—— 1963. Finance and politics in urban local government in England 1835–1900. *Hist.J* 6.
—— 1971. The sociological premises of the first Reform Act. *VS* 14.
—— 1973. *Fit and proper persons.* Arnold.

—— 1976. Poverty and social theory in England: the experience of the 1880s. *Soc.Hist.* 1.

—— 1982. Central/local government relations in England: an outline 1800–1950. *Urban Hist. Yearbook.*

Henriques, U. 1967. Bastardy and the new Poor Law. *P&P* 37.

—— 1970. An early Factory Inspector: James Stuart. *Scottish Hist.Rev.* 50 (1971).

—— 1971. The early Factory Acts and their enforcement. *Hist.Assn.*

—— 1972. The rise and decline of the separate system of prison discipline. *P&P* 54.

—— 1974. Jeremy Bentham and the machinery of social reform. In Hearder and Loyn 1974.

—— 1979. *Before the welfare state.* Longmans.

Herrick, F. 1948. The second reform movement in Britain 1850–1863. *JHI* 9.

Hexter, J. 1961. *Reappraisals in history.* Longmans.

—— 1978. Power struggle, Parliament and liberty in early Stuart England. *JMH* 50.

Hibbert, C. 1966. *The roots of evil.* Penguin.

Hill, C. 1940. The agrarian legislation of the revolution. In his 1958.

—— 1952. Puritans and the poor. Rev. in his 1958.

—— 1954. The Norman yoke. Rev. in his 1958.

—— 1955. *The English revolution 1640.* 3rd ed., L&W (1st published 1940).

—— 1956a. Social and economic consequences of the Henrician reformation. In his 1958.

—— 1956b. Recent interpretations of the Civil War. Rev. in his 1958.

—— 1958. *Puritanism and revolution.* S&W.

—— 1959. La révolution anglaise du XVIIe. siècle. *Revue Historique* ccxxi.

—— 1961a. Protestantism and the rise of capitalism. In his 1974.

—— 1961b. *The century of revolution 1603–1714.* Edinburgh, Nelson.

—— 1963. Puritans and 'the dark corners of the land'. In his 1974.

—— 1964. *Society and Puritanism in pre-revolutionary England.* S&W; rev. edn, Panther 1969.

—— 1965. *Intellectual origins of the English revolution.* Clarendon.

—— 1966. The many-headed monster in late Tudor and early Stuart political thinking. Rev. in his 1974.

—— 1967. Pottage for freeborn Englishmen: attitudes to wage labour in the 16th and 17th centuries. Rev. in his 1974.

—— 1969a. *Reformation to industrial revolution.* Rev. edn, Penguin (1st edn 1967).

—— 1969b. 'Reason' and 'reasonableness' in C17th England. Rev. in his 1974 (originally in *BJS* 1969).

—— 1970. *God's Englishman: Oliver Cromwell.* W&N.

—— 1974. *Change and continuity in C17th England. W&N.*

—— 1975. *The world turned upside down.* Rev. edn, Penguin (1st edn 1972).

—— 1977. *Milton and the English revolution.* Faber.

—— 1978a. Sex, marriage and the family in England. *Ec.HR* 31.

—— 1978b. From Lollards to Levellers. In Cornforth 1978.

—— 1980a. *Some intellectual consequences of the English revolution.* W&N.

—— 1980b. A bourgeois revolution? In Pocock 1980a.

—— 1981. Parliament and people in C17th England. *P&P* 92.

A very full – though still not exhaustive! – bibliography of Christopher Hill's writings, including reviews, 1938–78, can be found in Pennington and Thomas 1978. Harvester P. (1985 onwards) are publishing his *Collected Essays.*

Hilton, R. 1973. *Bondmen made free.* Temple Smith.

—— 1975. *English peasantry in the later middle ages.* OUP.

—— 1976 (ed.) *The transition from feudalism to capitalism.* NLB.

Hintze, O. 1906. Military organisation and the organisation of the state. In his 1975.
—— 1908. Origins of the modern ministerial system. In his 1975.
—— 1975. *Historical essays.* NY, OUP.
Hirschman, A. 1977. *The passions and the interests: political arguments for capitalism before its triumph.* Princeton UP.
Hirst, D. 1975. *The representatives of the people? Voters and voting in England under the early Stuarts.* CUP.
—— 1978. Unanimity in the Commons, aristocratic intrigue and the origins of the English Civil War. *JMH* 50.
—— 1979. Court, country and politics. In K. Sharpe 1979.
—— 1980. Parliament, law and war in the 1620s. *Hist.J* 23.
—— 1981. Revisionism revised: the place of principle. *P&P* 92.
Hobsbawm, E. (ed.) 1948. *Labour's turning point 1880–1900.* Repr. Harvester 1974.
—— 1959. *Primitive rebels.* Manchester UP.
—— 1968. *Labouring men.* Rev. edn, W&N.
—— 1969. *Industry and empire.* Penguin.
—— 1973. *Revolutionaries.* W&N.
—— 1983. Introduction and ch. 7 in Hobsbawm and Ranger 1983.
—— and Ranger, T. (eds) 1983. *The invention of tradition.* CUP.
—— and Rude, G. 1969. *Captain Swing.* L&W.
Holcombe, V. 1977. Victorian wives and property. In Vicinus 1977.
Holdsworth, W. 1924. *Influence of the legal profession on the growth of the English constitution.* Clarendon.
—— 1940. Bentham's place in English legal history. *California Law Rev.* 28.
—— 1972. *A history of the English law.* Rev. edn, 17 vols, Methuen/Sweet & Maxwell, 1972.
Hole, J. 1860. *Light, more light!* Longman, Brown.
Hollander, S. 1971. Adam Smith's approach to economic development. In Hughes and Williams 1971.
Hollis, P. 1970. *The pauper press.* OUP.
—— (ed.) 1973. *Class and conflict in C19th England.* RKP.
—— 1974. *Pressure from without in early Victorian England.* Arnold.
Holmes, C. 1980. The 'county community' in Stuart historiography. *JBS* 19.
Holmes, G. 1982. *Augustan England: professions, state and society.* A&U.
Holquist, M. 1983. Politics of representation. In S. Greenblatt (ed.) *Allegory and representation.* Johns Hopkins UP.
Horner, L. 1834. The Factories Regulation Act (explained). Glasgow, privately published.
—— 1837. 'Letter to Mr Senior', in the latter's Letters on the Factory Acts. London, printed R. Clay.
Hoskins, W.G. 1976. *The age of plunder: the England of Henry VIII, 1500–1547.* Longmans.
—— 1977. *The making of the English landscape.* Rev. edn, H&S.
Hughes, E. 1942. Civil service reform 1853–1855. Rev. in *PA* 32, 1954.
—— 1949. Sir Charles Trevelyan and civil service reform, 1853–1855. *EHR* 64.
Hughes, P. and Williams, D. 1971. *The varied pattern.* Toronto, Hakkert.
Hume, D. 1754. *History of Great Britain,* vol. 1. Penguin 1970.
Humphries, J. 1977. Class struggle and the persistence of the working class family. *Cambridge JEc.* 1.
—— 1981. Protective legislation. *FR* 7.
Humphries, S. 1979. Hurrah for England. *Southern Hist.* 1.
—— 1981. *Hooligans or rebels?* Oxford, Blackwell.

Hurstfield, J. 1966. Was there a Tudor despotism after all? *TRHS* 1967.
—— 1973. *Freedom, corruption and government in Elizabethan England.* Cape.
Hutchins, B. 1915. *Women in modern industry.* Repr. Wakefield, EP, 1978.
Hyndman, H. 1881. *England for all.* Repr. Harvester 1973.
Ignatieff, M. 1978. *A just measure of pain: the penitentiary in the industrial revolution 1750–1850.* Macmillan.
Inglis, B. 1971. *Poverty and the industrial revolution.* Rev. edn, Panther.
Ingram, J.K. 1878. The need for sociology. Presidential address, section F, BAAS. In Abrams 1968.
Jackson, T.A. 1971. *Ireland her own.* L&W.
Jaher, F.C. (ed.) 1972. *The rich, the well-born and the powerful.* Urbana, U. of Illinois P.
James, M. (ed.) 1973. *Bentham and legal theory.* Belfast, supp to *Northern Ireland Legal Qu.*
James, M.E. 1966. *A Tudor magnate and the Tudor state.* York U., Borthwick Inst.
Jameson, F. 1971. *Marxism and form.* Princeton UP.
Jeremy, D. 1977. Damming the flood: British government efforts to check the outflow of technicians and machinery 1780–1843. *Business Hist.Rev.* 51.
Jevons, W.S. 1882. *The state in relation to labour.* Murray.
Johnson, R. 1968. The Education Department 1839–1864. PhD thesis, Cambridge U.
—— 1969. Administrators in education before 1870. In Sutherland 1972.
—— 1970. Educational policy and social control in early Victorian England. *P&P* 49.
—— 1972. Elementary education. In *Guides to Parliamentary Papers: Education.* Dublin, Irish UP.
—— 1973. *The Blue Books and education 1816–1896.* CCCS.
—— 1975. *Peculiarities of the English route.* CCCS.
—— 1976. *Barrington Moore, Perry Anderson, and English social development.* CCCS.
—— 1977. Educating the educators: 'experts' and the state 1833–1839. In Donajgrodzki 1977.
Johnson, R.W. 1972. The British political elite. *AES* 14.
Johnston, H.J.M. 1972. *British emigration policy 1815–1830: 'shovelling out paupers'.* Clarendon.
Johnston, T. 1974. *The history of the working classes in Scotland.* Repr., Wakefield, EP.
Jones, D.J.V. and Brainbridge, A. *Crime in C19th Wales.* SSRC Report HR 2970. From this have appeared articles in *Llafur, Soc.Hist.* and *Welsh Hist.Rev.* (8, 1977), the latter an important piece on criminal vagrants.
Jones, E.L. and Mingay, G. (eds) 1967. *Land, labour and population in the industrial revolution.* Methuen.
Jones, G.S. 1974. Working-class culture and working-class politics in London. *JSoc.Hist.* 7.
—— 1977. Class expression vs. social control? *HWJ* 4.
Jones, W.R. 1973. Rex and ministri: English local government and the crisis of 1341. *JBS* 13.
Joseph, K. 1975. Is Beckermann amongst the sociologists? *NSt* 18 April.
—— 1976. *Reversing the trend: a critical reappraisal of Conservative economic and social policies.* Rose.
Jowell, J. 1979. Lords creating law. *Listener* 25 Oct.
Jowitt, Earl. 1977. *Dictionary of English law.* 2nd edn, 2 vols, Sweet & Maxwell.
Jung, H. 1983. Rhetoric, grammatology and political theory. *Reflections* 4.
Kamenka, E. and Neale, R.S. (eds) 1975. *Feudalism, capitalism and beyond.* Arnold.

Kay, J.P. (Kay-Shuttleworth from 1843 publications on).

—— 1832. *The moral and physical conditions of the working classes employed in the cotton manufacture in Manchester.* 2nd edn. Ridgway.

—— 1836. Report on the administration . . . Poor Law Amendment Act . . . Suffolk, and Norfolk. Appx B, PLC Rpt., Clowes.

—— 1838a. Report on the training of pauper children. Idem.

—— 1838b. On the establishment of County or District schools for the training of pauper children maintained in Union workhouses. *JStat.Soc.* 1.

—— 1838c. Notes . . . on the training in Schools of Industry of children. Idem.

—— 1839a. *Recent measures for the promotion of education in England.* 2nd edn, Ridgway.

—— 1839b. The training of pauper children. 2nd Rpt, Appx C. PLC Rpt, Clowes. Repr. 1839c.

—— 1839c. *The training of pauper children.* Repr. Manchester, Morten, 1970.

—— 1840a. On the training of pauper children. Supp. note. In PLC 1841 composite Rpt.

—— 1840b. An account of certain improvements in the training of pauper children. Idem.

—— 1841a. With E.C. Tufnell. On the training school at Battersea. Idem.

—— 1841b. *On the punishment of pauper children.* Repr. College of St Mark and St John 1961.

—— 1846. *The school in its relations to the state, the church, and the congregation.* Murray 1847.

—— 1853. *Public education as affected by the Minutes . . . from 1846 to 1852.* Longman, Brown, Green & Longman.

—— 1859. *Address . . . on the progress of civilisation in England.* Tr. NAPSS 1860.

—— 1860. *Address . . . on public education and the relations of moral and physical forces in civilisation.* Idem 1861.

—— 1862a. *Four periods of public education as reviewed in 1832 – 1839 – 1846 – 1862.* Longman, Green, Longman & Roberts.

—— 1862b. *Words of comfort and counsel of distressed Lancashire workmen . . . by a country squire, their neighbour.* Hatchard; Manchester, Abel Heywood.

—— 1866a. *Address . . . on economy and trade.* Tr. NAPSS 1867. Repr. as Laws of social progress, in his 1873.

—— 1866b. A sketch of the history and results of popular education in England. In his 1873.

—— 1868. *Memorandum on popular education.* Ridgway.

—— 1873. *Thoughts and suggestions on certain social problems, contained chiefly in address to meetings of working men in Lancashire.* Longman, Green & Co.

—— 1876. Some of the results of the Education Act and Code of 1870. *Fortnightly Rev.* 25.

Keith-Lucas, B. 1977. *English local government in the 19th and 20th centuries.* Hist.Assn.

Kellner, P. and Lord Crowther Hunt. 1980. *The civil servants: an inquiry into Britain's ruling class.* MacDonald.

Kelsall, R. 1938. *Wage regulation under the statute of artificers.* Methuen.

—— 1966. *Higher civil servants in Britain.* RKP.

Kennedy, W. 1957. Humanist vs. economist: the economic thought of Samuel Taylor Coleridge. *U of California Publications in Ec.* 17.

Kenyon, J. 1981. Holding the Whig line. *TLS* 4 Dec.

Kettle, M. 1979. Trying to make the verdicts fit the evidence; Several stones still unturned. *NS* 24 & 30 May.

Kieckhefer, R. 1976. *European witch trials.* RKP.

Kiernan, V. 1965. State and nation in W. Europe. *P&P* 31.

—— 1972. *Lords of human kind*. Rev. edn, Penguin.
—— 1976. Private property in history. In Goody 1976.
—— 1978. Working class and nation in C19th Britain. In Cornforth 1978.
—— 1982. *European empires from conquest to collapse 1815–1960*. Fontana.
King, P. 1974. *The ideology of order . . . Jean Bodin and Thomas Hobbes*. W&N.
Kinzer, B. 1982. *The ballot question in C19th English politics*. NY, Garland.
Kirby, J. 1957. The rise of the Under-Treasurer of the Exchequer. *EHR* 72.
Knights, B. 1978. *The idea of the clerisy in the C19th*. CUP.
Koeningsberger, H.S. 1977. Dominium regale or dominium politicum et regale? In *Der Moderne Parliamentarismus*, Duncker & Humboldt, Berlin.
Kristeva, J. 1981. Interview. *m/f* 5/6.
—— 1982. Women's time. *Signs* 7.
Kuczynski, J. 1945. *A short history of labour conditions under industrial capitalism*. 2nd edn, Muller, repr. 1972.
Kuhn, A. and Wolpe, A. (eds) 1978. *Feminism and materialism*. RKP.
Kundera, M. 1983. *The book of laughter and forgetting*. Penguin.
Langbein, J. 1977. *Torture and the law of proof: Europe and England in the Ancient Regime*. Chicago UP.
Larner, C. 1980. Crimen exceptum. In Parker and Gatrell 1980.
—— 1981. *Enemies of God: the witch-hunt in Scotland*. C&W.
—— 1982. *The thinking peasant: popular and educated belief in pre-industrial culture*. Glasgow, Pressgang.
Laski, H.J. 1928. The personnel of the English Cabinet 1801–1924. *Am.Pol.Sci.Rev.* 22.
Lazonick, W. 1974. Karl Marx and enclosures in England. *RRPE* 6.
—— 1978. The subjection of labour to capital. *RRPE* 10.
—— 1979. Industrial relations and technical change. *Cambridge JEc.* 3.
Le Carré, J. 1978. *The honourable schoolboy*. Pan.
Lee, J.M. 1963. *Social leaders and public persons*. OUP.
—— 1973. *The modernisation of Irish society 1848–1918*. Dublin, Gill.
—— 1974. Central capability. In B. Chapman and A. Potter (eds) *WJMM*. Manchester UP.
Lehman, W. 1930. *Adam Ferguson and the beginnings of modern sociology*. NY, Columbia UP.
—— 1952. John Millar, historical sociologist. *BJS* 3.
—— 1960. *John Millar of Glasgow*. CUP.
—— 1971. *Henry Home, Lord Kames, and the Scottish enlightenment*. Hague, M. Nijhoff.
Lehmberg, S. 1970. *The Reformation Parliament 1529–1536*. CUP.
Lenin, V.I. 1917. *The state and revolution*. Sel. works in 3 vols, vol 2. Moscow 1970.
Levey, M. 1971. *Painting at court*. W&N.
Lewenhak, S. 1978. *Women and trade unions*. Benn.
Lewis, R.A. 1950. Edwin Chadwick and the Administrative Reform Movement 1854–1856. *Birmingham UHist.J* 2.
Linebaugh, P. 1968. Tyburn. PhD Thesis, U. of Warwick.
—— 1975. The Tyburn riot against the surgeons. In Hay et al. 1977.
—— 1976. Karl Marx, the thefts of wood and working class composition. *Crime and Soc. Justice*.
—— 1983. All the Atlantic mountains shook. *Labour/Le Travail* 14.
Lipson, E. 1946. *Planned economy or free enterprise?* Black.
Lloyd, C. 1974. The Navy. In Barker 1975.
Loades, D. 1977. *Politics and the nation 1450–1660*. Fontana.
Lockwood, D. 1958. *The blackcoated worker*. A&U.

Lowe, R.A. 1878. Recent attacks on political economy. *Nineteenth Century* 4.
Löwith, K. 1982. *Max Weber and Karl Marx.* A&U (1st edn 1932).
Lubenow, W.C. 1971. *The politics of government growth.* Newton Abbot, David &
    Charles.
—— 1977. Social recruitment and social attitudes. *Huntington Library Qu.* 40.
Lucas, A. 1981. *Women in the middle ages.* Harvester.
Lukes, S. 1975. Political ritual. *Sociol.* 9.
Lyon, F.S.L. 1971. *Ireland since the famine.* OUP.
MacCaffrey, W. 1963. Elizabethan politics. *P&P* 24.
MacDonagh, O. 1955. Emigration and the state 1833–1855. *TRHS* ser.v. 5.
—— 1961. *A pattern of government growth, 1800–1860: the Passenger Acts and their
    enforcement.* M&K.
—— 1968. *Ireland.* Prentice-Hall.
—— 1977. *Early Victorian government 1830–1870.* W&N.
MacDonnell Commission. Royal Commission on the Civil Service, 1912–1914. Cd.
    6740.
McDowell, R.B. 1964. *Irish administration 1801–1914.* RKP.
Macfarlane, A. 1970. *Witchcraft in Tudor and Stuart England.* Clarendon.
—— 1978. *Origins of English individualsim.* Oxford, Blackwell.
McFarlane, K. 1952. *Wycliffe and English nonconformity.* Repr. Penguin 1972.
McGregor, O. 1951. Civil Servants and the Civil Service 1850–1950. *Pol.Qu.* 22.
—— 1957. Social research and social policy in the C19th. *BJS* 8.
Machin, G. 1977. *Politics and the churches in Great Britain 1832–1868.* Clarendon.
McIntosh, M. 1978. The state and the oppression of women. In Kuhn and Wolpe 1978.
    See also under Barrett, M.
Mack, M. 1955. The Fabians and utilitarianism. *JHI* 16.
McKendrick, N. (ed.) 1974. *Historical perspectives: studies in English thought and
    society.* Europa.
MacKenzie, N. 1976. The once and future Fabians. *NSt* 2 July.
McKibbin, R. 1974. *Evolution of the Labour Party 1910–1924.* OUP.
Mackie, J. 1952. *The early Tudors.* Clarendon.
MacKinnon, C.A. 1982. Feminism, Marxism, method and the state. *Signs* 7.
Macpherson, C.B. 1977. Do we need a theory of the state? *AES* 18.
Maine, H. 1885. Popular government. Longman, Green, Brown.
Maitland, F. 1897. *The constitutional history of England.* CUP 1963.
    See also under Pollock, S.
Malament, B. (ed.) 1980. *After the Reformation.* Philadelphia, U Pennsylvania P.
Malchow, H.L. 1976. Trade unions and emigration in late Victorian England. *JBS* 15.
Malcolmson, R. 1973. *Popular recreations in English society 1700–1850.* CUP.
Mannheim, K. 1936. *Ideology and utopia.* RKP 1960.
Manning, B. 1978. *The English people and the English revolution.* Penguin.
Mantoux, P. 1928. *The industrial revolution in the C18th.* Rev. edn, Methuen 1964.
Marchant, R.A. 1969. *The church under the law: justice administration and discipline
    in the diocese of York 1560–1640.* CUP.
Marshall, Dorothy. 1974. The role of the Justice of the Peace in social administration.
    In Hearder and Loyn 1974.
Marshall, David. 1984. Adam Smith and the theatricality of moral sentiments. *Critical
    Inquiry* 10.
Marshall, T. 1972. Value problems of welfare capitalism. *JSoc.Policy* 1.
Marson, D. 1973. *Children's strikes in 1911.* Oxford, Hist. Workshop Pamphlets 9.
Marx, K.
—— (and Engels, F.) *Collected Works.* To comprise 50 vols. Moscow, NY (Inter-
    national), London (L&W) 1975–.

—— 1842. Proceedings . . . thefts of wood. CW1, pp. 224–63.

—— 1843a. Contribution to the critique of Hegel's philosophy of law. CW3.

—— 1843b. On the Jewish question. Idem.

—— 1844a. Comments on James Mill. Idem.

—— 1844b. Economic and philosophical manuscripts. Idem.

—— 1850. Class struggles in France 1848–50. CW10.

—— 1852. 18th Brumaire of Louis Bonaparte. CW11.

—— 1855. The British constitution. In Marx & Engels 1971.

—— 1858. *Grundrisse*. Penguin 1973.

—— 1859. *Contribution to a critique of political economy*. L&W 1971.

—— 1863. *Theories of surplus value* (intended by Marx as vol. 4 of *Capital*). 3 vols, Moscow, 1963–71.

—— 1864. Inaugural address to the International Workingmen's Association. In Marx and Engels 1971.

—— 1865. *Capital*, vol. 3. L&W 1972.

—— 1867. Idem, vol. 1. L&W 1970.

—— 1871. Civil War in France [text and two drafts]. In *Writings on the Paris Commune*, ed. H. Draper, MRP 1971.

—— 1873. Afterword to 2nd German edn of his 1867. With the latter.

—— and Engels, F. 1846. *The German Ideology*. L&W, 1965 (our source; compare translation in CW5).

—— —— 1848. Manifesto of the Communist Party. CW6.

—— —— 1971. *Articles on Britain*. L&W.

For a detailed (though not exhaustive) bibliography of Marx in English see Sayer 1983a.

Massey, D. and Catalano, A. 1978. *Capital and land*. Arnold.

Mather, F. 1959. *Public order in the age of the Chartists*. Manchester UP.

Matthew, H.C.G. 1973. *The Liberal imperialists*. OUP.

—— McKibbin, R. and Kay, J. 1976. The franchise factor in the rise of the Labour *EHR* 91.

Matthews, D. 1948. *Social structure of Caroline England*. OUP.

Maudling, R. 1974. Self-discipline essential to a free society. *The Times* 20 Feb.

Meacher, M. 1974a. The coming class struggle. *NSt* 4 Jan.

—— 1974b. The widening wages gap. *The Times* 21 Jan.

Meek, R. 1973. *Precursors of Adam Smith: readings*. Dent.

—— 1976. New light on Adam Smith's Glasgow lectures on jurisprudence. *Hist. Pol.Ec.* 8.

Melosi, D. and Pavarini, M. 1977. *The prison and the factory*. Macmillan 1981.

Miall, F. 1851. The franchise as the means of a people's education. Cowes.

Middlemas, K. 1979. *Politics in industrial society: the experience of the British system since 1911*. Deutsch.

Middleton. C. 1979. Sexual division of labour in feudal England. *NLR* 113–14.

—— 1981. Peasant, patriarchy and the feudal mode of production in England. *Sociol. Rev.* 29.

Miliband, R. 1960. *Parliamentary socialism*. Merlin 1972.

Mill, James. 1826. State of the nation. *Westminster Rev.* 6.

Mill, John Stuart. 1838a. Bentham. *Westminster Rev.*, repr. in his 1950.

—— 1838b. Radical Party and Canada. *Westminster Rev.* 6.

—— 1840. Coleridge. *Westminster Rev.*, repr. in his 1950.

—— 1848. *Principles of political economy*. Books 4 and 5, Penguin 1970.

—— 1862. Centralisation. *Edinburgh Rev.* 115.

—— 1869. Chapters on socialism. *Fortnightly Rev.* 1879

—— 1950. *Mill on Bentham and Coleridge*. Ed. F. R. Leavis, C&W.

Milne, M. 1867. On the admission of the working classes as part of our social system. In *Essays on Reform* 1867.

Milsom, S. 1981. *Nature of Blackstone's achievement*. Selden Soc.

Mingay, G. 1975. *Arthur Young and his times*. Macmillan.

—— 1976. *The gentry*. Longman.

Misra, B. 1959. *Central administration of the E. India Co. 1773–1834*. Manchester UP.

Mitchell, G. 1968. *Hundred years of sociology*. Duckworth.

Mitchinson, R. 1962. *Agricultural Sir John: the life and times of Sir John Sinclair*. Bles.

Moir, E. 1969. *The justice of the peace*. Penguin.

Money, J. 1979. Extended review of Speck 1979. *Soc. Hist*. 4.

Montmorency, J. de. 1902. *State intervention in English education: a short history . . . to 1833*. CUP.

Moore, D.C. 1961. The other face of reform. *VS* 5.

—— 1965. The Corn Laws and high farming. *Ec.HR* 18.

—— 1966. Concession or cure? Sociological premises of the 1st Reform Act. *Hist. J* 9.

—— 1967. Social structure, political structure and public opinion in mid-Victorian England. In Robson 1967.

—— 1969. Political morality in mid-C19th Britain: concepts, norms, violations. *VS* 13.

—— 1971. Reply (to Hennock 1971). *VS* 14.

—— 1976. *The politics of deference*. Harvester.

Moore, J. Barrington Jr 1969. *Social origins of dictatorship and democracy*. Penguin.

More, T. 1515. *Utopia*. Everyman edn.

Morley, D. and Worpole, K. 1982. *The republic of letters*. Comedia.

Morrill, J.S. 1974. *Cheshire 1630–1660: county government and society during the 'English revolution'*. OUP.

—— 1976. *Revolt of the provinces: conservatives and radicals in the English Civil War 1630–1650*. Longmans.

—— 1979. Northern gentry and the great rebellion. *NH* 15.

Morris, W. 1893. *Communism: a lecture*. Fabian Soc. 1903.

Morton, A.L. 1979. *People's history of England*. Rev. edn. L&W.

Mowat, C.L. 1969. Social legislation in Britain and the US in the early C20th. *Hist. Studs*. 7.

Muldoon, J. 1975. Indian as Irishman. *Essex Historical Institutes* III.

Muller, V. 1977. Formation of the state and the oppression of women. *RRPE* 9.

Munsche, P. 1977. The game laws . . . In Cockburn 1977.

Myers, A. 1952. *England in the late middle ages*. Penguin.

Nairn, T. 1963a. The British political elite. *NLR* 23.

—— 1963b. The English working class. *NLR* 24.

—— 1964. Anatomy of the Labour Party. In R. Blackburn (ed.) *Towards socialism*, Fontana 1965.

Namier, L. 1957. *The structure of politics at the accession of George III*. Athlone P.

Neale, J.E. 1924. The Commons privilege of free speech. In Fryde and Miller 1970b.

—— 1953/7. *Elizabeth I and her Parliaments*. Vols 1 and 2. CUP.

—— 1958. *Essays in Elizabethan history*. Cape 1963.

—— 1976. *Elizabethan House of Commons*. Rev. edn, Fontana (1st edn. 1949).

Neale, R.S. 1975. Property, law and the transition from feudalism to capitalism. In Kamenka and Neale 1975.

Nettl, J.P. 1965. Consensus or elite domination. *Pol. Studs* 13. 1968. The state as a conceptual variable. *World Pol.* 20.

Newman, G. 1975. Anti-French propaganda and British Liberal nationalism in the early C19th. *VS* 18.

Newton, J.L. et al. (eds) 1983. *Sex and class in women's history*. RKP.

Nicholls, D. 1962. Positive liberty 1880–1914. *Am.Pol.Sci.Rev.* 56.

Nicholls, G. 1846. On the condition of the agricultural labourer. *J. Royal Agricultural Soc. of Eng.* Ser. i, 7.

—— 1898. *A history of the English Poor Law*. 2 vols, rev. with 3rd vol. by T. Mackay. King.

Nissel, M. 1980. Women in government statistics. *EOC Res.Bull.* 4.

Nossiter, T. 1970a. Aspects of electoral behaviour in English constituencies 1832–1868. In Allardt and Rokkan (eds) *Mass politics*, NY, Free P.

—— 1970b. Voting behaviour 1832–1872. *Pol.Studs.* 18.

—— 1970c. Recent work on English elections 1832–1935. Idem.

—— 1976. *Influence, opinions and party idiom*. Harvester.

O'Brien, M. 1981. *Politics of reproduction*. RKP.

—— 1983. Feminism and education. *Resources for Feminist Research* 12.

O'Day, R. 1979. *The English clergy . . . 1558–1642*. Leicester UP.

O'Faolain, J. and Martines, L. 1973. *Not in God's image*. Temple Smith.

Olsen, F.E. 1983. The family and the market: a study of ideology and legal reform. *Harvard Law Rev.* 96, pp. 1497–1578.

Ormond, R. 1977. *The face of monarchy*. Phaidon P.

Palliser, D. 1983. *The age of Elizabeth . . . 1547–1603*. Longmans.

Parel, A. and Flanagan, T. (eds) 1980. *Theories of property*. Wilfred Laurier UP.

Parker, G. and Gatrell, V. 1980. *Crime and the law: social history of crime in W. Europe since 1500*. Europa.

Parkin, F. 1971. *Class inequality and political order*. M&K.

Parris, H. 1960. The C19th revolution in government. *Hist.J* 3; repr. Stansky 1973.

—— 1968. Origins of the permanent civil service 1780–1830. *PA* 46.

—— 1969. *Constitutional bureaucracy: the development of British central administration since the C18th*. A&U.

Parry, N. et al (eds) 1979. *Social work, welfare and the state*. Arnold.

Parssinen, T. 1973. Association, convention and anti-Parliament in British radical politics 1771–1848. *EHR* 88.

Pascal, R. 1938. Property and society: the Scottish historical school of the C18th. *Mod.Qu.* 1.

Paul, E. 1979. *Moral revolution and economic science*. Westport, Conn., Greenwood P.

Pearl, V. 1979. Change and stability in C17th London. *London J.* 5.

Pearson, G. 1978. Goths and Vandals: crime in history. *Cont.Crises* 2.

Peel, J. 1971. *Herbert Spencer*. Heinemann.

Pelling, H. 1965. *Origins of the Labour Party*. Rev.edn. OUP.

—— 1976. *A history of British trade unionism*. 3rd edition. Penguin.

Pennington, D. and Thomas, K. (eds) 1978. *Puritans and revolutionaries: essays in C17th history*. Clarendon.

Percival, J. 1975. Papers of Sir Edwin Chadwick. Typescript in D. M. S. Watson Library, U. College London.

Perkin, H. 1969. *Origins of modern English society 1780–1880*. RKP.

Philips, D. 1977. *Crime and authority in Victorian England*. Croom Helm.
—— 1980. A new engine of power and authority . . . law enforcement in England 1780–1830. In Parker and Gatrell 1980.
Pinchbeck, I. 1930. *Women workers and industrial revolution*. Repr. Virago 1981.
Piper, D. 1977. *Personality and the portrait*. BBC.
Plucknett, T. 1949. *Legislation of Edward I*. Clarendon.
—— 1956. *A concise history of the common law*. 5th edn, Butterworths.
Plumb, J. 1950. *England in the C18th 1714–1815*. Penguin.
—— 1963. Idem. Rev.edn, Penguin.
—— 1967. *Growth of political stability in England 1675–1725*. Penguin 1973.
—— 1973. *Commercialisation of leisure in C18th England*. Reading UP.
Pocock, J. 1972. *Politics, language and time*. Methuen.
—— 1975. British history: a plea for a new subject. *JMH* 47.
—— (ed.) 1980a. *Three British revolutions*. Princeton UP.
—— 1980b. Mobility of property. In Parel and Flanagan 1980.
—— 1980c. Authority and property. In Malament 1980.
Polanyi, K. 1945. *Origins of our time: the great transformation*. Gollancz 1946.
Pollock, F. and Maitland, F. 1968. *History of English law*. 2 vols, CUP (repr. of 2nd edn, 1898).
Pons, V. 1978. Contemporary interpretations of Manchester. *Stanford J.Int. Studs*. 13.
Poor Law Report 1834. Ed. S. and E. Checkland, Penguin 1974.
Porter, G. 1836. *Progress of the nation*. 3 vols, 3rd edn 1851.
Porter, R. 1982. *English society in the C18th*. Penguin.
Poulantzas, N. 1978. *State, power, socialism*. NLB.
Pound, J. 1971. *Poverty and vagrancy in Tudor England*. Longmans.
Powell, K. and Cook, C. 1977. *English historical facts 1485–1603*. Macmillan.
Prebble, J. 1961. *Culloden*. Penguin 1967.
Preston-Thomas, H. 1909. *The work and play of a government inspector*. Edinburgh, Blackwood.
Prothero, I. 1979. *Artisans and politics in the early C19th*. Dawson.
Prouty, R. 1957. *The transformation of the Board of Trade 1830–1858*. Heinemann.
Pumphrey, R. 1959. Introduction of industrialists into the British peerage. *AHR* 65.
Purdy, F. 1860. The statistics of the English Poor Rate. *JStat. Soc*. 23.
Purvis, J. 1980. Women and teaching in the C19th. In Dale 1981.
—— 1981. Double burden of class and gender in the schooling of working-class girls in C19th England, 1800–1870. In L. Barton and S. Walker (eds) *Schools, teachers, teaching*. Falmer.
Putnam, B. 1906. Justices of labour in the C14th. *EHR* 21.
—— 1908. *Enforcement of the statutes of labourers*. King.
Quinault, R. 1974. The Warwickshire county magistracy and public order c.1830–1870. In Quinault and Stevenson 1974.
—— and Stevenson, J. 1974. *Popular protest and public order*. A&U.
Rabb, T.K. 1967. *Enterprise and empire*. Harvard UP.
—— 1981. Revisionism revised: role of the Commons. *P&P* 92.
Radzinowicz, L. 1948/68. *A history of English criminal law . . . from 1750*. 4 vols, Stevens.

Rae, J. 1890. State socialism and social reform. *Cont.Rev.* 58.

Rafter, N. and Stanko, E. (eds) 1982. *Judge, lawyer, victim, thief: women, gender roles, and criminal justice.* North Eastern UP.

Rapaport, A. 1967. The Galilean revolution. *Listener* 26 Oct.

Rapp, R. et al. 1983. Examining family history. In Newton 1983.

Read, D. 1964. *The English provinces c.1760–1960.* Arnold.

—— (ed.) 1982. *Edwardian England.* Croom Helm.

Reid, D. 1976. Decline of 'Saint Monday' 1760–1876. *P&P* 71.

Richards, E.S. 1973a. Structural change in a regional economy: Sutherland . . . 1780–1830. *Ec.HR* 26.

—— 1973b. *The Leviathan of wealth: the Sutherland fortunes.* RKP.

Richards, P. 1975. The state and the working class 1833–1841: MPs and the making of social policy. PhD thesis, U of Birmingham.

—— 1979a. R. A. Slaney, the industrial town and early Victorian social policy. *Soc.Hist.* 4.

—— 1979b. The state and early industrial capitalism. *P&P* 83.

—— 1979c. State formation and class struggle 1832–1848. In Corrigan 1980a.

Richardson, H.G. and Sayles, G. 1934. *The governance of medieval England.* Edinburgh UP 1963.

Richardson, J. 1974. *Local historians' encyclopedia.* New Barnet, Hist.Publications.

Richardson, R.C. 1977. *Debate on the English revolution.* Methuen.

Ritchie, D.G. 1902. *Principles of state interference.* 4th edn, G. Allen.

Roach, J. 1957. Liberalism and the Victorian intelligentsia. *Cambridge Hist.J* 13, repr. Stansky 1973.

—— 1959. Universities and national intelligentsia. *VS* 3.

Roberts, C. 1977. Constitutional significance of the financial settlement of 1690. *Hist.J* 20.

Roberts, D. 1960. *Victorian origins of the British welfare state.* Yale UP.

Robertshaw, P. and Curtin, C. 1977. Legal definitions of the family. *Sociol.Rev.* 25.

Robson, R. (ed.) 1967. *Ideas and institutions in Victorian England.* Bell.

Robson, W. 1934. The Factory Acts 1833–1933. *Pol.Qu.* 5.

Rodgers, B. 1952. The Social Science Association 1857–1886. *Manchester School* 20.

Rodgers, S. 1981. Women's space in the men's house: the British House of Commons. In Ardener 1981.

Rogers, N. 1973. Aristocratic clientage. *P&P* 61.

—— 1975. Popular disaffection. *London J* 1.

—— 1978. Popular protest. *P&P* 79.

—— 1979. Money land and lineage. *Soc.Hist.* 4.

Rollinson, D. 1981. Property, ideology and popular culture in a Gloucestershire village 1660–1740. *P&P* 93.

Rose, M.E. 1972. *Relief of poverty 1834–1914.* Macmillan.

Rose, R.B. 1961. C18th price riots and public policy in England. *IRSH* 6.

Rosenberg, N. 1960. Some institutional aspects of the 'Wealth of Nations'. *JPol.Ec.* 68.

Rosenblum, N. 1973. Bentham's social psychology for legislators. *Pol. Theory* 1.

—— 1978. *Bentham's theory of the modern state.* Harvard UP.

Roseveare, H. 1973. *The Treasury 1660–1870.* A&U.

Roskell, J.S. 1964. Perspectives in English Parliamentary history. In Fryde and Miller 1970b.

Ross, G. 1894. *The schools of England and Germany.* Toronto, The Ministry.
Rothblatt, S. 1975. *Trade and change in English liberal education.* Faber.
Routh, G. 1976. A straying philosopher. *THES* 16 June.
Rowbotham, S. 1977. *Hidden from history: 300 years of women's oppression and the fight against it.* 3rd edn, Pluto.
Rubinstein, W. 1976. Wealth, elites and class structure of modern Britain. *P&P* 76.
Rude, G. 1964. *The crowd in history . . . 1730–1848.* NY, Wiley.
—— 1970. *Paris and London in the C18th.* Fontana.
—— 1971. *Hanoverian London 1714–1808.* S&W.
—— 1978. *Protest and punishment.* Clarendon.
See also under Hobsbawm.
Rule, J. 1975. Wrecking and coastal plunder. In Hay et al. 1977.
—— 1979. Social crime in the rural south. *Southern Hist.* 1.
Rusche, G. and Kirscheimer, O. 1939. *Punishment and social structure.* NY, Russell, 1970.
Russell, C. 1979. *Parliaments and English politics 1621–1629.* OUP.
Russell-Smith, E. 1974. *Modern bureaucracy: the home civil service.* Longmans.
Ryan, A. 1974. *J.S. Mill.* RKP.
Sainty, J.C. 1972–81. *Office holders in modern Britain.* Athlone P.
 1: *Treasury officials 1660–1870* (1972).
 2: *Officials of the Secretaries of State 1660–1782* (1973).
 3: *Officials of the Board of Trade 1660–1870* (1974).
 4: *Admiralty officials 1660–1870* (1975).
 5: *Home Office officials* (1978).
 6: *Foreign Office officials* (1981).
Samuel, R. (ed.) 1981. *People's history and socialist theory.* RKP.
Sanderson, M. 1967. Education and the factory in industrial Lancashire 1780–1840. *Ec.HR* 20.
Saville, J. (ed.) 1954. *Democracy and the labour movement.* L&W.
Sayer, D. 1975. Method and dogma in historical materialism. *Sociol. Rev.* 23.
—— 1977. Precapitalist societies and contemporary Marxist theory. *Sociol.* 11.
—— 1978. Mao Tsetung's critique of Soviet economics. *C&C* 8.
—— 1979. Science as critique: Marx vs. Althusser. In J. Mepham and D. Ruben (eds) *Issues in Marxist philosophy,* vol. 3, Harvester.
—— 1983a. *Marx's method.* 2nd edn with new Afterword (1st edn 1979). Harvester/NY, Humanities.
—— 1983b. Karl Marx 1867–1883: a biographical note. In Shanin 1983.
—— 1985. Critique of politics and political economy: capitalism, communism and the state in Marx's writings of the mid-1840s. *Sociol.Rev.* 33(2).
—— and Corrigan, P. 1983. Late Marx: continuity, contradiction and learning. In Shanin 1983.
—— —— 1985. Revolution against the state: the context and significance of Marx's 'late' writings. *Dialectical Anthropology.*
—— and Shanin, T. (eds) forthcoming *Karl Marx: late writings.*
See also under Corrigan, P., Frisby, D.
Schaeffer, B. 1957. The idea of the ministerial department: Bentham, Mill and Bagehot. *Australian JPol. & Hist.* 3.
Schneider, L. (ed.) 1967. *The Scottish moralists.* Chicago UP.
Schofield, R. 1973. Dimensions of illiteracy 1750–1850. *Explorations in Ec.Hist.* 10.
Schulz, M. 1948. Development of the grant system. *Essays on local government,* I.
Scott, J. and Tilly, L. 1980. Women's work and the family in C19th Europe. In A. Amsden (ed.) *The economics of women and work.* Penguin.

Scull, A. 1979. *Museums of madness*. Allen Lane.

Seccombe, W. 1983. Marxism and demography. *NLR* 137.

—— (forthcoming) *Family forms and modes of production*. NLB.

Shahar, S. 1983. *The fourth estate: a history of women in the middle ages*. Methuen.

Shanin, T. (ed.) 1983. *Late Marx and the Russian road*. RKP/MRP.

Shanley, M.L. 1982. 'One must ride behind'. *VS* 25.

Sharp, B. 1980. *In contempt of all authority: rural artisans and riot in the west of England 1586–1660*. Berkeley, U. California P.

Sharpe, K. (ed.) 1979. *Faction and Parliament: essays in early Stuart history*. OUP.

Sheehan, W. 1977. Finding solace in C18th Newgate. In Cockburn 1977.

Shelton, W. 1973. *English hunger and industrial disorders*. Macmillan.

Shennan, J. 1974. *Origins of the modern European state 1450–1725*. Hutchinson.

Silver, A. 1967. The demand for order in civil society. In D. Bordua (ed.) *The police*, NY, Wiley.

Simon, B. 1960. *The two nations and the educational structure 1780–1870*. L&W.

—— and Bradley, I. (eds) 1975. *The Victorian public school*. Dublin, Gill.

Simon, D. 1954. Master and servant. In Saville 1954.

Simpson, A. 1961. *The wealth of the gentry 1540–1660*. Chicago UP.

Skinner, A. 1967. Natural history in the age of Adam Smith. *Pol.Studs*. 15.

—— and Wilson, T. (eds) 1975. *Essays on Adam Smith*. Clarendon.

Skinner, Q. 1978. *Foundation of modern political thought*. 2 vols, CUP.

Skultans, V. (ed.) 1975. *Madness and morals*. RKP.

Slack, P. 1974. Vagrants and vagrancy in England 1598–1664. *Ec.HR* 27. See also under Clark, P.

Smart, Professor. 1909. Notes . . . on the growth of Poor Law expenditure. Royal Commission on the Poor Laws, Stat. Appx, pt XII.

Smiles, S. 1859. *Self-help*. Sphere 1967.

Smith, A. 1759. *Theory of moral sentiments*. CW, Clarendon, 1976–, vol. 1.

—— 1763. *Lectures on justice, police, revenue, and arms*. CW.

—— 1776. *An inquiry into the nature and causes of the wealth of nations*. Routledge 1908.

Smith, D.E. 1974. Women's perspectives as a radical critique of sociology. *Sociol. Inquiry* 44.

—— 1983. Women class and family. *Socialist Register*.

Smout, T.C. 1964. Scottish landowners and economic growth. *Scottish JPol.Ec*. 11.

—— 1972. *History of the Scottish people 1560–1830*. Rev. edn, Fontana.

Snitnow, S. et al. (eds) 1983. *Powers of desire: politics of sexuality*. NY, MRP.

Speck, W. 1977. *Stability and strife: England 1714–1760*. Arnold.

Spence, J. and Corrigan, P. 1985. *Family album work book*. RKP.

Spencer, H. 1842. Proper sphere of government. *The Non-Conformist*, June.

—— 1851. *Social statics*. Kelley.

—— 1884. *The man and the state*. Penguin 1969.

—— 1899. Filiation of ideas. Appx to his 1908: II.

—— 1908. *Life and letters*. Ed. D. Duncan, 2 vols, Methuen.

Spitzer, S. 1975. Towards a Marxian theory of deviance. *Soc. Problems* 22.

Spring, D. 1953. Earl Fitzwilliam and the Corn Laws. *AHR* 59.

—— 1960. Some reflections on social history in the C19th. *VS* 4.

—— 1963. Aristocracy, social structure and religion in the early Victorian period. *VS* 6.

Spufford, M. 1974. *Contrasting communities*. RKP.

Stacey, M. and Price, M. 1981. *Women, power and politics*. Tavistock.

Stafford, P. 1983. *Queens, concubines and dowagers: the king's wife in the early middle ages*. Batsford.

Stafford, W. 1973. Man and Society in the thought of Coleridge and Disraeli. DPhil thesis, Oxford U.

Stansky, P. (ed.) 1973. *The Victorian revolution*. NY, Watts.

Statutes, The. For details see note 35 to chapter 6 above.

Statutes of the realm. See idem.

Statutes revised. See idem.

Steedman, C. 1984. *Policing the Victorian community: the formation of English provincial police forces*. RKP.

Steintrager, J. 1977. *Bentham.* A&U.

Stern, W. 1950. UK public expenditure by votes of supply 1793–1817. *Economica* 17.

Stevens, R. 1979. *Law and politics.* W&N.

Stevenson, J. 1979. *Popular disturbances in England 1700–1900.* Longmans.

Stigler, G. 1975. *The citizen and the state: essays on regulation.* Chicago UP.

Stone, L. 1948. Anatomy of the Elizabethan aristocracy. *Ec.HR* 18.

—— 1951. The political programme of Thomas Cromwell. *Bull.Inst.Hist.Research* 24.

—— 1965a. *Crisis of the aristocracy 1558–1641.* OUP.

—— (ed.) 1965b. *Social change and revolution in England 1540–1640.* Longmans.

—— 1969. Literacy and education in England. *P&P* 62.

—— 1973. *Family and fortune.* OUP.

—— (ed.) 1975. *The university in society.* I: *Oxford and Cambridge from the 14th to the early 19th centuries.* Princeton UP.

—— 1977. *Family, sex and marriage in England 1500–1800.* W&N.

—— and Stone, J. 1984. *An open elite? England 1540–1880.* Clarendon.

Storch, R. 1975. Plague of blue locusts. *IRSH.*

—— 1976. Policeman as domestic missionary. *JSoc.Hist.* 9.

Strachan, H. 1980. English Victorian army. *EHR.*

Strayer, J. 1970. *Medieval origins of the modern state.* Princeton UP.

Strong, R. 1963. *Portraits of Queen Elizabeth.* OUP.

—— 1973. *Splendour at court: renaissance spectacle and illusion.* W&N.

—— 1977. *The cult of Elizabeth.* T&H.

—— 1979. An Edwardian never-never land. *Listener* 9 Aug.

Stuard, S. (ed.) 1976. *Women in medieval society.* U Pennsylvania P.

Supple, B. 1971. The state and the industrial revolution. In Cipolla 1973.

—— 1974. Legislation and virtue . . . working class self-help and the state in the early C19th. In McKendrick 1974.

Sutherland, G. 1969a. Reform of the English civil service 1780–1914. *P&P* 42.

—— 1969b. Administrators in education after 1870. In her 1972.

—— (ed.) 1972. *Studies in the growth of C19th government.* RKP.

—— 1973. *Policy-making in elementary education 1870–1895.* OUP.

Tann, J. 1978. Marketing methods in the international steam engine market. *JEc.Hist.* 38.

—— and Breckin, M. 1978. International diffusion of the Watt engine 1775–1825. *Ec.HR* 31.

Tarn, J. 1973. *Five per cent philanthropy.* CUP.

Tawney, R. 1913. Assessment of wages in England by JPs. *Vierteljahrschrift für sozial- und Wirtschaftgeschichte* 11.

—— 1938. *Religion and the rise of capitalism.* Penguin.

—— 1941a. Harrington's interpretation of his age. *Proc. British Academy* 27.

—— 1941b. Rise of the gentry 1558–1640. *Ec.HR* 11.

—— 1954. Rise of the gentry: *Ec.HR*, 2nd ser., 7.

Taylor, A.J. 1972. *Laissez-faire and state intervention in C19th Britain.* Macmillan.

Taylor, B. 1983. *Eve and the New Jerusalem.* Virago.

Taylor, G. 1969. *Problem of poverty 1660–1834.* Longman.

Taylor, H. 1831. On the best mode of constituting public offices. *Pol.Studs.* 9 (1961).

Taylor, J.S. 1969. Mythology of the old Poor Law. *JEc.Hist.* 29.

Thane, P. 1978. Women and the Poor Law in Victorian and Edwardian England. *HWJ* 6.

Thirsk, J. 1978. *Economic policy and projects.* Clarendon.

Tholfsen, T.R. 1961. The transition to democracy in Victorian England. *IRSH* 6.

—— 1971. Intellectual origins of mid-Victorian stability. *Pol.Sci.Qu.* 86.

Thomas, D.N. 1969. Marriage patterns in the British peerage. MPhil. London U.

—— 1972. Social origins of marriage partners of the British peerage in the 18th and 19th centuries. *Population Studs.* 26

Thomas, K. 1958. The double standard. *JHI* 20.

—— 1959. Women and the Civil War sects. *P&P* 12.

—— 1971. *Religion and the decline of magic.* Penguin.

—— 1977. Age and authority in early modern England. *Proc. British Academy* 62.

—— 1978. Puritans and adultery: the Act of 1650. In Pennington and Thomas 1978.

Thomas, M. 1948. *Early factory legislation.* Leigh-on-Sea, Thames Bank.

Thomas, W. 1969. James Mill's politics: the 'Essay on government' and the movement for reform. *Hist.J* 12.

—— 1971a. John Stuart Mill and the uses of autobiography. *History* 56.

—— 1971b. James Mill's politics: a rejoinder. *Hist.J* 14.

—— 1974. The philosophic radicals. In Hollis 1974.

Thompson, E.P. 1965. Peculiarities of the English. Repr. in his 1978a.

—— 1967. Time, work-discipline and industrial capitalism. *P&P* 38.

—— 1968. *Making of the English working class.* Rev. edn, Penguin (1st edn 1963).

—— 1971. Moral economy of the English crowd in the C18th. *P&P* 50.

—— 1974. Patrician society, plebeian culture. *JSoc.Hist.* 7.

—— 1975. The crime of anonymity. In Hay et al. 1977.

—— 1976. Romanticism, moralism and utopianism: the case of William Morris. *NLR* 99.

—— 1977a. *Whigs and hunters: origins of the Black Act.* Rev. edn, Penguin (1st edn 1975).

—— 1977b. Happy families. *NS* 8 Sept, repr. *Radical Hist.Rev.* 20, 1979.

—— 1978a. *Poverty of theory.* Merlin.

—— 1978b. C18th English society. *Soc.Hist.* 3.

—— 1980. *Writing by candlelight.* Merlin.

Thompson, F.M.L. 1963. *English landed society in the C19th.* RKP.

—— 1981. Social control in Victorian Britain. *Ec.HR* 34.

Thomson, B. 1935. *Story of Scotland Yard.* Grayson & Grayson.

Thomson, D. 1950. *England in the C19th.* Penguin.

Thornhill, W. (ed.) 1975. *Modernisation of British government.* Pitman.

Tigar, M. and Levy M. 1978. *Law and the rise of capitalism.* MRP.

Tilly, C. (ed.) 1975. *Foundations of nation states in Europe.* Princeton UP.

Tomlinson, M. 1978. 'Prison palaces' . . . early Victorian prisons 1835–1877. *Bull. Inst.Hist.Research* 51.

—— 1981. Penal servitude 1846–1865. In Bailey 1981.

Torrance, J.R. 1968. Sir George Harrison and the growth of bureaucracy in the early C19th. *EHR* 83.

—— 1978. Social class and bureaucratic innovation. *P&P* 78.

Tremenheere, H.S. 1861. Submission to Newcastle Commision. PP 1861 (354) XLVIII.

—— 1865a. I: *Factory schools, and education under the Printworks Act;* II: *The Children's Employment Commission* (papers originally to NAPSS, Sheffield). Privately printed 1865.

—— 1865b. *The franchise: a privilege and not a right. Proved by the political experience of the ancients.* New edn. Murray.

—— 1880. State aid and control in industrial insurance. *Nineteenth Century* 8.
—— 1881. Thriftless thrift. *Fortnightly Rev.* 36.
—— 1893. *How good government grew up and how to preserve it.* Liberal Unionist Assn.
Trevelyan, G.M. 1962. *Shortened history of England.* Penguin (1st published 1942; abridged edn of his *History of England,* Longmans, Green & Co.).
Trevor-Roper, H. 1951. The Elizabethan aristocracy. *Ec.HR* 3.
—— 1953. The gentry, 1540–1640. *Ec.HR* supp., I.
—— 1967. *Religion, the reformation and social change.* S&W.
—— 1969. *European witch-craze of the 16th and 17th centuries.* Penguin.
—— 1976. *Princes and artists.* T&H.
Vallance, E.M. 1979. *Women in the House . . . women members of Parliament.* Athlone P.
Vicinus, M. 1977. *A widening sphere.* Indiana UP.
Vincent, D. 1981. *Bread, knowledge and freedom.* Methuen.
Walker, D. 1976. Fabians face financial crisis. *THES* 25 June.
Wallas, G. 1908. *Human nature in politics.* 3rd edn, repr. Constable 1948.
—— 1925. Bentham as a political inventor. *Cont.Rev.* 1926.
—— 1928. Jeremy Bentham. *Pol.Sci.Qu.* 38.
Wallerstein, I. 1974. *The modern world system.* NY, Academic P.
Ward, J.T. 1962. *The factory movement 1830–1855.* Macmillan.
—— 1970a. The factory movement. In his 1970b.
—— (ed.) 1970b. *Popular movements c.1830–1850.* Macmillan.
—— (ed.) 1970c. *The factory system.* 2 vols, Newton Abbot, David & Charles.
Webb, B. and Webb, S. 1929a. *English Poor Law history* Part II: *The last 100 years.* Vol. 1, Longman.
—— 1929b. Idem, vol. 2.
Webb R.K. 1955a. A Whig inspector. *JMH* 27.
—— 1955b. *The British working-class reader 1790–1848: literacy and social tension.* A&U.
Webb, S. 1890. *Reform of the Poor Law.* Longman.
Weber, M. 1905. *The Protestant ethic and the spirit of capitalism.* A&U 1974.
—— 1906. Protestant sects and the spirit of capitalism. In his 1948.
—— 1914a. Structures of power. Idem.
—— 1914b. Bureaucracy. Idem.
—— 1918. Politics as a vocation. Idem.
—— 1920a. Introduction to his 1905. In his 1978b.
—— 1920b. *General economic history.* Collier-Macmillan 1961.
—— 1920c. The meaning of discipline. In his 1948.
—— 1948. *From Max Weber.* Ed. H. Gerth and C. Wright Mills. RKP.
—— 1978a. *Economy and society.* 2 vols, Berkeley, U of California P (unfinished and posthumously published).
—— 1978b. *Selections.* Ed. W. Runciman. CUP.
—— 1983. *Max Weber on capitalism, bureaucracy and religion.* Ed. S. Andreski. A&U.
Weeks, J. 1976. Politics of pluralism. *BSSLH* 32.
—— 1981. *Sex, politics and society.* Longmans.
Wells, D. 1981. *Marxism and the modern state.* Harvester.
Wells, R. 1979. Development of English proletariat and social protest 1700–1850. *JPS* 6.
Westermarck, E. 1917. *Origins and development of moral ideas.* 2nd edn, Manchester, vol. 2.

White, R.J. 1957. *Waterloo to Peterloo*. Penguin 1968.

Widdowson, F. 1983. *Going up into the next class: women and elementary teacher training 1840–1914*. Hutchinson.

Wiener, M. 1971. *Between two worlds: political thought of Graham Wallas*. Clarendon.

Wilkinson, R.H. 1963. The gentleman ideal and the maintenance of a political elite. *Sociol. of Education* 37.

Williams, D. 1977. *History of modern Wales*. 2nd edn, Murray.

Williams, G. 1960. Making of radical Merthyr. *Welsh Hist.Rev.* 1.

—— 1978. *When was Wales?* BBC Annual Wales Lectures.

—— 1979. *The Merthyr rising*. Croom Helm.

Williams, P. 1963. The Tudor state. *P&P* 25.

—— 1979. *The Tudor regime*. Clarendon.

Williams, R. 1958. *Culture and society*. Rev. edn, Penguin 1963.

—— 1961. *The long revolution*. Penguin 1965.

—— 1973. Base and superstructure in Marxist cultural theory. *NLR* 82. Repr. in his 1980.

—— 1975. *The country and the city*. Paladin.

—— 1980. *Problems in materialism and culture*. Verso.

—— 1983. *Towards 2000*. C&W.

Willis, P. 1978. *Profane culture*. RKP.

—— 1981. Cultural production. *Interchange* 12.

—— and Corrigan, P. 1983. Orders of experience. *Social Text* 7. See also under Corrigan, P.

Wills, V. (ed.) 1972. *Reports of the annexed estates*. Edinburgh, HMSO.

Willson, F. 1955. Ministries and boards: aspects of administrative development since 1832. *PA* 33.

Winch, D. 1978. *Adam Smith's politics*. CUP.

Winter, J. 1974. *Socialism and the challenge of war*. RKP.

Wohl, A.S. 1968. Bitter cry of outcast London. *IRSH* 13.

—— 1977. *The eternal slum*. Arnold.

Wolfe, W. 1975. *From radicalism to socialism . . . Fabian social doctrines 1881–1889*. Yale UP.

Woodward, D. 1969. Assessment of wages by JPs 1563–1813. *Local Hist.* 8.

Woolrych, A. 1980. Court, country and city revisited. *History* 65.

Wootton, G. 1975. *Pressure groups in Britain 1720–1790*. Allen Lane.

Wright, D.G. 1969. A radical borough . . . Bradford 1832–1841. *NH* 4.

—— 1970. *Democracy and reform 1815–1885*. Longmans.

Wright, L.B. 1943. *Religion and empire . . . piety and commerce in English expansion 1558–1625*. U North Carolina P.

Wright, T. 1881. On a possible popular culture. *Contemp.Rev.* 40.

Wrightson, K. 1977. Aspects of social differentiation in rural England c.1580–1660. *JPS* 5.

Yates, F. 1974. *Astraea: the imperial theme in the C16th*. RKP.

Yelling, J. 1977. *Common field and enclosure in England 1450–1850*. Macmillan.

Yeo, E. and Yeo S. (eds) 1981. *Popular culture and class conflict 1530–1914*. Harvester.

Yeo, S. 1979. Working-class association, private capital, welfare and the state. In Parry 1979.

—— 1980. State and anti-state . . . social forms and struggles from 1850. In Corrigan 1980a.

—— 1984. Socialism, the state and some oppositional Englishness. In Colls 1985.

Young, G. 1867. The House of Commons in 1833. In *Essays on Reform* 1867.

Young, J.D. 1979. *Rousing of the Scottish working class 1770–1931.* Croom Helm.
Young, K. 1973. *Arthur James Balfour.* Bell.
Youngson, A. 1973. *After the '45.* Edinburgh UP.
Zagorin, P. 1959. Social interpretation of the English revolution. *JEc.Hist.* 19.
—— 1970. *The court and the country: beginning of the English revolution of the mid-C17th.* RKP.
Zangerl, C. 1971. Social composition of the county magistracy in England and Wales 1831–1887. *JBS* 11.

Index

What follows is a selective, thematic index. Themes indicated by our title and sub-title have *not* been indexed (e.g. state, state formation, culture, cultural revolution); neither, with a few exceptions, have the names of any writers and such related pervasive themes as bourgeois, masculinity, nation, politics etc. We have however indexed discussions of 'English, Englishness'.

Conventions: Terms surrounded by single quotation marks (e.g. 'official documentary system') are terms originating in this book, or used by us in a special way. Terms followed by page numbers with 'n' (e.g. 225–6n) indicates significant treatment in a note; page numbers followed by 'f' (e.g. 154f) indicate that the theme is treated and developed over several pages within a more general discussion, whereas continuous pagination (e.g. 21–4) indicates substantial treatment of the indicated theme; where the figures are in bold type (e.g. **21–2**) this indicates a major discussion and definition of the theme.